Your SCIENCE CLASSROOM

*We would like to dedicate this book to our children, Ginny, Kristin, and Michael,
for being our first students, and to all the students we have learned from and
whom we have taught. They inspired us to be better science teachers
than we ever thought we could be.*

Your SCIENCE CLASSROOM

Becoming an Elementary / Middle School Science Teacher

M. Jenice Goldston
The University of Alabama

Laura Downey
*Kansas Association for Conservation
and Environmental Education*

Los Angeles | London | New Delhi
Singapore | Washington DC

Los Angeles | London | New Delhi
Singapore | Washington DC

FOR INFORMATION:

SAGE Publications, Inc.
2455 Teller Road
Thousand Oaks, California 91320
E-mail: order@sagepub.com

SAGE Publications Ltd.
1 Oliver's Yard
55 City Road
London EC1Y 1SP
United Kingdom

SAGE Publications India Pvt. Ltd.
B 1/I 1 Mohan Cooperative Industrial Area
Mathura Road, New Delhi 110 044
India

SAGE Publications Asia-Pacific Pte. Ltd.
33 Pekin Street #02-01
Far East Square
Singapore 048763

Acquisitions Editor: Diane McDaniel
Assistant Editor: Rachael Leblond
Editorial Assistant: Megan Ann Koraly
Production Editor: Eric Garner
Copy Editor: Alison Hope
Typesetter: C&M Digitals (P) Ltd.
Proofreader: Joyce Li
Indexer: Wendy Allex
Cover Designer: Karine Hovsepian
Marketing Manager: Katharine Winter
Permissions Editor: Adele Hutchinson

Printed in the United States of America

Library of Congress Cataloging-in-Publication Data

Goldston, M. Jenice

Your science classroom : becoming an elementary/middle school science teacher / M. Jenice Goldston, Laura Downey.

p. cm.
Includes bibliographical references and index.

ISBN 978-1-4129-7522-3 (pbk.)

1. Science—Study and teaching (Elementary)—United States. 2. Science—Study and teaching (Middle school)—United States. 3. Science teachers—Training of—United States. I. Downey, Laura. II. Title.

LB1585.3.G65 2013
372.35′044—dc23   2011045609

This book is printed on acid-free paper.

12 13 14 15 16 10 9 8 7 6 5 4 3 2

BRIEF CONTENTS

DETAILED CONTENTS

PREFACE

When you think about teaching science in your classroom for the first time with twenty or more eager children looking at you ready to begin, how do you feel? Excited? Anxious? Happy? Expectant? Worried? Scared? Well, a great deal of how you feel about science and teaching science may be attributed to how you have experienced science in school and to some degree how you have been prepared to teach science. This book, designed for K–8 science methods instruction, is for teachers who desire to use inquiry in their classrooms. This textbook is written in a manner that invites you, the K–8 teacher, into science classrooms where inquiry experiences thrive while igniting student learning and science teacher enthusiasm.

Your Science Classroom: Becoming an Elementary or Middle School Science Teacher represents what we, as teachers of science, have learned through many years of classroom experiences with elementary and middle school students in rural and urban, public and private settings. It also represents thirty years of our experiences and passion for teaching science to graduates and undergraduates at the university level. As such, our purpose is to provide a practical science methods textbook that contains essential knowledge and skills that teachers need to begin to teach science to K–8 students using hands-on, minds-on approaches. Conceptually, our book emphasizes the importance of teachers as reflective, knowledgeable facilitators of standards-based, inquiry-based, constructivist practices. Along these lines, it also provides a practical presentation of relevant knowledge in the field. What makes *Your Science Classroom: Becoming an Elementary or Middle School Science Teacher* different from other science methods textbooks is that the chapters are actually designed using an inquiry approach, often referred to as the 5E inquiry instructional model. The stages of the 5E inquiry model have been modified slightly from its original intent for use in a book; by using this modified version, we provide the reader with multiple exposures to each phase of the instructional model through reflections, readings, and authentic activities embedded within each chapter. Our aim is to uncover key areas of science methods content well, without trying to cover everything.

It may be helpful to you to know a bit more about the 5E model used in the chapters. This model comprises five stages: Engage, Explore, Explain, Elaborate, and Evaluate. The following are brief descriptions of these stages:

1. **Engage**: Focuses on eliciting what the learners already know about the topic and invites inquiry. A variety of approaches can be used to accomplish these goals. These may include simple questions and KWL charts, to questions, story prompts, discrepant events, or other activities that are more sophisticated.
2. **Explore**: Uses a variety of investigative and inquiry experiences that actively involve students with science concepts and processes of science.

3. **Explain**: Develops students' understanding of scientific concepts and processes through teacher-facilitated questioning that draws on the inquiry activities. Labels and terminology associated with science concepts are introduced during this stage.
4. **Elaborate**: Applies the newly acquired science concepts and processes in new situations.
5. **Evaluate**: Examines through a purposefully designed task students' learning of the objective(s) taught.

Because the 5E inquiry instructional model is intended to be an interactive, dynamic model where students explore science phenomena firsthand, its use has been slightly adjusted here to fit the constraints of a textbook. In particular, the explain stage for each chapter is informational and has been modified from the 5E model simply because facilitating an interactive question-and-answer session about the explore activity and the associated science concepts is limited by the book format. However, if the explore activity becomes part of actual class instruction you may see the explain stage come to life as it is intended. Use of the 5E inquiry lesson model as a way of uncovering the information in this text will offer multiple opportunities for the reader to examine its format and the various strategies depicted in each of the stages. Each chapter invites the reader to participate in various tasks or activities as part of the 5E inquiry model. We encourage you to complete these active learning experiences to gain knowledge of each stage and thus experience firsthand a useful lesson plan model for inquiry in your science classroom. Each chapter gives you multiple opportunities to examine each phase of the 5E format, and to consider how it translates into science classroom inquiries with K–8 students.

Organization of the Text

Part I: The Nature of Science

As part of becoming an effective science teacher, you must have knowledge of science, children as diverse learners, and pedagogical approaches for teaching science. Chapters 1 and 2 deal with the nature of science, its evolving status in society, and how the work of scientists can be reflected through inquiry in the K–8 science classroom. The chapter activities challenge teachers to rethink the scientific method as well as how scientists come to know "what they know." Chapter 2 addresses the National Science Education Standards and scientific literacy as a goal for all students. The chapter also provides background knowledge of science as a contemporary enterprise that is closely interwoven with technology. Recognizing and understanding the relationship between science and technology in current society is important to all students as they develop scientific literacy.

Part II: The Nature of the Learner

When science content knowledge merges with a teacher's knowledge of the learner and the learning processes, effective teaching and substantial learning can take place. Chapters 3 and 4 examine current as well as emerging theories and findings on how students learn science. Chapter 3 considers the foundational work of cognitive and social psychologists, Piaget and

Vygotsky, whose work contributed to the contemporary view of constructivism. Examination of constructivist classrooms is contrasted with objectivism in Chapter 3 as a way to foster reflection on personal experiences in learning science and to bring to the forefront the many variables that influence when and how students learn. Chapter 4 explores the learning of science concepts from the perspective of constructivism, metacognitive thinking, and conceptual change approaches. These perspectives delve into additional strategies that uncover students' prior knowledge and sources of misconceptions while exploring science activities that actively challenge students' thinking to align with scientifically acceptable explanations. Children's alternative frameworks or misconceptions about a variety of science topics are discussed and resources for locating common misconceptions are cited.

Part III: The Nature of Science Teaching

Part III of this book is about science teaching and its many complexities. Though the chapters are presented separately, each represents aspects of teaching that are highly interwoven into the practices of science teaching. Chapter 5 addresses teacher questioning—the essence of inquiry teaching. The chapter examines types of questions, characteristics of effective questions, and research associated with questions, such as wait time. Chapter 6 centers on pedagogical approaches associated with inquiry teaching and the process skills students must acquire to conduct inquiry. The chapter distinguishes the varying roles of the students and the teacher in inquiry by examining different types of inquiry approaches used within K–8 science classrooms. These approaches are described and discussed by key features represented in an inquiry continuum. As students acquire process skills, they become more competent and capable of doing scientific experimentation on their own and of understanding scientific experimentation. Effective teaching by means of inquiry is always underpinned by effective planning, which is discussed in Chapter 7. Chapter 7 explores planning inquiry lessons using the 5E instructional model by taking the reader through inquiry planning using examples of phases that make up full lesson plans. The development of effective assessments and evaluations as important skills for science teachers is addressed in Chapter 8, which distinguishes between assessments *for* learning and assessments *of* learning. This knowledge provides teachers a lens for closely considering how and when to use formative or summative assessments for making decisions pertinent to student learning. The chapter provides descriptions and examples of a large variety of alternative, performance, and authentic assessments.

Part IV: The Nature of Diversity in Science Teaching and Learning

Chapter 9 focuses on variables that influence how students learn and learning style preferences. Readers can examine their own learning style and explore other learning style inventories, including Gardner's Multiple Intelligences. Understanding learning styles can promote the practice of offering a wide range of science experiences for all types of learners, ensuring science for all. Given the national impetus of science for all, Chapter 10 concentrates on student diversity in science classrooms and the relevance of that diversity in preparing scientifically literate citizens. Engaging all students in relevant science learning increases opportunities for diverse populations to pursue careers in science, technology, mathematics, or engineering (STEM) fields. Viewing diversity broadly, this chapter addresses useful practices for teaching learners with disabilities and English language learners (ELLs), as well as strategies that foster equity across gender, ethnicity, race, and culture in teaching science. Chapter 11, the final chapter, brings to light the pros and cons of integrating curricula and takes the reader through an example of integrating science with other disciplines using a thematic approach.

Key Features of the Text

Your Science Classroom: Becoming an Elementary or Middle Science Teacher uses the symbolic and familiar features of the classroom to provide organization of key concepts, practices, research findings, and teaching tips. The choice of this approach is to assist K–8 teachers to envision themselves within their own classrooms using features common to K–8 classrooms. Though not all classroom features are found in every chapter, the features represent and highlight different types of pertinent materials or information. The features included in the text include the following listed below:

Learning Objectives are stated to inform teachers of the intended learning outcomes of each chapter.

National Science Education Standards are stated at the beginning to each chapter to provide the teachers with the specific science teaching standards that are address as part of the chapter.

Key terms are bolded and defined at their first use in the text.

Teacher's Desk Tip is a feature that highlights, in brief, a variety of teaching issues involved with planning, science materials, or special needs, diversity information, and so forth.

Bulletin Board highlights key ideas, skills, assessment, guidelines, examples, or research findings.

My Science Classroom features narratives of teachers talking to teachers about classroom, pedagogical, content, or learning issues.

Tech Connect provides examples and ideas for integrating technology in your K–8 science classroom.

Chapter **Summary** found at the end of each chapter highlights important concepts and key topics.

Annotated Resources provide brief descriptions of the useful resources for teachers.

Chapter **References** provide a complete list of resource citations used in the chapter.

A **Glossary** at the end of the book lists and defines all of the bolded key terms in the text.

Appendices provide detailed information on how to write an instructional objective, safety in the science classroom, and setting up science inquiry learning centers.

Ancillaries

Instructor Teaching Site

A password-protected site, available at **www.sagepub.com/goldston**, features resources that have been designed to help instructors plan and teach their course. These resources include:

- An extensive test bank with multiple-choice, true/false, short answer, and essay questions
- Chapter-specific PowerPoint slide presentations which highlight essential concepts and figures from the text
- Chapter overviews which may be used for lectures and/or student handouts
- Class activities including handouts that relate to the activities presented in each chapter
- Access to recent, relevant full-text SAGE journal articles and accompanying article review questions
- A list of web resources including links to the annotated resources that appear in the text as well as state and national standards
- Several video clips for each chapter that apply to chapter topics

Student Study Site

A web-based study site is available at **www.sagepub.com/goldston**. This site provides access to several study tools including:

- eFlashcards which reinforce students' understanding of key terms and concepts presented in the text
- Web quizzes for student self-review
- A list of web resources including links to the annotated resources that appear in the text as well as state and national standards
- Several video clips for each chapter that apply to chapter topics
- Access to recent, relevant full-text SAGE journal articles and accompanying article review questions
- Sample lesson plans for the lessons presented in chapter 7

NATIONAL SCIENCE EDUCATION STANDARDS

Science Teaching Standards

The standards for science teaching are grounded in five assumptions.

- The vision of science education described by the Standards requires changes throughout the entire system.
- What students learn is greatly influenced by how they are taught.
- The actions of teachers are deeply influenced by their perceptions of science as an enterprise and as a subject to be taught and learned.
- Student understanding is actively constructed through individual and social processes.
- Actions of teachers are deeply influenced by their understanding of and relationships with students.

Teaching Standard A: Teachers of science plan an inquiry-based science program for their students. In doing this, teachers

- Develop a framework of yearlong and short-term goals for students.
- Select science content and adapt and design curricula to meet the interest, knowledge, understanding, abilities, and experiences of students.
- Select teaching and assessment strategies that support the development of student understanding and nurture a community of science learners.
- Work together as colleagues within and across disciplines and grade levels.

Teaching Standard B: Teachers of science guide and facilitate learning. In doing this, teachers

- Focus and support inquiries while interacting with students.
- Orchestrate discourse among students about scientific ideas.
- Challenge students to accept and share responsibility for their own learning.
- Recognize and respond to student diversity and encourage all students to participate fully in science learning.
- Encourage and model the skills of scientific inquiry, as well as the curiosity, openness to new ideas and data, and skepticism that characterize science.

Teaching Standard C: Teachers of science engage in ongoing assessment of their teaching and of student learning. In doing this, teachers

- Use multiple methods and systematically gather data about student understanding and ability.
- Analyze assessment data to guide teaching.
- Guide students in self-assessment.

- Use student data, observations of teaching, and interactions with colleagues to reflect on and improve teaching practice.
- Use student data, observations of teaching, and interactions with colleagues to report student achievement and opportunities to learn to students, teachers, parents, policy makers, and the general public.

Teaching Standard D:

Teachers of science design and manage learning environments that provide students with the time, space, and resources needed for learning science. In doing this, teachers

- Structure the time available so that students are able to engage in extended investigations.
- Create a setting for student work that is flexible and supportive of inquiry.
- Ensure a safe working environment.
- Make the available science tools, materials, media, and technological resources accessible to students.
- Identify and use resources outside the school.
- Engage students in designing the learning environment.

Teaching Standard E:

Teachers of science develop communities of science learners that reflect the intellectual rigor of scientific inquiry and the attitudes and social values conducive to science learning. In doing this, teachers

- Display and demand respect for the diverse ideas, skills, and experiences of all students.
- Enable students to have a significant voice in decisions about the content and context of their work and require students to take responsibility for the learning of all members of the community.
- Nurture collaboration among students.
- Structure and facilitate ongoing formal and informal discussion based on a shared understanding of rules of scientific discourse.
- Model and emphasize the skills, attitudes, and values of scientific inquiry.

Teaching Standard F:

Teachers of science actively participate in the ongoing planning and development of the school science program. In doing this, teachers

- Plan and develop the school science program.
- Participate in decisions concerning the allocation of time and other resources to the science program.
- Participate fully in planning and implementing professional growth and development strategies for themselves and their colleagues.

Source: From the National Science Education Standards, National Research Council, 1996a, excerpted from pages 27–53.

ACKNOWLEDGMENTS

We have had great support for this book from our friends and colleagues across the country, many of whom asked us to write a K–8 science methods textbook. Our thanks go out to all of you—your encouragements made this book a reality. Special thanks to our families for their patience, understanding, and love during the writing of this book. Last, but certainly not least, we would like to thank the teachers who work with us, invite us into their classrooms, and help us to "keep it real."

We would like to thank our colleagues who reviewed our book and provided thoughtful, constructive feedback. You all contributed more than you know.

Jeanne Andrioli, Marygrove College

Caroline Beller, Oklahoma State University

Jeanelle Bland-Day, Eastern Connecticut University

John Ellis, Missouri Western State University

Wendy Frazier, George Mason University

Mary Harris, Athens State University

Christy Heid, Chatham College

Fiona McDonnell, Emmanuel College

Margaret Ritson, Chatham College

Christine Royce, Shippensburg College

Paulette Shockey, Hood College

Mary Stein, Oakland University

Brenda Webb, University of North Alabama

John Yang, Lakeland College

And last, we'd like to thank SAGE Publications for their willingness to publish a science methods textbook that is different from the norm.

PART I

The Nature of Science

Chapter 1

I Know What Science Is!

It's an Experiment!

Learning Objectives

After reading Chapter 1, students will be able to

- Recognize and describe the basic tenets of science and scientific knowledge
- Identify the National Science Education Standards (NSES) associated with inquiry and the nature of science
- Describe science as a body of knowledge, processes, and a way of knowing

---

NSES TEACHING STANDARDS ADDRESSED IN CHAPTER 1

Standard B: Teachers of science guide and facilitate learning.
  In doing this, teachers

- focus and support inquiries while interacting with students;
- orchestrate discourse among students about scientific ideas; and
- encourage and model the skills of scientific inquiry, as well as the curiosity, openness to new ideas and data, and skepticism that characterize science.

Standard D: Teachers of science design and manage learning environments that provide students with the time, space, and resources needed for learning science. In doing this, teachers

- structure the time available so that students are able to engage in extended investigation;
- create a setting for student work that is flexible and supportive of science inquiry;
- make the available science tools, materials, media, and technological resources accessible to students; and
- identify and use resources outside of school.

Source: Reprinted with permission from the National Science Education Standards, copyright 1996, by the National Academy of Sciences, Courtesy of National Academies Press, Washington, DC.

Introduction

This book is for you, the K–8 science teacher. It is important that you understand the approach you will find here is different from other science methods textbooks. First, you will find that each chapter is organized around an inquiry approach supported by the National Science Education Standards (National Research Council [NRC], 1996) and advocated as an effective way to teach K–8 science through inquiry—an approach discussed in more detail in Chapter 8. The organizing framework for each chapter is an inquiry approach known as the 5E instructional **model**. The five "E's" of this approach refer to a sequence of phases: Engage, Explore, Explain, Elaborate, and Evaluate. In brief, the **engage** phase motivates students and seeks to uncover students' prior ideas of the concept to be taught. The **explore** phase is associated with student activities, and the **explain** phase follows with teachers' questioning students by drawing on the science activities conducted in the classroom. The **elaborate** phase requires a new application of the concepts learned, and the **evaluate** phase is an evaluation of student learning. Because the 5E model is highly student centered, each chapter embeds activities within each of the phases that are designed for you to examine or perform. In essence, the chapters are designed to be interactive, while bringing to life the 5E model for teaching K–8 science. Our vision, therefore, begins with you, and our goal for you is to broaden your understandings of science, scientists, and science teaching using the 5E model. As such, we will introduce ideas, concepts, and processes that you need to know and understand before we ask you to apply and use them with your students in your science classroom.

So, let the journey begin.

When you think of science, what do you think about? Do you think of your science experiences in school? Do you think of the science books, vocabulary, and concepts that you had to learn in school? Do you think of a science project you did in elementary, middle, or high school? Do you think about science experiences outside of school? We know that we ask a lot of questions, but your understanding of science as a field of study with its own characteristics is important. What you think and know about science will be reflected in what and how you teach shaping the K–8 science teacher you will become. In this chapter, we will explore those traits that define science and scientific knowledge as a discipline that is somewhat different from other disciplines. You also will examine how science and scientific knowledge are viewed in light of the NSES (NRC, 1996) for envisioning effective science teaching and learning.

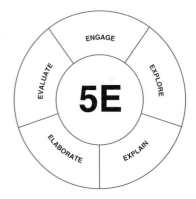

Let's start with you. Before you read further, take a few minutes to take a paper and pencil and draw a scientist or what you think a scientist might look like.

After you complete your drawing, share it with one of your classmates or ask a friend to draw a scientist and take a look at each other's drawing. Reflect on what details you and your peers have included or omitted. Write statements about what the drawing or drawings tell you about the individuals' images of a scientist (i.e., mad scientist). After having explored your image of a scientist, reflect further. What is the work of scientists really like? What would you say if one of your students asked, "What is science?" or "How is science done?"

Now that you have completed this activity, examine your drawing using the "Draw-a-Scientist Test" (DAST) checklist (Table 1.1) to gain insights into views of scientists and the stereotypical characteristics that individuals commonly imagine (Finson, 2002, 2003; Finson, Beaver, & Cramond, 1995). Keep these ideas in mind as you draw on your inner scientist in the following activity.

Table 1.1 Draw-a-Scientist Test (DAST) Checklist

Stereotype characteristics	In the drawing	Not in the drawing	Examples
Lab coat			
Eyeglasses or goggles			
Facial hair			
Symbols of Research • Science instruments • Lab equipment • Microscope, flasks, beakers, test tubes, animals, or others			
Symbols of Technology • Types: Computers, calculators. cell phones, television, etc. • Products: Rockets, etc.			
Symbols of Knowledge • Books, cabinets, clip board, pens in pockets			
Captions or Thought Bubbles • Formula, equations, classification, period charts, etc.			
Male			
Signs/posters/labels			
Unkempt appearance			
Caucasian only			
Middle-aged or elderly scientists			
Signs of secrecy or warning signs: (Private, Do not enter, etc.)			
Indications of danger			
Other images			
Evil or sinister (stereotypes), e.g., mad scientist			
Eccentric appearance (geek)			
Neutral			

Stereotype characteristics	In the drawing	Not in the drawing	Examples
Positive (smile, positive captions)			
Female			
Scientist working inside			

Note: Modified from Finson, K. D., Beaver, J. B., & Cramond, B. L. (1995), Development and field test of a checklist for the Draw-a-Scientist Test, *School Science and Mathematics*, *95*, 195–205.

Engage

Making Observations and Inferences With a Fossil

Now, think for a moment about a core skill needed to conduct scientific investigations. Did the word "observation" come to mind? It's a word you've heard many times before, but how would you define it? An **observation** is any information gathered through your senses or with instruments to extend your senses. Eighty-five percent of the observations made by sighted people come from one sensory organ, our eyes. However, when teaching students about the process of observation, it is important to stress that the best observations use more than one sensory organ to collect data. Be aware that when students make observations they also make explanations, generalizations, or draw conclusions based on their observations and experiences. These general statements are called **inferences**, and they may or may not be correct. Inferences are explanations, generalizations, or conclusions a person makes based on observations and experiences. As a science teacher, it is important to recognize the difference between the skills of observation and inference when teaching students. Consider the following sentence: "I ran into the kitchen and saw Mel standing by the table holding a cloth dripping water." To get you started, here is one observation: *There was a table*. Another observation is *Mel was standing*. An inference is an explanation that may or may not be correct. An inference you might make is that *Mel is a male*. Mel may or may not be a male. We do not know. Another inference is that *Mel spilled water and was cleaning it up*. So, look at the sentence again. What other observations and inferences can you make?

Making observations and inferences are fundamental skills in science; let's put those skills to work. Imagine you were fortunate enough that your paleontology professor, who needed a few extra assistants, offered you an opportunity to go on a dig to Morocco over the summer. During that trip, you found a most unusual fossil. You photographed the fossil and, with the help of your peers, you seek to find out what you've found. Now, look at the fossil you found (see Figure 1.1).

Teacher's Desk Tip: Addressing Diversity in Your Classroom

Consider adaptations for students with diverse needs. How would you adapt the fossil activity for a child who is visually impaired? Perhaps you could make clay model of the bones, or use actual fossils. Can you think of other adaptations?

Figure 1.1 Fossil bone

Make a concept web (graphic organizer that can be used to organize ideas, thoughts, concepts, and skills around a central topic or theme) or a list of statements about what you know about fossils. In making the web, consider the following questions: What are fossils? How do they form? Where do we find them? What process(es) create fossils? How do you think scientists reconstruct organisms from fossils? What tools do scientists use to reconstruct organisms from fossils? Next, look at the fossil pictured in Figure 1.1 and create a list of observations about it. What inferences can you make about the fossil? Describe the relationship between your observations and your inferences. Explain.

Explore

Digging Into the Nature of Science

Your exciting discovery has led you to pursue a dual degree in education and paleontology. You spend your summers at various archaeological digs, but that fossil you found remains on your mind. You're driven to know more. An opportunity to join a funded expedition back to Morocco and additional sites where similar fossils have been found becomes available through the National Observation System grant program. Fortunately, the university's scientific team was awarded a large grant and can assemble research teams to gather more information about your fossil find. You remember how excited your science methods peers were when you shared your pictures of the fossil. This time, you help arrange the research teams and invite some of your science methods peers to become a part of the teams.

The plan is to send out teams to the following places: Morocco, Siberia, the Badlands of South Dakota, Nigeria, and the Australian Outback. Based on past findings, each team is given GPS (global positioning satellite) coordinates for the location of its specific dig. Because of the remote locations and the political climates in some of the selected locations, digs must occur only at the approved sites. (We don't want to create any international incidents!)

As the summer ends and the school year is about to begin, the teams find they're not able to fully excavate the fossils and are forced to rely on pictures and sketches. Each team has a few more weeks on location before returning home, so, based on the sketches made (Figure 1.2), teams construct models using the "highly technical" tools of paper, pencils, and scissors (sorry, you didn't get *that* much funding) and begin working on models of the skeletal reconstruction. You, as a member of the team, will build a model and make a drawing of what you think the organism may have looked like. Answer the following questions to guide your investigation. Be prepared to discuss the evidences you have to support your reconstruction. The National Observation System program directors, Professors Eed Notsdlog and Arual Yenwod and hopefully your instructor, will arrange for a conference where the teams will meet to share their findings.

When you think of science, is this the kind of activity that comes to mind? What if we told you the activity is more than an exercise that simulates work done by paleontologists? In fact, it is intended to illustrate the nature of scientific knowledge and how it is produced. It is also an illustration of the way scientists may conduct research, depending on their field of study. So what does this activity reveal about scientific knowledge? How does this activity relate to the **nature of science** and scientists? Now, think about the scientist you drew. If you were to

---

Figure 1.2 Fossil Bone Set for Reconstructing a Mystery Organism

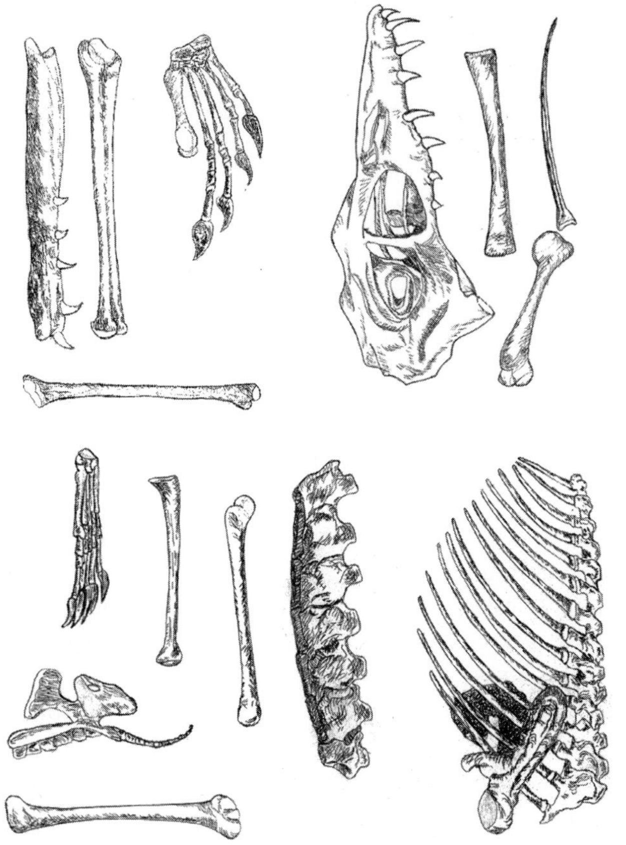

QUESTIONS

1. What are your observations?

2. What inferences did you make from the fossil sketches provided?

3. How would you describe your model (or drawing)? What are models? What role do you think models play in science?

4. What strategies or ideas did you use as you reconstructed the organism?

5. How confident are you about your reconstruction?

6. What do you think the organism looked like? Sketch it.

---

now draw the paleontologists for the fossil activity, would they look like the scientist you drew earlier? The DAST checklist (Table 1.1) reveals many stereotypical characteristics of scientists that are held by many individuals. The point is that many of the characteristics may not be representative of what a scientist looks like or the research he or she does. The activity should challenge you to rethink your views of science and scientists. As you read the next section, consider the focus questions to direct your thinking on the nature of scientific knowledge, the ways science is carried out, and how science is viewed in our society.

> *Science is the belief in the ignorance of the experts.*
>
> Richard Feynman
>
> How does this quote challenge your ideas about science? What type of disposition or attitude is Feynman advocating in the quote? Who is Richard Feynman?

Explain

Focus Questions

1. What is science?

2. What are the basic principles of the nature of science? How are these principles different from your experiences with science?

3. Describe **scientific theories and laws**. How are scientific theories and laws developed?

4. What is scientific inquiry?

5. How is scientific inquiry conceptualized by the NSES (NRC, 1996)?

The Nature of Science and Scientific Knowledge

As a K–8 science teacher, it is important that you recognize the nature of science, scientific knowledge, and the work of scientists to make the science taught in your classroom more relevant. This means examining aspects of science you may not have considered before. Imagine sitting on a high boulder surrounded by lush evergreen trees, listening to crystal-clear water rushing by or watching an eagle soar over the river below and swoop down for a trout. Do you hear and recognize a woodpecker tap-tap-tapping among the trees? Your sensory experiences are only the beginning of what is really happening around you. Why is the water moving so fast? What is the woodpecker really doing? How does it find food? How does the trout survive in fast-moving water? Why do the evergreens grow so tall? If we think about it as scientists, we might consider that everything in this scenario is centered on the energy of the sun. The trees compete for light to produce food through photosynthesis. The algae and plants found in the water and along the shore use sunlight to grow, and then become food for small fish and insects that in turn become food for the trout, and the trout for the eagle. When we stop and view the natural world or the universe, it generates questions that make us wonder and seek to explore its mysteries much as a child wonders how her favorite toy dinosaur roars or why stars appear to twinkle at night. The way in which *you* view the natural world shapes your views of science, scientists, and of how knowledge is generated through scientific activities.

So what is the nature of science? In general, it is a way of knowing guided by commonly held principles that result in scientific knowledge. Though some may disagree on the exact details or principles underpinning the nature of science, there are some principles or tenets on which most individuals would agree. These are described in the list below (Lederman, 1998).

1. *Scientific knowledge is developmental and subject to change* (National Science Teachers Association [NSTA], 2000). Scientific knowledge is not absolute.

Do you remember learning the names of all nine planets in our solar system? Did you use a mnemonic device like, "**M**y **V**ery **E**legant **M**other **J**ust **S**at **U**pon **N**ine **P**orcupines," to remember their order (the first letter of each word is the first letter of the planets in their proper order)? Within the past ten years, scientists have debated whether Pluto would remain a planet or be demoted to a Kuiper Belt Object (minor planets). In 2006, the

International Astronomical Union, which is charged with the classification of astronomical objects, reclassified Pluto to a dwarf planet. Older science textbooks, museum displays, and planet mobiles that include Pluto will need to be changed! So remember, scientific knowledge is not absolute; in fact, it is a work in progress that can be changed or even replaced. Guess it's time for a new mnemonic: "**M**y **V**ery **E**legant **M**other **J**ust **S**at **U**pon **N**eedles!" Consider the fossil reconstruction in the engage phase above. Do you think your model is absolute? Probably not: As new information in science arises, scientific knowledge is subject to change.

2. Scientific knowledge must be at least partially supported by empirical data.

Harold Varmus, Nobel Prize winner, with the National Institute of Health, stated at a 1996 Harvard University commencement address, "Science is a way of thinking—making judgments, often creative ones, that are based on evidence, not on desires, received beliefs or hearsay" (Varmus, 1996, p. 119). These "evidences" are empirical data from experiments or observations drawn from the senses or technological tools that extend the senses. Think about the fossil activity: What was your empirical data? Did you take measurements of the bone sockets? Did you compare shapes and sizes of the bones? Did you make careful, systematic observations of the joints? If you did, then you were gathering empirical data or "evidence" to support your reconstruction.

3. Scientific knowledge, in part, comes from the creativity and imagination of the scientists (NSTA, 2000). Scientific knowledge combines empirical evidence and creativity.

Did you use creativity and imagination in the fossil activity? Maybe you were creative and found that you had "extra bones" that were not part of the original organism. Instead, the bones were from something the organism ate. We have seen creative students take the paper bones and hold them up to the light to see if they could align the joints to match in shape and size. Scientists, too, use creativity in the way they ask questions, the methods they use, and even in the way they present the findings of their work.

4. Scientific knowledge is inherently subjective to some degree and therefore not objective, as is often assumed.

In the fossil activity, think of something you objectively know or observed about the bones (that is, something that is impartial, neutral, without bias)? You might take a measurement of the width, curve, or length of the bones and joints. Now, think of something you know about bones from a subjective stance (intuitive or instinctive). You may look at one bone and think, intuitively, that it looks like part of a jaw or a face or a tail or a hand. Both of these ways of knowing is important in understanding the nature of science. It's a myth to think that all science is objective.

5. Scientific knowledge involves both observation and inference.

Scientific knowledge comes about through observations made with the senses or with technology that extends the senses. Furthermore, it involves inferences that are statements based on observations that lead one to generalizations or conclusions. Did you make inferences based on observations of the teeth in the skull bone fossils you examined earlier? Did you infer the kinds of food the organism may have eaten? Did you make other inferences?

6. *Scientific knowledge is amoral—neither good nor bad.*

In a commencement address at Morgan State University in 1997, President Bill Clinton acknowledged this tenet by stating that science has no soul of its own. Clinton noted that, historically, scientific knowledge often emerges faster than our ability to understand its application. For instance, in April 2003, the entire gene sequence (genome) of the human species, *Homo sapiens*, was mapped. For the first time, scientists could decode and read the blueprints that make up human life. Now, what we do with this scientific knowledge is another matter. For instance, with this knowledge scientists have the opportunity to learn more about the genetic factors that cause diseases and to apply that knowledge to the prevention, diagnosis, and treatment of the diseases. Sounds very promising, doesn't it? On the other hand, what if insurance companies use this knowledge for genetic prescreening and only insure those individuals who do not show any propensity for a serious disease? Scientific knowledge, itself, is neither good nor bad. However, because the applications of scientific knowledge affect us, we must be scientifically literate.

7. *Science is influenced by social factors; it is a social endeavor* (McComas, Clough, & Almazroa, 1998).

It only takes looking back at the history of science to recognize that the directions that science progresses are often influenced by social needs and conditions. Recall what happened in the United States after the Soviet Union launched Sputnik I into space in October 1957. Research related to space and rocketry intensified so the United States could regain a competitive edge in the space race. Today, we see social influences on science as we look at the national emphasis on finding and developing economically feasible renewable or alternative energy sources. As a result of this social factor, it is likely we will see more funding shift toward research associated with these areas, which generally means a growth of scientific knowledge in these fields.

8. *There is no single set or sequence of steps in a scientific study* (NSTA, 2000). Scientists use a variety of methods to approach their questions and problems.

Think back to the fossil activity. Did you reconstruct the fossils in the same manner as others performing the task? Did you follow the scientific method you learned in school during the reconstruction? Our experience with this activity has repeatedly shown that students use many different approaches. Some individuals reconstruct the skeleton using trial and error. Others use more systematic approaches based on skeletal structures that they have studied previously, and still others are creative and put the bones in the most unusual positions. In short, not everyone uses the same approach in reconstructing the fossil bones. These different approaches to solving problems support the notion that there is no single scientific method. Throughout the history of science, there have been many debates regarding a single scientific method. Thomas Kuhn, in his influential book *The Structure of Scientific Revolutions* (1962), clearly suggests that scientists have worked within many paradigms or frameworks. Depending on the field of science and the researcher, the way scientific research methods are conducted will vary.

To understand how to teach science to children, it is important that you be aware of your understandings and perhaps a few misunderstandings surrounding the Nature of Science. For instance, recall the tenet that there is no single scientific method. Did you have to memorize the scientific method while you were in school? We suspect you did. Well, we did as well. Unfortunately, the notion that there is a single scientific method exists. It perpetuates a notion of a linear and hierarchical progression of the development of scientific knowledge from observation to law, which is not necessarily the case.

Viewing science and the development of scientific knowledge through the dynamic interactions between hypotheses, theories, and laws is more realistic than the traditional, linear or hierarchical view for a couple of reasons (see Figure 1.3). First, theories and laws are different kinds of scientific knowledge (McComas, 1996). For instance, a theory is an inferred "explanation of observable events," whereas "laws are statements about the relationships among the observable events" (Abd-El-Khalick, Bell, & Lederman, 1998; N. Lederman, 1994; Lederman & Lederman, 2010). Second, laws and theories cannot be absolutely proven. Simply stated, we cannot guarantee that some happening in the future would occur in the same manner as prescribed by the scientific law. Theories and laws can change. Consider the picture you drew of the organism from the fossil reconstruction: Can you prove that your model is the exact reconstruction of the live organism? Not likely, so when teaching K–8 science, it is important to acknowledge that multiple approaches for investigating scientific phenomena are important. In addition, K–8 science teachers should assist students in understanding that scientific theories and laws represent different kinds of knowledge that may change if the theories or laws do not explain the current findings.

Consider Figure 1.3 and the narrative in *Your Science Classroom: Team Meetings and Planning*. How does Table 1.2 provide evidence that theories do not necessarily become laws? What does this suggest about there being a single scientific method? As a teacher, how would you describe a theory and a law to your students? How do scientific theories

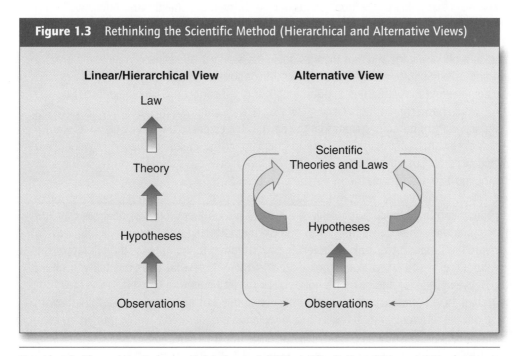

Figure 1.3 Rethinking the Scientific Method (Hierarchical and Alternative Views)

Note: Adapted with permission. Lederman, N. & Lederman, J. (2010), *Avoiding De-Natured Science: Activities that Promote Understandings of the Nature of Science.* Available at http://msed.iit.edu/projectican/.

support the nature of science principle that science is developmental or tentative? What example could you provide to your students?

As you examine the examples of theories and laws in Table 1.2, you will find that some laws such as the Law of Gravitation has no theory associated with it, and that some laws were developed long before the theory that explain the phenomena. As you may have surmised, one can identify the nature of science tenets throughout the history of scientific discoveries. Now that you have read some of the principles that underpin the nature of science, inquiry, and scientific knowledge, let's turn our attention to descriptions of science.

YOUR SCIENCE CLASSROOM:
Team Meetings and Planning

Ms. Sung Lee, the seventh-grade science instructor at Ridge Quarry Middle School, has been working on her master's degree in science education at the local university. In her "Science Trends and Issues" class, her instructor shared Table 1.1, then engaged the class in a discussion of theory,

> **Teaching Standard B: 3**
>
> How does this scenario reflect this standard?

law, and the Nature of Science. Ms. Lee was struck by her misunderstandings about the nature of science and wondered if her colleagues held the same ideas. At the weekly science team-planning meeting, Ms. Lee made copies of her class chart (see Figure 1.3) for her colleagues and asked, "How do you teach students about the scientific method? How do you handle teaching about theories and laws in your classrooms?"

Tom Alvarez, the eighth-grade science teacher replied, "I have them learn the scientific method as presented in the textbooks. The text doesn't cover a lot on this, but, from what I remember, it basically says theories are tested ideas that hold up over long periods of time. Given more time they become laws." Sung said, "Yeah, that's what I thought, too. I was using the same idea, but take a look at this chart my professor gave the class as we were discussing the nature of science. It surprised me that theories and laws refer to different kinds of knowledge and that theories don't necessarily become laws!" Tom had a puzzled look on his face and asked Sung to explain. "Well, if you think about the nature of science, theories, and laws through history we find that science is not absolute, but is self-correcting. Think about it: If it were absolute, a theory would never change, right? And a law would never change either. But they do. Consider Ptolemy's geocentric theory of the solar system that the earth is the center of the solar system. As science advances and new observations are made, we came to understand that Ptolemy's theory no longer held up under new evidences. So Copernicus' heliocentric theory that places the sun in the center of the solar system became the most comprehensive theory for the time period."

Tom replied, "Well, I understand what you're saying about that, but I am not sure how you're relating this to the scientific method." Sung said, "Well, there are different kinds of sciences that use different methods to address their questions and so a single method makes no more sense than having all theories turn into laws. Now, if you look at Table 1.2, pay attention to the dates and the relationship between them and it'll give you a few clues. Look closely at the dates—what does this tell you about the relationship between theories and laws? It's not as clear cut as we tend to teach it. These ideas not only make me rethink how I am teaching science in my classroom, but also makes me rethink how to teach students about the different ways that scientific knowledge is generated." With a grin on his face, Tom asked, "Hmm, how does evolutionary theory fit into this?" to which everyone chuckled and quickly noticed that their planning time was over. The two additional team members, Lynn and Sue replied, "Guess we'll have to continue this conversation next time, Tom!"

Table 1.2 Comparison of Theories and Laws	
Scientific Law	**Scientific Theory**
Boyles Law	**Kinetic Theory**
Robert Boyle, a physicist, stated that the pressure (p) of a given quantity of gas varies inversely to its volume (v) at constant temperature (1662). French physicist Edme Mariotte also discovered the relationship (1676).	Kinetic Theory proposes that the pressure of molecules is due to collisions between molecules moving about with a certain velocity. This theory underpins Boyle's Law, and is thought to have been first developed by Daniel Bernoulli (1738), though some suggest it was first developed by Rudolph Clausius and James Maxwell (1850s).
Law of Segregation and Law of Independent Assortment	**Chromosome Theory**
Mendel's Laws of Inheritance include the Law of Segregation and the Law of Independent Assortment (1865–1866). The Law of Segregation states that each pair of alleles separate when gametes are formed. A gamete will receive one allele of the pair. The Law of Independent Assortment states that two or more pairs of alleles segregate independently of one another during gamete formation.	The Chromosome Theory by Thomas Morgan and colleagues stated that chromosomes carry genes for each trait and chromosomes carry hereditary information (1915).
Law of Universal Gravitation	
Newton's Law of Universal Gravitation states that every mass in the universe attracts every other mass (1687). In his *Principia, The Mathematical Principles of Natural Philosophy,* he wrote that every particle in the universe exerts a force on every other particle along the line joining their centers. The magnitude of the force is directly proportional to the product of the masses of the two particles, and inversely proportional to the square of the distances between them.	None

Note: Adapted with permission. Lederman, N. & Lederman, J. (2010), *Avoiding De-Natured Science: Activities that Promote Understandings of the Nature of Science.* Available at http://msed.iit.edu/projectican/.

What Is Science?

Up to this point in the chapter, we've been talking about the nature of science and the processes by which scientific knowledge has been and is currently being developed. Now that you have a good idea of how scientific knowledge emerges, how can we apply that understanding to a definition of science? In other words, what do we mean when we refer to science?

If we asked any one of you for your definition of science, it is likely that we would get a variety of responses. For instance, most individuals think of school and view science as a body of knowledge related to the natural world. Some would define science as a way of viewing the world searching for explanations with the intent of understanding how the world works. Still others view science as a way of solving problems and using the solutions to explain how events, processes, and objects operate as they do. All of these definitions include dimensions of science.

Looking across the dimensions we find that science includes (a) a body of knowledge, (b) processes for conducting inquiry, and (c) ways of thinking reflected in the tenets that underpin the nature of scientific knowledge.

BULLETIN BOARD

Did you know the term "science" comes from the Latin word "scientia," or "knowledge"?

During the span of our careers, we have heard many definitions of science; one we find useful is simple and elegant. It came from a fellow science education professor, Dr. Steve Oliver, who was asked to describe his view of science. He replied, "Science is any activity that allows one to be intellectually independent with respect to the natural world." We find students' abilities to judge the evidences of an inquiry or read the findings of a study to determine the value of the evidences on their own captures the essence of science and scientific literacy that we must encourage when teaching K–8 students.

Connecting the Nature of Science, Classroom Inquiry, and the National Science Education Standards

At this point, you may be wondering why you need to know about the nature of science. Simply put, the answer is that your views of science and the nature of scientific knowledge will influence how your students come to view science. So, when you teach science, remember that scientists build concepts as they engage with and explore the world around them. The same should hold for students learning science. It is generally accepted by most educators that students, especially young students, learn through experience (Butts & Hofman, 1993; Dewey, 1998; Piaget, 1952, 1964). Teachers should plan explorations where students experience science and acquire knowledge as a process. This process draws on their observations and other information to form concepts about the phenomena under study. Over time, students should come to know that scientific knowledge is a work in progress that changes with new information. Therefore, scientific knowledge is always subject to change. However, it is important for students to know that, despite the possibility that the knowledge may change, it still represents the best explanations scientists have at the time.

Upon examining the nature of science and scientific knowledge, you may be wondering what science content is taught in K–8 classrooms. The state and national standards serve as your guide for answering this question. The NSES (NRC, 1996), which include both content and inquiry standards, is the go-to resource for all science teachers. The content standards are designed to provide a guide for teaching relevant science topics based on what students should know by the end of the fourth, eighth, and twelfth grades. Content standards include the core disciplines of life science, earth and space science, and physical science, with additional standards on science as inquiry, science in personal and social perspectives, and science and technology. The NSES are discussed in depth in Chapter 2, however, because science content goes hand in hand with inquiry let's take a moment to look at inquiry in the science classroom.

We all know that children are naturally curious about what they observe in their world. At times, they can ask what appears to be an endless string of questions in their search to find out how the world operates. Children, like scientists, seek explanations to the questions they pose. Students want to know how birds fly, why trees grow so tall, what causes rainbows, and why one ball dropped in the bathtub sinks another one floats, to name but a few.

Using students' questions and facilitating their search for explanations initiate students into the processes of inquiry (Duckworth, 1987; Johnston, 1996; Wray, 1999). So just how does one view inquiry? For some educators, like Cherif (1993), to inquire is to "seek knowledge and understanding by questioning, observing, investigating, analyzing and evaluating" (p. 26). In essence, his view suggests that scientific inquiry involves skills that allow the learner to experience the nature of science firsthand. Suchman (1966), an early leader in developing inquiry strategies and inquiry-based programs, suggested that inquiry strategies include presenting **discrepant events** where outcomes are unexpected or problematic situations where students observe, ask questions, test various hypotheses, and debrief through discussion. Teaching children science through inquiry involves providing opportunities and an environment for students to learn the skills necessary to conduct science explorations like a scientist (Layman, 1996; Wray, 1999). It also means that students learn key concepts and the language of science while experiencing inquiry opportunities.

Today, the NSES (NRC, 1996) serve as a guide for teaching science as inquiry. In particular, the standards provide guidelines to envision science as a body of knowledge, a process, and a way of thinking to gain understanding of the natural world. The standards for scientific **inquiry** stress that students have the

(1) abilities needed to conduct scientific investigations; and the

(2) understanding about science inquiry at all grade levels.

Children continually explore science through informal, everyday activities. Many children observe rainbows not only in the sky, but also in the spray of a garden hose.

In other words, according to the NSES, K–8 students should *acquire skills* by asking questions, conducting experiments, using scientific tools to collect data, analyzing data, developing explanations, and communicating their findings. In addition, elementary and middle school students should also *understand about* science inquiry. This includes (a) answering questions in light of knowledge already acquired, (b) designing investigations based on the questions, (c) using instruments, technology, and mathematics in conducting investigations, (d) recognizing that strong explanations are based on evidence, (e) communicating scientific findings for critique and review by other scientists that lead to acceptance or replacement of the ideas for better ones, and (f) acknowledging that advances in science through logical skepticism can result in new or different methods, technologies, questions, and investigations (see Figures 1.4 and 1.5). You might have noticed as you read through the list of the ideas in Figure 1.4 and 1.5 that they are

Author's Note:

National Science Education Standards: You can download and examine NSES free at National Academies Press Library at www.nap .edu.

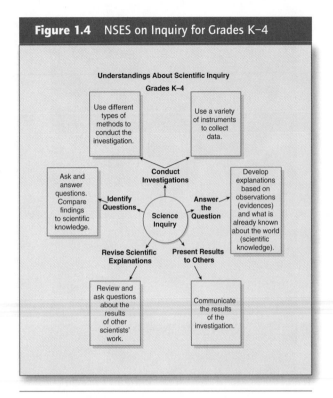

Figure 1.4 NSES on Inquiry for Grades K–4

Note: Adapted from National Research Council (1996), *National Science Education Standards*, Washington, DC: National Academies Press; and National Research Council (2000), *Inquiry and the National Science Education Standards*, Washington, DC: National Academy of Sciences.

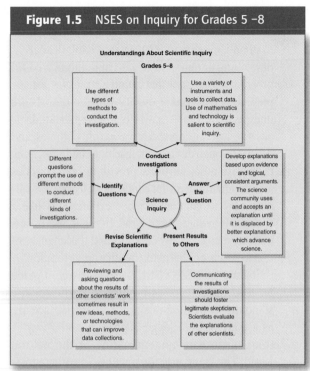

Figure 1.5 NSES on Inquiry for Grades 5 –8

Note: Adapted from National Research Council (1996), *National Science Education Standards*, Washington, DC: National Academies Press; and National Research Council (2000), *Inquiry and the National Science Education Standards*, Washington, DC: National Academy of Sciences.

reminiscent of the discussion about the nature of science earlier in the chapter. If you did, you're right! K–8 science teachers should create learning environments that assist students in developing ways of thinking and acting that are associated with scientific inquiry and reflect the nature of science.

Technology and Science

The last section of this chapter focuses on the roles of technology in science, which often go hand in hand. The NSES (NRC, 1996) address science and technology in both the content standards and the teaching standards. Within the content standards, a distinction is made between science inquiry and technology. Scientific inquiry is motivated by a desire to understand the natural world, whereas technology and technological design are driven by the desire to meet human needs and solve our problems. According to the NSES (NRC, 1996, p. 106), students should

1. distinguish between natural objects and objects made by humans (K–4),

2. develop the abilities of technological design (K–8), and

3. develop understandings about science and technology (K–8).

Like science, technological advances and technology are human endeavors that attempt to solve problems. Technology often adapts the environment and science seeks new knowledge. In science, inquiry skills such as identifying the problem and developing ways to test hypotheses help solve problems. In technology, skills focus on the design processes. Through technological design there are often multiple solutions to a problem or need. Based on the design criteria, one or more solutions may be selected to accomplish the task. For instance, a colleague who teaches in a sixth-grade classroom had a student who had a head injury as a result of a bicycle accident. She used that teachable moment to integrate technological design in her classroom. Students examined a variety of bike helmets to evaluate and redesign them to make them safer. In doing so, students used their understanding of the physics of motion, physical properties of materials, and human anatomy to address a real-life problem. This is an authentic example of the partnership between science and technology. From ancient times through today, scientific work has incorporated technologies that generate new scientific achievements, often evoking a need for new applications of technology.

It is because science and technology are so interrelated and interdependent that technology plays an important role in the K–8 science classroom. Concern for the interconnections between science and technology has been a major theme identified in recent educational reform documents. Reform documents, such as *The American Competitiveness Initiative*, address the connections in a variety of ways that range from students' achieving literacy in science and technology for daily life, to functioning competitively in global information-based work forces of science and technology (Domestic Policy Council, 2006).

Now here's where we're really going to try to confuse you. So far, we've been talking about technology as it relates to science (content understanding and skills) in the K–8 science classroom, but we also think it is important that you, as a teacher, understand the important role that technology can play in teaching and learning science, which is often referred to as educational technology.

BULLETIN BOARD

Guidelines for Using Educational Technology in the Science Classroom

Flick and Bell (2000) propose the following guidelines for technology use in science classrooms:

1. Technology should be introduced within science content.

2. Technology should address worthwhile science with appropriate pedagogy.

3. Technology instruction in science should take advantage of the unique features of technology.

4. Technology should make scientific views more accessible.

5. Technology instruction should develop students' understanding of the relationship between technology and science.

Today, technology as a teaching tool is influencing the way students learn. Technology for learning might include a variety of digital technologies that can open new options for students to learn science. Digital technologies have influenced science teaching in three areas (Flick & Bell, 2000). First, digital technologies have impacted science education K–16 by changing the ways in which interactions between teachers and students occur. Socially and psychologically, digital technologies influence the ways in which information is imparted, related, and organized. A second area of impact is the influence on instructional approaches that are driven by NSES and National Educational Technology Standards (International Society for Technology in Education [ISTE], 2008), both of which advocate the use of a range of digital technologies in teaching. Third, students and teachers are interacting with digital technologies in new and interesting ways on personal levels, as well as to conduct activities or deliver course content (teaching, advising, counseling, and mentoring) with the use of online discussions, Facebook, blogs, Second Life, Twitter, email, Glogster, Edmodo, GPS, texting, and others. These technological applications change rapidly.

It is not our intent to discuss all the possibilities for using educational technology in your science classroom. Nevertheless, we will include technology applications and tech connects like the following throughout the book.

TECH CONNECT: Podcasts

Make an audio tour of an outdoor classroom. Have students make observations and pose questions about natural outdoor features you select for them (plants, nests, flowers, water features, etc.). Have them research the features, write a script, and take turns recording salient points of interest for their designated area using a microphone and computer. Download audio recordings and make a class Podcast. These can be downloaded and combined to create a guided tour of the outdoor classroom for other classes and visitors.

The versatility of computers and digital technologies are everyday tools for today's youth, the digital generation.

For instance, a technology application for a science investigation may incorporate the use of a GPS to record the locations where your students are taking water samples along the steam. The data will allow students to accurately plot all the data collection locations on a map. Mapping the locations give students visual data of all the locations that assists them in making sense of their findings. Using this approach, they might explore where within the watershed their sample sites are located or whether their sample site was on a straight stretch or on a bend in the steam, and use that information to determine patterns that might influence water quality. Another example is using Twitter as a way to communicate information between the team leaders at the different sample collection sites.

As a science teacher, you're in a unique position not only to use technologies to enhance learning, but also, when appropriate, to explain the science associated with the technology. However, don't be misled: technology is an application of science, but technology can advance on its own. We urge you to use technology because it enhances the students' abilities to learn, understand, and conduct science, and not use it simply for its own sake. Sometimes, simple discussions enhance learning far more effectively than a technological tool.

Elaborate

Finding the Nature of Science in Everyday Things

At this point, you should be familiar with the basic principles of the nature of science. During the fossil activity you experienced some of the nature of science tenets (perhaps without even realizing it). In this task, we ask you to apply what you have learned about the nature of science. Read the following excerpt from a book by the late physicist Richard Feynman, and identify as many tenets of the nature of science as you can.

What principles did you find evidence for in Feynman's story? Did you find aspects of the nature of science that represent the notion that science is amoral? Did you find aspects of the nature of science that science is empirical? Did you find evidence that there are multiple approaches to conducting science? What other tenets are found in the story? Which of the principles seem most common in the story?

From "WHAT DO YOU CARE WHAT OTHER PEOPLE THINK?": FURTHER ADVENTURES OF A CURIOUS CHARACTER by Richard Feynman as told to Ralph Leighton. Copyright@1988 by Gweneth Feynman and Ralph Leighton. Used by permission of W. W. Norton & Company, INC., pp. 12–16.

Before I was born, my father told my mother, "If it's a boy, he's going to be a scientist." When I was just a little kid, very small in a highchair, my father brought home a lot of little bathroom tiles—seconds—of different colors. We played with them, my father setting them up vertically on my highchair like dominoes, and I would push one end so they would all go down.

Then after a while, I'd help set them up. Pretty soon, we're setting them up in a more complicated way: two white tiles and a blue tile, two white tiles and a blue tile, and so on. When my mother saw that she said, "Leave the poor child alone. If he wants to put a blue tile, let him put a blue tile."

But my father said, "No, I want to show him what patterns are like and how interesting they are. It's a kind of elementary mathematics." So he started very early to tell me about the world and how interesting it is.

We had the *Encyclopaedia Britannica* at home. When I was a small boy he used to sit me on his lap and read to me from the *Britannica*. We would be reading, say, about dinosaurs. It would be talking about the *Tyrannosaurus rex*, and it would say something like, "This dinosaur is twenty-five feet high and its head is six feet across."

My father would stop reading and say, "Now let's see what that means. That would mean that if he stood in our front yard, he would be tall enough to put his head through our window up here." (We were on the second floor.) "But his head would be too wide to fit in the window." Everything he read to me he would translate as best he could into some reality.

It was very exciting and very, very interesting to think there were animals of such magnitude—and that they all died out, and that nobody knew why. I wasn't frightened that there would be one coming in my window as a consequence of this. But I learned from my father to translate: everything I read I try to figure out what it really means, what it's really saying.

We used to go to the Catskill Mountains, a place where people from New York City would go in the summer. The fathers would all return to New York to work during the week, and come back only for the weekend. On weekends, my father would take me for walks in the woods and he'd tell me about interesting things that were going on in the woods. When the other mothers saw this, they thought it was wonderful and that the other fathers should take their sons for walks. They tried to work on them but they didn't get anywhere at first. They wanted my father to take all the kids, but he didn't want to because

(Continued)

(Continued)

he had a special relationship with me. So it ended up that the other fathers had to take their children for walks the next weekend.

The next Monday, when the fathers were all back at work, we kids were playing in a field. One kid says to me, "See that bird? What kind of bird is that?"

I said, "I haven't the slightest idea what kind of bird it is."

He says, "It's a brown-throated thrush. Your father doesn't teach you anything!"

But it was the opposite. He had already taught me: "See that bird?" he says. "It's a Spencer's warbler." (I knew he didn't know the real name.) "Well, in Italian it's a *Chutto Lapittida*. In Portuguese, it's a *Bom da Peida*. In Chinese, it's a *Chung-long-tah,* and in Japanese, it is a *Katano Tekeda*. You can know the name of that bird in all the languages of the world, but when you're finished, you'll know absolutely nothing whatever about the bird. You'll only know about humans in different places, and what they call the bird. So let's look at the bird and see what it's *doing*—that's what counts." (I learned very early the difference between knowing the name of something and knowing something.)

He said, "For example, look: the bird pecks at its feathers all the time. See it walking around pecking at its feathers?"

"Yeah."

He says, "Why do you think birds peck at their feathers?"

I said, "Well, maybe they mess up their feathers when they fly, so they're pecking them in order to straighten them out."

"All right," he says. "If that were the case, then they would peck a lot just after they've been flying. Then, after they've been on the ground a while, they wouldn't peck so much any more—you know what I mean?"

"Yeah."

He says, "Let's look and see if they peck more just after they land."

It wasn't hard to tell: there was not much difference between the birds that had been walking around a bit and those that had just landed. So I said, "I give up. Why does a bird peck at its feathers?"

"Because there are lice bothering it," he says. "The lice eat flakes of protein that come off its feathers."

He continued, "Each louse has some waxy stuff on its legs, and little mites eat that. The mites don't digest it perfectly, so they emit from their rear ends a sugar-like material, in which bacteria grow."

Finally he says, "So you see, everywhere there's source of food, there's *some* form of life that finds it."

Now, I knew that it may not have been exactly a louse, that it might not be exactly true that the louse's legs have mites. That story was probably incorrect in *detail*, but what he was telling me was right in *principle*.

Another time, when I was older, he picked a leaf off a tree. This leaf had a flaw, a thing we never look at much. The leaf was sort of deteriorated; it had a little brown line in the shape of a C, starting somewhere in the middle of the leaf and going out in a curl to the edge.

"Look at this brown line," he says. "It's narrow at the beginning and it's wider as it goes to the edge. What this is, is a fly—a blue fly with yellow eyes and green wings has come and laid an egg on this leaf. Then, when the egg hatches into a maggot (a caterpillar-like thing), it spends its whole life eating this leaf—that's where it gets its food. As it eats along, it leaves behind this brown trail of eaten leaf. As the maggot grows, the trail grows wider until he's grown to full size at the end of the leaf, where he turns into a fly—a blue fly with yellow eyes and green wings—who flies away and lays an egg on another leaf."

Again, I knew that the details weren't precisely correct—it could have even been a beetle—but the idea that he was trying to explain to me was the amusing part of life: the whole thing is just reproduction. No matter how complicated the business is, the main point is to do it again!

Not having experience with many fathers, I didn't realize how remarkable he was. How did he learn the deep principles of science and the love of it, what's behind it, and why it's worth doing? I never really asked him, because I just assumed that those were things that fathers knew.

My father taught me to notice things. One day I was playing with an "express wagon," a little wagon with a railing around it. It had a ball in it, and when I pulled the wagon, I noticed something about the way the ball moved. I went to my father and said, "Say, Pop, I noticed something. When I pull the wagon, the ball rolls to the back of the wagon. And when I'm pulling it along and I suddenly stop, the ball rolls to the front of the wagon. Why is that?"

"That, nobody knows," he said. "The general principle is that things which are moving tend to keep on moving, and things which are standing still tend to stand still, unless you push them hard. This tendency is call 'inertia,' but nobody knows why it's true." Now, that's a deep understanding. He didn't just give me the name.

He went on to say, "If you look from the side, you'll see that it's the back of the wagon that you're pulling against the ball, and the ball stands still. As a matter of fact, from the friction it starts to move forward a little bit in relation to the ground. It doesn't move back."

I ran back to the little wagon and set the ball up again and pulled the wagon. Looking sideways, I saw that indeed he was right. Relative to the sidewalk, it moved forward a little bit.

That's the way I was educated by my father, with those kinds of examples and discussions: no pressure—just lovely, interesting discussions. It has motivated me for the rest of my life, and makes me interested in *all* the sciences. (It just happens that I do physics better.)

I've been caught, so to speak—like someone who was given something wonderful when he was a child, and he's always looking for it again. I'm always looking, like a child, for the wonders I know I'm going to find—maybe not every time, but every once in a while.

From "WHAT DO YOU CARE WHAT OTHER PEOPLE THINK?": FURTHER ADVENTURES OF A CURIOUS CHARACTER by Richard Feynman as told to Ralph Leighton. Copyright@1988 by Gweneth Feynman and Ralph Leighton. Used by permission of W. W. Norton & Company, INC.

Evaluate

Nature of Science in the News

Feynman's narrative illustrates many examples of the nature of science. Now we want you to identify some on your own. Focusing on global climate change, you will use resources and technologies to locate information (i.e., news articles, journal articles, websites, and other resources) to illustrate the nature of science. Find three different sources of information to demonstrate three different the nature of science tenets (see pages 8–10). Identify the source of information and describe how it depicts global climate change. Then explain how the information typifies the nature of science tenet you select. For example, you might locate a newspaper article that *describes* how scientists are designing and testing huge reflective sheets of plastic to lay down over large areas of the polar ice caps. The researchers hypothesize that the sheets will decrease or eliminate the rate of melting. You *decide* that the newspaper article represents science as a "creative endeavor" and *explain* how this aligns with the tenet selected. In this case, you begin by stating that the scientists creatively used knowledge of the properties of inexpensive materials to design a potentially useful technology for slowing down the melting of the ice caps due to global climate change.

Summary

As you began this chapter, we asked you to consider what "science" means to you. Do you still think of science as mostly experiments? Do you think of science as concepts and terms students must memorize? Do you see science as a fixed sequence of steps that scientists and students use to carry out an experiment? Did reading the chapter challenge some of your ideas about science? We hope so. A major goal of K–8 teachers of science is to foster the development of students who are able to make informed decisions about science that influences their lives. This is referred to as "scientific literacy." You will not be able to accomplish this goal in a single year, but you can begin this journey by teaching students about the nature of science and the use of technologies, as well as by teaching them the skills for investigating science via inquiry. In closing, this chapter addressed science as a body of knowledge, a process or method, and a way of knowing the natural world. The nature of science as a way of knowing was emphasized in this chapter because it is the most neglected of these aspects in teaching science. Your task as a K–8 science teacher is to teach all aspects of science. Furthermore, these aspects of science should be continually addressed throughout the K–12 curriculum (AAAS, 1993; NRC, 1996).

Annotated Resources

University of California's Museum of Paleontology

http://evolution.berkeley.edu/evosite/nature/index.shtml

This website was created by the University of California's Museum of Paleontology with support provided by the National Science Foundation and the Howard Hughes Medical Institute. It is an excellent resource for both teachers and students. The site explores the nature of science with an interactive quiz to challenge your abilities to draw on your knowledge of the nature of science. For teachers, this site includes a variety of excellent grade level activities that can be used in K–8 science classrooms to teach the various tenets of the nature of science.

American Association for the Advancement of Science website has free online access for the book. *Science for All Americans* (AAAS, 1991)

http://www.project2061.org/publications/sfaa/online/chap1.htm

This website provides a chapter on the nature of science and inquiry, which is appropriate reading for teachers. It provides further examples and insights into a scientific worldview, the nature of science, and the scientific enterprise. Chapter 1 points out key ideas about scientific knowledge and the scientific endeavor which form the requisites for scientific literacy.

Nature of Science Podcasts

http://vmsstreamer1.fnal.gov/VMS_Site_03/Lectures/NOSPodcasts/

This website offers a number of Podcasts with eight early-career scientists from a variety of different science disciplines working at the University of Chicago or at the Fermilab in Chicago. These Podcasts put a human face on scientists who talk about what it is like to be a scientist and what science is. They talk about science and its role in controversies such as evolution and the Big Bang Theory. They also discuss what it is that makes science so exciting in the work they do as scientists. These Podcasts are easy to use and can be listened to using iTunes or another MP3 device.

International Society for Technology in Education

http://www.iste.org/

This website is for technology educators, teachers, and administrators. The site provides the National Educational Technology Standards (NETS) and performance indicators for students, teachers, and administrators. You will also find articles and books related to educational technology on the website.

Great Fossil Find (by Randak and Kimmel)

http://www.indiana.edu/~ensiweb/lessons/gr.fs.fd.html

This is a website with a variation of the explore phase activity used in the chapter. The activity on this website is appropriate for upper-elementary and middle school students.

American Museum of Natural History

http://www.amnh.org/ology/index.php?channel=paleontology#channel

This website is colorful and informative, and has hours of exploration embedded within. The site has a wide age-level appeal with information including fossil hunting, exploring timelines, interviews with a Protoceratops, and exploring a contemporary dig in the Gobi Desert with scientists. Students of all ages will find this site a delightful learning experience. This is an excellent site for teachers emphasizing inquiry, the nature of science, and content areas across several disciplines.

American Institute of Physics. (1997). *The best of wonderscience: Elementary science activities.* New York: Delmar Publishers.

This is an inquiry-based activity book rich in physical science activities. Activities target fourth- to eighth-grade students. Materials needed to conduct the activities are inexpensive and easy to locate for purchase. Some background information accompanies the units.

Assessing scientific inquiry by Erin Peters in *Readings in Science Methods, K–8.* Arlington, VA: National Science Teachers Association. 2008.

This short article discusses the elements of the nature of science and its ways of knowing as well as process skills involved with inquiry. It provides useful approaches to the assessment of inquiry with peer-reviewed sample questions, rubrics, and student products.

Annenberg Media Learner.org

http://www.learner.org/resources/series129.html?pop=yes&pid=1452

The website has a range of videos on a variety of issues related to science teaching and learning. The inquiry-based science workshop (Series 129) shows inquiry teaching and learning with practicing teachers and students within their K–8 classrooms. This one-hour video highlights teachers using inquiry to enhance student learning. This video workshop is useful for preservice and practicing teachers exploring the inquiry process and how that process benefits students, and provides teachers with strategies to use within the classroom.

References

Abd-El-Khalick, F., Bell, R., & Lederman, N. (1998). The nature of science and instructional practice: Making the unnatural natural. *Science Education, 82*(4), 417–436.

American Association for the Advancement of Science. (AAAS). (1991). *Benchmarks for science literacy.* New York: Oxford University Press.

American Association for the Advancement of Science. (AAAS). (1993). *Benchmarks for science literacy.* New York: Oxford University Press.

Butts, D., & Hofman, H. (1993, February). Hands-on, brains-on. *Science and Children, 30*(5), 15–16.

Cherif, A. (1993, December). Relevant inquiry: Six questions to guide your students. *The Science Teacher, 60*(9) 26–28.

Dewey, J. (1998). *Experience and Education: 60th anniversary edition.* Indianapolis, IN: Kappa Delta Pi.

Domestic Policy Council (2006). American competitiveness initiative: Leading the world in innovation. Available at http://www.linearcollider.org/newsline/files/aci06-booklet.pdf.

Duckworth, E. (1987). *'The having of wonderful ideas' and other essays on teaching and learning.* New York: Teachers College Press.

Feynman, R. (1988). *What do you care what other people think?* New York: Norton.

Finson, K. (2002). Drawing a scientist: What we do and do not know after fifty years of drawings. *School Science and Mathematics, 102*(7), 335–345.

Finson, K. (2003). Applicability of the DAST-C to the images of scientists drawn by students of different racial groups. *Journal of Elementary Science Education, 15*(1), 15–26.

Finson, K. D., Beaver, J. B., & Cramond, B. L. (1995). Development and field test of a checklist for the Draw-a-Scientist Test. *School Science and Mathematics, 95*, 195–205.

Flick, L., & Bell, R. (2000). Preparing tomorrow's science teachers to use technology: Guidelines for science educators. *Contemporary Issues in Technology and Teacher Education* [Online serial], *1*(1). Available at http://www.citejournal.org/vol1/iss1/currentissues/science/article1.htm.

International Society for Technology in Education (ISTE). (2008). *National technology standards and performance indicators for teachers.* Available at http://www.iste.org/Content/NavigationMenu/NETS/ForTeachers/2008 Standards/NETS_T_Standards_Final.pdf.

Johnston, J. (1996). *Early explorations in science.* Philadelphia: Open University Press.

Kuhn, T. (1962). *The structure of scientific revolutions.* Chicago: University of Chicago Press.

Layman, J. (1996). *Inquiry and learning.* New York: College Entrance Examination Board.

Lederman, N. G. (1994). Scientific hypotheses, theories, laws, and other dangerous ideas. Paper presented at the National Convention of the National Science Teachers Association, Anaheim, CA.

Lederman, N. G. (1998). The state of science education: Subject matter without context. *Electronic Journal of Science Education, 3*(2). Available at http://unr.edu/homepage/jcannon/ejse/ejsev3n2.html.

Lederman, N., & Lederman, J. (2010). Avoiding denatured science: Activities that promote understanding of the nature of science. Available at http://msed.iit.edu/projectican/.

McComas, W. (1996). Ten myths of science: Reexamining what we think we know. *School Science & Mathematics, 96*(1), 10.

McComas, W., M. Clough, & H. Almazroa (1998). The role and character of the nature of science in science education. In W. F. McComas (Ed.), *The nature of science in science education: Rationales and strategies* (pp. 41–52). Boston: Kluwer Academic Publishers.

National Research Council (NRC). (1996). *National Science Education Standards.* Washington, DC: National Academies Press.

National Research Council (NRC). (2000). *Inquiry and the National Science Education Standards.* Washington, DC: National Academy of Sciences.

National Science Teachers Association (NSTA). (2000). Position statement: The nature of science. Available at www.nsta.org/positionstatement&psid=22.

Piaget, J. (1952). *Origins of intelligence in children.* New York: International Universities Press.

Piaget, J. (1964). *Judgment and reasoning in the child.* Paterson, NJ: Littlefield, Adams.

Suchman, R. J. (1966). *Developing inquiry: Inquiry development program.* Chicago: Science Research Associates.

Varmus, H. (1996, November). Science as a way of thinking. *Journal of College Science Teaching, 26*(2), 119–122.

Wray, D. (1999). *Inquiry in the classroom: Creating it, encouraging it, enjoying it.* Toronto, ON: Pippin.

Chapter 2

Are You Scientifically Literate?

Why We Teach Science

Learning Objectives

After reading Chapter 2, students will be able to

- identify and describe science content standards appropriate to grade levels,
- describe scientific literacy and give illustrations and examples of how scientific literacy skills could be integrated into science classrooms, and
- explain the contributions of significant science reform documents and initiatives on science classrooms today.

NSES TEACHING STANDARDS ADDRESSED IN CHAPTER 2

Standard B:Teachers of science guide and facilitate learning. In doing this, teachers

- encourage and model the skills of scientific inquiry; and
- recognize and respond to student diversity, and encourage all students to participate.

Standard E: Teachers of science develop communities of science learners that reflect the intellectual rigor of scientific inquiry and the attitudes and social values conducive to science learning. In doing this, teachers

- display and demand respect for diverse ideas, skills, and experiences for all students; and
- model and emphasize the skills, attitudes, and values of scientific inquiry.

Source: Reprinted with permission from the National Science Education Standards, copyright 1996, by the National Academy of Sciences, Courtesy of National Academies Press, Washington, DC.

Introduction

In Chapter 1, you explored the nature of science and inquiry in ways we hope challenged and expanded your views of science and scientific knowledge. We intend to continually challenge your ways of thinking about science and science teaching throughout this book. In this chapter, you will explore and examine the National Science Education Standards (NSES; National Research Council [NRC], 1996) and the history behind their development. We understand that you may wonder why including a history of science education is important to you as a K–8 Science teacher, but it is. Recall from the first chapter that science is a social endeavor that is driven by social, economic, political, and human endeavors or events. Education is also a social endeavor and it is important for you to know how past reform initiatives and policies influence the state of science education today. It gives you perspective on how these initiatives have led to the national vision and goal of scientific literacy for all (American Association for the Advancement of Science [AAAS], 1993; NRC, 1996; Rutherford & Ahlgren, 1990). So what does being scientifically literate mean to you? The NSES (NRC, 1996) state, "Scientific literacy is the knowledge and understanding of scientific concepts and processes required for personal decision making, participation in civic and cultural affairs, and economic productivity" (p. 2). As you read this chapter, ask yourself, "What does it mean to be scientifically literate? Am I scientifically literate? What strategies can I use to assist students in becoming scientifically literate?" Let's begin exploring these questions with the following contemporary example.

Engage

Are You Scientifically Literate?

When we were children, the only time we got to choose what we ate or drank was when our families ate out at a restaurant, and even then our choices were edited by parents who selected healthier foods and drinks. As adults, what we eat and drink is our choice. So, how do you decide what to eat or to drink? Do you consider flavor, nutritional value, additives, calories, or whether it is organic? Do you think about what is healthy? What influences your choices? What sources of information do you use to make your choices? Let's apply these questions to something many of us personally enjoy, diet sodas. Are you a diet drink fan? For this activity, we will assume you are, or that you have a friend or family member who is. Have you ever really considered the health trade-offs of diet drinks? Have you considered whether they are healthy for you? Answer the following: On a scale of 1 to 10 (10 being most knowledgeable and 1 having little to no knowledge), how would you rate your scientific knowledge and understandings of the artificial sweeteners found in your favorite diet soda? What are artificial sweeteners? How healthy are these ingredients for humans? Do artificial sweeteners have side effects? If so, what are they? Can they be harmful to people? Should you drink them?

Explore

You Make the Decision: Should You Drink Diet Soda?

We all know that soft drinks have become common to many of our diets. So imagine this: while taking a study break, you open a can of your favorite diet soda and sit down to catch up on your email. You read the following chain email that was forwarded to you by a friend (this is an actual email we received several years ago).

RE: Your Health

From: Your Friend

Sent: May 1998 3:30pm

To: You

**Teaching Standard
B: 1 and E: 2**

How does this narrative encourage the development of the scientific literacy through these standards?

I have spent several days lecturing at the World Environmental Conference on "Aspartame" used in many diet products. In the keynote address by the EPA, they announced that there was an epidemic of multiple sclerosis and systemic lupus, and they did not understand what toxin was causing this to be rampant across the United States. I explained that I was there to lecture on exactly that subject.

When the temperature of aspartame exceeds 86 degrees Fahrenheit the wood alcohol, aspartame, converts to formaldehyde and then to formic acid, which in turn causes metabolic acidosis. Formic acid is the poison found in the sting of fire ants. The methanol toxicity mimics multiple sclerosis; thus people are being diagnosed with having multiple sclerosis in error. The multiple sclerosis is not a death sentence, where methanol toxicity is.

In the case of systemic lupus, we are finding it has become almost as rampant as multiple sclerosis, especially in diet soft drinks. Also, with methanol toxicity, the victims usually drink three to four 12-ounce cans of them per day–some even more. In the cases of systemic lupus, which is triggered by aspartame, the victim usually does not know that the aspartame is the culprit. The victim continues its use aggravating the lupus to such a degree, that sometimes it becomes life threatening.

When we get people off the aspartame, those with systemic lupus usually become asymptomatic. Unfortunately, we cannot reverse the disease. On the other hand, in the case of those diagnosed with multiple sclerosis (when in reality, the disease is methanol toxicity), most of the symptoms disappear. We have seen cases where their vision has returned and even their hearing has returned. This also applies to cases of tinnitus. During a lecture I said, "If you are using aspartame and you suffer from fibromyalgia symptoms, spasms, shooting pains, numbness in your legs, cramps, vertigo, dizziness, headaches, tinnitus, joint pain, depression, anxiety attacks, slurred speech, blurred vision, or memory loss–you probably have aspartame disease!"

People were jumping up during the lecture saying, "I've got this, is it reversible?" It is rampant. Some of the speakers at my lecture even were suffering from these symptoms. In one lecture attended by the Ambassador of Uganda, he told us that their sugar industry is

(Continued)

(Continued)

adding aspartame! He continued by saying that one of the industry leader's son could no longer walk, due in part by product usage!

We have a very serious problem. Even a stranger came up to Dr. Espisto (one of my speakers) and myself and said, "Could you tell me why so many people seem to be coming down with MS? During a visit to a hospice, a nurse said that six of her friends, who were heavy diet soft drink addicts, had all been diagnosed with MS. This is beyond coincidence."

Here is the problem. There were Congressional Hearings when aspartame was included in 100 different products. Since this initial hearing, there have been two subsequent hearing, but to no avail. Nothing has been done. The drug and chemical lobbies have very deep pockets. Now there are over 5,000 products containing this chemical, and the patent has expired!!!

At the time of this first hearing, people were going blind. The methanol in the aspartame converts to formaldehyde in the retina of the eye. Formaldehyde is grouped in the same class of drugs as cyanide and arsenic deadly poisons!! Unfortunately, it just takes longer to quietly kill, but it is killing people and causing all kinds of neurological problems. Aspartame changes the brain's chemistry. It is the reason for severe seizures. This drug changes the dopamine level in the brain. Imagine what this drug does to patients suffering from Parkinson's disease. This drug also causes birth defects.

There is absolutely no reason to take this product. It is not a diet product. The Congressional record said, "It makes you crave carbohydrates and will make you fat." Dr. Roberts stated that when he got patients off aspartame, their average weight loss was 19 pounds per person. The formaldehyde stores in the fat cells, particularly in the hips and thighs.

Aspartame is especially deadly for diabetics. All physicians know what wood alcohol will do a diabetic. We find that physicians believe that they have patients with retinopathy, when in fact it is caused by the aspartame. The aspartame keeps the blood sugar level out of control, causing many patients to go into a coma. Their physicians could not get the blood sugar levels under control. Thus, the patients suffered acute memory loss and eventually coma and death.

Memory loss is due to the fact that aspartic acid and phenylalanine are neurotoxic without the other amino acids found in protein. Thus it goes past the blood brain barrier and deteriorates the neurons of the brain. Dr. Russell Blaylock, neurosurgeon said, "The ingredients stimulate the neurons of the brain to death, causing brain damage of varying degrees." Dr. Blaylock has written a book entitled, *Excitotoxins: The Taste That Kills* (Health Press, 1.800.643.265). Dr. H. J. Roberts, diabetic specialist and world expert on aspartame poisoning, has also written a book, *Defense Against Alzheimer's Disease* (1.800.814.9800). Dr. Roberts tells how aspartame poisoning is escalating Alzheimer's disease, and indeed it is. As the hospice nurse told me, women are being admitted at 30 years of age with Alzheimer's disease. Dr. Blaylock and Dr. Roberts will be writing a position paper with some case histories and will post it on the Internet. According to the Conference of the American College of Physicians, "We are talking about a plague of neurological diseases caused by this deadly poison."

Dr. Roberts realized what was happening when aspartame was first marketed. He said, his "diabetic patients presented memory loss, confusion, and severe vision loss." At the Conference of the American College of Physicians, doctors admitted that they did not know. They had wondered why seizures were rampant (the phenylalanine in aspartame breaks down the seizure threshold and depletes serotonin which causes manic depression, panic attacks, rage and violence).

Just before the conference, I receive a fax from Norway asking for a possible antidote for this poison because they are experiencing so many problems in their country. This poison is now available in ninety-plus countries worldwide. Fortunately, we had speakers and ambassadors at the conference from different nations who had pledged their help. We ask that you help too. Print this article out and warn everyone you know. Take anything that contains aspartame back to the store. Take the "no aspartame test" and send us your case history.

After reading the chain email, ask yourself whether you accept it at face value or do you question its claims. Here are some additional questions to consider:

1. What are your thoughts on the use of aspartame in diet drinks? What questions do you have after reading this email?

2. What can you determine about the source of this email? What are your sources of information?

3. According to the email, what are the potential risks associated with aspartame consumption? How reliable do you think these claims are? Are there other sources of information you can find on aspartame that are more reliable? How do you know if these other sources are reliable?

4. What kinds of information need to be presented to make a science-related document credible or reliable? Are these present in the email?

5. As a scientifically literate citizen, you have to make a decision about whether to use aspartame in your drinks. What are you thinking as you look at the soda you opened? Will you finish it?

6. How could you use this sort of activity with students in your science classroom? What decisions do children make in their everyday lives that make being scientifically literate is important? (For instance, you could create a chart of the class preferences of drinks and examine the sugar content in light of obesity issues in youth today.)

The aspartame email is an example of widely disseminated information that should be questioned and researched for its credibility in a number of ways. For instance, you could seek the identity of the author(s) of the email. You could look at terms such as "methanol toxicity," "wood alcohol," "lupus," and "acidosis," and locate medical studies to determine relationships of these to aspartame, if any. You could locate and examine actual research studies conducted on aspartame. This activity was selected to plunge you into a real-life example where being scientifically literate allows you to make decisions that are informed. Media, advertisements, and news reports about science are frequently at the heart of scientific literacy for most of us, and can also be used with students. As teachers, we have to be able to teach children the content, skills, and habits of thinking necessary to be scientifically literate in a world that is increasingly driven by science and technology.

Teacher's Desk Tip:
Go "Green" to Teach Scientific Literacy

Our students hear a lot about being "green," but being green isn't as simple as it seems. It often requires investigation or research. Here are some questions you may use in your classroom to foster going green and scientific literacy:

1. When shopping, what do you use to carry out your purchases? Do you choose paper, plastic, or reusable bags? What are the advantages and disadvantages of choosing one over the other regarding environmental impact?

2. What are the environmental impacts of the choices made for the school cafeteria? Are the serving utensils made of paper or plastic, or are they washable dishes? What are the advantages and disadvantages of choosing one over the other?

So whether you or your students are involved in an experiment or reading and discussing an advertisement, email, or a science news report, being able to judge the merit of the event or reading about a science phenomena in an informed way is one illustration of scientific literacy.

> *Science is an integral part of culture. It's not this foreign thing,*
> *done by an arcane priesthood. It's one of the glories of the*
> *human intellectual tradition.*
>
> Stephen Jay Gould

How do you see this quote in light of scientific literacy? How are science and scientific literacy part of human culture?

Explain

Focus Questions

1. According to the NSES, what is scientific literacy?

2. What are the traits of a scientifically literate person?

3. What major historical educational initiatives or events have led up to the NSES?

4. What are the NSES and why are they relevant to K–8 science teachers?

5. What do you think the NSES standards mean by "science for all"?

Scientific Literacy and Society

The Gould quote emphasizes the important role of science in our lives. The aspartame email is just one example of how one's ability to think scientifically and process information is critical to making choices and decisions in our lives. As teachers, we often hear, "Why do we need to learn this? Why is science important?" When we hear these questions from students, it always makes us stop and take stock of the many reasons for teaching and learning science in K–8 classrooms. Yes, all states require K–8 science be taught to meet the outcomes of the state standards, so that is one reason students need to learn science. But we also need a certain level of understanding and knowledge about science to operate in our world. In fact, we often take our role as "everyday scientists" for granted. Consider this: You've had a wonderful home-cooked meal and are now facing a huge sink full of greasy, dirty dishes. You fill up the sink with some cold water and wash the dishes without soap, right? No, that doesn't work very well, does it? Why not? How do you know that? We rarely ever stop to think about science while washing dishes, but we are applying scientific knowledge to ordinary daily routines when we use hot water and soap to wash them. As Gould so eloquently stated in the earlier quote, science is so interwoven into the culture of our lives we seldom think of it. Having a basic scientific understanding of the world around us is important on many levels. Scientists and science educators believe science understanding is so relevant that during the past twenty years a national goal of science education has emerged. The goal underscores a need for teaching students science in powerful, meaningful ways throughout their school experiences. The goal is a B-HAG—a "big, hairy, audacious goal" but one we strive to attain. The goal is "scientific literacy for all." But what exactly does that mean?

BULLETIN BOARD:

Environmental Literacy

Environmental literacy is one context for scientific literacy. Did you know most Americans can't pass a basic environmental knowledge test (National Environmental Education and Training Foundation [NEETF] and Roper Starch Worldwide, 2001)? Test your environmental IQ at http://www.neefusa .org/resources/roper2001-b .htm. Explore the full report and see how your environmental IQ compares to others at http://www.neefusa.org/ resources/roper2001-a.htm.

Scientific Literacy and Your Classroom

As we stated earlier, scientific literacy is "the knowledge and understanding of scientific concepts and processes required for personal decision making, participation in civic and cultural affairs, and economic productivity" (NRC, 1996, p. 22). Translating this definition into practical science teaching ideas is not always easy. The aspartame email and the Teacher's Desk Tip: Go "Green" to Teach Scientific Literacy are examples to assist you in conceptualizing what a scientifically literate individual should be able do.

Most state science standards are based on the National Science Education Standards, therefore both state and national standards are important guides for selecting appropriate grade-level concepts for teaching K–8 science.

When teaching students, you will notice that besides content, many scientific literacy skills focus on interpreting investigations and scientific reports as well as using available resources to research information for decision making.

The following are examples from the NSES (NRC, 1996) of practical approaches that can be used with students to foster scientific literacy:

> Read newspapers, articles or media presentations regarding science to be able to make informed conclusions, implications, or appropriate decisions based upon the source(s).
>
> Reflect critically on information included in or omitted from information sources.
>
> Ask questions and seek resources for solutions to queries or experiences in the natural world.
>
> The ability to analyze and evaluate arguments, based on evidences and draw conclusions for informed personal decisions.
>
> Recognize and analyze scientific and technological concerns and the potential implications on society (locally as well as globally) based on the evidence and the origin of the information sources. (NRC, 1996)

What does this mean for your science classroom? It might mean your students discuss a recent article in the newspaper that alleges a well-known baseball player has been enjoying an unfair advantage through his use of a specially designed bat. You engage the students in a discussion of bats used in girls' softball and boys' baseball. Teams of students research bat designs, discuss their findings, and make charts for class discussion that eventually lead to conclusion statements for determining whether a certain bat design gives an unfair advantage. Another possibility is that students who bring bottled water to school ask a question about whether bottled water is better than tap water. You examine the different kinds of bottled water seeking information on the source of the water. Is the information available on labels? If not, why? How do we know which is better? Is bottled water different from regular tap water? Does the government regulate tap water and bottled water? Is that information included on the bottle labeling? To be scientifically literate, students must acquire the ability to question events, information, and materials in their world and to seek answers to their questions.

TECH CONNECT: Wikispace and Scientific Literacy

Create a class Wikispace and post information about current global events or science issues (e.g., volcanic eruption, tsunamis, or earthquakes). Pose a question related to the event (e.g., What are effects of nuclear radiation leaks on the environment?) appropriate for your students. Set up a blog for students to post their ideas. This takes science beyond the classroom into real-world scenarios. A free site is located at www.wikispaces.com and information on blogs is at www.blogger.com.

Clearly, science is a part of our daily life and a logical reason for supporting the teaching of science and promoting scientific literacy in the early grades. Scientific literacy skills—such as learning to think like a scientist, acquiring knowledge of the natural world, and becoming **intellectually independent** (the ability to judge the evidences and findings of research for one's self)—require time to develop (Munby, 1977; Oliver & Nichols, 2001). Using scaffolding strategies, science teachers build on what students already know to move them toward learning something they do not know (Benson, 1997; Wood, Bruner, & Ross, 1976). In this case, most individuals would agree that if we start teaching science early in the primary grades, we can **scaffold** students' skills and knowledge of the processes of inquiry over time, building a depth and breadth of science understanding.

As teachers of K–8 science, scientific literacy is the ultimate goal for all our students. In achieving this goal, we open the door for more of our students, especially those who are currently underrepresented, including women and minorities (see Figure 2.1), to enter science, technology, engineering, or mathematics (STEM) fields as a chosen career. No matter what career paths students choose, teaching our students to be scientifically literate gives them the ability to actively participate in informed ways on local, national, or global issues related to science. As the late Carl Sagan once said, "Our species needs, and deserves, a citizenry with minds wide awake and a basic understanding of how the world works."

So when your students ask the proverbial question, "Why do I need to know this?" You could simply say, "Because Carl Sagan said so." We doubt, however, that this will convince them. Instead, you might say that being scientifically literate opens doors. It opens doors for each of us every day, allowing us to make informed, responsible choices and decisions about science and technology in our lives. So how did we arrive at this national goal and the national standards for teaching and learning science? Let's take a look back at the history of science education as it relates to scientific literacy for all (see Figure 2.2).

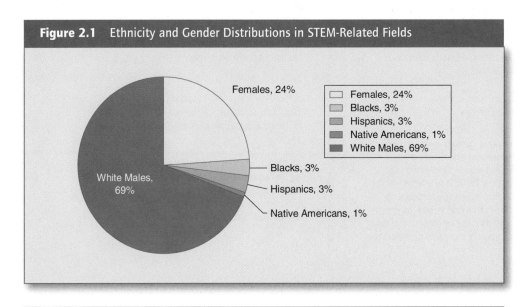

Figure 2.1 Ethnicity and Gender Distributions in STEM-Related Fields

Females, 24%

Legend:
Females, 24%
Blacks, 3%
Hispanics, 3%
Native Americans, 1%
White Males, 69%

Blacks, 3%
Hispanics, 3%
Native Americans, 1%
White Males, 69%

Note: Adapted from National Science Foundation (NSF, 2002), *Women, minorities, and persons with disabilities in science and engineering,* Arlington, VA: NSF, Division of Science Resources.

Figure 2.2   Science Education Reform: A Snapshot

1864 Herbert Spencer advocated inquiry teaching such that students conduct their own inquiry and draw their own inferences.

Early 1900s John Dewey, proposed child-centered and experiential-based education, perhaps one of the most influential educational reforms in the last century.

1890 Committee of Ten brought forth the idea of a common curriculum or what we might refer to as a national curriculum.

1957 The Soviet Union launched Sputnik I satellite into space which created a response by the United States for more funding in schools to enhance math and science. This push was an effort to ensure that the United States was the most technologically advanced country in the world.

1970s Despite the push for more math and science in schools, test scores continue to decline.

1983 The NCEE published *A Nation at Risk,* that cited the critical need for state and local schools to raise test scores in all areas, but particularly in math and science.

1981 National Commission on Excellence in Education (NCEE) is formed to address declining test scores in math and science.

1985 Project 2061 was established with the goal of scientific literacy for all Americans by 2061.

1989 Project 2061 publishes *Science for All Americans* which presents a unified vision for scientific literacy in the United States.

1989 National Council for Teachers of Mathematics publishes national mathematics standards.

1993 Project 2061 publishes *Benchmarks for Science Literacy.*

1996 The National Research Council publishes the National Science Education Standards.

2001 Congress passes a reauthorization of the Elementary and Secondary Education Act entitled No Child Left Behind (NCLB). NCLB is the first federal legislation that mandates standards-based educational outcomes, leading many states to more tightly control how and what is being taught in classrooms.

2001 Project 2061 publishes *Atlas of Science Literacy,* a set of tools to help educators understand how students develop skills and ideas that lead to scientific literacy.

Science Education Through Time

It is not our intent to examine in any depth the roots of science and its reform in the United States. However, knowing a bit of history is useful in understanding where K–8 science education is today. It also helps us to understand the social and political influences that affect how and what we teach. If you look back through history, you will see that early education did not traditionally include science as a part of the core curriculum. The core curriculum was the "Three R's"—reading, writing, and arithmetic. As our society grew more dependent on science and technology, teaching science became more a part of the regular school day. It is interesting to note, however, that many present-day ideas about how to teach science were advocated in the past. Look at our timeline (see Figure 2.2) and you will notice that science teaching as inquiry has a long history, yet we still find science educators calling for inquiry to take a central place in teaching science today. Another example is seen in 1890, when the Committee of Ten suggested a common curriculum for all students. Though the U.S. does not have a national science curriculum, common core standards in English language arts and mathematics introduced in 2010 have been adopted by the majority of states. Furthermore, the No Child Left Behind Act of 2001, a federal law that influences curriculum at the national, state, and local levels, reflects aspects of a national common curriculum with respect to reading.

According to DeBoer, if there has been any real change in science education over the past hundred years, it has been "to accommodate the child and the curriculum, to find ways to connect the interests, experiences, and capacities of the child to the subject matter that has been organized by adult minds" (2006, p. 9). These child-centered, experientially based ideas represent the essence of Dewey's philosophy (1902, 1916); the popularity of these ideas has repeatedly waxed and waned throughout the twentieth century. Though child-centered, hands-on approaches are currently embraced by science educators, they have yet to be fully realized within many K–8 classrooms. As we moved into the 1950s, social and political events, specifically the launch of Sputnik by the Soviet Union in 1957, moved science and mathematics to the forefront of educational politics. Why? At the time, it was unthinkable that another country could be more scientifically advanced than the United States. So with the launch of Sputnik, the United States moved rapidly to maintain, or some might say regain, its leadership position in the international space race. During this time, federal dollars found their way into public school systems and higher education—specifically to promote science and mathematics while encouraging greater interest in science and mathematics careers.

Despite the push for science and mathematics in the 1950s, the 1970s saw declining student test scores, and again concern focused on science. The National Commission on Excellence in Education (NCEE) was established in 1981 to identify the problems plaguing U.S. education and to generate potential solutions. The Commission worked at a time when there was great concern nationally about the competitive status of U.S. business and commerce. Once more today, we find ourselves concerned about our international competitiveness, as

---

Author's Note:

No Child Left Behind Act of 2001: To find out more, go to www.ed.gov/nclb.

Common Core Standards: To find out more, go to www.commoncore.org.

seen in the American Global Competitiveness Initiative (American Global Competitiveness Initiative, 2007). So, you might ask, "How are students across the nation doing in science today?" When examining U.S. student achievement in science, we usually look to the National Center for Education Statistics (NCES) for two key reports on assessments done nationally and internationally. These include *The Nation's Report Card: National Assessment for Educational Progress* (NAEP) and the *Trends in International Mathematics and Science Study* (TIMSS). TIMSS and NAEP are generally administered about once every four or five years. If you look at the NAEP data, you can examine for yourself the scores of fourth- and eighth-grade students' science achievement attained since 1995 (see Tables 2.1 and 2.2). You'll also find information on student achievement internationally on the TIMSS assessment in the Bulletin Board: Trends in International Mathematics and Science Study Assessment. What trends do you see in the data? What are the implications for teaching science in the K–8 classroom?

In addition to the assessments, there are two important documents that have been instrumental in moving science education to where we are today—*A Nation at Risk*, the report of the National Commission on Excellence in Education (NCEE, 1983), and *Educating Americans for the Twenty-First Century* (National Science Board, 1983). These two documents advocated high standards for all, recommended more-rigorous expectations of academic performance, and emphasized more exposure to science. For instance, the Commission recommended that science students should be taught (a) the concepts, laws, and processes of science, (b) methods or processes of scientific inquiry, and (c) application of scientific knowledge to daily life. In addition, the Commission

Table 2.1   National Assessment for Educational Progress (NAEP): The Nation's Report Card on Fourth-Grade Level Trends in Science

Fourth graders' level of science achievement on the NAEP

Year	Below basic	At or above basic	At or above proficient	At advanced
1996	37%	63%	28%	3%
2000	37%	63%	27%	3%
2005	32%	68%	29%	3%
2009	29%	72%	32%	1%

Note: NAEP science tests are scaled from 0–300. Levels of performance for fourth grade include Basic (138), Proficient (170), and Advanced (205).

The NAEP science assessment was updated in 2009 to keep the content current. Due to the recent changes with the assessment, the results from 2009 cannot be compared to those from previous assessment data). National Center for Education Statistics (NCES). (2009), NAEP Science Assessment: 2009 Science Results Available at NCES at http://nationsreportcard.gov/science_2009/.

Adapted from National Center for Education Statistics (NCES). (2005). *The Nation's Report Card: Science 2005 Executive Summary*. Available at NCES at http://nationsreportcard.gov/science_2005/s0101.asp.

Fourth-grade students' scores show an increasing trend at the basic level from 1996 to 2005. Fourth-grade students' scores show little difference between 1996 and 2005 at the proficient and advanced levels.

Table 2.2   National Assessment for Educational Progress (NAEP): The Nation's Report Card on Eighth-Grade-Level Trends in Science

Eighth graders' level of science achievement on the NAEP

Year	Below basic	At or above basic	At or above proficient	At advanced
1996	40%	60%	29%	3%
2000	41%	59%	30%	4%
2005	41%	59%	29%	3%
2009	38%	63%	28%	2%

Note: NAEP science tests are scaled from 0–300. Levels of performance for eighth grade include Basic (143), Proficient (170), and Advanced (208).

Eighth-grade students' scores show little difference at (or above) the Basic level or Proficient levels from 1996 to 2005. Eighth-grade students' scores at the Advanced levels were lower in 2005 than in 1996

The NAEP science assessment was updated in 2009 to keep the content current. Due to the recent changes with the assessment, the results from 2009 cannot be compared to those from previous assessment data (NAEP, 2009).

Adapted from National Center for Education Statistics (NCES). (2005). The Nation's Report Card: Science 2005 Executive Summary. Available at NCES at http://nationsreportcard.gov/science_2005/s0101.asp; National Center for Education Statistics (NCES). (2009). NAEP Science Assessment: 2009 Science Results. Available at NCES at http://nationsreportcard.gov/science_2009/.

Eighth-grade students' scores show little difference at (or above) the Basic level or Proficient levels from 1996 to 2005. Eighth-grade students' scores at the Advanced levels were lower in 2005 than they were in 2000.

recommended that science students should recognize social and environmental consequences of scientific and technological innovations (NCEE). Both reports provided a vision as well as strategies for science education reform. The Commission also recommended national testing by state governments and local school districts to raise the academic achievement of students with respect to science and mathematics, as noted earlier.

Closely following these earlier reform initiatives, Project 2061 began in 1985 and was sponsored by the AAAS. Project 2061 got its name from the year that Halley's Comet will to be visible again on earth, seventy-six years after its last appearance, in 1985. Project 2061 is a massive and long-term reform effort designed to promote scientific literacy in the United States by 2061. One of the early products of this reform initiative was the publication of *Science for All Americans* (Rutherford & Ahlgren, 1990). *Science for All Americans* represents the first thorough report that outlines the principles for effective teaching and learning to achieve scientific literacy for all. However, it does not describe what students should know and when they should know it. *Science for All Americans* opened discussions locally and nationally that focused on reshaping science education with the goal of scientific literacy for all in mind. A year later, as Project 2061 progressed, *Benchmarks for Scientific Literacy* (AAAS, 1991) was published. This book describes a framework of ideas that could be used in the development of science curriculum models. However, once published, *Benchmarks for Scientific Literacy* was thrust into the standards movement and was

BULLETIN BOARD

Trends in International Mathematics and Science Study Assessment

- The TIMSS assessment has been administered to students every four years since 1995. In 2007, the TIMSS science achievement scores of fourth graders included thirty-six countries. According to TIMMS data, a score of 500 is considered the average, or mean. The following apply to the 2007 TIMSS:

- U.S. fourth graders scored an average of 539 in science, which was higher than twenty-five of thirty-five other countries.

- U.S. fourth-grade students' scores showed no detectable gains in science achievement compared to scores in 1995.

- U.S. fourth-grade students' scores were lower than in 1995. (Fourth graders scored 542 in 1995, and 539 in 2007.)

- Eighth graders scored an average of 520 in science achievement, which was higher than thirty-five of forty-seven countries. The eighth-grade students scored below nine other countries.

- U.S. eighth-grade students' scores show no detectable change compared to scores in 1995.

- U.S. eighth-grade students' science achievement scores were 520, compared to 513 in 1995 (National Center for Educational Statistics [NCES], 2007).

viewed as a standards document—not because that was its intent, but because the nation was primed and ready for national standards in science education.

Science Education Today

By now you should recognize that by examining the history of science education reform the stage is set for the development of the NSES. As we have mentioned, the late 1980s saw a push to provide specific grade-level learning outcomes or standards. Professionals in mathematics led the way by publishing the first set of national standards for K–12 students, the *Curriculum and Evaluation Standards for School Mathematics* (National Council of Teachers of Mathematics [NCTM], 1989). Shortly thereafter, the National Science Teachers Association (NSTA), the American Association for the Advancement of Science (AAAS), the National Research Council (NRC), and other associated professional organizations began the process of creating national science standards. They started the process by asking these questions, among others: (a) Does our present science curriculum and ways of teaching prepare students for the twenty-first century? (b) Is science education staying abreast of technological advancements worldwide? (c) Are teachers being prepared in both science content and **pedagogy** for teaching in the twenty-first century? (d) Are we preparing students to become scientifically literate? (e) What must the average citizen need to know to make informed decisions that affect her or her communities? (e) Does the science curriculum embrace diversity and opportunities that allow *all* students access to STEM careers? and (f) What role do administrators and community members embrace to support improved science education? These questions, thoroughly explored by scientists, science educators, and teachers served as a guide for developing the science content and inquiry standards known as the NSES (NRC, 1996).

It may seem that we took the long route to get to the discussion of the NSES and we did. We wanted you to have more insight into how societal and political activities influence science education. The NSES have become a framework for raising expectations for learning and teaching science. Though the standards are nationally agreed on, they do not prescribe a national curriculum. The NSES describe appropriate science content and successful K–12 science practices that support student learning. The standards also provide a guide and impetus for change by envisioning science for all students and defining what it means to be scientifically literate. Most recently, *A Framework for K–12 Science Education: Practices, Crosscutting Concepts, and Core Ideas (2011)* was published. This document is intended to serve as a conceptual guide for developing new science education standards (the first since the NSES, 1996) that envision the nature of education in science, engineering and technology for the 21st century.

Figure 2.3

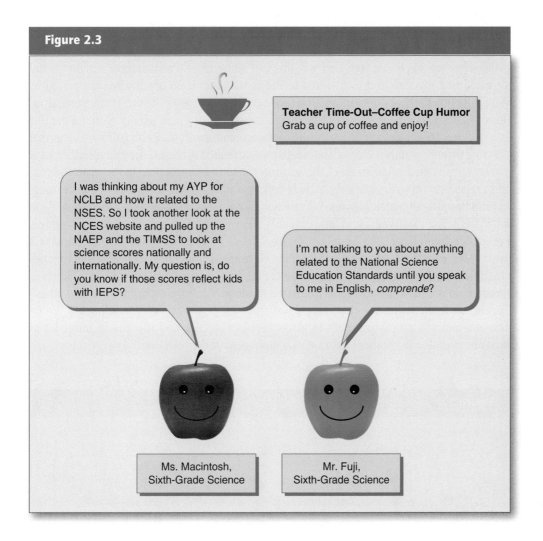

Understanding the National Science Education Standards for Your Classroom

The NSES present guidelines and goals for science teaching, science programs, professional development, assessment standards, and K–12 science content as a whole unit. Because the bulk of what we teach children is science content, we will begin by focusing on the science content standards. At this point, you may be wondering what content and skills you will need to teach your students. The NSES describe content that students should know and be able to do by the end of their K–12 education. The science content standards are organized around grade-level bands K–4, 5–8, and 9–12. The standards can guide your teaching no matter where you teach in the United States, because most local curriculum is based on the state standards, which are generally modeled after the NSES (NRC, 1996). So when we talk about teaching the science concept standards, we are referring to teaching scientific content knowledge, which includes commonly used terms fundamental to content—facts, concepts, principles (generalizations), and theories.

Facts are generally defined as discrete information substantiated through evidences (e.g., observations or measurements) that are supported by sensory inspection. Opinion and beliefs have no place in a fact. Can you think of some facts? For instance, a penny is not attracted to a magnet. Iron is attracted to magnets. A fact is an observation supported by visual and other sensory inspection. **Concepts** are ideas or notions derived from generalizations of facts and experiences. For instance, a concept in physical science is that a magnet exerts a force on ferromagnetic materials (metals containing iron). **Principles** are ideas that describe the often multifaceted relationships among related concepts. For example, the closer a magnetic material is to a magnet, the stronger the force of attraction. In this case, the concepts related to this principle may include concepts of magnetic fields, lines of force, magnetic material, and magnetic poles. When teaching students science, take care to show them how facts relate to concepts and how concepts relate to principles as they develop scientific knowledge (see Figure 2.4). Moreover, as teachers of science, we know that an important aspect of science that leads to scientific literacy is to assist students to recognize that theories are the most comprehensive explanations of the current observations and evidence. However, theories are not incontrovertible, as discussed in Chapter 1. Jim Ritter may have said it best: "Science is littered with the dead corpses of theories" (*Chicago Sun Times*, April 7, 1996). Theories can and do change. With facts, concepts, principles, and theories in mind, let us turn our attention to another fundamental component of the NSES, unifying concepts.

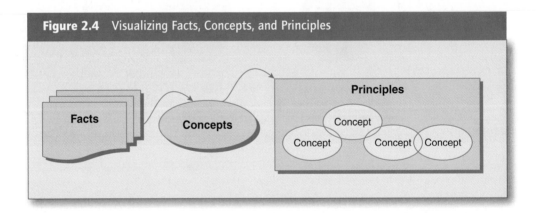

Figure 2.4 Visualizing Facts, Concepts, and Principles

Unifying concepts refer to those ideas or processes that connect scientific ideas across the disciplines. A unifying concept within constancy, change, and measurement can be illustrated using the concept of energy. As you learned in your science classes, potential energy is stored energy and kinetic energy is energy of motion. Energy is a unifying concept because it crosses the scientific disciplines. In physical science, a ball poised at the top of a hill (stored energy) may roll downhill (energy in motion). In biology, food (stored chemical energy) is converted by the muscles cells for cellular function or movement (energy of motion). In geology, pressure (stored energy) on a fault line due to layers of rock and soil deposited over time may be released by means of earthquakes (energy in motion). These concepts are repeatedly addressed in more depth as students advance through the various grade levels and study the different science disciplines. In each case, potential or kinetic energy connects and unifies the different scientific disciplines, providing students with a more comprehensive view of scientific concepts. With an understanding of how the unifying concepts serve as a framework for connecting all science content standards, next we will examine the content standards.

Remember as you examine the NSES content standards that content is just one part of teaching science effectively. At first glance, the NSES can be quite overwhelming and confusing. So let's begin by examining how the standards are organized.

First, we start with the most familiar categories that include the three content standard strands of (1) life, (2) earth and space, and (3) physical science. Less familiar are four other content standard strands. These include science as inquiry, science and technology, science in personal and social perspectives, and the history and nature of science. In Chapter 1, we spent time discussing two of these content standards strands. Take a look at Table 2.3. Do you recall which two? (They are science as inquiry, and the nature of science.) As a K–8 teacher, it is helpful to know that the standard strands are identified by grade-level bands (K–4, 5–8, and 9–12). If you explore the entire NSES, under each individual grade-level standard you will find a description of the content that should be learned by the end of that grade band. For example, under the K–4 standard strand, "Personal and Social Perspectives" is the standard "Changes in the Environment." Under that standard, are fundamental concepts and principles students should know. In this example, it states that "Environments are space, conditions and factors that affect an individual's and a population's ability to survive and their quality of life" (NRC, 1996, Content Standard C: Grade 4, p. 140). Combined, these content standards set the stage for scaffolding learning science content that leads toward scientific literacy. You might notice as you explore the NSES Content Standards in Table 2.3 that we've included the standards for students in grades nine to twelve. We have done this intentionally to point out the entire scope and sequence of content and skills that students should know by the end of twelfth grade. The following outline of the NSES is designed as an overview and a quick reference (see Table 2.3).

First graders make weather observations using a data sheet.

Suppose you were asked during your classroom field experiences to plan and teach lessons on weather. Your cooperating teacher specifically wants you to teach the seasons along with temperature and precipitation to first graders. What content standards might be appropriate for the lessons? If you selected "objects in the sky" or "changes in earth and sky" you would be on the right track. But you aren't done yet. You also have to identify specifically what part of the standard you will address based on the topics of the lessons. Now, use the online website (www.nap.edu/html/nses/) for the National Academies Press Library and locate which of the three parts of the standard are most appropriate for this task. Free access to the NSES makes this a very useful website.

Author's Note:

NSES standards can be downloaded at no charge at www.nap.edu/html/nses/.

Table 2.3   National Science Education Standards

UNIFYING CONCEPTS AND PROCESSES STANDARDS		

- System, order, and organization
- Evidence, models, and explanation
- Change, constancy, and measurement
- Evolution and equilibrium
- Form and function

STRAND: SCIENCE AS INQUIRY STANDARDS		
Levels K–4 Standards	**Levels 5–8 Standards**	**Levels 9–12 Standards**
Abilities necessary to do scientific inquiry	Abilities necessary to do scientific inquiry	Abilities necessary to do scientific inquiry
Understanding about scientific inquiry	Understanding about scientific inquiry	Understanding about scientific inquiry

STRAND: PHYSICAL SCIENCE STANDARDS		
Levels K–4 Standards	**Levels 5–8 Standards**	**Levels 9–12 Standards**
Properties of objects and materials	Properties and changes of properties in matter	Structure of atoms
Position and motion of objects	Motion and forces	Structure and properties of matter
Light, heat, electricity, and magnetism	Transfer of energy	Chemical reactions
		Motions and forces
		Conservation of energy and increase in disorder
		Interactions of energy and matter

STRAND: LIFE SCIENCE STANDARDS		
Levels K–4 Standards	**Levels 5–8 Standards**	**Levels 9–12 Standards**
Characteristics of organisms	Structure and function in living systems	The cell
Life cycles of organisms	Reproduction and heredity	Molecular basis of heredity
Organisms and environments	Regulation and behavior	Interdependence of organisms
	Populations and ecosystems	Matter, energy, and organization in living systems
	Diversity and adaptations of organisms	Behavior of organisms

STRAND: EARTH AND SPACE SCIENCE STANDARDS		
Levels K–4 Standards	**Levels 5–8 Standards**	**Levels 9–12 Standards**
Properties of earth materials	Structure of the earth system	Energy in the earth system
Objects in the sky	Earth's history	Geochemical cycles
Changes in earth and sky	Earth in the solar system	Origin and evolution of the earth system
		Origin and evolution of the universe

STRAND: SCIENCE AND TECHNOLOGY STANDARDS		
Levels K–4 Standards	**Levels 5–8 Standards**	**Levels 9–12 Standards**
Abilities to distinguish between natural objects and objects made by humans	Abilities of technological design	Abilities of technological design
Abilities of technological design	Understanding about science and technology	Understanding about science and technology
Understanding about science and technology		
STRAND: SCIENCE IN PERSONAL AND SOCIAL PERSPECTIVES		
Levels K–4 Standards	**Levels 5–8 Standards**	**Levels 9–12 Standards**
Personal health	Personal health	Personal and community health
Characteristics and changes in populations	Populations, resources, and environments	Population growth
Types of resources	Natural hazards	Natural resources
Changes in environments	Risks and benefits	Environmental quality
Science and technology in local challenges	Science and technology in society	Science and technology in local, national, and global challenges
STRAND: HISTORY AND NATURE OF SCIENCE STANDARDS		
Levels K–4 Standards	**Levels 5–8 Standards**	**Levels 9–12 Standards**
Science as a human endeavor	Science as a human endeavor	Science as a human endeavor
	Nature of science	Nature of scientific knowledge
	History of science	Historical perspectives

Source: Reprinted with permission from the National Science Education Standards © 1996 by the National Academy of Sciences, Courtesy of National Academies Press, Washington, DC, pp. 104–110. Table adapted from Ostlund and Mercier (1996), *Rising to the Challenge: The Processes of Science Inquiry.*

Elaborate

National Science Education Standards Scavenger Hunt

We know the NSES are not the most exhilarating part of learning to teach science. However, activities that actively engage the learner can change boring into exploring. This exercise models one way to learn more about the NSES that may be a bit more challenging than just reading about them. So get ready to go on a scavenger hunt! First, you will need to go to www.nap.edu/html/nses/ and use the NSES standards to answer the following:

1. In the introduction, the NSES states two reasons why science literacy is important. Describe the reasons.

2. In what chapter do you find the full version of the Science Teaching Standards? How many teaching standards are listed?

3. Besides the Science Content Standards and Science Teaching Standards, what other standards are included in the NSES? In the content standards, you will find classroom examples that illustrate the standards. Where would you find the classroom example entitled "Willie the Hamster"? What standard does it address?

4. In the Grades 5–8 standards, you will find the following concept and principle: "An object that is not being subjected to a force will continue to move in a straight line." Identify the content strand and the content standard for this example.

5. In the K–4 standards, you will find the following statement within a content standard: "Although men and women using scientific inquiry have learned much about objects, events and phenomena in nature, much more remains to be understood. Science will never be finished." Identify the content strand and the content standard for this example.

By using the NSES as a guide, you will find illustrations, examples, and descriptions of scientific literacy, science content, and inquiry standards to guide your curriculum and the science you choose to teach. To teach a standards-based science curriculum, it is imperative that you become knowledgeable and familiar with the NSES. Next, bringing together our discussion of scientific literacy and the standards, we shift the focus to your science classroom.

Evaluate

How Sweet It Is

Ms. Sanders, your cooperating teacher, teaches seventh grade and has asked you to assist her in identifying the content standards and evidences of scientific literacy associated with the following activity (modified from Physical Science Resources, J. H. Bedenbaugh, A. O. Bedenbaugh, located at www. usm.edu.) On the home page, search key words "Sugar concentration in soft drinks." The activity is identified on the site as http://www.usm.edu/psr/Determining_Concentration_of_Sugar_Using_Time_of_Fall_Apparatus.pdf).

The activity: As a part of your teaching unit on personal health, the seventh-grade students are asked to evaluate the sugar content in their favorite drinks. They will be using density and a drop-time apparatus. First, the students are assigned to cooperative groups and each group is asked to choose his favorite drink and bring a sample to class. You work with Ms. Sanders prior to beginning the activity to create five transparent drop-time tubes (Ht = 3 ft). Each contains a plastic density ball obtained from an antifreeze tester and you prepare sugar solutions (3%, 6%, 9%, 12%, and 15%). You demonstrate how to **measure** the drop-time for each of these standardized solutions to the entire class. You do at least three trials for each tube with the resulting data measuring the time that it takes the ball to travel from the top drop point to the bottom of the tube with the following results (Table 2.4):

Table 2.4 Average Drop-Time for Percentages of Sugar Solutions

Sugar solution	Trial 1	Trial 2	Trial 3	Average Drop-Time
3%	5.1 sec	4.9 sec	5.0 sec	5.0 sec
6%	7.4 sec	7.9 sec	7.5 sec	7.6 sec
9%	8.0 sec	8.6 sec	8.3 sec	8.3 sec
12%	11.1 sec	11.3 sec	11.5 sec	11.3 sec
15%	13.5 sec	13.7 sec	13.3 sec	13.5 sec

Now that the students have the calibrated measurements for comparison, each group gathers the following materials:

- One three-foot-long plastic tube
- One group of plastic density balls
- One group of stop watches
- Two rubber stoppers
- Group's sample of favorite drinks

The students are instructed on how to construct their drop-tubes with their favorite drink and each team then conducts three or more drop-time trials on their sample. The team recorder enters data on the team chart and determines the average drop-time for the team's drink. The team recorders add the data to a class chart. Then the teams compare their data to the calibrated data of sugar solution percentages (see Table 2.4) and **estimate** the percentage of sugar in the team's drinks. The resulting class chart is in Table 2.5.

Each student is asked the following question: Drawing on what we've learned so far about personal health and the data we gathered about our favorite drinks, what would you choose to drink and why? Students are asked to support their explanations with details, references, and data. Students are encouraged to use their science textbook and outside resources to defend their decisions. The following is Brandon's response:

Table 2.5 Percentages of Sugar (Team Results)

Team	Trial 1	Trial 2	Trial 3	Average Drop-Time	Percentage of Sugar
Coke	10.8 sec	10.0 sec	10.4 sec	10.4 sec	~11%
Sprite	10.5 sec	10.4 sec	10.3 sec	10.4 sec	~11 %
Orange soda	12.0 sec	12.0 sec	12.0 sec	12.0 sec	~13%
Welch's Strawberry	12.9 sec	13.0 sec	13.0 sec	13.0 sec	~14%
Mountain Dew	11.9 sec	12.1 sec	12.0 sec	12.0 sec	~13%

When we had the list of drinks on the board, I thought the orange soda would be healthiest to drink because it has fruit juice in it. Before we did the test, that's what I would have picked. But after we did it, I changed my mind. And, well, I shouldn't drink any of them because we learned that having too much sugar can make you gain too much weight and you won't be healthy. That was in our science book. That can be hard on your body and your organs. My mom says it can lead to heart problems and I looked it up on the web on the American Heart Foundation and she's right! So I started looking around for what other problems I might have from too much sugar. I checked out this one website called www.nancyappleton.com and it had a whole long list of bad things that can happen with too much sugar. But when I looked more on this website, I found a bunch of books and stuff she's trying to sell, so I'm not sure that this information is all correct. So I guess, to be on the safe side, I am going to try to drink just one Coke a day, since Coke's my favorite.

Using Brandon's response and the details of this activity, respond to the following:

1. How does Brandon's response provide evidences of what a scientifically literate person should do? What's missing?

2. How does this investigation help to scaffold students' learning related to being scientifically literate?

3. Ms. Sanders asked you at the start of this activity to identify all the NSES content standards that this activity addresses. Prepare a list of the strands and standards you think fit this activity. Be prepared to defend your choices.

Summary

This chapter focused on insights into science education reform afforded through the history of science education and the creation of the NSES designed to achieve scientific literacy for all students. The goals for teaching and learning science, viewed through the NSES, make clear that students in K–12 classrooms should be active inquirers. In addition, teachers should provide students with experiences that mirror the ways scientists conduct science as well as their ways of thinking. Elementary students are innately curious about the world around them. Teaching science content by means of inquiry in the elementary years as advocated by NSES can foster students' positive dispositions toward science and inquiry. By doing so, elementary teachers pave the way for the middle and high school years, preparing students to be informed citizens capable of making their own decisions with respect to science issues throughout their lives. In other words, as a teacher you will play a vital role in achieving the goal of scientific literacy for all initially set forth in Project 2061. As you plan for and teach science to students, we hope you revisit the NSES and other associated documents as you continue to develop your skills and knowledge as a K–8 science teacher.

Annotated Resources

Science for All Americans (1990)

http:www.project2061.org/.

This website takes you to the homepage for Project 2061. The book, *Science for All Americans*, is free online and located at http://www.project2061.org/publications/sfaa/online/sfaatoc .htm emphasizes that knowing and understanding should be the focal point of learning science. It deemphasizes traditional lecture, where memorizing definitions and vocabulary take precedence. In addition, one will find a discussion of the nature of science and technology with a historical perspective. It also illustrates ways of thinking that are considered necessary for scientific literacy.

Benchmarks for Science Literacy (Project 2061)

http:www.project2061.org/.

The book *Benchmarks for Science Literacy* is free online and located at http://www.project 2061.org/publications/bsl/online/index.php, follows *Science for All Americans* and describes what students should learn and skills they should be able to perform at the end of the second, fifth, eighth, and twelfth grade. This book is useful in describing the nature of science and technology.

Atlas of Science Literacy: *Project 2061*, Vol. 1 (AAAS, 2001).

Atlas of Science Literacy: Project 2061, Vol. 2 (AAAS, 2007).

The *Atlas of Science Literacy* is a two-volume set of books that provides an image-based visual web of content strands representing the various grade bands. The Atlas illustrates the connections and interconnections of concepts that lead to scientific literacy.

No Child Left Behind 2001 Act

http://www.ed.gov http://www2.ed.gov/policy/elsec/guid/states/index.html

The first link takes you to U.S. Department of Education home page. The second link is a web page that features No Child Left Behind, a federal law and its policies. Selecting the topics related to No Child Left Behind takes you to quick links that address several aspects directed toward education. One component of the document is that all teachers meet the highly qualified status. Another component is that all states adopt state standards and conduct statewide accountability testing with annual yearly progress reports.

Inquiry and the National Science Standards: A Guide for Learning and Teaching

http://www.nap.edu/ http://www.nap.edu/openbook.php?isbn=0309064767

Inquiry and the National Science Standards is a free online book located at http://www .nap.edu/openbook.php?isbn=0309064767. The link is found at the National Academies Press Library homepage at http://www.nap.edu/.

Inquiry and the National Science Standards is an addendum to the NSES. It provides further insights into the NSES and inquiry through practical applications using the content standards with examples, narratives, and illustrations.

ScienceNetLinks

http://www.sciencenetlinks.com/matrix.php

This website has a rich variety of lesson plans that span many concept and inquiry standards associated with *Benchmarks for Science Literacy*. Each lesson is categorized by grade level and aligned with the appropriate benchmark.

Department of Education (located within each state)

State standards are generally found at each state's Department of Education website. Locate your state's education department and you will likely find web links to state standards for science and other disciplines. If you are interested in the state assessments or students' performances on state assessments identified by school, you can usually find this information on the state Department of Education website as well.

National Science Education Standards (1996)

http://www.nap.edu/

This site is the home page for the National Academies Press Library and it provides free access to many important science education resources. Some of the resources include the science standards, assessment, professional development, teaching standards, and content standards across the K–12 grade levels.

Annenberg/CPB Foundation Professional Development Videos on Science

http://www.learner.org/resources/series129.html

These videos may be viewed from the website. After registering, go to browse teacher resources and then click the video icon you wish to view. These videos involve authentic classroom contexts with range of content and grade levels addressing issues of misconceptions, cooperative inquiry, the nature of science, diversity, questioning, process skills, integration, and outdoor experiences, to name a few. Series 129 focuses on scientific processes, ways of thinking, and inquiry.

National Center for Educational Statistics (NCES)

http://nces.ed.gov

This website keeps current student data on national and international assessments for science and mathematics. NAEP reports scores for students in grades four, eight, and twelve. It publishes the Nation's Report Card giving data on mathematics, science, and reading. The TIMSS data may also be found on this site.

References

American Association for the Advancement of Science (AAAS). (1991). *Benchmarks for science literacy*. New York: Oxford University Press.

American Association for the Advancement of Science (AAAS). (1993). *Benchmarks for science literacy*. New York: Oxford University Press.

American Association for the Advancement of Science (AAAS). (2001). *Atlas of science literacy*, Vol. 1. New York: Oxford University Press.

American Association for the Advancement of Science (AASS). (2007). *Atlas of science literacy*, Vol. 2. New York: Oxford University Press.

American Global Competitiveness Initiative. U.S. Department of Education. (2007, April 24). Available at http://www.ed.gov/about/inits/ed/competitiveness/index.html.

Benson, B. (1997). Scaffolding (coming to terms). *English Journal, 86*(7), 126–127.

DeBoer, G. (2006). History of the Science Standards Movement in the U.S. In D. Sunal & E. Wright (Eds.), *The impact of state and national standards on K–12 science teaching* (pp. 1–49). Greenwich, CT: InfoAge Publishing.

Dewey, J. (1902). *The child and the curriculum*. Chicago: University of Chicago Press.

Dewey, J. (1916), *Democracy and education: An introduction to the philosophy of education*. New York: Macmillan.

Munby, H. (1977, March 22–24). Analyzing teaching: The quality of the intellectual experience and the concept of intellectual independence. Paper presented at the annual meeting of the National Association for Research in Science Teaching. Cincinnati, OH.

National Commission on Excellence in Education (NCEE) (1983). *A nation at risk: The imperative for educational reform*. Washington, DC: U.S. Department of Education.

National Council of Teachers of Mathematics (NCTM). (1989). *Curriculum and evaluation of school mathematics*. Reston, VA: Author.

National Center for Education Statistics (NCES). (2005). *The nation's report card: Science 2005 executive summary*. Available at NCES at http://nationsreportcard.gov/science_2005/s0101.asp.

National Center for Education Statistics (NCES). (2007). *Trends in International Mathematics and Science Study (TIMSS)*. Available at NCES at http://nces.ed.gov/timss/results07_science07.asp.

National Center for Education Statistics (NCES). (2009). *NAEP Science Assessment: 2009 Science results* Available at NCES at http://nationsreportcard.gov/science_2009/.

National Environmental Education and Training Foundation and Roper Starch Worldwide. (2001, May). *Lessons from the environment: Why 95% of adult Americans endorse environmental education*. Available at http://www.neefusa.org/pdf/roper/Roper2000.pdf.

National Research Council (NRC). (1996). *National science education standards*. Washington, DC: National Academies Press.

National Research Council (NRC). (2011). *A Framework for K–12 Science Education: Practices, Crosscutting Concepts, and Core Ideas*. Washington, DC: National Academies Press.

National Science Board (U.S.). (1983). Educating Americans for the twenty-first century: A plan of action for improving mathematics, science and technology education for all American elementary and secondary students so that their achievement is the best in the world by 1995. Washington, DC: National Science Board Commission on Precollege Education in Mathematics, Science and Technology.

National Science Foundation (NSF). (2002). Women, minorities, and persons with disabilities in science and engineering. Arlington, VA: Author, Division of Science.

Oliver, J. S., & Nichols, K. B. (2001). Intellectual independence as a persistent theme in the literature of science education: 1900–1950. *School Science and Mathematics, 101*(1), 49–56.

Ostlund, K., & Mercier, S. (1996). *Rising to the challenge: The processes of science inquiry*. Squaw Valley, CA: S & K Associates.

Rutherford, F. J., & Ahlgren, A. (1990). *Science for all Americans*. New York: Oxford University Press.

PART II

The Nature of the Learner

We planted our seeds on Wed. April 26th been growing

Chapter 3

Children's Construction of Science

Learning Objectives

After reading Chapter 3, students will be able to

- describe the theories of learning developed by Piaget and Vygotsky,
- compare and contrast constructivism and objectivism as related to teaching science, and
- analyze science classrooms scenarios using constructivist and objectivist perspectives.

NSES TEACHING STANDARDS ADDRESSED IN CHAPTER 3

Standard B: Teachers of science guide and facilitate learning. In doing this, teachers

- focus and support inquiries while interacting with students;
- orchestrate discourse among students about scientific ideas;
- challenge students to accept and share responsibility for their own learning;
- recognize and respond to student diversity and encourage all students to participate fully in learning; and
- encourage and model the skills of scientific inquiry, as well as the curiosity, openness to new ideas and data, and skepticism that characterize science.

Source: Reprinted with permission from the National Science Education Standards, copyright 1996, by the National Academy of Sciences, Courtesy of National Academies Press, Washington, DC.

Introduction

How do you define knowledge? Have you ever *really* pondered what it means to learn? Do you wonder how children learn science? Have you wondered how you learn science? In answering these questions it will become clear that many individuals have contributed ideas and theories to how students learn science. For instance, Dewey advocated experiential, interactive learning. Bruner supported reflection on learning, while Ausubel emphasized structuring ideas through connections as one participates in science, and Kohlberg suggested safe learning climates. Today we find that all of these perspectives have contributed to how one learns science. In this chapter, we focus on a perspective that builds on many of these contributions and is grounded strongly in the work of Piaget and Vygotsky. Both the work of Piaget (cognitive development) and Vygotsky (social interactions) underpin what is referred to today as **constructivism**. According to von Glasersfeld (1989), one of the earliest accounts of constructivism came from Giambattiste Vico (1668–1744), a historian and philosopher who stated in his early works that knowledge is *verum et factum convertuntur*, or that "the true and the made are convertible" (Vico, n.d.). In other words, what is known—knowledge—is connected to the one who knows it.

As a K–8 science teacher, it is important that you have a broad knowledge about learning to enable you to make informed decisions about how to provide the best possible science instruction to your students. Piaget's and Vygotsky's learning theories underpin the constructivist perspective and serve as a point of reference for teaching K–8 science. It is important to note, however, that constructivism is not a theory—it is an **epistemology** that gives teachers a framework for looking at how students "know and make sense" of their experiences in science. Simply put, constructivism is a way of looking at how children construct meaning of the world around them. Now, consider for a moment that as human beings we all have a great capacity for learning. What does your image of a student learning science look like? Think back to your experiences as a student in science class. What was a typical day like in your science class? How was science taught to you? What activities did you experience? What approaches did the teacher use? What content did you study? What do you think your teacher believed about how children learn? What did you learn? How did you learn? How do you want to teach science to maximize learning? Keep these questions in mind as you read and contemplate the theories of **cognition** that are presented in this chapter. To start, consider the following quote:

Intelligence organizes the world by organizing itself.

Jean Piaget

What does this quote say about cognition or thought processes and learning? What does this quote say about teaching? How would you rephrase Piaget's words? What experiences or interactions help us organize our knowledge of science and how the world works? What experiences or interactions influence our pedagogical knowledge of how a science classroom works? In what contexts and in what ways do students and teachers maximize or constrain science learning?

Research findings have suggested that a teacher's beliefs about teaching and learning are drawn from their own experiences as students (Haney, Czerniak, & Lumpe, 1996; Kagan, 1992). Take a moment to consider the many teachers you have had during your education. If we asked you whether they all used the same instructional approaches you would probably tell us, "No." If you had to draw your two favorite science teachers and illustrate the ways they taught, what would the images of their science instruction look like? Rather than draw your image of science teaching analyze two preservice teachers' images of "science teachers at work," found in the following engage phase.

Engage

Teacher-Centered or Student-Centered Classrooms?

Examine the following two preservice teachers' drawings of "science teachers at work" (Figures 3.1 and 3.2). Pay attention to the details of each image. Write a description of your interpretation of each teacher's approach to teaching. How would you describe the teacher's interactions with students? How might you determine whether the depiction of the teacher's instruction is student centered or teacher centered? What are the students doing? What kinds of science content are depicted in the drawings? What do you think each artist believes about science teaching and learning? How are the drawings alike and how are they different? Which classroom would you want to learn in?

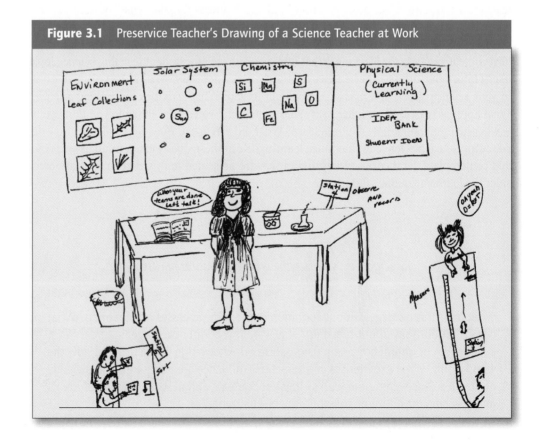

Figure 3.1 Preservice Teacher's Drawing of a Science Teacher at Work

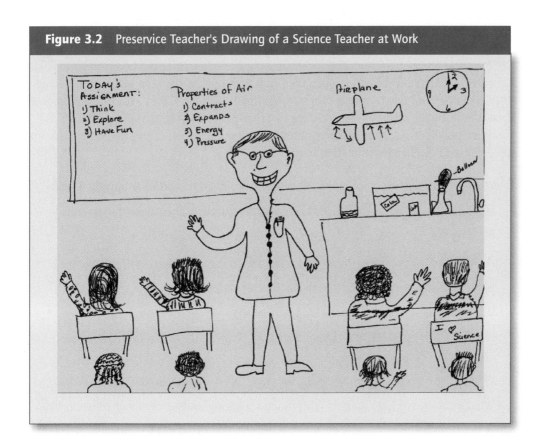

Figure 3.2 Preservice Teacher's Drawing of a Science Teacher at Work

Use the questions provided as a guide to analyze the drawings. Describe how your analysis of the drawings reveals clues about how the artist perceives the teaching of science. We will return to these drawings and identify visual clues that provide insight into the predominant teaching approach depicted in each classroom scenario. For now, let's consider how we can learn from practicing teachers.

Explore

Tales of Science Teaching: Learning Through Observation

Now that you've examined the drawings of science teachers at work, your next mission is to conduct a mini-classroom research project entitled, "Tales of Science Teaching." Your task is to observe a K–8 science teacher. You will want to take notes and even sketch the physical arrangement of the room. You may also want to use a tape recorder or a video camera to assist you in capturing what occurs as the science lesson unfolds, but it is not necessary to do so. Using your data and observation notes, write a "Tale of Science Teaching" from your observations to share with your peers. Make sure you give the school, teacher, and students pseudonyms. Also remember, you are not critiquing the teacher or the teaching. Without intensive interviews with the teacher, one brief teaching observation only gives you a glimpse into a teacher's view of how students learn science. Use the questions below to describe how you think the teacher you observed views how students learn science.

If you are unable to observe a science classroom, an alternative method is to go to www.learner.org (Annenberg Learner site), then click "science" on the menu bar. Scroll through the list of titles and find "Science: K–6 Investigating Classrooms." Select the title "All Sorts of Leaves" to view the fifty-minute videotape of a first-grade classroom.

When making the science teaching observation use the following questions as a guide for collecting data needed for your summary:

What grade level did you observe? What time did class start and what time did it end?

What did the classroom look like? Where was the teacher? Where were the students?

What was the objective or main purpose of the lesson or activity?

How did the teacher begin the science lesson?

What strategies were used by the teacher during the lesson?

What were some of the questions the teacher used?

What kinds of questions did the students ask? How did the teacher respond to students' questions?

What did the teacher say or do during the class? What content did the teacher cover?

What were the students doing? Were students working independently or collaboratively?

What activities were used with students in the lesson? Were the students involved in investigative inquiries?

Did the teacher appear to address students' prior knowledge and experiences?

What strategies were used to address issues of access, equity, and diversity?

Were the activities related to real-life situations?

What resources or materials were used in the lesson? How did the lesson end?

Using the data you have collected from observing the teacher, summarize your ideas about how the classroom teacher thinks students learn science.

> *The single most important factor influencing learning is what the learner already knows.*
>
> David Ausubel
>
> Do you agree with this quote? Why or why not?

Note: If you observe the science teacher, your instructor will provide you with instructions and tips for gaining the permission of a classroom teacher. Some teachers may not wish to be recorded or videotaped, so be certain to have his or her permission before you use recording equipment.

Explain

Focus Questions

1. What is Piaget's theory of cognitive development? How does it inform your understanding of science teaching?

2. What is Vygotsky's theory of social constructivism and how does it expand on Piaget's theory?

3. What is constructivism? What is objectivism?

4. How are Piaget's and Vygotsky's theories related to constructivism?

5. What teaching strategies support constructivism?

Learning: An Active Process

As you read this chapter, think carefully about how you perceive the processes of learning in light of Piaget's and Vygotsky's theories as well as how your views align with the ideas of constructivism. By now you have surely heard of Jean Piaget and Lev Vygotsky. In fact, they are "household names" in the field of education. Piaget's theory of cognitive development emphasized children's construction of reality and their developmental level, whereas Vygotsky's work brought to the foreground the influence of language and interactions with other individuals within the social world as important in learning. Both men have contributed theories of how children learn and how we all come to know. Both have influenced educational practices in science for several decades. What you might not know is that both men were contemporaries born in 1896, and they both viewed learning as an active process of building knowledge. In fact, they both were constructivists in their orientation to learning. Let's begin with our examination of constructivism with Piaget's views of knowledge development.

Piaget: A Theory of Cognitive Development

Piaget's theory grew out of his passion for biology and cognition. An assumption underpinning his theory of cognitive development is that humans have the ability to connect thinking processes into coherent, logically linked systems he referred to as "organization." For instance, a very young child might experience that a puppy and a kitten have fur and that the puppy and the kitten are animals, and therefore infer that all animals have fur. Such an example supports Piaget's notion that during development a child builds **cognitive schemes** that are systematic patterns of thinking or behavior that make up the child's image of reality. Piaget also proposed that individuals have the ability to adjust to different environments, which he called **adaptation**. For instance, a child might believe that heat comes from warm clothes. After experiencing activities with heat in school, the child's idea is challenged. In fact, the child learns that heat comes from his or her body and not from the clothes. With this new information, the child may make a cognitive adaptation with respect to prior knowledge and restructure his or her thinking about heat.

We all know that as children grow, they constantly encounter new adventures and experiences. Some of their experiences align with the prior conceptions of reality (schemes).

Other experiences do not, and may lead to adaptations in which the child changes preexisting schemes to match the new experience. According to Piaget, this adaptation process may occur through either **accommodation** or **assimilation**. Accommodation is the process of adaptation whereby the child changes the preexisting scheme to align with the new encounter. Assimilation occurs when the new encounter aligns with the preexisting scheme. So what happens when there is a mismatch or imbalance between what one already understands and what is perceived in a new experience? Piaget refers to this mismatch as **cognitive disequilibrium**. The disequilibrium is accommodated until a balance is regained, a state called **equilibration**. These mismatches between prior schemes and new experiences are important to the processes of learning. Piaget's work on cognitive development culminated in his conceptualization of stages of cognitive development (see Table 3.1).

Table 3.1   Piaget's Stages of Cognitive Development

Stage and Age	Description of Stages	Stage-Appropriate Science Activities
Sensorimotor Birth to 2 years	• Early development of intelligence is illustrated via sensory and motor skill activities. • Knowledge limited by physical interactions. • By the end of this stage, object permanence of object develops and symbolic skill via language develop.	
Preoperational 2 to 7 years	• Knowledge construction via language (symbols) • Memory and imagination develop. • Mental operations are nonreversible and illogical. • Children learn using direct experiences and manipulating objects. • They are capable of simple observations, sorting, and classifying.	Learners need many hands-on experiences using common items such as hand-made fans, windsocks, rain gauges, thermometers, rulers, measuring cups, magnifiers, and other simple tools. Using these simple tools, students need time to explore, manipulate, or test the items, as well as talk about their findings. For example, children may observe the way the wind blows using a weather vane or a windsock. They may also read rain gauges and record amounts of rainfall over a period of time. Talking about their findings and ideas allows the teacher to move them toward conceptualizations of the targeted weather phenomena.
Concrete Operational 7 to 11 years	• Children are capable of reversible mental operations. • Conservation has developed in children. • They have a more systematic and logical use of knowledge. • They can understand another's point of view. • Learning requires concrete examples or experiences.	Learners can pose simple science questions (e.g., What season has the most rainfall? Least rainfall? What is the average rainfall or temperature for a particular season? What types of clouds produce sudden summer thunderstorms?). What happens to wind speed near buildings? Learners should investigate in direct, concrete ways whenever possible. Use of cooperative groups to explore science concepts via laboratories, fieldwork, technology, videos, or authentic problem solving offers students the opportunity to discuss, listen, and negotiate meanings with their peers.

Stage and Age	Description of Stages	Stage-Appropriate Science Activities
Formal Operational 11 years to adulthood	• Individuals use symbols logically in abstract thinking. • They engage in metacognitive thinking. • They reason abstractly and make generalizations.	Formal operational thinkers can take on abstract concepts such as condensation or finding dew point temperature. In the weather example, student exploration may involve finding the dew point of air inside and outside. Formal operational thinkers are able to begin to design experiments more independently by building on previous experiences (i.e. stating hypotheses, operational definitions, identifying variables and drawing conclusions based on findings).

Note: Modified from Kuhn, D., Langer, J., Kohlberg, L., & Haan, N. S. (1977), The development of formal operations in logical and moral judgment, *Genetic Psychology Monograph, 95*, 97–188.

A major component of Piaget's theory is that the stages of children's development follow sequentially and children must come to terms with the preceding stage before moving to the next one. As a K–8 teacher you will teach students whose cognitive development generally falls within the concrete operational stage. This means that it is important that you provide your students multiple, firsthand concrete experiences to assist them in building knowledge of science concepts. It is also pertinent to be aware, as stated by Piaget, that the age ranges associated with the cognitive stages are not fixed and that some children reach the stages earlier or later than the ages in the chart indicate.

Vygotsky: Social Interaction and Cognitive Development

Lev Vygotsky, a sociolinguist, and Piaget, his contemporary, believed that individuals actively construct knowledge of the world in which they live. While Piaget focused on cognitive stages of children's development, Vygotsky emphasized cognitive growth through social interactions. Although Piaget did not research the social influence on cognitive development, he did acknowledge that social interactions influence cognitive development. Vygotsky, on the other hand, stated that social experiences and interactions play an important role in the cognitive development of a learner. He said:

> "Every function in the child's cultural development appears twice: first, on the social level, and later, on the individual level; first, between people (interpsychological) and then inside the child (intrapsychological)." (1978, p. 57)

Vygotsky's theory of learning is centered on the following premises: (a) learners actively construct knowledge, (b) learning takes place in the zone of proximal development (cognitive development is limited to a certain range), and (c) development cannot be separated from social interactions. Vygotsky proposed that children's social interactions with a variety of individuals, including adults who are more knowledgeable, assist learners in gaining knowledge.

Based on his view that social interactions hold a pivotal role in students' constructions of knowledge, Vygotsky suggests school learning experiences could and should be organized in

Learning science involves active, social interaction.

ways that promote active student learning. He further advocated that teachers support and guide students in the cognitive processes. For teachers this means science lessons are structured for active student learning based on the learner's "zone of proximal development." The **zone of proximal development** is described as the difference between what a child can do without assistance and what the child can do with assistance. Therefore, if you have knowledge of what students already know and can do, you are more likely to engage them in science activities and learning goals that are appropriate for the learner's zone of proximal development. Having awareness of students' zones of proximal development and creating lessons with the zone of proximal development in mind can guide students to greater cognitive development.

An important teaching approach based on Vygotsky's zone of proximal development is scaffolding. Scaffolding is a process of guiding the learner from what he or she presently knows to what you want the student to learn through support. For Vygotsky (1978), student abilities fall into three categories:

1. Skills that the student cannot perform

2. Skills that the student might be able to perform with help

3. Skills that the student can perform

According to Vygotsky, our role as science teachers is to scaffold tasks by breaking them down and providing supportive information or collaborative engagement to allow students to perform at a level that would normally be slightly beyond their ability without assistance and guidance.

A student's advancement through the zone of proximal development requires social interactions. Accordingly, a learner can move his or her knowledge development further with social interaction involving teacher guidance or peer collaboration, than he or she could alone. The role of the teacher is to provide support and assistance with scaffolded opportunities as students move toward the targeted knowledge or skill. With scaffolding, teachers begin by finding out and drawing on the skills and knowledge students already have. Next, they plan activities that move students toward skills and knowledge that students can perform or attain with assistance from the teacher or other students. Finally, the teachers withdraw scaffolding as students independently perform the skills or use the concepts. Scaffolding to support students learning, based on Vygotsky's zones of proximal development, is an important characteristic of constructivist learning and teaching.

YOUR SCIENCE CLASSROOM:
Scaffolding Student Learning in Science

Ms. Hernandez, a first-year teacher, is teaching her third-grade students about the states of matter. She remembers learning about scaffolding concepts in her science methods class but is really not sure how to proceed. She has already explored with her students the properties of solids, liquids, and gases. She is confident her students can identify objects that naturally exist in each of those states, but her objective

> **Teaching Standard**
> **B: 1 & B: 2**
>
> How does this scenario reflect these standards?

is to move students toward the concept that matter changes states with the addition or subtraction of heat (energy). She enters the teachers' workroom and finds another science teacher, Ms. Telker, and asks for advice. Ms. Hernandez says, "I really need some help. I know my students struggle with abstract ideas and the idea of energy in changing states of matter is difficult for them. Can you help me with some ideas for scaffolding their learning?" Ms. Telker asks, "What do they already know about matter?" Ms. Hernandez replies, "Well, they really do know the properties of matter and they know things like, ice is solid water. But they don't really have any idea of what causes changes in states to occur." "Okay," says Ms. T, "what I would recommend for scaffolding is that you begin by focusing on what they know about water and ice. For instance, you might revisit the properties of water in its liquid state and ask if they have ever seen water as a solid. I suspect they will say yes. Then I would ask, How do you think the water becomes solid or ice?" Ms. Hernandez ponders this and says, "Okay, so then I can do some activities with the children on changing water to ice and ice to water focusing on what you need to make the change happen." Ms. Telker agrees, "Right. For instance, you could put an ice cube on a hot plate and heat it and have students make observations. Then you could provide small groups with an ice cube on a plate on their desks and have them discuss and record observations every ten minutes. Both interactions with you and with other students help to scaffold student understanding of changes in states of matter with the addition of heat through their direct observations and discussions. Then with less assistance have them work through changes of state by taking heat away. This sets the stage for you to assist students in scaffolding their learning to understand changes in states of matter with other materials." She goes on to say, "You know, scaffolding serves as a temporary support for student learning with the goal of students adding these concepts to those they can perform independently." Ms. Hernandez smiles and says, "I really appreciate you! Being able to talk these things through has helped me to understand scaffolding so much better. I think you have scaffolded my learning of this process."

> In Your Science Classroom: Scaffolding Student Learning in Science, Ms. Hernandez talks with Ms. Telker about how to teach her students that the addition or subtraction of heat causes a change in the state of matter. Within the scaffolded experiences suggested by Ms. Telker, what might you expect to hear from the students about what causes ice to melt? What other activities could Ms. Hernandez do with the students to further scaffold the concepts?

Constructivism

Return to the explore activity for a moment. What did your classroom observations reveal about the teacher's view of how students learn? As you reflect on the pedagogical or teaching approaches you saw, what might you infer about the stage or stages of cognitive development the teacher targeted in the lesson? Can you determine the stages of cognitive development from the way the teacher designed and taught the lesson? Did you note Vygotsky's scaffolding being used? Did the teacher appear to have some sense of what the learners could do and what might be too challenging for them (zone of proximal development)? Again, ask yourself, "What is my image of how students learn?" In other words, if student learning is at the heart of teaching, then shouldn't teachers reflect on their views of how students learn to guide the way they teach? We believe the answer is, "yes." In addition, it has been documented within the research that teachers tend to teach as they have been taught (Prawat, 1992; Richardson, 2003). So be cognizant of how you were taught and your own ideas of how students learn because your views influence how you design lessons and teach science. In the next section, we will explore two very different perspectives from which to view science teaching: constructivism and objectivism.

BULLETIN BOARD

Key Aspects of Constructivism

- Prior knowledge influences learning.

- Individuals construct their own view of the world through experience with the physical environment and social interaction.

- Linking prior knowledge to new knowledge is a continuous, active process.

- Learning may require reorganizations of existing knowledge.

- Existing concepts are extremely resistant to change.

- Individuals are ultimately responsible for their own learning.

Constructivism has a long history and has been advocated by the National Science Education Standards (NSES) and science education reform initiatives for the last couple of decades as a way to make sense of how students learn science. As noted earlier, constructivism is not a learning theory: Constructivism is an epistemology that refers to the origin of knowledge. In other words, constructivism is useful in explaining how we know what we know. In teaching, a constructivist perspective can assist you in making sense of what students experience, see, think, and how they act in your classroom. So what is constructivism? Constructivism embraces the stance that individuals actively construct knowledge of the world through interactions and experiences. In a constructivist classroom, you might see students engaged in cooperative learning groups actively exploring their own questions through investigation and experimentation. You might also see a teacher listening and questioning students to ascertain prior knowledge before a lesson, while facilitating science investigations using a variety of approaches such as questions, concept maps, or journal reflections. Do these strategies sound novel? Probably not—they are examples of active learning, a concept first introduced by John Dewey in 1933. Dewey, Vygotsky, and Piaget were all constructivists. In a constructivist classroom, knowledge and its construction arise from experiences, but knowledge resides within each individual. Now let's consider another perspective, objectivism.

Objectivistic approaches have historically dominated U.S. classrooms. Unlike constructivism where knowledge is a construction that resides within the knower and cannot be separated from the knower, an objectivist view is one where knowledge is presumed to be outside of the individual. Therefore, the knowers are separated from the known. In short, you might say that knowledge is out there somewhere and learners must seek to find and understand it. Associated with the objectivist view are the traditional teaching approaches typified by students passively receiving knowledge from teachers. This is mirrored in the expression that students are like a blank slate and the role of the teacher is to fill that slate. From an objectivist perspective, students experience concepts, events, and other phenomena in science presented as absolutes and, in many cases, as absolutes that are not open to questioning. In many objectivistic science classrooms you might see teachers lecturing and students taking notes, reading textbooks, and answering questions. Or you might see teachers demonstrating a science concept so that students can repeat the procedures in a laboratory setting. Objectivistic strategies may be very familiar to you through your own experiences as a student. In general, traditional teaching approaches that are teacher centered often reflect an objectivistic nature.

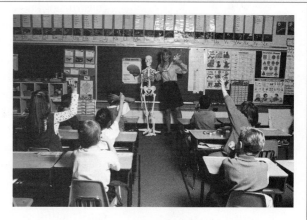

Does this science classroom appear to be more constructivistic or objectivistic in approach?

Clearly, objectivism and constructivism have very different orientations toward learning and teaching. Objectivism presumes that knowledge can be passed in an identical form to another individual. In contrast with constructivism, where knowledge lives within the person, it is not possible for knowledge to be transferred in its exact form into another individual. From a constructivist stance, learners use their senses and experiences within the environment to create images of their world and how it works. This means that each of us construct knowledge based on observations and experiences that are unique to us. Therefore, constructivist teachers cannot assume that the knowledge they impart to their students is taken in by the learners in the same form given. In a constructivist classroom, using collaborative activities that provide learners with opportunities to carry out activities or to try out their ideas within a group of peers assists students to shape and reshape the concepts. It is through social interactions that students constrain or expand their thinking and knowledge. The use of language and sharing one's thoughts are part of the interactions of a classroom where individuals are constantly constructing meaning. So, collaborative interactions among students and the teacher are important to sense making and learning in science. It is through interactions with others that each learner constructs and makes adaptations that fit with new experiences.

With constructivism, the experiences and interactions of the individual within the world are carried out by the senses. For each of us, our personal knowledge constructions represent our view of how the world operates and allows us to operate in that world. Science as seen from the objectivistic view is a search for truth and from the constructivist view it is about making sense of the world. While recognizing the objectivistic view, the NSES focus on constructivist inquiry practices that engage students in the ways of knowing and scientific processes that parallel the world of scientists and what they do. Thus the NSES emphasize learning science as a participatory, active, social enterprise that seeks to make sense of observations and experiences, both individually and collaboratively.

If one follows the constructivist viewpoint, learning science becomes an active process wherein learners build knowledge through their social and individual interactions with the natural world. Constructivist teachers recognize that learners come into their classrooms with prior knowledge and therefore it becomes critical that the teacher uncover prior knowledge in order to facilitate knowledge construction in the classroom (Driver, 1989; Driver, Asoko, Leach, Mortimer, & Scott, 1994; Posner, Strike, Hewson, & Gertzog, 1982). We have found from our experiences that children's notions of science are often very different from what is scientifically acceptable. This is not that surprising—remember, your students have been

BULLETIN BOARD

How to Create a Constructivist Classroom Environment

- Provide experiences that foster appreciation for multiple perspectives (experiences that range from directed to full inquiries).

- Position learning experiences in realistic, authentic, and relevant contexts.

- Encourage ownership and voice in the learning process.

- Make learning a social experience (cooperative and interactive).

- Encourage the use of multiple modes of representation.

- Encourage self-awareness in the knowledge construction process.

Modified from P. Honebein (1996), Seven goals for the design of constructivist learning environments. In B. Wilson (Ed.), *Constructivist learning environments* (pp. 17–24). Englewood Cliffs, NJ: Educational Technology Publications; and Ernest, P. (1995), The one and the many. In L. Steffe & J. Gale (Eds.), *Constructivism in education* (pp. 459–486). Hillsdale, NJ: Lawrence Erlbaum.

constructing knowledge and making sense of the world around them on their own since birth. The point we wish to make here is that the prior knowledge children bring with them into the science classroom can lead them to create meanings that are different from the meaning the teacher intended. In fact, students may find they are learning things that conflict with what they initially thought (dissonance). They may resolve the tension by accommodating the new information and restructuring their cognitive schema, or they may compartmentalize the knowledge schema into the "science they constructed from previous experiences" and the "science they learned in school." This suggests that an individual's prior constructions have a strong hold on an individual's thinking and are not easily changed by science activities in school. In any case, constructivist teachers view children as actively constructing or reconstructing their knowledge of the natural world through their personal and social interactions.

Active Learning and Constructivism

Constructivism goes hand in hand with the notion of active learning. The simplistic model of active learning taps into students' experiences and dialogue either individually or through social interactions (Figure 3.3). For instance, as students construct meaning, they actively engage in "internal talk" that involves the ideas and questions they hold based on their observations. For example, a student may observe the phases of the moon and through internal dialogue construct the idea that the moon actually changes shape. Thus the student is learning and constructing ideas in a self-reflective process. However, active learning may be at its best when it also involves dialogue with others. Active inquiry in a constructivist science class occurs because the teacher creates a classroom environment that nurtures group dynamics allowing for free, back and forth discussion of students' ideas and shared activities. Within the moon example, imagine a teacher bringing in models of the moon and earth as well as several light sources. The teacher has the students working in groups and using the models to simulate the phases of the moon. Students manipulate the models by moving the sun (light source), Earth, and moon, visually representing their positions for full, new, and half-moon phases. After the activity, the students talk with each other about what they saw and how they figured out the positions needed to get the different phases of the moon. Through the interactive explorations and group discussions, students find out that the changing positions of these celestial bodies cause the phases, or what appears to be changes in the shape of the moon. Through these interactions, student learning is enhanced and richer conceptual development occurs.

The example of active inquiry above fits the constructivist view of teaching. As stated throughout this chapter, the NSES advocate a constructivist stance with active learning and inquiry at its foundation. Teaching in constructivist ways often means that teachers have to rethink the ways they view teaching and learning. Research findings even suggest that if teachers make a belief shift from objectivism to constructivism, their teaching practices change dramatically (Lorsbach, Tobin, Briscoe, & LaMaster, 1992; Tobin, 1990). For these teachers, using traditional passive strategies for teaching and learning just don't make sense anymore. They recognize that students need time to explore and experience science while

Figure 3.3 Active Learning

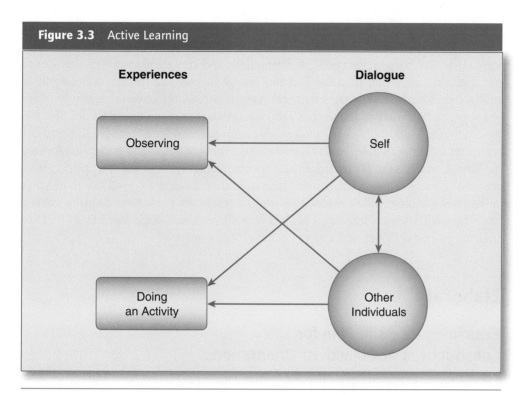

Note: Modified from D. Fink, University of Oklahoma Instruction Development Program (1999), http://honolulu.hawaii.edu/intranet/committees/FacDevCom/guidebk/teachtip/active.htm.

resolving differences in what they already know and what they are learning. Constructivist teachers ultimately realize that the construction of knowledge occurs within the learner. Therefore, constructivist science teachers employ collaborative, active learning experiences that incorporate discussions, clarification, and negotiation for building shared meaning among its participants.

TECH CONNECT: Using Real-Time Data

Activity 1: Student teams collaborate and collect real-time data for weather studies using webcams located all over the world. The site is called EarthCam.com. You may select and assign two to three cam sites for students to check daily (e.g., London; São Paulo, Brazil; and New York City). Students can track the wind speed, humidity, and temperature at their cam site for two to three weeks. The data can be graphed and plotted for comparisons.

Activity 2: Students use the weather data to analyze trends over the two weeks. Students write a weathercast for a specified day at the end of two weeks at each location.

Another excellent resource site for teachers who wish to conduct real-time projects or collaborative partnership lessons on various topics is located at Center for Innovation in Engineering and Science Education located at http:/ciese.org with curriculum projects found at http://www.ciese.org/currichome.html.

Recall your earlier images of how students learn science. Did your image include the kinds of experiences and opportunities that students need to make sense of science in active ways? Did your image reflect student interactions and conversations about the science investigations conducted in class? Did your image include the teacher exploring what students already know about the science concepts to be taught? Finally, think of your image of how students learn. Was the teacher a sage on the stage or a guide on the side? Now it is time to think about the drawings you were asked to analyze in the engage phase. Figure 3.1 represents a classroom drawing that is a more constructivist view of learning. The clues are the cooperative pairing of the students, students interacting, and the multiple, student-centered activities. The teacher's caption also suggests that discussion will follow activities and students' findings will be the focus. Figure 3.2 represents a classroom drawing that is a more objectivistic view of learning. The clues show students working independently, a lack of student-centered activities, and a more teacher-centered image.

Elaborate

Examining a Lesson Plan for Constructivist or Objectivist Orientations

It's now time for you to apply what you have learned about constructivism, objectivism, active learning, and learning theories. Go to Science NetLinks at http://www.sciencenetlinks .com/. On this website, find a science lesson plan of interest to you. Once you select a lesson plan, spend some time reading and reviewing it, and then consider the following:

1. What elements of the science lesson plan reflect a constructivist stance? What elements of the lesson plan reflect an objectivist stance?

2. Compare and contrast the lesson plan elements from both the constructivist and objectivist orientations.

3. In light of what you learned about Vygotsky and Piaget, answer this question: What elements of the lesson plan reflect aspects of their theories of student learning?

4. How would you modify this lesson to maximize student learning?

Evaluate

Photonarratives: Visualizing Objectivistic and Constructivistic Science Teaching

Examine the summary chart of objectivism and constructivism in Table 3.2.

In this evaluation activity, you'll be creating a photonarrative—a tool you may want to use in your own science classroom. Your photonarrative will take the viewer on a visual journey that compares and contrasts objectivism and constructivism. To create your photonarrative, make your own digital photographs or locate photographs and other images on the web. Select eight to ten pictures that exemplify elements of constructivism and objectivism in teaching and learning science. Use the table above to help guide you in selecting your images, but also consider the work of Piaget and Vygotsky as you create or select your images. Put your selected images into a PowerPoint presentation. Write a brief script about the images you chose and why you chose them. You may voice record your script to play as the images are displayed.

Table 3.2 Objectivism vs. Constructivism

Objectivism Supports	Constructivism Supports
The mind as "tabula rasa" or the mind at birth is without innate conceptions.	Since birth, individuals actively construct knowledge to make sense of their world via personal experiences, social interactions, beliefs, and preexisting knowledge.
Knowledge is received and memorized.	Knowledge is actively constructed, which requires receiving, interpreting, and relating it to prior knowledge.
Teacher acts as the authority and transmitter of knowledge.	The teacher facilitates and orchestrates students' experiences and provides opportunities for discussion of phenomena via their observations and engagement in activities.
Students are passive receiver of knowledge.	Students actively construct knowledge.
Knowledge is absolute.	Knowledge is tentative and relative due to the learner's own mental actions.
Knowledge is static.	Knowledge is sense making and changes through discussion and interaction.

TECH CONNECT: Using Digital Technology

Using digital cameras and computers, students can demonstrate their knowledge of science processes or content individually or as a team. All you need are a few relatively inexpensive digital cameras or camera phones.

Second graders: Have students photograph three natural objects and three designed objects. Assist them to download the images and put into them into a PowerPoint slide show. Have them write about how their photographs represent each category.

Fourth graders: Have students take photographs that represent the processes involved in the water cycle (condensation, evaporation, precipitation). Have them write the story of the cycle, linking the processes to their pictures in a slide show or in Photo Story 3. (You can down load Photo Story 3 free. Google search: "Digital Photo Story.")

Eighth graders: Have students take photographs to demonstrate two different kinds of physical change and three examples of chemical change. Have them download images and explain how each example represents each type of change, using Photo Story 3.

Depending on their computer skills, student may decide to add quotes, music, and other creative components to their slide show or to their digital Photo Story 3 project.

Summary

Knowledge of constructivism and objectivism provides teachers with two common frameworks for viewing student learning. A constructivist view maintains that student knowledge is built when individuals learn in active ways. Therefore, a constructivist classroom is one that fosters social interaction and active participation in learning experiences; the teacher facilitates learning experiences and discussions as students negotiate science understandings and meanings. With constructivism, the knower constructs what is known. Objectivism posits that knowledge is "out there" to be learned. An objectivist classroom is one where the teacher is the authority who transmits information to the students, information that is passively received, memorized, and learned. Objectivism and constructivism stances evoke different images of the classroom and perspectives of how students learn. Therefore, it is important that science teachers critically think about their views of how students learn science. Having knowledge of constructivism and objectivism provides a framework for viewing our beliefs of how students learn. Reflecting on our own views of how we believe students learn is important because it shapes our personal teaching knowledge and practices. This self-reflective process is a complex, ongoing endeavor that is essential in becoming an effective teaching professional.

Examining Piaget's and Vygotsky's views of learning and how they are related to constructivism provides support for teaching science in active ways that are advocated by the NSES (NRC, 1996). In closing, as you reflect on this chapter ask yourself, What do I think about Vygotsky's and Piaget's cognitive development theories? What do I think about the constructivist and objectivist views as related to science teaching? Where do my views fit in with respect to each perspective? As a K–8 science teacher, your responses to these questions may take shape in the ways you teach science to your students.

Annotated Resources

Homage to Piaget

http://www.oikos.org/Piagethom.htm

This website provides a comprehensive overview of Piaget's work and theories about child development and learning. Written by Ernst von Glasersfeld.

The Learning Classroom: Theory Into Practice

http://www.learner.org/resources/series172.html

This website offers a series of videos that explore classroom learning and the role of the teacher in that process. Though the series offers thirteen videos exploring various topics, of particular interest and related to this chapter are the first three, which explore constructivism and other learning perspectives, as well as Vygotsky's work.

Also, Session 7 explores the social contents of learning with additional focus on Vygotsky.

Brooks, M., & Grennon Brooks, J. (1999) The courage to be constructivist. *Educational Leadership 57*(3), 18–24.

http://www.ascd.org/publications/educational_leadership/nov99/vol57/num03/The_Courage_to_Be_Constructivist.aspx

This article explores constructivist teaching in light of high-stakes testing. It provides a good overview of constructivism across the curriculum as well as a good discussion of what constructivism is and what it isn't.

Duschl, R., Schweingruber, H., & Shouse, A. (2008). *Taking science to school: Learning and teaching science in grades K–8.* **Washington, DC: National Academies Press.**

http://www.nap.edu/catalog.php?record_id=11625

This book provides the essentials for K–8 science teaching that supports students' learning. It provides details and descriptions of how we know what we know about children's learning of science with questions that address child development related to scientific concepts. It also provides an examination of what tasks are more appropriate for traditional approaches or inquiry approaches. This book is a useful resource for anyone involved in K–8 science education and teaching.

References

Dewey, J. (1933). *How we think: A restatement of the relation of reflective thinking to the educative process.* Boston: D.C. Heath.

Driver, R. (1989). Changing conceptions. In P. Adey, with J. Bliss, J. Head, & M. Shayer (Eds.), *Adolescent development and school science* (pp. 79–99). Lewes, UK: Falmer Press.

Driver, R., Asoko, H., Leach, J., Mortimer, E. F., & Scott, P. (1994). Constructing scientific knowledge in the classroom. *Educational Researcher, 23*(7), 5–12.

Ernest, P. (1995). The one and the many. In L. Steffe & J. Gale (Eds.), *Constructivism in education* (pp. 459–486). Hillsdale, NJ: Lawrence Erlbaum Associates.

Fink, D. (1999). Active learning. Oklahoma Instruction Development Program. Search Google for "active learning theory." Available at http://honolulu.hawaii.edu/intranet/committees/FacDevCom/guidebk/teachtip/active.htm.

Giambattista Vico (n.d.). *The Stanford encyclopedia of philosophy* (Summer 2008 ed.). Available at http://plato.stanford.edu/entries/vico/.

Haney, Czerniak, & Lumpe. (1996). Teachers beliefs and intentions regarding the implementation of science education reform strands. *Journal of Research in Science Teaching, 3*(9), 971–993.

Honebein, P. (1996). Seven goals for the design of constructivist learning environments. In B. Wilson (Ed.), *Constructivist learning environments* (pp. 17–24). Englewood Cliffs, NJ: Educational Technology Publications.

Kagan, D. (1992). Professional growth among preservice and beginning teachers. *Review of Educational Research, 62*(2), 129–169.

Kuhn, D., Langer, J., Kohlberg, L., & Haan, N. S. (1977). The development of formal operations in logical and moral judgment. *Genetic Psychology Monograph, 95,* 97–188.

Lorsbach, A., Tobin, K., Briscoe, C., & LaMaster, S.U. (1992). An interpretation of assessment methods in middle school. *International Journal of Science Education, 14*(3), 305–317.

Posner, G. J., Strike, K. A., Hewson, P. W., & Gertzog, W. A. (1982). Accommodation of a scientific conception: Toward a theory of conceptual change. *Science Education, 66*(2), 211–227.

Prawat, R. (1992). Teachers' beliefs about teaching and learning: A constructivist perspective. *American Journal of Education, 100*(3), 354–395.

Richardson, V. (2003). Preservice teachers' beliefs. In J. Raths & A. R. McAnnich (Eds.), *Teacher beliefs and classroom performance: The impact of teacher education* (pp. 1–22). Greenwich, CT: InfoAge Publishing.

Tobin, K. (1990, April). Conceptualizing teaching roles in terms of metaphors and belief sets. Paper presented at the annual meeting of the American Educational Research Association, Boston, MA.

von Glasersfeld, E. (1989). Cognition, construction of knowledge, and teaching. *Synthese, 80*(1), 121–140.

Vygotsky, L. S. (1978). *Mind in society: The development of higher psychological processes.* Cambridge, MA: Harvard University Press.

Children's Alternative Frameworks and Conceptual Change

Learning Objectives

After reading Chapter 4, students will be able to

- describe misconceptions and instructional approaches associated with conceptual change,
- explain and demonstrate strategies that elicit students' prior knowledge about science concepts, and
- analyze the role of prior knowledge and metacognition learning and conceptual change.

NSES TEACHING STANDARDS ADDRESSED IN CHAPTER 4

Standard B: Guide and facilitate learning. In doing this, teachers

- orchestrate discourse among students about scientific ideas.

Standard C: Engage in ongoing assessment of their teaching and of student learning. In doing this, teachers

- use multiple methods and systematically gather data on student understanding and ability.

Standard D: Design and manage learning environments that provide students with time, space, and resources needed for learning science. In doing this, teachers

- structure the time available so that students are able to engage in extended investigations.

Standard E: Develop communities of science learners that reflect the intellectual rigor of scientific inquiry and the attitudes and social values consistent with science learning. In doing this, teachers

- display and demand respect for the diverse ideas, skills, and experiences of all students.

Source: Reprinted with permission from the National Science Education Standards, copyright 1996, by the National Academy of Sciences, Courtesy of National Academies Press, Washington, DC.

Introduction

All of us construct meaning of the physical world. From the time we are born, we begin to create views about our environment. As each of us grows and develops, we have a need to make meaning of how and why things act as they do. So, long before entering school or a science classroom, each child attempts to make sense of how the natural world behaves. In essence, your students have been constructing ideas, expectations, and explanations about science phenomena as it relates to their daily experiences since birth. The conceptions, ideas, and explanations that children create form complex conceptual frameworks for thinking about the world that makes sense to them. However they are frequently different from the views of scientists (Blosser, 1987; Driver, Squires, Rushworth, & Wood-Robinson, 1994; Treagust & Duit, 2008). Children's explanations of natural phenomena at variance with those that are scientifically acceptable are referred to as **alternative frameworks**, prior notions, naive ideas, or preconceptions, among other terms. Fisher (1985) and other researchers refer to explanations that differ from the scientific views as **misconceptions** (Feller, 2007; Larrabee, Stein, & Barman, 2006; Odom & Barrows, 1995). Regardless of the term used, recognizing that students come into your science classroom with ideas about how the natural world operates is relevant because research findings have shown that students' prior knowledge and beliefs influence what they learn in school (Duit, Treagust, & Widodo, 2008; Kyle & Shymansky, 1989; Osborne & Gilbert, 1980; Stein, Larrabee, & Barman, 2008; Treagust & Duit, 2008; Trowbridge & Mintzes, 1985). As you prepare lessons, it is important to find out what students know about the science content before you teach it. Why? Having knowledge of what students already know allows you to use this information in ways that assists them in learning new concepts with greater relevancy and understanding. Equally important, it allows students to connect what they know to what they will be learning, drawing them into active learning at the start of a lesson. When tapping into students' prior knowledge of the science content, more often than not you will find they have incomplete or inaccurate understandings. This chapter focuses on the importance of attending to students' prior knowledge, their science misconceptions, and the associated instructional approaches. Drawing on constructivism, **conceptual change** includes instructional approaches that challenge students' misconceptions and prior knowledge, while encouraging them to rethink their ideas in light of new evidences through inquiry activities.

> *What you do about what you don't know is, in the final analysis, what determines what you will ultimately know.*
>
> Eleanor Duckworth (1987)

What does Duckworth mean with this quote? Do you agree or disagree? How might ascertaining what students already know about science concepts before you teach them relate to this quote? Rewrite this quote in your own words.

Reflecting on your thinking by examining what you know or do not know is essential for continued learning. Recognizing what we do not know is the core of metacognitive thinking. **Metacognition** refers to thinking about thinking. It is linked to students' ability to control their own cognitive processes. Students regulate their learning by finding and using strategies to achieve their learning goals (Flavell, 1979; Schraw, Crippen, & Hartley, 2006). So how does metacognition relate to students and your science teaching? Think about your K–8 science experiences as a student in school. Did you study plants? How did you study plants? What did you learn about them? What do you know about plants today? A fundamental curricular area of study for K–8 students is plant structure and function. In fact, the following section, "Engage," is intended to reveal your prior knowledge and address the National Science Education Standards (NSES) standards at the K–4 level that focus on characteristics of organisms as well as their environments. It also addresses standards related to regulation and behavior as well as the structure and function in living systems at the 5–8 grade level. As you read the following, draw on what you know of plants to answer the questions.

Engage

What Happens When Plants Grow in the Dark?

Fourth-grade students planted and germinated a variety of seeds as part of a unit on plants. The students also examined the structures of seeds, sprouts, and seedlings. On this day, the class was talking about **variables** they thought might influence corn growth. Marquis said, "My mom uses fertilizer, so if we put fertilizer on the plants they will grow taller." Carlie suggested, "If we grow corn in the dark, it won't get any light and it won't grow much." This idea prompted a lot of discussion among the students. For the remainder of the class, the teacher focused on and recorded students' questions on what the students thought would stimulate plant growth. The students, however, were unsure about the necessary elements required for corn to grow. In particular, students wondered whether or not corn would grow in the dark. The students asked the teacher to tell them what would happen. Ah! With such a teachable moment, she chose to have them conduct the experiment with corn seeds grown in the light and the dark. For the engage phase, you will reflect on your own prior knowledge on plant growth and consider the importance of prior knowledge in teaching science using the questions below.

> In the previous discussion with students, what did the teacher do to get at students' prior knowledge of plant growth? What did she do with this knowledge? Think about what you were taught about plants. What do you know about the requirements for seed growth? Predict which environment will grow the tallest plants (the dark or the light environment)? Write or illustrate what the corn plants will look like grown in the light and the dark.

Explore

Comparing Seedlings Grown in Darkness or Light

Your instructor may challenge you or assign teams to design a test with sunflower or corn seeds to compare what happens when the seeds are grown with and without light. You will need to prepare the seeds for germination, prepare soil in pots, decide how and when you will make observations, and decide how you will measure the growth for a given length of time. Remember, you are designing a test to compare whether the seeds grow taller in the dark or in the light, so you will need to control the remainder of your variables. In addition, the experiment will require the pots be set up in two different environments (light and dark). An alternative to actually conducting the experiment is to go to the website (see Author's note below) and view time-lapse photography of the plant growth.

Were your predictions correct, or were you surprised by the results? The purpose of this engage was twofold. First, it models an approach to access students' prior knowledge and models how teachers can use this knowledge to select science inquiry activities. Second, it prompts each of you to examine your own prior knowledge regarding how plants grow in the dark and light. This is the same form of metacognitive thinking you want to encourage your students to use. To challenge you further, ask yourself what differences may occur in students' learning if they view the experiment on a video or if they actually conduct the experiment themselves.

Explain

Focus Questions

1. What are alternative frameworks or misconceptions in science?

2. How can misconceptions pose barriers to learning science?

3. What are useful strategies for eliciting student's prior knowledge of science concepts?

4. What is a conceptual change approach to teaching science?

5. How is metacognition important to conceptual change in science?

What Are Misconceptions?

In the engage phase, you were asked to reflect on your thinking. Did you think that the seeds planted and grown in the light would be taller than those grown in the dark? If you did, you hold an alternative framework or misconception about an aspect of plant growth. You are not alone: there are many individuals who think plants grown in the light will be taller. Why? It is logical, especially when you consider what children, even very young children, hear, observe,

---

Author's Note:

Comparing Plant Growth in the Dark vs. the Light

http://plantsinmotion.bio.indiana.edu/plantmotion/earlygrowth/photomorph/photomorph.html and learn about plants. For instance, early in their schooling children are taught that plants need light to grow into healthy organisms over time. It is therefore expected that one might predict that light will produce a healthier plant and that such a plant would grow taller than one grown in dark. However, if you actually start plants from seeds in light and dark conditions, you will notice the plants grown in the dark are generally taller (or at least the same height) as those grown in the light. This phenomenon increases the probability of a plant reaching a light source; however, if continually deprived of light and food reserves, it will eventually die. Were you surprised? This phenomenon is referred to as **etiolation**, and is characterized by an elongated stem and a lack of chlorophyll due to reduced light or an absence of light. What other observations were made? What color(s) were the plants that were grown in the dark? How does the size of the leaves grown in the dark compare to those grown in the light?

TECH CONNECT: Video Technology with Science Projects and Experiments

Videos and video clips used as authentic assessments for documenting science experiments and projects are exciting learning alternatives for students. Armed with digital camcorders, or phones or iPads with embedded cameras, students can demonstrate aspects of their projects or experiments like the one on plant growth seen at Schooltube.com (http://www.schooltube.com/video/1a37da89dfcc49cd 8159/Plant-Growth-and-Development).

This experiment was focused on plant height, not a comparison of the color of the stem or the smaller leaves per se; lack of color and small leaves are additional characteristics that occur when plants are grown in the dark. Scientifically, what is happening? The plant's hormones (**auxins**) produced in the tips of the shoots undergo rapid cell production in the absence of light, resulting in faster growth in stem height. When light is present, the auxin (indolacetic acid) is inhibited at the tip of the stem and the stem grows more slowly. The lack of light inhibits photosynthesis and the production of chlorophyll, which gives plants their yellowish or whitish color.

Think back to the engage phase. You may wonder why you were asked to predict what you thought would happen in the experiment. The reason was to elicit your ideas about plant growth and encourage you to think about your own thinking. Having students make predictions is a useful strategy for uncovering prior knowledge in instances like this one. Next, you were encouraged to investigate the question through an experiment or video clip. After seeing the video clip or actually conducting the experiment, did you question your earlier ideas? The findings from the seed experiment or video should have done one of two things: (1) verified or (2) challenged your prior notions of plant growth. In either case, the engage stage was designed to elicit prior knowledge and the explore stage to challenge your ideas and provide direct evidences needed to answer the question.

Using this example with students, you may find that many children predict that the plants "won't grow" or will only "grow a little bit" in the dark, while stating that plants will grow "taller or bigger" in the light. These responses when probed suggest that the learners have prior knowledge of plant growth from their experiences both in and out of school. The concept of plant growth in the light and dark was selected here because teachers can easily do this experiment with students. Furthermore, students' ideas can be challenged concretely by having them conduct a relatively simple experiment. Students see the results with their own eyes. Unfortunately, not all science concepts can be addressed or challenged in concrete ways. It is hard work and takes time for science teachers to facilitate activities that foster students to rethink their alternative frameworks of science phenomena. Begin small, listen to your students, and no matter what science concepts you teach, always begin by providing learners the chance to share or reveal their prior knowledge about the concept. Once you have that, you have an idea of what ideas to reinforce and what ideas to challenge. So, remember to ask what they think!

Sources of Misconceptions

At this point, you may be wondering where or how students develop alternative frameworks or misconceptions. We cannot tell you how they actually originate, but we can identify some common sources of misconceptions. Believe it or not, textbooks and the images used in them can unintentionally foster students' misconceptions about science concepts, especially when students misconstrue the images, causing them to construct inaccurate understandings. For instance, some textbooks represent the solar system with the planets circling the sun from a side view (see Figure 4.1) and not a bird's eye view (see Figure 4.2), which makes the orbital paths appear as very narrow elliptical orbits.

This, of course, is not the case. Other sources of misconceptions may come from individuals close to the student. These credible others include a variety of individuals such as their peers, parents, grandparents, and teachers. These individuals may inadvertently provide partial answers or even incorrect answers to children's questions. Clearly, students' experiences related to science inside and outside of the classroom lead them to develop understandings and misunderstandings of the natural world.

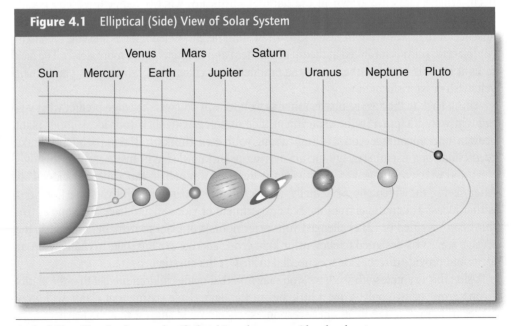

Figure 4.1 Elliptical (Side) View of Solar System

Author's Note: Pluto has been reclassified and is no longer considered a planet.

Figure 4.2 Bird's Eye View of Solar System

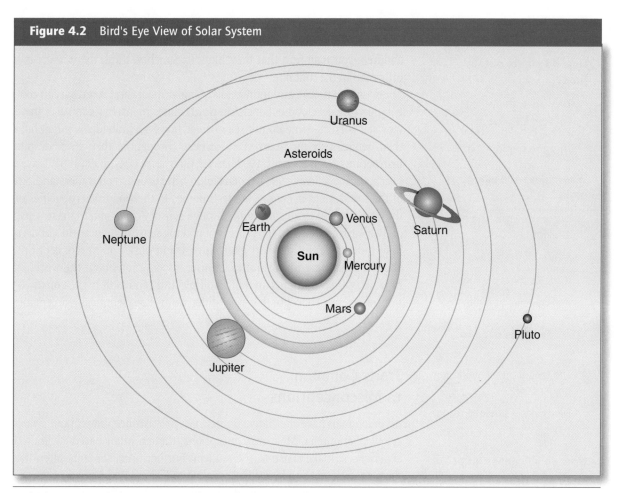

Author's Note: Pluto has been reclassified and is no longer considered a planet.

Consider the notion of the "man in the moon." We've all seen storybooks or cartoons with this image. During discussion about misconceptions in a science methods class, one preservice teacher shared this about her experiences with "the man in the moon." Ms. Sanchez said when she was about six years old her "grandmamma" told her and her siblings a story about the man in the moon. She loved her grandmama's stories, and recalled her grandmamma saying that if you looked carefully you could see the man in the moon. Laughing, Ms. Sanchez said she would go out in the evenings to look at the moon, but she never saw the "man in the moon." She said, "I looked for the man in the moon for more years than I want to admit." It was many years later before she realized that her grandmama meant that "the man in the moon" was actually an "image of a face" on the moon's surface. She said, "All that time I was looking for a 'little man' and not the image of the face." The "face of the man in the moon" is a result of the pattern of dark patches known as seas called "maria" (which are lava plains with no water) and the light areas are mountains and craters of the moon's surface. Recall our point here: Books and significant others can and

BULLETIN BOARD

Some Common Misconceptions

Where does rain come from?

Rain comes from holes in clouds.

Rain comes from shaking clouds.

Rain comes when clouds sweat.

(Continued)

(Continued)

How do plants obtain food?

They use water as food.

They use plant food.

They use soil for food.

Where does the sun go at night?

It goes down in the ground at night.

It flies off in space at night.

It goes behind the moon.

It disappears at night.

What do seeds need to grow?

The seed drinks water to get bigger.

Seeds need sunlight to get taller.

How do volcanoes erupt?

A volcano is a deep hole that goes to the center of the Earth.

It gets very, very hot and then the water boils out.

What causes the seasons?

The sun is closer in the summer and farther away in the winter.

The sun going around the Earth

What is magnetic?

All shiny metals are attracted to a magnet.

Large magnets are stronger than small magnets.

do influence a child's images of the world. As you can see in a child's constructions of the world, misconceptions will arise. If you teach young children, you may find that they, like Ms. Sanchez, think there really is a little man in the moon.

As with textbooks and individuals, popular media and language can contribute to the development of children's misconceptions. In many cases these may self-correct; some do not self-correct, however. Individuals might hold them tenaciously for many years or even throughout their lives, despite instruction (Black & Lucas, 1993; Driver, Guesne, & Tiberghien, 1985; Driver, Leach, Millar, & Scott, 1996). When children are young, their understandings of the world, right or wrong, are testimonies to the wondrous capacities of the human brain to give meaning through sensory input and to make sense of their surroundings. In the process of making sense of their world, children may independently develop alternative frameworks or misconceptions. Human senses are important to gaining information about the world—however, sensory organs are not infallible and can result in the construction of science concepts that may differ from the scientifically acceptable concepts we teach.

Traits Common to Misconceptions

All individuals have alternative frameworks or misconceptions about a variety of phenomena. Most misconceptions, though often based in limited experiences, make sense to the student. Furthermore, students often use them consistently and logically. According to Fisher (1985), misconceptions serve a need for the person holding them. As such, teachers should respect students' misconceptions or alternative frameworks. Fisher has suggested that misconceptions share some commonalities: for instance, they are very resistant to change. Even after individuals have been instructed in the scientifically accurate explanation, individuals may still hold on to their misconceptions about the science concept. Another commonality is that the same misconception is often held by many individuals. For instance, many individuals incorrectly think the seasons are due to the Earth being closer to the sun in the summer and farther away in the winter. In fact, the opposite is true. The seasons are caused by the tilted axis of the Earth in its revolution around the sun, which creates the unequal heating of the Earth's surface. Another commonality is that misconceptions often parallel ideas held by scientists historically. For instance, ancient astronomers believed the sun circled the Earth (geocentric theory). This misconception was accepted for more than a thousand years until Copernicus presented data on planetary alignment that challenged the geocentric theory by suggesting that the planets actually circled the sun (heliocentric theory). Young children today, when asked whether the Earth goes around the sun or the sun goes around the Earth, often state that the sun goes around the Earth, as did early scientists. After all, they observe it moving across the sky on most clear days, and rising and setting each day as if it were circling the Earth.

Not only are there commonalities among misconceptions, but there are also many common sources for misconceptions. For instance, misconceptions can arise from student constructing ideas from books, media, people close to the learner, and everyday language. Because constructions of science are based on personal observations, if individuals experience similar observations, they may independently construct similar misconceptions. The following narrative provides a humorous glimpse into one child's thinking and the way some misconceptions manifest themselves in the classroom through language. As you read the narrative, consider how a student's everyday language and a teacher's language can lead to confusion and misconceptions in any of the disciplines. What did this teacher do to untangle the students' confusion? How effective was it? What else, if anything could be done? In this instance, the student's confusion is not limited to the definitions of the two terms—it is also related to what the child thinks he hears (not what was actually said) and the meaning he associates with it. As science teachers, the point is to recognize that children are not always thinking about the language a teacher uses in the same way it is intended.

Ptolemy's Geocentric Map of the Solar System

What Do Students Think? Prior Knowledge and Students' Science Conceptions

By now, we have established that teaching should begin with discovering what the student already knows about the topic. For meaningful learning to occur, science concepts must be taught in ways that encourage learners to connect new knowledge to those relevant existing concepts in the learner's cognitive schema. Therefore, eliciting prior knowledge from the students is critical in the learning process. Learning is not just the addition of new information, or even correcting misinformation. In any classroom, learning

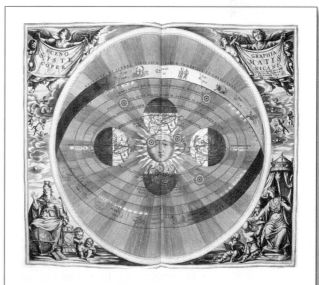

Copernican Heliocentric Universe

YOUR SCIENCE CLASSROOM:
Language and Misconceptions

Teaching Standard C: 1

How does this scenario reflect this standard?

Julie James
Journal Entry

Hi Dr. G,

I was thinking about what we talked about in class last week, and your words that "children are not always thinking the same thing we are when we are teaching" hit home. It really rang true and the following experience came to mind.

One day while I was working as a classroom aide for first grade at Franklin Elementary School, the teacher, Ms. Wilhite, was discussing with the children that a story can have different endings. Ms. Wilhite went on to say that the same story may be written in different ways with different events and endings. She was showing the class the library shelves and pointed out the different versions of Snow White found in their school library. In a blink of an eye, one little boy, Jared, exclaimed, with eyes the size of saucers and mouth open wide, "You mean there's virgins in them stories?" Ms. Wilhite, two years from retirement, calmly said (with a sparkle of laughter in her eyes), "Yes, here's one version of Snow White (emphasizing ver<u>shion</u>), and here's another version of Snow White." At this point, the little boy was slowly shaking his head from side to side in disbelief as she pointed to the shelves of big books and reiterated, "On these shelves we have many versions of a lot of different stories you can read." The boy just stared, and then slowly turned away. As he walked past me I heard him say under his breath, "My mom's never gonna believe this." We laughed over this and so many other misconceptions that year.

My own daughter, Suzanne, would often substitute words she didn't know or was not familiar with for the words she thought we meant to say. She often made us laugh when she would come in from playing and inform us that it sure was "human" out today instead of "humid." We enjoyed her way of saying things so we sometimes let her go on saying them that way for a while. Sometimes she would correct herself and sometimes we would reluctantly "enlighten" her.

science means acquiring understandings of scientific topics by successfully integrating accurate scientific knowledge with personal knowledge of the world. Sounds simple, but the process may not always occur as teachers expect. In fact, research findings suggest that sometimes students simply view scientific knowledge learned in school as being separate from their personal knowledge (Kyle & Shymansky, 1989; Trowbridge & Mintzes, 1985; Watson & Konicek, 1990). In these instances, science is merely a collection of unconnected vague facts rather than a system of conceptual schemes for understanding. In other cases, learning science involves a process of changing prior knowledge and the interpretative frameworks that learners use to make sense of the natural world.

So, what does all this mean in terms of teaching science to K–8 learners in schools? More often than not, science is taught in elementary and middle school as if students have no prior experiences or knowledge of the science (**tabula rasa**). Tabula rasa is Latin and refers to the mind as a "blank slate." The term was used by philosopher John Locke, who maintained that individuals were born without innate ideas. In contrast, a constructivist orientation suggests that students hold ideas and misconceptions about science phenomena that are viable and that work for them. Many of these ideas develop at an early age and students continue to hold them tenaciously throughout their K–12 schooling (Bransford, Brown, & Cocking, 1999; Donovan & Bransford, 2005). Because prior misconceptions or alternative frameworks can be a barrier to learning science, teaching strategies that uncover and challenge misconceptions are critical in assisting students to acquire scientific understanding that aligns with acceptable explanations. This approach is known as conceptual change (Osborne & Freyberg, 1985; Posner, Strike, Hewson, & Gertzog, 1982; Smith, 1991; Watson & Konicek, 1990).

Fortunately, teachers can draw on a solid body of research exploring children's conceptions about science to guide science instruction. The origins of research exploring children's ideas about science concepts come from work by Osborne and Freyberg (1985) and the Learning in Science Project. Many additional researchers have explored students' views of various science concepts (Arnaudin & Mintzes, 1986; Driver, 1983; Driver & Easley, 1978; Minstrell, Anderson Kraus, & Minstrell, 2008; Stepans, 1985, 1996). From this research, we find that children are constantly observing their world and developing a variety of ideas for explaining science phenomena long before they are formally exposed to science in school. As noted earlier, their ideas may be correct, incorrect, or simply incomplete, and students may hold these beliefs throughout schooling and beyond. Therefore, many of the same misconceptions held by young children are also held by older students. So assuming children's minds are "blank slates" is problematic for science teachers. Why? Because students come to your classroom with ideas, and to be effective in your teaching, you first must address those ideas. If not addressed, students may recall what you teach for a test, but leave your classroom believing what they originally thought. Think for a moment about magnets. Many of you may recall conducting investigations with magnets and various materials testing each material to see if would "stick" to a magnet (though the term "attract" would be a better word because "stick" refers to adhesive properties). What if you were only provided metal objects that are attracted to magnets and you were never presented metal items that were not magnetic? You might develop the conception that magnets are attracted to all metals; if it is never challenged, you may hold this notion and never consider other possibilities. At this point, are you asking yourself whether this notion is accurate? Think about a copper penny or a piece of aluminum foil. Are these items metal? Yes. If you test these metals, you will find they are not attracted to magnets and this experience may cause you to adjust your ways of thinking about magnets to those more closely aligned with scientific explanations. That all metals are attracted to magnets, however, is a common misconception held by many children. This misconception can create barriers to developing scientifically acceptable understandings about magnets if nonmagnetic metals and other materials are not part of the testing activities.

In this chapter, some common misconceptions have already been discussed. However, numerous other misconceptions exist on a variety of science concepts and many have been researched and documented (Arnaudin & Mintzes, 1986; Barman, Barman, Cox, Newhouse,

Child's drawing in response to the question, "What is your favorite season?"

& Goldston, 2000; Endreny, 2006; McClelland & Krockover, 1996; Osborne & Freyberg, 1985; Philips, 1991; Rice, 2005; Stepans, 1985). Research findings on children's understandings of science concepts have contributed to a number of useful websites for teachers to examine students' alternative ideas about particular science concepts. For example, the Operation Physics website listed in the annotated resources is quite comprehensive for physical science concepts. Examining the sites like those listed in the annotated resources and becoming familiar with commonly held misconceptions can provide useful insights into how children view particular science concepts, which can guide instructional activities.

As you examine the sample misconceptions in this chapter, you should become aware that the ideas that students hold are related to their personal experiences and observations. Consequently, the students' views make a lot of sense to them. So how do teachers prepare lessons that bring students' ideas about science concepts to light and challenge students' misconceptions as they teach?

Getting at Students' Prior Science Conceptions

As a teacher, you will find that formative assessment plays an important role in getting at students' prior knowledge because it can direct your "instruction to help students bridge their initial ideas to more formal, scientific thinking" (Minstrell and van Zee, 2003, p. 72). According to Donovan and Bransford, "Teachers will need to engage [students'] ideas if students are to understand science" (2005, p. 399). So what kinds of preassessment or elicitation strategies can be used to ascertain student's ideas for subsequent learning? Strategies for accomplishing or eliciting prior knowledge can be as direct as asking a question. Another direct approach often used by teachers in the elementary grades is a KWL chart. With a KWL chart, you begin by asking students what they "Know" about a concept before beginning activities. This is often prompted by the question, "What do you think some people could or would say they know about this topic?" At this time, *all* student ideas are respected (right or wrong) and recorded publicly for class viewing. Next, students are asked, "What" they want to know and again, their ideas and questions are recorded on a class chart. Some teachers add

Figure 4.3 What I Know, What I Want to Know, and What I Learned

KWL charts are commonly used by teachers for (a) ascertaining prior knowledge, (b) motivating students to generate questions for exploration, and (c) assessing what students have learned after lessons. The following is an example of a chart developed around energy and its uses.

What I Know	What I Want to Know	What I Learned
It is like electricity.	Where does it comes from?	Energy is stored.
It's what I need to play.	How do we use it?	Energy of motion is kinetic.
Cars need it.	What is it?	
Toys need it.		
Batteries have energy.		

an "H" to the KWL chart (making it KWHL). The "H" refers to "How will we learn?" Resources for how they will learn are listed in this category. Finally, after the lessons are completed, students are asked what they "Learned," and this is recorded. At this time, the categories are revisited and the teacher facilitates questioning as students share their new "best thinking" on the topic. Students' ideas are either accepted or rejected based on the activities conducted and classroom discussions. KWL charts can quickly reveal prior misconceptions that can be discussed after instruction and students can reflect on their old ideas, comparing them to the new evidence from their current investigations. An example of a KWL chart is found in Figure 4.3.

Finding out what your students already know isn't limited to direct questioning. Suppose that you were planning to teach lessons on animals and their characteristics to third-grade children. You could get at what students know of animals by asking them to give you a list of three different animals and describe how they know their choices are animals. This gives you insight into their ideas about animals that they know, but it may not reveal what they do not know. So, a more useful approach may be to put together a wide variety of animal pictures (people, insects, spiders, sea urchins, octopuses, rats, lizards, birds, and clams) and nonanimals (fungi, trees, flower, moss, bacteria, etc.). Then have students select pictures that represent animals and explain their reasons for selection (Barman, Barman, Berglund, & Goldston, 1999; C. Barman et al., 2000). This strategy of asking children, "What is?" and "What isn't?" can quickly give you more insights into what the students know or do not know about the topic. This kind of knowledge helps you decide which activities to use or modify, based on what your students reveal about what they know.

Another example for eliciting prior knowledge might involve students creating graphic organizers (webs, concept maps, feedback loops, or cycles) with selected terms. Students may then arrange the science terms in ways that show their connections and meanings. A free trial of a concept mapping software program can be downloaded at www.inspiration. com. Figures 4.4 and 4.5 provide classroom examples of concept maps.

Think back to the seeds grown in the dark and light. We presented the investigation as a discrepant event that began with students predicting (in writing or drawing) what was going to happen and explaining their reasoning. Another example of a discrepant event might occur when a person would predict an inflated balloon would pop if a bamboo skewer were pushed through it. But what if it doesn't pop? Common sense suggests that it should pop, but a discrepant event activity turns out differently than expected and challenges conceptual frameworks of the individual (Wright & Govindarajan, 1992). Demonstrations may or may not be a discrepant event but they are also useful at getting at students' prior knowledge. A demonstration often used with fifth- and sixth-grade students who are embarking on an exploration of the process of evaporation as part of a weather unit is to hang up wet pieces of cloth on a line. The students are asked to predict what will happen to the cloth when they return the next day. In addition, students write an explanation within their science journal of how they think the change happens. The journal writing focuses on explaining the changes student predict rather than naming the change.

As you might imagine, uncovering students' prior knowledge and alternative conceptions can take a variety of forms. These include, but are not limited to, the following: (a) the use of charts like the KWL, (b) quick writes to questions, (c) class discussions,

Figure 4.4 Plant Concept Map

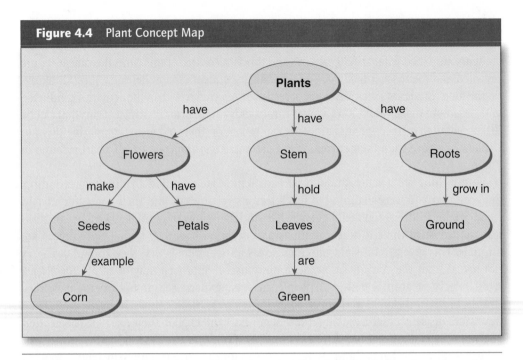

Note: This concept map was constructed with second graders during class. The teacher facilitated a discussion on plants to demonstrate the characteristics of a concept map. Key elements for the concept map include a hierarchical ranking with the broadest concept at the top and examples at the bottom. Arrows show the direction of the proposition statements (e.g., Leaves are green). When completed, concept maps illustrate constructions of relationships between science concepts and terms.

Figure 4.5 Student Concept Map of Natural Resources

This concept map was made by a third grader, Tim, who was demonstrating his knowledge of characteristics of natural resources studied during classroom activities. He created this concept map in his science notebook as part of the lesson assessment. Students were given the terms "water, fresh, salty, lakes, oceans, and rivers." The children were encouraged to add their examples. Tim added catfish and whales.

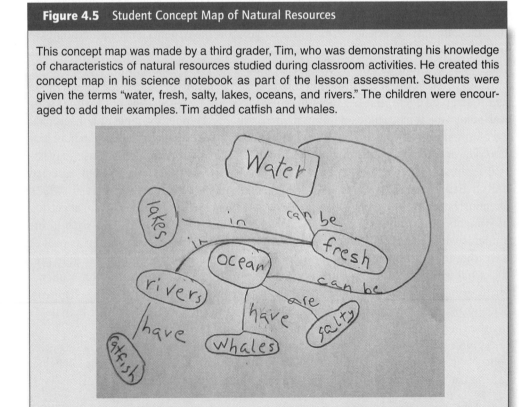

(d) journaling, (e) demonstrations, (f) the development of webs or concepts maps, (g) surveys and questionnaires, and (h) classification activities sorting items such as "What is living" and "What is not living." These activities provide important insights about what your students know as well as their misconceptions, and serves as a guide for instruction. Without determining what your students already know and what misconceptions exist, your science instruction is more likely viewed by students as something to simply be learned in school, rather than as a useful tool in interpreting the natural world around them.

In the annotated resources at the end of this chapter, you will find resources for preassessing students' understandings of science concepts, including a five-volume set of assessment probes that cover a variety of science topics and may be useful tools as you prepare to teach. To get you thinking about strategies you might use to ascertain prior knowledge and potential misconceptions, read "Your Science Classroom: Investigating Sinking and Floating in Ms. Silva's First-Grade Classroom." As you do so, try to identify strategies that she is using to explore prior knowledge and misconceptions her students appear to hold.

You may have noted that Ms. Silva used several strategies to uncover the preconceptions and prior knowledge her students held regarding sinking and floating. She listened carefully and valued their ideas. She tapped into prior knowledge by having the students identify items they thought would either sink or float and guided a discussion about "rules" that students could use to make

Posing a question about a science concept and recording students' responses is one way to uncover students' prior knowledge which assists teachers to plan effective inquiry strategies that can challenge erroneous views students may hold.

predictions. She had students make predictions and provide their explanations. In addition to conducting a preassessment of students' understandings, the choice of the items she had the students test were selected to begin the process of challenging science misconceptions.

Teaching Science for Conceptual Change

Posner and colleagues (1982) proposed instructional strategies for addressing alternative conceptual frameworks that have led to what is known today as a conceptual change approach to teaching science. Changing students' alternative views or misconceptions to those that are scientifically acceptable is much more than simply giving students the correct explanation. It means offering students multiple opportunities to grapple with the concepts they hold and with the scientific explanations. Students' cognitive schemata and beliefs about how the world works are held strongly, and why not? They have held them several years and have used them successfully to operate in an often confusing world. Why should they give up their ideas unless there is a reason to do so? In order for students to change their misconceptions related to specific science concepts, certain conditions must exist. Let's take a look.

YOUR SCIENCE CLASSROOM:
Investigating Sinking and Floating in Ms. Silva's First-Grade Classroom

Ms. Silva is a first-grade teacher who loves to integrate science with other subjects in her classroom, so when her class read the book *Who Sank the Boat?* by Pamela Allen, Ms. Silva knew this would be a perfect time to do some sink-or-float investigations in her classroom. Ms. Silva began by asking her students to help her brainstorm definitions for sink and float. Once students had a common definition for both terms, Ms. Silva asked her students to brainstorm a list of items that sink or float; she created the following chart on the board from student responses:

> **Teaching Standard**
> **B: 1, C: 1, D: 1, and E: 1**
>
> How does this scenario reflect this standard?

Sink	Float
Rocks	Beach balls
Bowling balls	Sticks
Pennies	Plastic bottles
Marbles	Toy boats
Bar of soap	Apples

After examining the brainstormed list, the students were divided into groups and asked to create a "rule" that would help them decide whether new items would sink or float. Ms. Silva wandered around the room to hear the groups' discussions and helped each group record their rule. Each group shared their rule and Ms. Silva recorded them on the board:

Heavy (big) things sink and light (little) things float

Things made of metal sink

Things made of plastic float

Ms. Silva discussed with her class how scientists test their ideas and the class decided to test the rule: heavy (big) things sink and light (little) things float. Recognizing that many of the students had misconceptions about sinking and floating, Ms. Silva gathered items for the students to test that would challenge the students' ideas about what sinks and what floats. The following day, Ms. Silva brought in the following items: rock, marble, paper clip, pumpkin, foil, bar of soap, penny, piece of firewood, ping pong ball, and golf ball. She asked the groups to complete a prediction chart with their explanation. Then she gave them sticky notes. They put their names on their sticky notes (one sticky note for each student per item) and then placed the sticky note under the sink or float column beside each item to be tested on the whiteboard.

Groups shared their predictions and rationales for which items they believed would sink and which would float. Although responses varied between groups, there were clear patterns that indicated to Ms. Silva that most students held the misconception that the weight or size of an item determined whether or not the item would sink or float. Ms. Silva set up stations for team rotation. Teams rotated to each station that contained some of the items to be tested and a tub of water to test the items. Needless to say, most groups were surprised when the pumpkin and the piece of firewood floated—they were the heaviest and biggest items, after all! Some students had predicted that the golf ball would float and again were surprised when it sank while the ping pong ball floated. Several students thought the paper clip was light and would float, but it sank. The foil floated when left in a flat sheet, but sank when it had been crushed into a little ball.

Ms. Silva discussed the test results with the class and they decided to create a new rule. After some more discussion, the students came up with the following new rule: Some heavy (big) items sink and some float. Some light (little) items sink and some light items float. As science ended for the day, Ms. Silva wondered if any of the children would mention that the shape of an item might influence whether an item would sink or float during the next activity.

> How does she determine the students' prior knowledge of sink and float? Why do you think Ms. Silva chose the items she did for her students to test? How might you assist students to alter their understandings of a science concept to be compatible with scientific explanations? What other strategies could be used to get at students' science misconceptions? What would you do next if you were Ms. Silva?

Conditions and Teaching Strategies for Conceptual Change

According to Posner and colleagues (1982), students must first be dissatisfied with their misconceptions before they are willing to consider a more appropriate explanation. This makes sense—as long as what students believe works for them and with what they're experiencing, the misconceptions held will continue to exist because there is no reason for them to rethink their understandings. Through challenging investigations, students can become self-aware that what they observe during class activities is different from what they initially believed. Thus begins the process of dissatisfaction with their previous inaccurate or incomplete views on the science topic. Furthermore, discussing their observations and having them conduct experiments can lead to compelling arguments that foster dissatisfaction with their prior alternative frameworks opening up the possibilities for new scientific explanations. It is naive to think that a single class activity is enough to change students' long-held conceptions. However, if students are to alter their understandings to more scientifically acceptable explanations, they first must be dissatisfied with their own ideas.

First, remember that changing students' alternative frameworks is not easy and takes time. So, let's assume students become dissatisfied with their alternative frameworks. What other conditions must occur? Students must have an intelligible (understandable) scientific explanation available to them to replace existing ideas or they may still hold on to their preconceived notions despite its flaws. We are reminded of a classic article featuring Deb O'Brien's fourth-grade class where most of the children believed that when their parents told them to put on "warm clothes" that the warm clothes alone gave off heat (Watson & Konicek, 1990). After students conducted several experiments using thermometers placed in rolled rugs, comforters, sweaters, and caps, Ms. O'Brien's students were disappointed. They saw no temperature increases as they had predicted. Following a week of testing, the class discussed the reasons for their results. Despite evidence to the contrary, many students held on to their original misconception, rationalizing that something was wrong with the thermometers they had used or the experiments they conducted. Even with testing, observing, and class discussion some students did not accept the view that the heat comes from the body and is transferred to clothing. They did not accept the scientific explanation and held on to their original erroneous ideas. This illustrates how tenaciously a student can hold on to a misconception, which is why it often takes multiple experiences and time to correct students' misconceptions. With concepts such as heat and other abstract science concepts, it may be more difficult to establish scientific explanations that are intelligible to students. Even if intelligible explanations are provided through activities, some students may still not change their misconceptions. Posner and colleagues (1982), suggest that there are additional conditions necessary for conceptual change to occur.

BULLETIN BOARD

Teaching Strategies Used to Foster Conceptual Change (Generative Learning Model)

- Ascertain students' ideas, expectations, and explanations prior to instruction. Make ideas public in a risk-free environment. Have students discuss ideas without judging right or wrong.

- Provide contexts or experiences to challenge their ideas (multiple hands-on inquiries and discussions on the concept).

- Facilitate the exchange of learners' views and challenge students to compare ideas, evidences, and scientific perspectives.

- Provide opportunities for students to use new science concepts or explanations in familiar or everyday settings.

(Osborne & Wittrock, 1985)

When faced with changing one's beliefs about how natural phenomena work, students must also view the new scientific explanation as plausible. This means, for a student to change their beliefs, the scientific explanation must be believable. In other words, they may ask, "Is it more reasonable or believable than my original beliefs or does it help me to understand better?" A final condition is that the new scientific explanation must be usable in many new situations. Classroom activities and discussions must be convincing enough that students accept the new scientific explanations as more productive in their daily experiences. Think back for a moment to Ms. Silva's activity with sink and float. The selection of items she had students test not only challenged their prior knowledge (e.g., all metals sink, big items sink, small items float), but also the test results offered evidence for an alternative explanation. This set the stage for the class to revise their rules about sinking and floating to align more closely with the scientific explanation. So what finally happened with Ms. O'Brien's students who were investigating heat? After more discussion of their findings and retesting, Ms. O'Brien's asked her students to make a choice. Students chose one of the following statements to demonstrate what they believed about clothes and heat: (a) Warm clothes give off heat. (b) Clothes do not give off heat. Our bodies give off heat, which warms the clothes we wear. (c) I am unsure of the reason. In the end, there were students who stood in each group. Not all of the children chose the new scientific explanation as the right choice, and some were simply unsure.

In summary, Posner and colleagues (1982) stated that the conditions needed for an individual to undergo conceptual change include dissatisfaction with prior ideas. In addition, new scientific explanations must be intelligible, plausible, and useful in a variety of contexts. Teaching strategies for conceptual change are supported by research (Osborne & Freyberg, 1985; Osborne & Wittrock 1985; Watson & Konicek, 1990) and are found to be powerful strategies that, if given time, may allow learners to identify their own misconceptions, to examine the soundness and usefulness of their ideas in light of scientifically accurate explanations, and to reflect on them to resolve the gaps or differences. Whether conceptual change occurs or not, the strategies are useful approaches for science teachers because they encourage students to be active participants in their own learning as they seek to construct and acquire new knowledge (see Bulletin Board: Teaching Strategies Used to Foster Conceptual Change [Generative Learning Model]).

Elaborate

Interviewing a Child: Uncovering Prior Knowledge

Teachers should practice using a variety of strategies to decode and understand what children know and what they are learning within their classrooms. Several strategies have been discussed in this chapter so far; an additional strategy that can be used to decode student's knowledge is the interview. Interviewing all students in a class is not usually as practical as other approaches, but interviewing children is an important skill for teachers for several reasons. First, for teachers of young children it is used extensively as a form of assessment with students who have yet to develop writing skills to determine what they know. Interviewing children can also uncover students' ideas about science prior to and after instruction. Preparing an interview requires thoughtful questions and flexibility to adjust questions as children reveal their ideas. The following will provide you with information about using interviews to ascertain students' prior knowledge.

Why Conduct Interviews?

Before you begin interviewing, it is useful to understand what can be gained through interviewing your students. An interview can be a form of assessment not unlike that used by a physician. Physicians need to get information from a patient in order to assess the illness and prescribe effective and appropriate treatment. It is reasonable to assume that a teacher needs to be aware of what the students already know in order to design effective instruction. Second, science textbooks and classes on human development can provide you information on what students can do at different age ranges, but interviewing your students provides insights on what your students know and can do. Finally, interviewing is a practical way to develop questions and questioning skills while refining your listening skills. Interviewing here is intended to provide you with a tool for researching children's misconceptions about science concepts and processes.

The Nature of Interviews

Interviews can be a purposeful conversation initiated by one person to find out what another knows about a particular topic. Your goal is to find out what a student knows about a science concept. The focus of conversational interviews is not to judge whether the student gives right or wrong answers, but rather to determine the child's understandings of the subject matter. Finding out what children really think is not easy. Children spend a large part of their childhood figuring out how to please adults and they are adept at fastening on to small visual cues as to what is expected of them. Teachers may unintentionally use leading questions, reject an incorrect answer by quirking an eyebrow, or shift a question to another student rewarding the "correct" answer. So for a good interview, put the child at ease and make it clear that you want to know what they really think, and you are not judging their answers. Interviews between a student and teacher can assist the teacher in determining whether the learner has a misconception, partial understanding, or complete understanding of the concept under consideration.

Tips on Conducting an Interview With a Child

Before beginning the interview, take some time to just talk with the child. Let the child operate the tape recorder and listen to their voice on tape so that the child has a moment to become comfortable talking with you while using the recording equipment.

Interviewing Tips

- When beginning the interview be open and clear about what you want to achieve. Tell the children your reasons for doing the interview.
- Audiotape the interview. Turn it on (or let them turn it on) while you sit alongside them, not face to face. Place the tape recorder by the students and tell them you will remove any parts they don't want to keep in it at the end of the interview.
- Have your questions written out before you conduct the interview. Keep your questions neutral and ask probing questions when appropriate. Examples of probing questions might be, "You used the word _____. What does that mean to you?" or "Can you think of some examples of what you're describing that would help me understand better?" Use the phrases "What do you think" or "Can you tell me more?" when asking questions. Avoid leading questions that imply to the child that there is one answer you're looking for. An example of a leading question on the topic of weather might be, "So, in order for it to snow, the temperature in the atmosphere needs to be?" Instead you might ask, "What do you think causes precipitation to come down as snow?"
- Watch your tone, voice, and expressions. Encourage but avoid being suggestive in word or action that might signal to the children that you are indicating they are right or wrong, such as saying "Great answer!" after a response. Instead, use "okay," or smile to let the children know you are listening without influencing what they are saying.
- Use open-ended questions (requiring more than a one-word response) more often than closed-ended questions. Start with simple questions and move to questions that are more difficult.
- Listen carefully and use follow-up question prompts. Again, it may be helpful to write out examples of these prompts prior to conducting your interview. Examples might include, "Tell me more about what you mean when you say," or "Give me an example of that."
- Sincerely restate your interest in the children's words and ideas.
- Repeat unexpected or contradictory responses by restating them, as if you are mulling them over and pause to encourage the children to clarify.
- If you don't understand the response, repeat their words and ask them to "tell you more." Another tactic is to simply pause and wait for them to give you more information.

The following is an actual interview conducted with a first-grade student on the topic of weather. Read the interview and then answer the questions that follow.

An interview with a first-grade student: (I) interviewer, (S) student

I: Tell me how you describe weather.

S: Weather is how it is feeling outside. Like if it's windy or if it's sunny or it's cloudy or if it's rainy.

I: Okay, so weather is how it is feeling outside. Can you tell me more about that?

S: Well, it's what is happening outside.

I: Okay. How is the weather today?

S: Sunny.

I: Um. It's sunny. Okay, does weather change?

S: Uh-huh. It changes. Because sometimes it's sunny when it's summer. That's my birthday and when it's summer it's really hot. But when it's Christmas, that's not my birthday and when it's Christmas it's really cold. And there is a difference between those.

I: Okay, so can you tell me about the seasons?

S: The seasons?

I: Yes

S: Seasons. Hmmm. Let me think. No. What is it?

I: No? When it's your birthday, what is it?

S: Summer, is that a season? Oh yeah, summer, fall, winter.

I: Is there another one?

S: Summer, fall, winter, spring!

I: Good job! So how is the weather in the winter?

S: Cold and snowy.

I: Can you tell me why it's cold and snowy?

S: Because that's when it's Christmas.

I: Can you tell me more about why it might be cold?

S: No.

I: How is the weather in the spring?

S: In the spring, hmmm, let's see. Maybe sunny, a little bit windy, though.

I: Why do you think this?

S: Well, because the wind is blowing softly and it is still sunny.

I: How's the weather in the summer?

S: Hot! Really hot! But it's fun, too, because that is when my birthday is and then I can go to Disneyland!

I: What do you think causes it to be hot in the summer?

S: Well, because I'm always sweaty when I play.

I: What's the weather like in the fall?

S: In the fall. Hmmm. Cold.

I: Why do you think it's cold?

S: I don't know. I'm just taking a guess.

I: Okay. Is it fall right now?

S: No.

I: What season is it right now?

S: I don't know. Sometimes we don't have seasons.

I: So sometimes there isn't a season?

S: Yeah, I will have to think about that.

I: Okay, so is temperature the same as weather?

S: No. Yes, yes, yes.

I: How are temperature and weather connected?

S: They are the same because the. Hmmm. Because temperature and temperature might be snowy and temperature is cold and the weather is cold. They mean the same thing.

I: When do you think it is the hottest time of the day?

S: In the middle of the day. Because that is the only time I get sweaty.

I: Okay, can you tell me what are clouds?

S: They are things that float up in the air and they're close by the sun.

I: Okay, so they are close to the sun. What do you think clouds are made of?

S: Hmmm. Hey! Clouds aren't made of anything. God just made them. He just said, "Let there be clouds," and there they were.

I: Okay, do clouds change when the weather changes?

S: No.

I: They're always the same?

S: Oh no, no, no! They change like when it's stormy they're black, but when it's sunny they're white.

I: Why do you think that is?

S: I don't know. I can't tell you. Because the weather is different so they're different.

I: Okay, what is rain?

S: Rain is just a little water dripping down.

I: Dripping down from where?

S: From the sky.

I: Are you saying that rain comes from the sky?

S: I don't know. Rain just comes down from the sky.

I: Why is that?

S: Just to feed the plants down here to make them grow.

I: Okay, so what is rain made of?

S: Rain is made of water.

I: Okay, so what is snow?

S: I don't know. That's too hard.

I: Thanks so much, I think it is time to stop. You were very helpful and thank you for sharing your ideas with me.

> How well does this interviewer get at the student's understandings of weather concepts? Be specific. How could the interview be improved or what would you have done differently? What does the interview tell you about what the child knows about weather? Do you detect possible misconceptions? What are they? How might the information from this interview inform your teaching of weather concepts to first graders?

Evaluate

Interviewing Children About Science

Now it is your turn to conduct an interview with a child. Your first task is to select a science topic that you have studied and understand well. Next you will develop ten to fifteen interview questions that focus on the science concept. You may also want to jot down some follow-up questions and prompts to assist you. Identify a child (relative, family friend, a student you tutor, etc.) and obtain permission from their parent or guardian to interview them. You will want to audiotape the interview, so be sure you have a tape recorder that you have tested so you know it is working properly. Audiotape the interview and take notes, since sometimes the tape recorder stops or jams.

Analyze the interview for the learner's understanding of the science concepts or processes. To analyze the interview, listen to the tape recording and type up the questions and the child's responses. Include notes about what you observed while conducting the interview. For your analysis, first describe the child you interviewed (gender, age, where you interviewed the child, and any other pertinent information). Next, analyze the responses as they relate to the child's understanding of the topic using these questions. The following questions may be useful as you complete this analysis. Did the children have more understanding than you expected? What did you expect them to tell you? What did they know about the topic? Did they hold misconceptions of the science concept? What were those misconceptions? Now that you have an idea of what the child thinks about the concept, consider how you would design instruction to teach them the concept. How would you begin a unit on your selected topic? Identify the strategies you would you use and explain your selection of strategies. What activities would you select to provide the learners with evidence to challenge or enhance their ideas about the concept? How would teaching strategies for conceptual change be useful in planning the lessons? Finally, to improve your interviewing skills, critique your interview using the questions in the elaborate section above.

Summary

Students are constantly observing the world around them, clustering observations with other similar information, forming "rules" about how things work, connecting it to prior experiences, and ultimately constructing ideas to make sense of the world. Learning is always taking place, both in and out of the classroom. Recognizing that students come to school with a variety of understandings about the world means acknowledging and respecting their prior ideas, providing experiences to support or challenge their thinking, and discussing their prior ideas in light of explanations that are scientifically accurate. As discussed in this chapter, the erroneous ideas about science concepts that students bring to classrooms are known by a variety of names—preconceptions, alternative frameworks, misconceptions, or naive ideas; they can pose barriers to subsequent learning. Because children hold tightly to their misconceptions and it takes time to provide numerous experiences to change their misconceptions, conceptual change may seem time consuming and impractical. However, as described in this chapter, conceptual change strategies can assist teachers in moving past barriers and focus students toward new patterns of thinking that align with acceptable science explanations. Instructional strategies used in teaching for conceptual change can support new thinking patterns and are underscored by providing students with hands-on experiences that challenge misconceptions, create dissatisfaction, and generate alternative explanations. Teaching science for conceptual change is intended to enable students to emerge from learning science with ways of understanding the world that are more accurate, and to build a solid foundation for continued new learning.

Annotated Resources

SciLinks Plant Activities

http://www.scilinks.org/MyScilinks/SearchByCode.aspx?Enc=1&Scilink=YeocUq+G7oak=&EntPt=YwkU/jb1sML+8JeNA+6MA/s3bOrjucxkz

This site provides a variety of activities and lessons for teachers to use with students (teacher guide included). Activities are on topics that range from plant structure to growing gardens.

Misconception Resources

The listed websites are useful resources for seeking information of alternative frameworks held by students. They cover a wide range of science topics.

Operation Physics: Children's Misconceptions About Science

http://www.eskimo.com/~billb/miscon/opphys.html

Science Misconceptions Directory

http://www.huntel.net/rsweetland/science/misconceptions/

New York Science Teacher Website: Common Science Misconceptions

http://www.newyorkscienceteacher.com/sci/pages/miscon/subject-index.php

Saginaw Valley State University Regional Math and Science Center: Resources

http://www.svsu.edu/mathsci-center/uploads/science/gspsk.htm

Science Myths in K–6 Textbooks and Popular Culture

http://www.eskimo.com/~billb/miscon/miscon.html

Science Hobbyist: Science Misconceptions in K–6 Texts

https://www.msu.edu/user/boswort9/attempt1/cep817web/amasci/scimis.htm#mis.

Minds of Our Own (Annenberg series)

http://www.learner.org/resources/series26.html

This excellent website provides two hour-long videos (Can We Believe Our Eyes? and Out of Thin Air) that explore classroom learning and challenge the assumptions we have on how students learn science in the classroom. The science topics addressed include conceptions related to electricity, photosynthesis, and air.

Private Universe Project in Science (Annenberg series)

http://www.learner.org/resources/series29.html

This website provides a series of eight ninety-minute video workshops on science topics of astronomy, physics, biology, and chemistry. Each video focuses on a pertinent science issue such as hands-on approaches, appropriate experiences for learners, and origins of students' ideas on a variety of topics related to learning science concepts.

Uncovering Student Ideas in Science: Formative Assessment Probes

Keeley, P., Eberle, F., & Farrin, L. (2005). *Uncovering Student Ideas in Science: 25 Formative Assessment Probes.* Volume 1. Arlington, VA: NSTA Press.

Keeley, P., Eberle, F., & Tugel, J. (2007). *Uncovering Student Ideas in Science: 25 More Formative Assessment Probes.* Volume 2. Arlington, VA: NSTA Press.

Keeley, P., Eberle, F., & Dorsey, C. (2008). *Uncovering Student Ideas in Science: Another 25 Formative Assessment Probes.* Volume 3. Arlington, VA: NSTA Press.

Keeley, P., & Tugel, J. (2009). *Uncovering Student Ideas in Science: 25 New Formative Assessment Probes.* Volume 4. Arlington, VA: NSTA Press.

Keeley, P., & Harrington, R. (2010). *Uncovering Student Ideas in Physical Science: 45 New Force and Motion Assessment Probes.* Volume 1. Arlington, VA: NSTA Press.

Keeley, P. (2011). *Uncovering Student Ideas in Life Science: 25 New Formative Assessment Probes.* Volume 1. Arlington, VA: NSTA Press.

This is a series of books that provides assessment probes for ascertaining students' preconceived ideas about a variety of science concepts and ideas. The probes are applicable across a variety of grade levels and generally easy to use. The six volumes available cover a number of physical, life, Earth, and space science concepts.

References

Arnaudin, M., & Mintzes, J. (1986). The cardiovascular system: Children's conceptions and misconceptions. *Science and Children, 23*(5), 48–51.

Barman, C., Barman, N., Berglund, K., & Goldston, M. (1999). Assessing students' views about animals. *Science & Children, 37*(1), 44–49.

Barman, C., Barman, N., Cox, M., Newhouse, K., & Goldston, M. (2000). Students' views about animals: A national study. *Science & Children, 38*(1), 42–47.

Black, P. J., & Lucas, A. M. (Eds.). (1993). *Children's informal ideas in science.* London: Routledge.

Blosser, P. (1987). Science misconceptions research and some implications of the teaching of science to elementary school students. ERIC/SMEAC Science Education Digest, 1, 1–6.

Bransford, J., Brown, A., & Cocking, R. (1999). *How people learn: Brain, mind, experience, and school.* Washington, DC: National Academies Press.

Donovan, S., & Bransford, J. (2005). *How students learn: History, mathematics, and science in the classroom.* Washington, DC: National Academies Press.

Driver, R. (1983). *The pupil as scientist?* Milton Keynes, UK: Open University Press.

Driver, R., & Easley, J. (1978). Pupils and paradigms: A review of literature related to concept development in adolescent science students. *Studies in Science Education, 5*, 61–84.

Driver, R., Guesne, E., & Tiberghien, A. (Eds.). (1985). *Children's ideas in science.* Milton Keynes, UK: Open University Press.

Driver, R., Leach, J., Millar, R., & Scott, P. (1996). *Young people's images of science.* Philadelphia: Open University Press.

Driver, R., Squires, A., Rushworth, P., & Wood-Robinson, V. (1994). *Making sense of secondary science: Research into children's ideas.* New York: Routledge.

Duckworth, E. (1987). *The having of wonderful ideas and other essays on teaching and learning.* New York: Teachers College Press.

Duit, R., Treagust, D., & Widodo, A. (2008). Teaching science for conceptual change: Theory and practice. In S. Vosniadou (Ed.), *International handbook of research on conceptual change* (pp. 629–646). New York: Routledge.

Endreny, A. (2006). Children's ideas about animal adaptations: An action research project. *Journal of Elementary Science Education, 18*(1), 33–42.

Feller, R. (2007). 110 Misconceptions about the oceans. *Oceanography, 20*(4), 170–173.

Fisher, K. (1985). A misconception in biology: Amino acids and translation. *Journal of Research in Science Teaching, 22*(1), 53–62.

Flavell, J. H. (1979). Metacognition and cognitive monitoring: A new area of cognitive-developmental inquiry. *American Psychologist, 34*, 906–911.

Kyle, W., & Shymansky, J. (1989). *Enhancing learning through conceptual change teaching. Research matters. To the science teacher.* National Association for Research in Science Teaching monograph, No. 21.

Larrabee, T., Stein, M., & Barman, C. (2006). A computer-based instrument that identifies common science misconceptions. *Contemporary Issues in Technology and Teacher Education, 6*(3), 306–312.

McClelland, A., & Krockover, G. (1996). Children's understandings of science: Goldilocks and the three bears revisited. *Journal of Elementary Science Education, 8*(2), 32–65.

Minstrell, J., Anderson Kraus, P. & Minstrell, J. E. (2008). Bridging from practice to research and back: Tools to support formative assessment. In J. Coffey, R. Douglas & C. Sterns (Eds.), *Science assessment: research and practical approaches* (pp. 37–68). Arlington, VA: NSTA Press.

Minstrell, J., & van Zee, E. (2003). Using questioning to assess and foster student thinking. In J. Atkin & J. Coffey (Eds.), *Everyday assessment in the science classroom* (pp. 61–73). Arlington, VA: NSTA Press.

Odom, A. L., & Barrow, L. H. (1995). Development and application of a two-tier diagnostic test measuring college biology students' understanding of diffusion and osmosis after a course of instruction. *Journal of Research in Science Teaching, 32*(1), 45–61.

Osborne, R., & Freyberg, P. (Eds.). (1985). *Learning in science: The implications of children's science.* London: Heinemann.

Osborne, R., & Gilbert, J. (1980). A technique for exploring students' views of the world. *Physics Education, 15*(6), 376–379.

Osborne, R., & Wittrock, M. (1985). The generative learning model and its implications for science education. *Studies in Science Education, 12*, 59–87.

Philips, W. (1991, February). Earth science misconceptions. *The Science Teacher, 58*(2), 21–22.

Posner, G. J., Strike, K. A., Hewson, P. W., & Gertzog, W. A. (1982). Accommodation of a scientific conception: Toward a theory of conceptual change. *Science Education, 66*, 211–227.

Rice, D. C. (2005). I didn't know oxygen could boil! What preservice and inservice elementary teachers' answers to "simple" science questions reveals about their subject matter knowledge. *International Journal of Science Education, 27*(9), 1059–1082.

Schraw, G., Crippen, K., & Hartley, K. (2006). Promotion self-regulation in science education: Metacognition as part of a broader perspective on learning. *Research in Science Education, 36*(1–2), 111–139.

Smith, E. (1991). A conceptual change model of learning science. In S. Glynn, R. Yeany, & B. Britton (Eds.), *The psychology of learning science* (pp. 43–63). Hillsdale, NJ: Lawrence Erlbaum.

Stein, M., Larrabee, T., & Barman, C. (2008). A study of common beliefs and misconceptions in physical science. *Journal of Elementary Science Education, 20*(2), 1–11.

Stepans, J. (1985). Biology in elementary schools: Children's conceptions of life. *The American Biology Teacher, 47*(4), 222–225.

Stepans, J. (1996). *Targeting students' science misconceptions: Physical science concepts using conceptual change model.* Clearwater, FL: Ideas Factory.

Treagust, D., & Duit, R. (2008). Conceptual change: A discussion of theoretical, methodological and practical challenges for science education. *Cultural Studies of Science Education, 3*, 297–328.

Trowbridge, J., & Mintzes, J. (1985). Students' alternative conceptions of animals and animal classification. *School Science and Mathematics, 85*(4), 304–316.

Watson, B., & Konicek, R. (1990, May). Teaching for conceptual change: Confronting children's experience. *Phi Delta Kappan, 71*, 680–685.

Wright, E., & Govindarajan, G. (1992). Stirring the biology teaching pot with discrepant events. *The American Biology Teacher, 54*(4), 205–207.

PART III

The Nature of Science Teaching

Chapter 5

Classroom Teaching Practices
Questioning and Inquiry

Learning Objectives

After reading Chapter 5, students will be able to

- discuss and defend the use of wait times during questioning,
- analyze the types of questions used in a science inquiry activity and determine the range of cognitive levels,
- evaluate questions associated with a given science inquiry, and
- summarize key characteristics of effective questioning.

NSES TEACHING STANDARDS ADDRESSED IN CHAPTER 5

Standard B: Teachers of science guide and facilitate learning. In doing this, teachers

- focus and support inquiries while interacting with students;
- orchestrate discourse among students about scientific ideas;
- challenge students to accept and share responsibility for their own learning;
- recognize and respond to student diversity and encourage all students to participate fully in science learning; and
- encourage and model the skills of scientific inquiry as well as the curiosity, openness to new ideas and data, and skepticism that characterize science.

Source: Reprinted with permission from the National Science Education Standards, copyright 1996, by the National Academy of Sciences, Courtesy of National Academies Press, Washington, DC.

Introduction

The afternoon sunlight was passing through a beveled windowpane on the partially opened classroom door. Lily was staring at the rainbow of colors seen on the classroom wall as Ms. Simons walked in, noticed Lily, and asked, "Are you looking at the colors on the wall?" Lily nodded. Ms. Simons continued, "How do you think the colors got on the wall?" Lily shrugged and said, "I don't really know." Ms. Simons then explained the refraction of light to her. Now, let's pause a moment. What if Ms. Simons had asked Lily a different question. What if she had asked, "What do you think you would observe if you closed the door?" or "What do you think you would see if you opened the door wider?" These types of questions would encourage Lily to carry out her own simple inquiries. Lily may have opened the door wider or closed the door to see what would happen. By doing so she could gather more information about the conditions of refraction. She may have even come up with a question or two of her own in the process.

While supervising, we have seen wonderful inquiry activities by preservice teachers. Unfortunately, when it came time to discuss the concepts with the students, the lesson sometimes stalls out. On one occasion, a seventh-grade class was exploring the water cycle by moving to different stations as part of a Project WET lesson (www.projectwet.org). During the lesson, students roll a cube at each station that sends them on their journey as a water drop. The six surfaces on the cube send students to places such as clouds, lakes, rivers, glaciers, soil, oceans, animals, plants, and ground water. The activity allows students to explore a range of places involved in the water cycle and the changes in state associated with water moving through the cycle. The students were totally immersed into the activity. We heard one student, Steve, say, "Hey, I've been stuck in this glacier for five rolls!" Xavier laughed and said, "I'm moving right along. I've been in the ground, the lake, and now the clouds." Cyndi chimed in and whispered, "You need to evaporate or melt, Steve!" Other students chuckled, but it was clear they were anticipating where the roll of the cube would send them next in the water cycle. After a bit of time passed, the teacher flipped the light switch, a signal to wrap up, and said, "Let's summarize, class! And pull this together. I have a diagram of the water cycle on the board we need to complete." She proceeded, "Jim, would you please define evaporation?" After Jim's textbook response, she asked, "Joy, what is condensation?" Following Joy's response, she asked, "Sheree, can you tell us what we call rain, hail, sleet, and snow?" Unfortunately, the teacher orchestrated a series of questions like these until an accurate water cycle diagram was completed. Initially animated, students became quiet jotting down notes as requested. What is wrong with this picture? Where are the questions that have students drawing on their experiences in the activity? Where are the students' questions? In this brief example, the questions asked were not related to what the students had just experienced as "waterdrops." None of the students had the opportunity to discuss what they experienced in the simulated water cycle activity, nor did they have an opportunity to ask questions about the cycle. Could the teacher have used questions from the activity to lead to the same concepts but in ways that were part of the students' "waterdrop" experiences? The answer is "Yes." What if the teacher had begun the discussion by asking students if they had any questions? What if the discussion had included the questions, "What did you experience as a waterdrop? Do you have any questions about what happened to you as a waterdrop?" or "What did you observe as you moved through the water cycle?" Becoming a good questioner (and listener) takes time and practice. Science questions should foster student inquiry and learning. As you teach science, remember to find time to elicit students' questions and motivate them to investigate their own questions and inquiries. It is important that you recall the discussion of the nature of science and scientific inquiry, because it is impossible to talk about questions and questioning without talking about inquiry. In fact, questioning is at the heart of science inquiry practices in the classroom.

TECH CONNECT: Science Games for Your Science Classroom

"Droplet and the Water Cycle" is a game found at the NASA site http://kids.earth .nasa.gov/games/. Though the game is not built around a lot of questions based on the hydrologic cycle, it does require students to answer key questions to move to the next level, which involves additional questions. The game can be played in teams at school or individually at home to see who can complete all four stages.

Another site with interactive activities, games, and songs for the hydrologic cycle and other science topics can be found at neok12 Educational Video, Games and Lessons for K–12 School Kids located at http://www.neok12.com/Water-Cycle.htm.

Can it be that asking questions is teaching? I am just beginning to see what is behind all your questions. You lead me on by means of things I know, point to things that resemble them, and persuade me that I know things that I thought I had no knowledge of.

Socrates, quoted in Xenophon's *Oeconomicus*

Examine Socrates' statement. What would Socrates say is the purpose of questions? Considering this quote, what questions would Socrates have asked Lily regarding the spectrum of light on the wall?

Engage

Do You Know Your Questions?

One of the most basic approaches for examining different types of questions is to sort them according to whether they are convergent or divergent. **Convergent questions**, often called closed-ended questions, have one answer. Two examples might be, "What is a diffraction grating?" or "Who coined the term, 'spectrum'?" Divergent or open-ended questions are those that have multiple responses or answers. An example might be, "If you could create an item for humankind, what would it be?" For science teachers, an important part of lesson planning is related to designing questions for lessons. Effective teachers make it look easy, but be aware that it takes much practice. In the following engage phase you are provided with three content areas specified in the standards for K–8 science. Write one divergent and one convergent question for each content area identified. The first one is done for you.

Here's an Example: Level K–4 Organisms and Their Environment

Standard: "All animals depend on plants. Some animals eat plants for food. Other animals eat animals that eat the plants" (NRC, 1996, p. 129).

Convergent: What is the name of the herbivore (plant eater) in the diagram of the food chain?

Divergent: If you could remove all humans from any ecosystem on the planet, what do you think the impact would be on food chains? Explain the changes in the predator–prey relationships you think would occur in your selected ecosystem.

Strand One: Level K–4 Organisms and Their Environment

Standard: "Humans depend on their natural and constructed environments. Humans change environments in ways that can be either beneficial or detrimental for themselves and other organisms" (NRC, 1996, p. 129).

Convergent: _____

Divergent: _____

Strand Two: Level 5–8 Transfer of Energy

Standard: "Heat moves in predictable ways, flowing from warmer objects to cooler ones, until both reach the same temperature" (NRC, 1996, p. 155).

Convergent: _____

Divergent: _____

Strand Three: Level 5–8 Earth in the Solar System

Standard: "The sun is the major source of energy for phenomena on the earth's surface, such as growth of plants, winds, ocean currents, and the water cycle. Seasons result from variations in the amount of the sun's energy hitting the surface, due to the tilt of the earth's rotation on its axis and the length of the day" (NRC, 1996, p 161).

Convergent: _____

Divergent: _____

How well did you do? How easy was it for you to craft each type of question? Which questions, divergent or convergent, were easier to write? Crafting questions for wide-open topics is probably a bit easier than creating them for designated science topics as you have done here. In everyday life we ask numerous convergent questions. For instance, one might ask, "Where do you place the stamped envelopes for sorting?" or "Who starred in the role of Bella Swan in *Twilight*?" For a **divergent question** one might ask, "If you could rewrite the book *Gone With the Wind*, how would it end?" So, if you struggled with writing the convergent or divergent science questions, practice writing convergent and divergent questions on everyday topics. Another tactic is to take convergent questions and rephrase them to be divergent questions. Being able to write and recognize divergent and convergent questions is a much-needed skill that effective science teachers work hard to acquire. It takes thoughtful practice. Keep this in mind as you explore why questions are so important to science teaching and inquiry activities.

Explore

Cognitive Levels of Questions

If, as Socrates suggested, questioning is at the heart of teaching, then your skill level as a questioner is central to effectively teaching science. The National Science Education Standards (National Research Council [NRC], 1996) advocate teaching science in ways that foster critical thinking; teachers therefore must be able to identify whether a question is designed to tap into lower or higher levels of thinking. Read the following narrative modified from an interview with Dr. Luiz Moura, who was a colleague of Alexander Fleming. After reading the narrative, determine whether each question stimulates lower- or higher-level thinking, and label them accordingly. As you label the questions, ask yourself how you are defining higher- and lower-level thinking questions.

The Story: Alexander Fleming and the Discovery of Penicillin

Alexander Fleming's father was the gardener's son for Lord Randolph Churchill, Sir Winston Churchill's father. When Winston was eight years old, he fell into a well and would have drowned if Alexander, who was then ten years old, had not pulled him out. Lord Churchill was so grateful for his son's life that he told the gardener he could ask for anything. He even said that if he needed a house he would give him one. Alexander's father said, "No, I don't need a house." He said, "I have four children. Three of them will do work like me, but Alexander has always wanted to do research and be a doctor. I don't have the funds to help him fulfill his desires." With Lord Churchill's support and Alexander's aptitude, he graduated with a degree in medicine and later discovered penicillin.

However, there is more to the story. Lord Churchill offered Alexander Fleming space to set up a laboratory in one of his mansion's rooms; instead Fleming set up a laboratory under two staircases in the mansion. His lab was humid. His bacteria cultures, the focus of his work, were often contaminated with fungi that grow well in high humidity. During his years of research, he found a fungus (later identified as *Penicillium notatum*) growing in a bacterial culture (*Staphlococcus aureus*) that destroyed the bacteria. As a researcher, he might have been disgusted that his bacteria were destroyed, but he didn't throw the culture out. Instead, he pondered why there was a halo of "no growth" around the fungus. Later research showed that this fungus secreted a material, penicillin, that kills bacteria. Fleming began testing the substance on cows and horses sick with pneumonia and other infectious diseases. Then, during the Second World War, the Royal Air Force commander sought out Dr. Fleming and asked him to come with him to administer penicillin to Winston Churchill who was seriously ill with pneumonia and who had little chance of getting medical assistance in North Africa. Churchill was in Africa providing support for Montgomery who was fighting Rommel, the Desert Fox. So, the commander and Fleming traveled to Africa to find Churchill. Thinking about what he was about to do, Fleming supposedly said to say to the commander, "What, Churchill, our prime minister? Well, it's all or nothing." He pondered the situation a moment longer and went on to say, "Winston Churchill will be the first human being to have a penicillin injection." Turns out that Alexander Fleming saved Winston Churchill's life a second time.

Modified from a YouTube video conversation with Dr. Luiz Moura presented by Ana Martinez and Luiz Fernando Sarmento, November 2009.

Using this story, identify the following questions as lower- or higher-level questions:

1. Who are the key characters in the story?

2. If you could create a new ending for the story, what would it be?

3. How would you retell Fleming's story?

4. What is your perspective on whether Fleming's choice to inject Churchill with untested penicillin was ethical?

5. What type of organism is penicillin?

6. Why was Lord Churchill grateful to his gardener?

7. How were Fleming's scientific experiences similar to and different from those of Louis Pasteur?

8. What is your stance on whether testing antibiotics on mammals such as horses and cows is ethical?

9. How would one of Fleming's siblings tell the story?

10. Where was Fleming's early laboratory located?

11. What parts of the story could possibly happen to you?

12. What might have happened if Fleming had tossed out all of the contaminated cultures?

(Continued)

(Continued)

13. Why did Fleming go to North Africa?

14. What are the events in the story that indicate scientific inquiry?

15. Does this story raise any questions in your mind?

Note: This story, while presented as true within the YouTube video referenced, is indeed fiction. Fleming discovered penicillin by accident in 1928 when he left bacteria cultures out while away on a monthlong vacation. When Fleming returned from vacation, he was sorting through his cultures and found one where mold had begun to grow. He noticed that the bacteria immediately around the molded area had died. Because of his careful observations, Fleming was able to discover a mold that was used as the first antibiotic. If you read this story with skepticism, then you're practicing one of the tenets of science! As with any Web-based source, it is important to check sources and verify information.

As you read the narrative, which questions did you identify as requiring lower levels of thinking? Which questions were identified as the higher-level questions? Which type of question was easiest to identify? What did you use as a guide to sort the questions? Which questions challenge students to think critically? What do you think is the best question? After you read the following section you will be able to answer these questions and identify the types and levels of questions associated with the story of Alexander Fleming.

> *Learn from yesterday, live for today, hope for tomorrow.*
> *The important thing is not to stop questioning.*
>
> Albert Einstein

Interpret Einstein's quote. What do his words say to teachers today? Based on this quote, what question(s) would you like to ask Einstein?

Explain

Focus Questions

1. What is meant by lower- and higher-level cognitive thinking questions?

2. How are the lower- and higher-levels of cognition reflected in Bloom's Taxonomy (1956)?

3. What is the role of a science teacher with respect to questioning?

4. How are productive questions important for supporting inquiry activities in science?

5. How can questioning be used to bridge students' learning and understanding of science?

6. What are the benefits of wait time?

7. What strategies and techniques make questioning effective?

Inquiry and Questions

The nature of science teaching activities should not be about students generating static knowledge; instead, it should be a dynamic process of inquiry that requires students to think critically and problem solve. Cherif's (1993) description of inquiry is useful from this stance. He stated that to inquire is to "seek knowledge and understanding by questioning, observations, investigating, analyzing, and evaluating" (p. 26). Inquiry often begins with a question, a need, or a problem. For individuals to solve or answer questions with sound scientific thinking requires a range of skills. Although the definition of inquiry appears to be simple, it implies many other skills such as predicting, interpreting, hypothesizing, classifying, inferring, and more. As you teach science, ask yourself if your questions motivate students to investigate phenomena to gain understanding of the concepts or ideas being taught. Do your questions lead toward scientific literacy and intellectual independence, which refers to a student's ability to judge the evidences for one's self (Munby, 1980)? Given the goal of scientific literacy and intellectual independence, how do we know what kinds of questions to ask students? How do we examine questions and questioning so we can become more-effective teachers of science and science inquiry?

Questioning in Science Classrooms

A useful place to begin our inquiry into questions and questioning is Bloom's Taxonomy of educational objectives (1956). This system has had a powerful influence on education and teachers across the disciplines since the 1950s, and is still used widely today.

Bloom's Taxonomy of Educational Objectives

Benjamin Bloom and a team of educational psychologists identified three areas or domains related to learning and educational activities (Bloom & Krathwohl, 1956). The areas associated with learning include the cognitive (mental) domain, affective (feelings and emotions) domain, and psychomotor (physical) domain. All of these areas are important to learning science, but for our purposes the focus is on the cognitive domain. Bloom's work revealed that the vast majority of test questions used in schools required students to think only at the lowest cognitive level—mostly recall. He also found that teachers asked lower-level questions 80%–90% of the time. So, how do you learn to think critically if you are rarely asked to do so? Bloom's system provides a way for science teachers to look at questions that span a wide range of cognitive skills from the lower level (knowledge, comprehension, and application) to the higher level (analysis, synthesis, evaluation). His classification system comprises six cognitive levels (from lower level to higher level): knowledge, comprehension, application, analysis, synthesis, and evaluation. The cognitive levels of thinking are associated with various "action verbs" that should be considered when teachers plan questions for class activities, develop lesson objectives, and create test questions.

Although Bloom's Taxonomy has influenced teacher questioning for fifty years, during the1990s, one of Bloom's former students, Lorin Anderson, reexamined the cognitive taxonomy while working with David Krathwohl, one of Bloom's partners in the creation of the original taxonomy. The new taxonomy was a group effort that included expertise from individuals in cognitive psychology, curriculum and instruction, and educational testing, measurement, and assessment. Anderson and Krathwohl led the effort revising the classification system (see Table 5.1).

Table 5.1   Bloom's Taxonomy of Questioning Skills and Cognitive Levels With Revised Levels

Bloom's Taxonomy (1956)			Anderson & Krathwohl (2001)
Cognitive levels	**Questioning verbs**	**Examples of questions or assignments**	**Revised taxonomy**
Knowledge: Learners recall, recite, list knowledge previously learned	Explore What, Why, When, How, and/or Who, Cite, Define, Describe, List, Label, Name, Match, Select, Choose, Order	What is a spectrum? Define metamorphosis. List the body parts of insects. Describe plant cell organelles. Name the parts of a flower. Who discovered penicillin?	Remembering: Retrieving, recalling, or recognizing knowledge based in memory. Refers to use of memory for definitions, facts, items, or lists.
Comprehension: Learner grasps, understands, or explains the meaning of knowledge	Interpret, Expand, Explain, Demonstrate, Convert, Infer, Illustrate, Estimate, Predict, Summarize, Classify, Relate	Explain the process of photosynthesis. What can you infer from the project findings? Interpret the bar graphs on types of organisms. Predict to which group the organism belongs. Summarize the key factors of the rock cycle.	Understanding: Refers to meaning derived from different types of operations, whether written or graphic. It includes interpreting, exemplifying, classifying, summarizing, inferring, and explaining.
Application: Learners use acquired information or ideas in new situations	Solve, Construct, Identify, Develop, Utilize, Organize, Plan, Select, Experiment, Build, Apply, Classify Manipulate, Adapt	What examples of energy can be associated with this room? Select the evidence that is most supportive of the conclusion. Organize the data in a chart. How will you solve the density problem? Identify the variables in the design.	Applying: Associated with executing or implementing procedures or processes. Using learned material through products like models, presentations, interviews, or simulations.
Analysis: Learners break down the information into key parts. Makes inferences and evidences to support claims	Dissect, Compare, Contrast, Examine, Deduce, Include, Reason, Diagram, Differentiate, Distinguish, Assume	Compare/contrast theories on how dinosaurs became extinct. How are mitochondria related to respiratory function? How do you distinguish between a Monarch and Viceroy butterfly? What can you infer from the graph? Examine the igneous rocks and differentiate between intrusive and extrusive. Diagram the simple machines in the toy.	Analyzing: Breaking down tasks or concepts into parts while determining how the parts relate based upon the purpose. It involves differentiating and organizing between the elements or parts. Creating spreadsheets, surveys, charts, diagrams, or graphic representations.

Bloom's Taxonomy (1956)			Anderson & Krathwohl (2001)
Cognitive levels	**Questioning verbs**	**Examples of questions or assignments**	**Revised taxonomy**
Synthesis: Learners bring together information in new ways or proposes alternative outcomes	Build, Combine, Compile, Construct, Formulate, Develop, Generate, Discuss, Propose, Invent, Change	What change would you make to improve the tower's support? What is another way you could design the experiment? What would happen if the light were left on the flower buds for a longer time? Using the items and a wooden spool, invent a way to make it move on the stretched wire. How would you test the quality of water with only these items?	**Evaluating:** Use criteria and standards in making judgments via critique. Critiques, position papers, recommendations, and various kinds of reports are useful for evaluation products. In Anderson and Krathwohl's taxonomy, evaluation comes before creating. Why? Because it is a necessary precursor to creating something new.
Evaluation: Learners judge or critique information or the quality of items, ideas, or works	Measure, Conclude, Critique, Decide, Rate, Interpret, Establish criteria, Determine, Recommend, Prioritize, Grade, Appraise, Conclude	How would you prioritize the list of scientific achievements given and explain? How did you decide which solution was best, and why? Summarize your criteria in selecting the key elements needed for photosynthesis. How would you rate your partner's reaction time? Examine the graph and interpret the most salient findings.	**Creating:** Putting ideas or items together in new ways. Reorganizing information or materials by planning and constructing a novel item. This is the highest cognitive level in the new taxonomy.

Note: Adapted from Bloom, B. S. (1956), *Taxonomy of Educational Objectives, Handbook I: The Cognitive Domain*. New York: David McKay; and Anderson, L. W., & Krathwohl, D. R. (Eds.) (2001), *A Taxonomy for Learning, Teaching, and Assessing: A Revision of Bloom's Taxonomy of Educational Objectives*, Boston, MA: Allyn & Bacon (Pearson Education Group).

As noted in Table 5.1, one obvious difference between the two taxonomies is the rewording of the levels. This change was based on the current view that thinking is always an active process. This point of view led to using verbs instead of nouns for all the levels. In the revised form, the last two levels are known as evaluating and creating (Anderson & Krathwohl, 2001). The categories "synthesis" and "evaluation" switched places in the original taxonomy and "synthesis" was renamed and modified to become the last category "creating" in the Anderson and Krathwohl version. The changes occurred because it was argued and supported that to create something new one must first evaluate the existing item or phenomena. Given the discussion of Bloom's Taxonomy, go back to the explore activity with the fictional Fleming story and identify the questions according to Bloom's cognitive levels. How well did you do? The questions posed in the explore phase were classified as follows:

1. knowledge (lower)

2. application (lower)

3. synthesis (higher)

4. evaluation (higher)

5. knowledge (lower)

6. comprehension (lower)

7. analysis (higher)

8. evaluation (higher)

9. application (lower)

10. knowledge (lower)

11. analysis (higher)

12. synthesis (higher)

13. comprehension (lower)

14. analysis (higher)

Science teachers engage students by asking questions for a variety of purposes. Whether a science teacher asks questions to foster critical thinking or support student understanding of science concepts, planning questions in advance is important.

Clearly, Bloom's Taxonomy builds a foundation for looking at questions for their ability to stimulate cognitive processes. What other dimensions of questions and questioning do science teachers need to develop to become more effective?

Questioning With a Purpose

To become a more effective science teacher you must be able to facilitate the progression of students' learning and skills toward the specified learning objectives. Careful attention to questions and questioning by teachers can help students reach these goals and foster their learning while the activities are still under way. One way to expand your understanding of questions is to understand that questions that are asked have an underlying purpose.

Blosser's (1990) work centered on the types of questions science teachers ask and their associated purposes. She states that many classroom questions serve a managerial purpose to guide science class activities. A second purpose is to reinforce facts or concepts. This type of questioning may require a student response or it may be rhetorical and not require a response. A third purpose for questioning is to stimulate student thinking. The fourth purpose for asking questions is to arouse curiosity or even create a mind-set for classroom inquiry. Blosser acknowledges that teachers may have other purposes for questions, but these categories, though not exhaustive, are quite common. What these common categories do is provide a good starting point for us to reflect on the types and purposes of our own questions in the K–8 science classroom. A savvy teacher is one who is aware of the purpose behind a question and knows when to use it.

While noting the purposes for questions, Blosser's (1990) review of research found that questions in most science classrooms centered on textbook content and were teacher centered. Furthermore, about a third of the classroom questions asked by teachers were managerial (Hastings, 2003). To foster students' involvement in investigations and problem solving we must shift our thinking about how we use questions in science teaching. We must move away from the entrenched image of teacher as the information giver to a view of the teacher as a guide and facilitator. This shift is not easy; after all, each of you have been apprenticing for a teaching career by observing your teachers. It is likely you have experienced learning science where teachers and textbooks were the authorities. Resisting the urge to teach in the traditional ways in which you may have been taught and rethinking your science classrooms as places where students, questioning, and inquiry are center stage is imperative. One way to accomplish this shift is to consider the purpose of a question before asking it, and to choose your question accordingly. Another way in which to make the shift toward student-centeredness is to ask questions that encourage students to investigate questions and share their understandings of science concepts or processes. Jos Elstgeest's (2001) work on questioning paves the way for the shift.

Science Inquiry and Questions

With respect to inquiry and questioning, Elstgeest (2001) separates questions into two broad categories: (a) nonproductive questions that are often wordy and lead to even wordier textbooks answers, and (b) productive questions that lead the learner to engage in mental or physical activity. Productive questions invite students to further examine an idea or pursue a fresh perspective on the topic or concept. In other words, productive questions require or stimulate productive activity whereby students demonstrate, rather than state the answer—because they can inquire and find out for themselves. Used carefully and in a timely manner, productive questions can help science teachers support student learning, maintain student interest, and assist students in generating their own productive questions. Elstgeest's five types of productive questions for student inquiry include (1) attention focusing, (2) measuring and counting, (3) comparing and contrasting, (4) action, and (5) problem posing.

Attention-Focusing Questions

Questions that focus student attention are intended to support student learning by redirecting their activity to an important detail or details they may have overlooked. During science inquiry activities, a teacher may need to pose questions that support learning the concept by having student activity focus on relevant details they may have missed. For example, a teacher might ask a student, "What do you notice about the direction the paper helicopter's propellers spin?" or "What do you notice about the angles of the structure supporting the most weight?" or "What can you see that could help you figure out which end is the anterior (head) of a worm?" By directing students to make a particular observation, attention to pertinent aspects of the phenomena under study are not overlooked. Thus, attention-focusing questions most commonly assist students to more carefully make observations.

BULLETIN BOARD

Blosser's Types of Questions and Examples

Managerial: Has your team neutralized the lemon juice? Are you ready to move to the next station? Have you completed the classification of the mystery animal? Is your name on your paper?

Rhetorical: Dew point is the temperature at which water vapor changes to a liquid, right? Amphibians live part of their lives on land, correct?

Stimulate thinking: I wonder what happens if I add another pulley to the system. I wonder what happens to the breathing rate of a goldfish if I increase the temperature. How can I make the pendulum swing at one-second intervals?

Create mind-set: Tell me what you know about energy. Look at this unusual shell. What do you want to ask about the shell?

Stimulate curiosity or inquiry: What do you think will happen to the pumpkin if you put it into the tub of water? How might I get the boiled egg out of the bottle?

Children need many opportunities to estimate and measure length, volume, time, temperature, and mass. A variety of equipment such as scales, meter sticks, balances, graduated cylinders, and thermometers are important tools to help them develop these science skills.

Measuring and Counting Questions

Measuring and counting questions are exactly the kinds of questions you might expect them to be. For instance, taking young children on a nature walk may begin with a question like, "How big is this tree?" In another activity you may ask, "How many marbles could you hold in your hand?" Students' responses at this point may be only rough estimations, but as students grow older they gain experiences that can lead them toward more accuracy. Questions should then include more quantitative information, such as "How far does the ball move the paper dragon?" "How frequently did the spider eat?" "What is the count of flower blooms?" or "What is the mass of the pennies?" As children learn how to use rulers, balances, graduated cylinders, stopwatches, and other scientific apparatus, they can answer measuring and counting questions with a greater degree of accuracy through their learned skills. As students become more skilled with measuring and counting, they are ready for comparing and contrasting questions.

Comparing and Contrasting Questions

Both **qualitative** and **quantitative** descriptions are important to scientific discovery. Comparing and contrasting questions can involve both descriptive and numerical information. An obvious example for their use is when students are classifying items. A common question might be, "How are butterflies and moths alike? How are they different?" Children may at first focus on the qualitative aspects such as the color or shape of the organisms, but may shift to quantitative descriptions related to the number of legs or the number of body divisions the organisms exhibit. Other examples of compare and contrast questions might include, "How is granite like gabbro? How are they different?" or "How are the processes of evaporation and condensation alike? How are they different?" If you ponder these examples carefully, you will notice that they have the potential to draw on both qualitative and quantitative information. The next type of question can be used at any time, but often follow other questions. Action questions can lead to new investigations and new outcomes.

Action Questions

If you are wondering what type of questions evoke action through simple investigations, these are the "What happens if?" questions. Some examples are seen in the following: "What happens if we place a vial of cold water (colored red) into a tub of clear warm water?," "What happens if we hang a magnet from the ceiling?," or "What happens if we put a colored jaw breaker in a petri dish of water?" What if we put three different-colored jaw breakers in a petri dish of water? Having students conduct simple investigations based on action questions can have either multiple or singular solutions. In both cases, these are the "cool" questions that students are always ready and excited to explore. In fact, students frequently ask this type of question themselves. Elstgeest (2001) refers to them as "What happens if?" questions. As productive questions, they encourage basic investigations or experiments. If students are supported to pursue them, they enrich students' repertoire of science experiences. In addition, many action questions promote students' **predictions** (statements of a future events based on a pattern or consistency of evidence [data]) prior to conducting their investigative activities. Even young children can make predictions, though at first they are generally more like guesses because of their limited experience. Practicing this skill through science activities will improve their prediction abilities.

Problem-Posing Questions

Problem-posing questions are questions that involve thinking and skills that are more complex; these usually come after students have experience with other productive questions. Problem-posing questions involve asking students the "Can you find a way to?" or "Can you figure out how to?" questions. Selection of appropriate problem-posing questions will generate a lot of excitement if the questions are at the appropriate cognitive and skill level of the students. Don't be surprised, however, when you hear your students ask their own problem-posing questions, because they often do. Supporting their questions by allowing them to investigate in teams or on their own provides opportunities that are often some of the most powerful learning experiences in science classrooms.

In a simple machine unit, a problem-posing question often used with fourth graders is, "Can you find a way to balance two small washers on a ruler with only one small washer as a counterbalance weight?" Once given the materials, the students immediately begin "messing around" with the washers, using available dowel rods and pencils as fulcrums. Students move the washers toward and away from the fulcrum, or they move the fulcrum to solve the challenge. As some of the pairs of students begin to solve the challenge, other questions such as, "Can you balance three washers?" are posed to challenge them further. Sometimes, the questions shift from problem solving to attention focusing, as the teacher refocuses thinking with questions like, "What do you notice about the position of the fulcrum?" As the students continue to meet the challenge, questions shift to get them to show what they are finding out, so the teacher can determine the range of their conceptualizations and understandings. With the simple machine activity, we find some students may have difficulty working systematically to move the fulcrum or washers. In doing so, they may not pay attention to the results of their changes. For them, teacher questions such as, "What happens if we put two washers on one end and the other washer on the other end of the ruler, then move the fulcrum closer to the two washers?" are useful. This question, though direct, may be needed to assist the students in developing the idea that levers do work using less effort by applying force over a greater distance.

BULLETIN BOARD

Examples of Problem-Posing Questions

Can you think of a way to make the canister rocket go higher?

Can you find a way to keep the paper helicopter in the air longer?

How might you arrange the candies in the dish to get the same color dispersion pattern shown?

Can you come up with a way to find the strength of a magnet?

Can you figure out a way to measure the height of a tree?

You may have noticed there has been little discussion of *why* or *how* questions. According to Elstgeest (2001), the use of *how* and *why* questions are important, but they should be used with care because they generally require explanations that may be beyond the scope of the students' experiences. Recall Lily's response to Ms. Simons' questions at the beginning of the chapter. Instead of asking *how* or *why* the colors of light appeared on the wall, it is more useful to rethink the questions so they can result in hands-on activities and experiences for students. In many cases, *why* questions are best used by transforming them into "Why do you think that?" questions. Adding the simple phrase, "Do you think?" to a question makes it appear less intimidating and opens it up to multiple responses that allow teachers to move instruction in a productive direction. Recognizing the purposes and uses of questions that range from managing a class to inspiring student inquiry is very useful in planning and developing questions for your science classroom. Having this knowledge is not enough however; there are other skills related to questioning you still need to know and practice, and one such skill is wait time.

TECH CONNECT: Online "Science in the News"

Introducing current scientific findings and processes is an authentic way to evoke discussions and generate science questions about contemporary science. It can also be used to extend classroom inquiries. "Science News for Kids," a website by the Society for Science & the Public (http://www.sciencenewsforkids.org/), provides science news article on a range of topics written for students ages nine to fourteen.

Wait Time

Wait time is exactly what it sounds like it should be. A discussion on questioning is not complete without discussing Mary Budd Rowe's research (1986, 1996) on wait time. Effective science teachers who use wait time, a questioning-teaching technique, allow five seconds or more of silence (think time) after asking a question. This may sound like common sense, but research has shown that the average time a teacher waits for a student's response after asking a question is just one second (Rowe, 1996). As you observe teachers in schools today, you may find that some teachers still question students without adequate wait time. This is surprising given that the benefits of using wait time have been known for twenty years. However, teachers have their reasons. They may be concerned that if they slow down and give students more time, the students will become bored, the class will become noisy, or there may be a perception that if there is silence the students do not know the answer. No matter what the teachers' reasons, adequate wait time is a highly effective technique for asking students to think and respond to questions. The research by Rowe held another surprise. Did you know there is a second wait time? According to Rowe (2003), after the child responds to a question, another wait time (the second wait time) should occur. What she found is that most teachers wait less than a second before asking another question, repeating or rephrasing the original question, or reiterating what the child just said. The findings on wait time research reveal many interesting aspects related to how teachers ask questions. For instance, if a teacher uses longer wait times, students' will give more-elaborate answers and you will have fewer shoulder shrugs and "I don't know" responses. Another finding was that using longer wait times allows students to make more speculative comments like, "The car could be moving faster because of the type of surface we used or it could be the wheels?" Furthermore, students use evidence to support or oppose ideas more frequently when their teachers use longer wait time. Another interesting positive outcome of longer wait times is that students, who may not normally respond to questions, begin to volunteer. In addition, a common strategy, Think, Pair, Share (TPS), used after asking a question allows students time to think individually about a question, turn to a partner to discuss their answers to the question and finally share their best response with the class. The benefits of TPS parallel Rowe's findings and include the following: (a) students focus on the question and each other more frequently with the TPS strategy, (b) more students are willing to speak up with a partner, and (c) students recall more information better.

Mary Budd Rowe was a pioneer in the field of science questioning; in addition to identifying the benefits of using wait time for students, she also identified the benefits of wait time for teachers. For instance, using wait time provides teachers the opportunity to actually listen to the students, think about their responses to create more flexibility in determining which responses they consider appropriate. In contrast, with little wait time teachers are often more rigid about accepting only a single "correct" answer. Another benefit of using wait time is related to changing teachers' perceptions of students who are high or low achievers in class. Rowe studied fifty science teachers who were given students that were grouped into high verbal, low verbal, and a high-low combination of verbal skills. Teachers who used increased wait time taught science knowing that the students were grouped as described, but did not know who was in each group or which group they were teaching. At the conclusion of the lesson, the teachers had to determine which group they taught. Surprising to everyone, the teachers often misjudged the low verbal group as the highly verbal group (Rowe, 1996). Research suggests that teachers' expectations of students influence the ways they perceive how students will interact and perform. Unfortunately these perceptions may inhibit student opportunities. In other words, if a teacher doesn't think a student can answer a higher-level question, it is unlikely the teacher will ask the student one. Such a student rarely has the opportunity to show higher levels of thinking. But with adequate wait time this can change because the student actually has time to think through the question and respond. Thus, all learners can contribute and learn. In this study, the findings show that when using wait times, a teacher's expectations of students' abilities in science change and all students are given opportunities to share their thinking and knowledge.

Asking Science Questions Effectively

In this chapter, we have talked about questions based on purposes, cognitive levels, and types of inquiry questions as well as the effects of wait time for students and teachers. But are you aware that as a teacher, you will ask around four hundred questions a day (many of them managerial), and that one third of your time is spent on asking questions? If you do the math, that means you ask a lot of questions (approximately seventy thousand) each year. If you are going to ask that

BULLETIN BOARD

Wait Time Research—Student Benefits

1. Increase in student volunteers with appropriate responses.

2. Students do more task-related talking.

3. Students' responses to questions increase in length.

4. Student confidence is reflected in the decrease of responses with a questioning tone inflection.

5. Frequency of student questions increases.

6. Fewer students fail to respond to questions.

Wait Time Research—Teacher Benefits

1. Teacher disciplinary moves decrease.

2. Teachers use a greater variety (level and types) of questions.

3. Teacher expectation of less apt students improves.

Modified from Rowe, M. B. (1996). Science, silence, and sanctions. *Science and Children, 34*(1), 35–37.

BULLETIN BOARD

Strategies for Effective Questioning

1. Prepare your questions in advance of the lesson.
2. Use different cognitive levels for your questions.
3. Use simple, direct, and clear wording for questions.
4. Do not ask "rapid fire" questions.
5. Avoid repeating questions.
6. Use "think time" after each question (five seconds or more).
7. Provide wait time after students respond (five seconds or more).
8. State questions before you call on a student.
9. Plan a strategy to call on all students.
10. Ask questions for learning, not punishments.
11. Encourage students to be questioners.
12. Avoid answering your own questions.
13. Encourage students to complete their answers.
14. Handle wrong answers with respect: Use mistakes to extend student learning.
15. Let students think, pair, and share with a partner to answer some questions.
18. Use thumbs up or thumbs down as a means to survey the class and have a visual of every student's answer.
19. Respect student questions.

Source: Modified from Gridley, C., & Robert, R. *Asking better classroom questions: A teacher's mini-workbook*. Portland, ME: J. Weston Walch, Publishers, c 1992.

many questions, don't you think it is worth making sure you select the appropriate questions and use questioning techniques that are effective? So what can you do to improve your questions and questioning skills? What can you do to encourage your students to ask questions so that the classroom becomes an interactive community of learners? Addressed here are some of the characteristics of effective questioners. One characteristic of effective questioners is that they plan their questions in advance. By doing so, they can make sure to include (a) a mix of divergent and convergent questions, (b) both higher- and lower-level cognitive thinking questions, (c) questions arranged from lower- to higher-level questions, and (d) questions that are stated simply and precisely. Once questions are planned, teachers can focus on the actual performance of questioning. Planning questions in advance allows teachers to pay attention to the following: (a) wait times, (b) whole-class questioning, (c) students who volunteer and students who don't volunteer, (d) asking questions more slowly, and (e) addressing other issues that arise during class discussions. (See Bulletin Board: Strategies for Effective Questioning.) Finally, one powerful way to improve questioning skills is to videotape yourself leading a class discussion. There is nothing more eye opening than to actually analyze and evaluate your own questioning skills.

Elaborate

Questions About Questions

In the elaborate phase of any lesson, the purpose is to move students toward the application of new concepts in a different context. Therefore, this elaborate activity places you in the role of instructor for this chapter. As the instructor, you have finished teaching this chapter on questions, questioning, and inquiry. Before going on, you want students to apply what they have learned about questioning in a new situation. So the task you assign is to have the students write a question for each of the following. As the instructor, provide one example for your students on each of the following:

1. Write two questions that foster speculative thinking about wait time for the following question types.
   a. Compare and contrast
   b. Attention focusing

2. Write two questions that reveal the purposes underpinning questions.
   a. Divergent
   b. Convergent

3. Write two questions that foster higher-level thinking about questions or questioning techniques.
   a. Analysis
   b. Synthesis

4. Write two questions that promote inquiry.
   a. Action
   b. Problem posing

5. Write two questions for teaching effective questioning.
   a. Problem posing
   b. Compare and contrast

An alternative elaborate phase is to videotape yourself while teaching. After you have done that, conduct a self-analysis of your questioning. Being able to study ourselves and reflect on our own skills is a reflective learning tool. It is well established that videotaping yourself teaching a science lesson is a practical way to analyze and improve questioning techniques. First, watching the videotape makes you aware of what you do well and what you don't do so well. At first it may be a bit painful to watch yourself, but it is a practical method that can help you reflect on your strategies and assist you in improving your teaching and questioning skills. After you videotape yourself questioning students, watch the tape and make a list of the questions you asked. Use Bloom's Taxonomy to analyze the questions for cognitive levels used. Which type of question did you ask the most? Use Blosser's categories to analyze your questions. Did you ask more convergent or more divergent questions? Finally, don't forget to analyze your wait time.

Evaluate

Investigating Science Classrooms:
A Teacher's Questions

For this task you will go to Science K–6: Investigating Classrooms at http://www.learner.org/resources/series116.html. Scroll down and locate the video *Completing the Circuit: A Conversation About Teaching* with fourth-grade students. Click on the video. The video is about fifty minutes long. We encourage you to watch the entire video of a teacher using inquiry to build a science community of young learners. However, for this task your focus is only on the time frame beginning at thirty-one minutes and ending at thirty-eight minutes. During the assigned time frame, you will examine the fourth-grade teacher, Ms. Block, with regard to her questions. First, write down the questions that she asks within the time frame. Second, analyze the questions for the following:

Part 1. Wait time: About how much wait time does Ms. Block use when asking questions of students? How much time does she use after a student responds? Does she provide more wait time with higher-level thinking questions? Who does most of the talking?

Part 2. Productive Questions: Which questions does Ms. Block use as attention focusing? Which does she use as compare and contrast questions? Which as action questions? Which as problem-posing questions? Did she ask any nonproductive questions?

Part 3. Imagine that Ms. Block asked you to observe her teaching a lesson to help her improve her questions and questioning skills. What characteristics of an effective questioner would you say she already exhibits? What suggestions would you make for her to improve her questions or questioning technique? An alternative to watching the video is to actually observe a classroom teacher teaching a science lesson. Write down the teacher's questions and analyze the questions and wait time as you would have done for the video in Part 1 and Part 2.

Summary

There are many ways to look at questions and questioning, but for teachers the art of selecting and asking questions is central to daily life in a science classroom. In science, Mary Budd Rowe's groundbreaking research with wait time opened up many issues related to questions, questioning, and inquiry in the classroom. As a leader in the field of science education she tells of visit to Princeton University as a seventh-grade student. While there she noticed a man standing by a water fountain looking at water droplets. She moved closer to see what he was doing and she noticed that he was looking at the water droplets by quickly moving his fingers back and forth in front of his face. The man turned and asked her "Can you do it? Can you see the individual drops?" She copied his technique and with a little practice the fountain of water seemed to "freeze frame" into single drops. She was amazed and stood there with him practicing her "strobe technique." The man, a professor, turned to leave but before he left, he said to her, "Never forget that science is just that kind of exploring and fun" (Rowe, 1995, p. 177). The man, the professor, was Albert Einstein. One can learn as she did from Einstein's curiosity about the world and his ability to ask questions. In his brief encounter with Mary Budd Rowe, he asked two excellent questions. His questions invited inquiry by asking an action question followed by an attention-focusing question. In the end, they both pursued the simple joy of inquiry.

Drawing on research, the chapter emphasized knowledge needed for the development of skills necessary for effective questioning in your science classroom. The research addressed types of questions and their purposes, cognitive levels for questioning, types of inquiry questions, as well as the effects of wait time on students and teachers. Make no mistake—these skills require practice and continual reflection for improvement. As noted, videotaping yourself while questioning, as well as practicing thoughtful questions in advance of teaching a science lesson are approaches for improving your questioning skills. Therefore, to enhance your growth as a science teacher, continual self-examination, practice, and experience must be part of the process, and the process begins with you.

Annotated Resources

***Quality Questioning: Research-Based Practice to Engage Every Learner* (2005), by J. A. Walsh, & E. D. Sattes. Thousand Oaks, CA: Corwin.**

This book is a research-based scholarly resource with many realistic, practical examples for both novice and experienced classroom teachers. Readers will find the book has a conversational approach with simple ways to implement quality questioning strategies. The book includes many "thinking and probing questions" that challenge and engage learners. This text is a comprehensive "questioning" resource that offers techniques that enhance instruction in any classroom.

The Art of Inquiry: Questioning Strategies for K–6 Classrooms (1995), by Nancy Cecil. Winnipeg, MB, Canada: Penquis Publishing.

Nancy Cecil's book offers readers numerous examples of types and levels of questions that are easily translated into classroom practice with students. This book includes a wealth of questioning ideas and strategies that span the primary to upper elementary grades within the identified subject discipline. She provides insights that enrich teachers' ways of thinking about questions and questioning with the inquiry approach center stage.

Learning to Question, Questioning to Learn: Developing Effective Teacher Questioning Practices (2000), by M. Dantonio & P. C. Beisenherz. Boston: Allyn & Bacon.

This book provides a model designed to increase student learning of content by intentionally engaging students in their own thinking and learning of concepts. Teachers using this strategy will explore how and why their students think the way they do since students must explain in detail their thoughts about and their reasons for their answers to questions. There is a de-emphasis on rote-memorized answers to content questions and more emphasis on students as active participants in the learning process. Through questioning, students are encouraged to draw on new knowledge and ideas while connecting to information and experiences already known. This is a good resource for teachers who want to improve their questions and questioning.

Questioning Techniques

http://teachertools.londongt.org/index.php?page=questioningTechniques

This narrated PowerPoint presentation provides a good overview of effective questioning strategies in the classroom.

YouTube.com

You Teach Learning Strategies~Questioning

http://www.youtube.com/watch?v=9vEKZilguGQ&NR=1

This short clip offers a unique idea for questioning in the classroom that is motivating!

Asking Better Questions in the Classroom

http://www.youtube.com/watch?v=NFMfEVdfDys&feature=related

This clip highlights an instructor discussing convergent versus divergent questions with associated examples.

Questioning Styles and Strategies (Dr. Harvey Silver)

http://www.youtube.com/watch?v=5uKqs3D0Z0M&feature=related

The instructor models questioning strategies with students on _Terabithia_, a novel by Katherine Paterson. Students respond with varying levels of understanding. What children are asked the questions? Who is asked the higher-level thinking questions? Who is asked the lower-level thinking questions? The instructor uses various questions to motivate the students and engage them in different styles of thinking that foster differentiated instruction.

Compare and Contrast Strategy (Dr. Harvey Silver) Hannah Compton's Fifth-Grade Class

http://www.youtube.com/watch?v=54F6Gy9R4kg&feature=channel

The instructor uses compare and contrast as a powerful technique that builds students' memories, reduces confusion, and highlights critical similarities and differences.

Bloom's Taxonomy, from matloobtalib xvid

http://www.youtube.com/watch?v=6vl5xddPzPE&feature=related

This is a clever digital photonarrative of Bloom's Taxonomy by students who created it as a class project.

Wait Time (A Teacher's Perspective)

http://www.youtube.com/watch?v=tj6eZGu8NfA&feature=PlayList&p=25D9204B409FD0E2&playnext_from=PL&index=0&playnext=1

This short video presentation highlights three teachers who describe how they incorporate wait time (or think time) strategies into their classrooms. Benefits of using wait time are also discussed.

Wait Time II or Wait Time Extended

http://www.youtube.com/watch?v=2zQ_hosc5eY&feature=PlayList&p=25D9204B409FD0E2&playnext_from=PL&index=1&playnext=2

This demonstration video addresses a common habit of responding too quickly after a student answers a question. In doing so, a teacher may unintentionally stifle other student input and ideas. The video encourages teachers to become comfortable with silence. This short video shows how asking an open-ended question and incorporating wait time after student responses generates further student discussion.

References

Anderson, L. W., & Krathwohl, D. R. (Eds.). (2001). *A taxonomy for learning, teaching and assessing: A revision of Bloom's Taxonomy of educational objectives: Complete edition.* New York: Longman

Bloom, B. S. (1956). *Taxonomy of educational objectives.* Handbook I: *The cognitive domain.* New York: David McKay.

Bloom, B. S., & Krathwohl, D. R. (1956). *Taxonomy of educational objectives: The classification of educational goals, by a committee of college and university examiners.* Handbook I: Cognitive domain. New York: Longmans, Green.

Blosser, P. (1990). *Using questions in science classroom.* Research matters. To the science teachers. NARST Monograph.

Cherif, A. (1993). Relevant inquiry. *Science and Children, 60*(9), 26–27.

Elstgeest, J. (2001). The right question at the right time. In W. Harlen (Ed.), *Primary science. Taking the plunge* (pp. 25–35). Portsmouth, NH: Heinemann.

Gridley, C., & Robert R. (c. 1992). *Asking better classroom questions: A teacher's mini-workbook.* Portland, ME: J. Weston Walch.

Hastings, S. (2003). Questioning. Available at http://www.tes.co.uk/article.aspx?storycode=381755.

Munby, H. (1980). Analyzing teaching for intellectual independence. In H. Munby, G. Orpwood, & T. Russell (Eds.), *Seeing curriculum in a new light: Essays from science education* (pp. 11–33). Toronto: OISE Press.

Rowe, M. B. (1986). Wait time: Slowing down may be a way of speeding up. *Journal of Teacher Education, 37*(1), 43–50.

Rowe, M. B. (1995, October). Teach your child to wonder. *Reader's Digest,* 177–184.

Rowe, M. B. (1996, September). Science, silence, and sanctions. *Science and Children, 34*(1), 35–37.

Rowe, M. B. (2003). Wait-time and rewards as instructional variables, their influence on language, logic, and fate control: Part one—Wait time. *Journal of Research in Science Teaching, 40*(1), 19–32.

Chapter 6

Inquiry Teaching Approaches and Science Process Skills

Learning Objectives

After reading Chapter 6, students will be able to

- discuss and describe inquiry-based approaches advocated by the National Science Education Standards,
- identify and apply process skills needed to carry out science inquiry,
- describe and distinguish basic and integrated process skills, and
- analyze an inquiry approach and modify it into different forms of inquiry (structured, guided, open).

NSES TEACHING STANDARDS ADDRESSED IN CHAPTER 6

Standard A: Teachers of science plan an inquiry-based science program for their students. In doing this, teachers

- select science content and adapt and design curricula to meet the interests, knowledge, understanding, abilities, and experiences of students.

Standard B: Teachers of science guide and facilitate learning. In doing this, teachers

- encourage and model the skills of scientific inquiry, as well as the curiosity, openness to new ideas and data, and skepticism that characterize science.

Standard D: Teachers of science design and manage learning environments that provide students with the time, space, and resources needed for learning science. In doing this, teachers

- structure the time available so that students are able to engage in extended investigations;
- create a setting for student work that is flexible and supportive of science inquiry;
- ensure a safe working environment;
- make available science tools, materials, media, and technological resources to students; and
- identify and use resources outside schools.

Standard E: Teachers of science develop communities of science learners that reflect the intellectual rigor of scientific inquiry and the attitudes of social values conducive to science learning. In doing this, teachers

- enable students to have a significant voice in decisions about the content and context of their work and require students to take responsibility for the learning of all members of the community; and
- model and emphasize the skills, attitudes, and values of scientific inquiry.

Source: Reprinted with permission from the National Science Education Standards, copyright 1996, by the National Academy of Sciences, Courtesy of National Academies Press, Washington, DC.

Introduction

The National Science Education Standards describe inquiry as "the diverse ways in which scientists study the natural world and propose explanations based upon evidence" (National Research Council [NRC], 1996, p. 23). Central to the definition of scientific inquiry is the term "evidence." Just as scientists seek understanding of the natural world, students should seek understanding of natural phenomena by gaining knowledge and evidences in a variety of ways (Wittrock & Barrows, 2008). Throughout this chapter you will learn about how to encourage student inquiry and incorporate a variety of standards-based inquiry instructional strategies as part of your science classroom. By promoting student inquiry and using inquiry as a teaching technique you will assist students in acquiring the knowledge and skills for carrying out scientific inquiry for themselves.

YOUR SCIENCE CLASSROOM:
Children's Investigations

It was one of the last, warm, glorious days of summer with the air carrying a crispness that heralded autumn. However, with the sun shining brightly, thoughts of autumn were a far distance memory in the students at Claremont Elementary School who talked and played ball during their lunch break. Some of the students were

> **Standard B-1 and D-3**
>
> How does this scenario reflect these standards?

playing soccer in the school yard that was surrounded by a green space filled with native plants. This natural green space was used by teachers and their classes for various types of field studies. Two students, Sam and Josh, were chasing down a runaway ball at the edge of the garden when the ball got wedged between two rocks. Sam and Josh pushed one of the rocks out of the way so they could get the ball when they noticed small creatures moving across the damp ground where the rock was pushed away. They called to their classmates to come over and look. They decided to catch the creatures and take them back inside. Josh took off his ball cap to hold the creatures they quickly scooped up. They were excited and anxious to take their living discovery to their teacher, Ms. Jacobs. They wondered what the creatures were and they were sure Ms. Jacobs, their fourth-grade teacher, would know and tell them. One thing they did know was that Ms. Jacobs would tell them to wash their hands.

Suppose you were Ms. Jacobs and you recognized the creatures as pill bugs (sowbugs, woodlice): Would you tell the students what they were or would you give them some clues and send them searching for the answers? What would you have done with the creatures? Would you allow them in the classroom? Would you have the students research the characteristics of an appropriate habitat for the pill bugs? Would you let students observe the pill bugs over a period of time? What other things might you have the students investigate with their "living" discovery?

Engage

Who Wants to Be a K–8 Science Teacher?

You have been out of middle school for some time now. How well do you remember your science textbooks? This activity should evoke your memories. Just imagine that you have been

> *Children should be led to make their own investigations,*
> *and to draw their own inferences. They should be told as little as possible,*
> *and induced to discover as much as possible.*
>
> Herbert Spencer, *Education: Intellectual, Moral, and Physical* (1864)

What is your position on students conducting their own inquiries in science class? As teachers of science, "to tell or not to tell" students the answers to their questions poses some interesting dilemmas for teachers using inquiry. What do you think some of the dilemmas might be?

selected for a game show, "Who Wants to Be a K–8 Science Teacher?" You have sixty seconds to list as many features of a typical science textbook chapter as you can recall. For example, the chapter's title would be worth one point. The winner is the individual who has the longest list. Your sixty seconds begins now!

How long is your list? If you had to describe the teaching approaches represented in the textbooks you have used, how would you describe them? Do you recall science textbooks focusing on skills that students need to conduct inquiries? Did you include any inquiry activities in your list? Sometimes what is *not* present is as important as what is. What features do you think science textbooks should have in them? Now that you have your list of chapter features, what are your memories of how textbooks were used in your science classroom?

Some of you probably recalled textbook features that involved doing hands-on activities in class, others probably did not. Still others may recall activities that involved seeking answers to questions in other ways. Scientific inquiry activities are intellectual endeavors that involve a range of activities from active, hands-on experiences to reading and researching. Today, alignment with the National Science Education Standards (NSES) means that it is important that student inquiry be a big part of your science classroom, whether it involves hands-on activities or information seeking in other ways. So let's see what inquiring minds do.

> *When you make the finding yourself—even if you're the last*
> *person on Earth to see the light—you'll never forget it.*
>
> Carl Sagan

What kinds of learning experiences are those you never forget? How does Sagan's quote support constructivist learning? What would Herbert Spencer say to Carl Sagan about this quote (see earlier quote by Spencer)? Overall, do you think the use of science textbooks in science classrooms foster "finding out for yourself"?

Explore

Inquiry in Your School Yard

Pill bugs, sow bugs, or woodlice are different names for the same organism. These gregarious organisms can be found globally with many species found in the oceans.

Borrowing from Sagan's and Spencer's stance, you will explore some interesting characteristics about an organism that is known by many names. It is called a pill bug, roly-poly, sow bug, and sometimes a wood louse.

No matter what you choose to call these organisms, they are curious little creatures that can often be found in backyards, gardens, and woodpiles living under brush, rocks, pots, and stones. It is simple to keep your own culture of pill bugs, and easy to maintain.

According to Joseph Joubert, "To teach is to learn twice." In this case, preparation for classroom inquiry activities is an important part of science teaching. Therefore, one teaching practice you want to remember is to conduct science activities yourself to learn what may or may not happen during the activity before using them with students. Here is your chance—let's proceed.

Though this activity was originally designed for fifth-grade students, we use it with many ages, making only minor modifications.

Part 1: Observing your pill bugs: Take out a pill bug and put it on a white piece of paper. Observe and write down the characteristics of your pill bug. How many legs does it have? Does it have antennae? How would you describe its color? How big is it (take a measurement)? Does it make any sounds? Does it smell? What happens if you touch it gently with a pencil? Use a magnifying glass for more observations. Try to find ways to answer the questions. Record your observations and include labels and drawings of your pill bug.

Teacher's Desk Tip: Resources for Your Classroom

Pill bugs, also known as sow bugs and wood lice, can be purchased at http://www.carolina.com and http://www.wardsci.com.

TECH CONNECT: Inquiry and YouTube

Enrich and enhance classroom inquiry with short video clips. YouTube posts many video clips on various science topics that can enrich your classroom inquiry discussions and further develop process skills. For the pill bug activity, you can find many video clips showing different pill bug species and the behaviors of the organisms. For instance, "Bug Island 9" is a video featuring a pill bug at http://www.youtube.com/watch?v=QeufyNGeKhQ.

Part 2: Do pill bugs have a preference for light or dark areas? Let's find out. Cover one half of a container (petri dishes work well) with a piece of old newspaper or black construction paper. Take six pill bugs and put them on the uncovered side of the container.

Place the container near a brightly lit area outside or near the window. Observe your pill bugs for ten minutes. What do they do? Do they stay where you put them? Do they move to a darker area? Do some stay in the light and others in the dark? Record your findings in a data table (see Table 6.1). Based on your evidence, do pill bugs have a light or dark preference? Support your answer with evidence from your tests in a short written conclusion.

Part 3: Do pill bugs have a preference for dry or damp conditions? Take six pill bugs from their habitat and put them on a damp paper towel covering half of the inside of the dish.

Observe your pill bugs for ten minutes. Do they stay where you placed them? Do they move to the side with the damp paper towel? Do some stay on the damp towel and some move to the dry side? Record your findings in a data table (see Table 6.1). Based on your data, do pill bugs have a preference for dry or damp conditions? Record your ideas. Are there other preferences that you might explore? Are there other inquiries you have about pill bugs? Ask your own question about pill bugs and design an investigation to explore. Be sure to record your data and findings. To assist students with other tests on pill bugs as a teacher, you must do your own research and investigate the characteristics, behaviors, habitats, and survival needs of pill bugs.

Table 6.1   Pill Bug Data Table

PILL BUG DATA TABLE		
Observations (and Drawing) of Pill Bugs in Light/Dark Conditions	**Observations (and Drawing) of Pill Bugs in Dry/Moist Conditions**	
Light/Dark Investigation	Number of pill bugs on the light side at the end of 10 minutes.	Number of pill bugs on the dark side at the end of 10 minutes.
Moisture Investigation	Number of pill bugs on the damp paper towel at the end of 10 minutes.	Number of pill bugs on dry surface at the end of 10 minutes.
My New Question(s):		

Safety note: When you have finished observing your pill bugs, wash your hands.

Note: If you no longer wish to keep them in their temporary habitat and care for them, release them outdoors so they can continue to help break down dead plants and insects. If you don't have pill bugs in your vicinity you can do this same activity with earthworms and mealworms.

Using the data from pill bug inquiries, you may wish students to build a pill bug habitat for further study. First, find an old container that has a flat bottom and clear sides at least a few inches tall—small plastic food storage containers work well. All living things need air, so if you

A couple of third graders are looking for insects and other invertebrates. Pill bugs are crustaceans often found under stones, brick, logs, and other items in the environment that provide for their needs.

use a lid, be sure to first create some holes in it to allow air to enter or cover the top of your container with a piece of cloth, old nylons or other porous materials.

Next, gather some roly-polys or pill bugs by looking under rocks, clay pots, stones, bricks, or old piles of leaves or debris in your yard or garden. They are generally found in shady, moist habitats. If they are not common to your locale they can be purchased from science companies (see Teacher's Desk Tip: Resources for Your Classroom). Create a habitat for your pill bugs by putting a layer of soil, some dead leaves, twigs, and stones into your container. Using a spray bottle, lightly mist the habitat. Mist the habitat every few days. Pill bugs will eat dead leaves, especially maple leaves, but try small pieces of well-cleaned lettuce, cabbage, apples, or potatoes and observe. Remember to handle the pill bugs with care; if you keep them for any length of time use a variety of food types and be sure to remove any items that become moldy. When you are finished studying the pill bugs, they may be released back into the areas in which they were found.

Explain

Focus Questions

1. What are the variations for teaching inquiry in the K–8 science classroom?

2. What are the essential features of classroom inquiry teaching approaches?

3. According to the NSES, how is scientific inquiry described in terms of what students need to know and do?

4. What are basic process skills for teachers of K–8 science? What are integrated process skills?

5. Why are process skills important for K–8 learners to know and be able to do?

6. How are investigative activities and experiments alike? How are they different?

7. How do common classroom curricula and resources support inquiry in the classroom?

Having completed the hands-on inquiry activity with pill bugs, now consider the structure of the inquiry activity. Answer the following questions about the pill bug activity with either "teacher/text" or "students."

Who or what determined the questions that were investigated?

Who or what designed the procedures?

Who or what determined what data or evidence to collect?

Who or what determined what explanations were made?

Who or what determined how the findings were communicated, explained, and supported?

Who or what determined what and how information was shared?

These questions provide a general framework for determining the type of inquiry-based instruction represented in the pill bug activity as well as other science activities. Answering these questions you will find that the teacher or the text determined and directed most of the activity. As such, the pill bug inquiry is considered **directed** or **structured inquiry**. It is only at the end of the pill bug inquiry that the teacher provides opportunities for student choices as seen in the question, "Ask your own question about pill bugs and design an investigation to explore." According to the NSES (NRC, 1996), the questions above set the stage for determining and understanding the continuum of inquiry approaches in teaching science. Keep these questions in mind as you examine the following inquiry-based instructional approaches.

Inquiry-Based K–8 Science Instruction

Despite decades of educators advocating inquiry teaching methods in the science classroom, you may have noticed that inquiry methods are not the predominant method of teaching science in most K–8 classrooms (Weiss, 2006; Wells, 1995). According to researchers (Hodson, 1988; Welch, Klopfer, Aikenhead, & Robinson, 1981; Pomeroy, 1993; Slotta, 2004), there are many reasons practicing teachers give for not using inquiry approaches. The reasons include these: (a) Inquiry is difficult to manage. (b) Inquiry takes too long to carry out. (c) Inquiry is for advanced students. (d) I feel uncomfortable and unprepared for student questions due to a lack content knowledge. (e) Teaching science is factually based and must prepare students for their next grade level. Furthermore, inquiry can be confusing because it refers to science teaching approaches and the actions of students seeking answers to questions by means of investigations, experimentation, and other methods (Colburn, 2008). Moving past the reasons for not using inquiry-based instruction, let's look at how you can make your classroom inquiry based.

The directed inquiry teaching approach with pill bugs instructs students to observe, collect and record data, and draw conclusions based on the evidence collected. For students, the inquiry journey begins with you assisting them in gaining the ability to use a variety of scientific techniques, processes, and skills to answer questions or solve problems. Because teaching science with inquiry methods is considered an important focus of the national science education standards, the National Research Council (NRC; 2000) identified several "essential features" that provide a framework for determining the type of inquiry approach. These "essential features" used in determining inquiry teaching approaches include (a) engaging with a scientific question, (b) participating in developing the procedures, (c) giving priority to evidence, (d) formulating explanations, (e) connecting explanations to scientific knowledge, and (f) communicating as well as justifying explanations (NRC, p. 29). The essential features of inquiry teaching form a continuum ranging in degrees from teacher-centered to student-centered inquiry where students pursue questions or problems in a variety of ways. Table 6.2 describes the variations of inquiry methods of teaching.

Table 6.2 Essential Features of Classroom Inquiry and Their Variations

Essential Feature Variations

Learner engages in scientifically oriented *questions*	Learner poses a question	Learner selects among questions, poses new questions	Learner sharpens or clarifies question provided by teacher, materials, or other source	Learner engages in question provided by teacher materials or other source
Learner gives priority to *evidence* **in responding to questions**	Learner determines what constitutes evidence & collects it	Learner directed to collect certain data	Learner given data and asked to analyze	Learner given data and told how to analyze
Learner *formulates* *explanations* **from evidence**	Learner formulates explanation after summarizing evidence	Learner guided in process of formulating explanations from evidence	Leaner given possible ways to use evidence to formulate explanation	Learner provided with evidence
Learner connects explanation to scientific knowledge	Learner independently examines other resources and forms the links to explanations	Learner directed toward areas and sources of scientific knowledge	Learner given several possible connections	
Learner communicates and justifies explanations	Learner forms reasonable and logical argument to communicate explanations	Learner coached in development of communication	Learner given broad guidelines to sharpen communication	Learner given steps and procedures for communication

More _____ Amount of Learner Self-Direction_____ Less

Less _____ Amount of Direction From Teacher or Material _____More

Source: Reprinted with permission from *Inquiry and the National Science Education Standards: A Guide For Teaching and Learning* (p. 29) © 2000 by the National Academy of Sciences, Courtesy of the National Academy Press, Washington, DC.

Directed or Structured Inquiry

With directed or structured inquiry methods of teaching, the teacher often provides the students with a question or questions to investigate in a hands-on manner, much like the pill bug activity. The teacher centered approach provides students with the question, procedures (including instructions on what data to collect and tables for recording data) and materials to conduct the activities. The expected outcomes, of course, are not given to the students. Therefore, the students must explore the question or problem using the directions from the text or the teacher to discern what, if any, connection or pattern is notable. Often called cookbook activities these are examples of directed (structured) inquiry. Directed inquiry activities are predominantly orchestrated by the teacher or text with respect to the essential features in Table 6.2 of the inquiry continuum. Which columns represent directed inquiry? The columns to the far right which are also teacher centered. Recall the end of the pill bug activity: Students were encouraged to generate questions and design experiments. What columns represent this type of inquiry? The columns to the left are student centered. When teaching young students, you might expect the predominant teaching method to be directed inquiry and it often is because young students have few skills for investigating on their own. However, directed inquiry experiences often lead to further questions about a given phenomenon, which sets the stage for additional investigations where students can use their newly acquired skills. As appropriate, science teachers should take these opportunities to allow students to explore and investigate their questions with guidance. When this occurs, the inquiry method of teaching moves from directed toward guided inquiry.

Guided Inquiry

Look at the essential features in the inquiry continuum again. **Guided inquiry** is typified by more student choice with respect to the essential features than direct inquiry. For instance, think about the pill bug activity. Instead of following specific directions to test the pill bugs in light/dark and damp/dry conditions, what if students were asked to chose one of three questions to investigate (e.g., Do the pill bugs prefer light or dark environments? Do the pill bugs prefer wet or dry surfaces? Do the pill bugs prefer rough or smooth surfaces?). Presenting students with choices is a subtle shift away from directed inquiry to guided inquiry. With this example, although students choose a question to investigate on their own, the teacher may still guide the investigations by providing some or all of the procedures for investigating, collecting data, recording data, or communicating findings for students to complete the investigations.

For instance, a teacher may give students a question to explore and provide opportunities for student teams to write up their own procedures for conducting their investigations. After the teacher reviews the students' plans, they begin the activity or investigation. In other examples, a teacher may provide some of the procedures and offer several ways to analyze data, or allow students the opportunity to decide on the procedures and how they wish to analyze the data. These are only a few variations that demonstrate a shift from directed to guided inquiry approaches. However, as with any inquiry, an effective science teacher continues to provide students support and guidance where needed by providing appropriate options for the activities, based on the essential features. If you examine Table 6.2, you will notice the middle two columns represent varying levels of guided inquiry by providing variations for student-centered activity and investigation.

Full or Open Inquiry

Have you ever participated in a science fair project? Did you come up with the questions? Work on the procedures yourself? Did you decide what data to collect and how to record it? Did you make sense of the data collected and report it? Did you make the major decisions in the inquiry? If so, you were conducting full inquiry and your teacher probably provided useful insights, questions, suggestions, feedback, and resources to assist you in accomplishing the goal. Full inquiry in its purest form involves students or student teams independently asking questions, developing procedures for testing, deciding what data to collect and how the data should be analyzed, and then making sense of their evidences and communicating it. Full inquiry is similar to science fair experiments, and parallels at times the work of some scientists. With full inquiry the choices and decisions regarding the investigation are determined by the students rather than the teacher. The teacher's role is to assist and facilitate the students' investigations and experiments. Full inquiry is designed to give students' opportunities for independent experimentation and investigation—much like a scientist. This doesn't mean that the teacher leaves the students solely to their own devices, but it does mean that the teacher monitors the progress of students and guides them when necessary. Examples of directed, guided, and full inquiry are seen in Bulletin Board:

BULLETIN BOARD

Examples of Inquiry-Based Instruction

Directed or structured inquiry: The teacher poses the question, "How can we change the pitch of sound?" He passes out straws and blunt-nosed scissors needed to produce a change in pitch. The students are given a set of specific instructions on making the instrument. They are given an activity sheet with questions that direct them on how to cut the straws and record the observed changes in pitch in a table.

Guided inquiry: The teacher gives student teams the following materials: rulers, straws, scissors, rubber bands, wood blocks, thumb tacks, cans, balloons, scissors, string, wire clothes hangers, Styrofoam cups, and metal spoons. Students are asked to demonstrate changes in the pitch of sound. They are asked to demonstrate a change in the pitch of sound in as many ways as they can with the materials available. Students are later asked to demonstrate how their instruments changes pitch. Students are required to record their observations and explain how the instruments produce a change in pitch.

Open inquiry: Students are shown rulers, straws, scissors, cans, water, bottles, rubber bands, wood blocks, balloons, and a variety of other materials. Students are then asked to generate testable questions about sound and changes in pitch. Students check their questions with the teacher and then are directed to write their testing procedures and to describe what data they will collect and how they will organize it. Again, these are checked. Following approval, the students begin their testing.

Examples of Inquiry-Based Instruction. Challenge yourself to identify the essential features as being either teacher or student centered.

Inquiry and Process Skills

Up to this point, we have discussed variations on inquiry methods for teaching science in K–8 classrooms. Now let's turn our attention to student inquiry and science process skills. As far back as Aristotle and Socrates, students have engaged in inquiry for problem solving. Dewey popularized a view of inquiry in the mid 1930s as a way for students to become aware of science facts through data collection that allows them to draw conclusions based on their evidences. Today as in the past, using inquiry methods to teach science and foster students' development of science process skills necessary for inquiry is a priority. Furthermore, educators advocate that science process skills should be taught in conjunction with learning science content (Wolff & Roychoudhury, 1993). What this means is that whenever possible as you teach science concepts you should have students practice using the process skills appropriate for the activity. For instance, if you are teaching the concept of velocity in a physical science activity using marbles and ramps, you might have students measure distance and time in completing their explorations. This activity provides an appropriate venue for using the skill and, and discussing the importance of measurement to inquiry.

So what are the science process skills? Science process skills usually fall into two broad categories. The first category, known as the **basic science process skills**, includes common everyday skills such as observing, inferring, predicting, estimating, classifying, and measuring. The second category, entitled **integrated process skills**, builds on the basic process skills. Integrated process skills are often more specialized and are associated with experimentation (Padilla, 1990). Science process skill development should begin with young children in the primary grades and continue throughout high school. Younger children should be introduced to the basic process skills and allowed to practice using them through a variety of directed and guided inquiries. As students develop mastery with these skills, fair testing and other integrated process skills should be introduced. As students move through the grade levels, with continued opportunities to practice and build proficiency with the basic and integrated science process skills they become more capable of designing experiments independently (Table 6.3).

Table 6.3 Experimentation and Integrated Process Skills: A Guide for Teachers		
Grades K–2	**Grades 3–5**	**Grades 6–8**
Recognize and define the problem	Recognize and define the problem	Recognize and define the problem
1. Define the problem ask a question. 2. Hypothesize guess an answer	1. Choose a problem, and ask a question about the problem. 2. Research the problem look in books, get advice, confer with teacher, make observations. 3. Develop hypotheses form hypotheses from a simple question, use the words "if" and "then."	1. Craft a testable, defined question 2. Recognize and define relevant variables (independent, dependent variables are stated). 3. Generate hypotheses based on question (If/then statements). 4. Search literature to support research area (cite sources).
Design procedures or problem-solving strategy		
1. Experiment observe, communicate, compare.		
Implement	Design process	Design process
1. Write it down record data, organize. 2. Make a picture graph, display data.	1. Design the experiment, write procedures, sequence each step to be taken, control variables, list the materials needed.	1. Design an experiment that addresses the hypothesis (identify and show understanding of and control for the variables in plan). 2. Describe appropriate method(s) of collecting information (independent and dependent variables are measurable).
Interpret and communicate findings	Implement	Implement
1. Draw conclusions answer the question.	1. Test the hypotheses follow procedures, make observations, collect data in a notebook. 2. Organize the data make a chart, table, or graph of the procedures or results, use pictures or photographs to show the procedures or results, write a statement of what happened in the experiment.	1. Use procedures in the design. 2. Use equipment to measure and record data. 3. Record data accurately and clearly. 4. Apply mathematical techniques to data preparation (use averages, graphs, tables to present data).
	Interpret and communicate findings	Interpret and communicate findings and conclusions
	1. State conclusions share what has been learned, make connections to real-life applications (accept/reject hypotheses).	1. Make clear, reasonable conclusions from data (supported with data in text, graphs, tables, or charts applying appropriate mathematical analysis). 2. Explain the experiment and conclusions (accept/reject hypotheses) clearly. 3. Present results and conclusions and their significance (relate to everyday environment). 4. Identify needs for additional data and limitations of the experiment.

As pointed out above, it is your role to assist students in gaining these skills by actively engaging them with science activities and experiments. By creating learning environments that allow your students to learn science process skills and to practice them while they construct knowledge of science concepts, students become active participants in science. The following discussion presents both basic and integrated process skills followed by examples. Let's begin with basic science process skills that are commonly used by individuals on a daily basis and found across other disciplines.

Basic Process Skills

Observing

Do you hear it? What do you see? Can you smell that? What does it taste like? Did you feel the material? Questions such as these lead students to gather information through their five senses to gain understanding about objects and phenomena. Which of the five senses do you perceive as used most often? Did vision come to mind? About 85% of all information processed by individuals is obtained through vision. However, it is important to encourage students to use all their senses (vision, auditory, tactile, olfactory, and taste when appropriate) to provide maximum information when observing science events or phenomena, simply because the senses are not infallible. Furthermore, it is important to provide students opportunities to observe with technology that extends their senses using equipment such as magnifying glasses, microscopes, telescopes, balances, rulers, compasses, and computers, to name a few. It is scientists' use or invention of new technologies that often prompts reexamination of current scientific knowledge in light of new findings.

Here are a couple of examples related to making observations:

Ask students to make observations using sight, smell, hearing, and touch (no tasting).

One activity centers on students observing through sight and smell. In this activity students observe a chemical reaction that occurs when sugar and sulfuric acid are combined. Under teacher supervision have students use their sense of touch to feel the jar which it is very warm.

> **Teacher's Desk Tip: Addressing Diversity in Your Classroom**
>
> Be sensitive to the students in your classroom. Students with visual or hearing impairments will need this activity modified so they can focus on other sensory input.

Safety

Conduct this as a demonstration only and do so with proper ventilation in a fume hood.

Check out this video to see this demonstration before you begin: http://www.youtube.com/watch?v=-b9EZjTugao

No eating or tasting in science labs.

Another example that fosters the development of observation skills is providing students with "shakers." These sealed, plastic, opaque containers hold various items hidden inside that student describe. Students observe by listening and touching. Then they describe the sounds of the mystery items. Encourage students to only make observations using their senses. We encourage students to avoid telling us what they think the mystery item is because that information is an inference. An extension activity (Sound Shakers/Noise Makers) can be found at http://faculty.washington.edu/chudler/chhearing.html.

Inferring

Now if you ask students to identify the mystery items used in the previous example, then your students are making inferences. Inferences are attempts to make sense of or explain an event through observations and experiences. Specifically, inferences are statements associated with experiences or direct observations. They extend our thinking by predicting, explaining, or generalizing about an observed object, process, or event. An inference may result when you observe a puddle of water and say, "It must have rained." In this example the observation leads to a possible explanation. Now, consider the following statement: "I walked into the room and saw Pat sitting on the couch with a red face." What are some observations that can be made? Okay, a couple of obvious observations are that Pat was sitting and Pat had a red face. What other observations can you make? What are some inferences that can be made? One inference might be that Pat's face was sunburned. Can you think of others? Inferences may or may not be correct, but they are based upon observations and experiences. Furthermore, the ability to make inferences is an amazing example of how the human brain quickly attempts to make sense of an individual's observations and experiences.

At this point, it is important for teachers to know that students often struggle with communicating their observations. Furthermore, students often confuse observations and inferences. For instance, if you teach a sound unit and students shake containers with mystery items inside, don't be surprised if students give the observation, "Coins are inside" (an inference) instead of describing their sound observations. An observation might be, "When I shake it, I feel more than one thing inside hit in different places." Another observation might be, "It makes a clinking sound." In short, the brain processes stimuli gained through our observations and translates it into possible explanations (inferences) very quickly as we attempt to make sense of the world. So, it should not be surprising that observations and inferences are difficult to distinguish. Both practice and explicit discussion with students about these skills will help them understand the difference. Be aware that young children will struggle with the distinction. Now, consider the observations and inferences in the examples and then make some of your own.

Example: Observations and inferences

> **Teacher's Desk Tip: Addressing a Language Connection and Science Process Skills**
>
> Create a word wall of the terms used as students make observations, then list their inferences. Make comparisons between the lists to reinforce the differences between observations and inferences. These examples are from students using mystery sound containers.
>
> ### Students' Observations
>
> | **Sight** | **Sound** | **Touch** | **Smell** |
> |-----------|-----------|-----------|-----------|
> | shiny | clinks | bumpy | stinky |
> | black | thumps | sharp | sweet |
>
> ### Students' Inferences
>
> Coins are inside.
> The object inside is round.
> There is sand inside.

1. Students are working with test tubes containing a clear liquid, bubbles, and *Elodea*, a water plant.

   (a) There are many bubbles in the test tube with the water plants. (observation)

   (b) The plants must be creating the bubbles. (inference)

2. Look at the graphic.

   (a) What observations can you make of the graphic?

   (b) What inferences can you make after observing the graphic?

Classifying

In science, classification systems are developed based on the similarities and differences of objects or processes with the purpose of showing relationships. In daily life, we often **classify** for convenience by grouping similar items. Think about how you locate milk, bread, or fresh produce in a grocery store. Your experiences in grocery stores make it easy to find these items in other stores because the foods are organized according to the similarities and differences of the food products. In addition to grouping by similarities, important traits of a good classification system are that they should be flexible enough to accommodate new items and easy to use, and that they can be used to serve as a quick reference.

In science, we often use **binary classification** systems and **dichotomous classification keys** to group and identify organisms. Binary classification is an approach to classification whereby the objects or events are sorted into two groups based on a selected trait. The objects either have the trait or they do not have the trait, so each time a specific trait is selected the items fall into one group or the other (see Figure 6.1).

Figure 6.1   Binary Classification With Everyday Materials

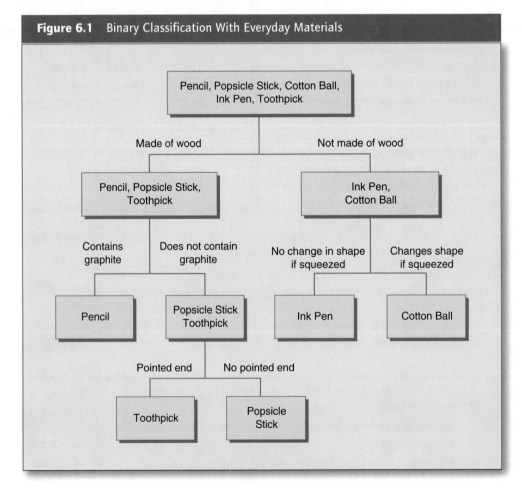

A dichotomous key is a tool that is generally used to identify an unknown organism or object. "Dichotomous" is a Greek term that means "divided in two parts." A dichotomous key is a series of paired statements about the traits of organisms. For each set of paired statements, the examiner decides which of the two statements is correct based on the traits of the organism or object. Once the choice is made about the trait, the examiner is directed to the next pair of statements until the item or organism is identified by name. Check out the dichotomous key examples found at the websites noted in the Tech Connect: Dichotomous Keys.

It is best to have students classify with a purpose in mind. If they are simply classifying general items such as shoes or clothing to understand the classification structure, then do so sensibly. Recall that when teaching process skills, such as classifying, you should do so while teaching science concepts whenever appropriate. For instance, when studying the key characteristics of animal groups (reptiles, amphibians, mammals, and birds) student learning can be enhanced by classifying various animals based on their characteristics. Another useful example for incorporating classifying skills into science content is when teaching the processes of volcanism. Student understanding of volcanism can be supported by examining and classifying igneous rocks as intrusive (formed underground) or extrusive (formed at the surface).

Measuring

Measuring is the process that deals with quantities or "amounts." This skill requires describing quantitatively the dimensions of an item, event, or process with their appropriate units. Dimensions commonly used include length, area, volume, mass, time, and temperature, to name a few. Measuring requires comparing the amount of an item to either arbitrary units (nonstandard) or to standard units. In general, we find students have very little experience with measurements in either the International System of Units (SI) or the English system. Scientists all around the world use the SI system. As teachers of science, it is important to have students conduct measurements using the SI (metric) system during activities and experiments. It is often interesting and useful to explore measurement by starting with nonstandard units. Students quickly find the inconsistency of their measurements and see the need for standard units. The value of standard units of measurement becomes apparent and gives relevancy to subsequent measurements. When teaching young children, we find that they first think about measurement in descriptive terms. For instance, when asked about size, it is common for very young learners to say, "Joe is big" or "Joe is bigger than Jim." With practice they learn how to measure using whole units (liters, meters, seconds, Celsius, etc.); as they gain more skill, students make more detailed measurements (e.g., Joe is 170.3 centimeters tall and Jim is 162.5 centimeters tall). Be alert to science content that provides students experience with measuring.

> **TECH CONNECT:**
> **Dichotomous Keys**
>
> To find classification keys, search "dichotomous keys" online to find a variety of examples. Each of the examples below fosters students' ability to use classification keys.
>
> 1. Ms. Hayhurst's Sci-Page Dichotomous Key Activity, http://www.lnhs.org/hayhurst/ips/dichot/.
>
> 2. Leaf: What Is a Dichotomous Key?, http://www.uwsp.edu/cnr/leaf/Treekey/tkframe.htm.

Example: Measuring

1. Student teams place a wooden 30 centimeter stake in the ground. They mark and measure the length of the shadow (in meters) cast by the stick every hour throughout the day. Time and length are recorded and examined to identify patterns in the sun's movement.

2. Students measure the volume of their lungs (in liters) by blowing into a small rubber hose inserted into a calibrated jar filled with water. Blowing into the tube displaces water in the jar with exhaled air. The water line is then measured using the calibrated lines on the jar.

3. Students measure the mass of the apple slices before and after dehydration, and find the difference in the mass.

Estimating

Estimating is a skill that is associated with measurement. An estimate is an approximation of a quantity given a unit of reference. Whenever you ask students to make estimates, make sure that they know the unit for the estimation. For instance, if you ask them to estimate the length of a piece of yarn in centimeters, they must have knowledge of the distance a centimeter represents. No one can make an estimate if they do not understand the referent for which the estimate is to be made. Below are activities that emphasize students' use of estimates in science activities.

Example: Estimating

1. Using scaled distances, estimate the distance between Jupiter and the sun in centimeters.

2. Estimate 80 milliliters of cornstarch needed for making the mixture.

3. Estimate the mass of 25 grams of salt needed to make the saline solution.

4. Estimate the distance in meters from your classroom door to the lunchroom door.

Predicting

A prediction is a statement of a future event based on a pattern or consistency of evidence (data). Predictions in science are made based on a relationship between variables and are forecasts that are based on many observations (Misiti, 2001). Though often confused with inferences, predictions are different from inferences. Inferences are based directly on a given observation. Consider the following statement: "It is hot, humid, and overcast this morning; it will most likely rain sometime today." The first part of the statement is an observation, while the second half of the statement is an inference. It is not a prediction because it is not based on a pattern of consistent observations. Consider the following examples.

Example: Predicting

1. Predict the length of plant root growth during the fourth week based on a graph of growth data recorded during the previous three weeks.

2. After taking ten data points of temperature during a chemical reaction, look at the pattern and predict the temperature for the eleventh measurement.

Communicating

Communication takes any number of forms (verbal and nonverbal) to convey information about processes, events, or objects. Communicating is an important part of scientific inquiry, as it is in daily life. There are key characteristics of effective communication. These include (a) receiving and sending accurate perceptions of objects, (b) selecting proper word choice, and (c) knowing when the message is sent and that it conveys ideas accurately through social interchanges. Verbal communication is only one way to present one's knowledge of science, and is not enough for any science teacher. The use of multiple forms of communication is needed to maximize student understanding of science concepts and processes. Students also need to develop various forms of communication. So when teaching communication skills, you should provide opportunities for students' to communicate science in a variety of ways. These may include having students communicate through words and graphic representations such as pictographs, histograms, charts, tables, songs, models, stories, diagrams, graphs, photographs, maps, symbols, illustrations, and reports.

Example: Communicating

(1) Draw and label the parts of the insect you observed.

(2) Use Glogster (http://www.glogster.com/) to create a poster on the phases of the moon for class presentation.

(3) Create a graph showing monthly temperature and rainfall averages for Atlanta, Georgia.

Integrated Process Skills

Building on the basic process skills, the integrated process skills take the students into the realm of a scientific experimentation. The integrated process skills include hypothesizing, identifying variables, controlling variables, operationally defining objects or processes, designing procedures, testing, collecting data, organizing data, drawing conclusions, communicating findings (oral, graphical, pictorial), and even making models (Ostlund & Mercier, 1999; Padilla, 1990).

Generally speaking, experiments are driven by a question or problem that leads to the acceptance or rejection of a **hypothesis**. The question might be, "Which battery lasts the longest time?" or it might be, "What happens to the speed of a toy if we wind it more times?" Once a question is determined and made testable, integrated science process skills come into play through the testing process, although the skills are not addressed in any specific order. Understanding these skills and how they contribute to a **fair test** where all the variables are kept the same except for the variable being tested is essential if students are to conduct and interpret experiments. Next, we begin with experimentation and discuss the other integrated skills essential to fair testing.

Experimenting

You may have heard students say that eating chocolate causes pimples. Or, perhaps, students have shared their curiosity about an idea that some plants grow better near magnets. These and many other questions are asked of science teachers quite frequently. Taking these questions and assisting students in turning them into testable questions can be the beginning of individual, group, or class experimentation. With primary elementary students you may use directed inquiry approaches to teach the children how to design and conduct fair tests in whole class projects. In the upper elementary or middle grade levels you may shift your approach to guided or full inquiry with students working more independently either alone or in groups. In either case, experimentation means asking a testable question, stating hypotheses, and conducting a fair test to answer it. The experiment includes designing the steps or procedures for the fair testing, describing **operational definitions**, identifying variables, determining what data to collect, interpreting the data, drawing conclusions, and communicating the findings.

Example: Experimenting

1. Experimentation includes all the processes (developing a question, writing hypotheses, procedures, determining data collection methods, recording results and drawing conclusions) needed to determine the effects of vitamin B on *Planaria* regeneration.

2. Experimentation includes all the processes needed to determine whether plants grow better with the addition of three-month-old or six-month-old compost.

3. Experimentation includes all the processes needed to determine whether the respiration rate of gold fish change when the water temperature changes.

Hypothesizing

Though you may have often heard and been taught that a hypothesis is an educated guess, it is not. What is an educated guess? How can a guess become educated? It cannot. Not to be confused with a prediction, a hypothesis is a falsifiable "if-then" statement designed to be tested. Do you recall learning to write a hypothesis? If so, you may have been taught to write just one hypothesis; many experiments have more than one hypothesis, however. We find it is useful to have students come up with at least three hypotheses, if possible. One way to begin is by asking students to think of all the possible outcomes of the experiment. For instance, think back to the pill bug experiments. One hypothesis (H_1) might be, "If there is a relationship between pill bug behavior and the amount of light, then more pill bugs will be under the covered side of the dish after ten minutes." Another possible outcome or hypothesis (H_2) might be, "If there is a relationship between pill bug behavior and the amount of light, then more pill bugs will remain in the uncovered side of the dish after ten minutes." There is still another possibility; what might it be? Well, it is possible that the pill bugs are found equally distributed in both the covered and uncovered sides of the dish. So, a third possibility known as the null hypothesis (H_0) might state, "If there is no relationship between pill bug behavior and the amount of light, then the pill bugs will be equally distributed on covered and uncovered sides of the dish after ten minutes." The results of an experiment will allow students to accept only one hypothesis. Now, depending on the question, some experiments may not have three hypotheses; all hypotheses, however, have the independent and dependent variables stated within them.

Remember the discussion on the nature of science in Chapter 1 pointing out that a hypothesis never proves anything? Well, they do not prove anything but they are testable and are either accepted or rejected. With three hypotheses stated for the experiment only one can be accepted based on the findings of the experiment. If students only write one hypothesis and their data doesn't support it—what do they do? They have no hypothesis to accept. So by writing three hypotheses they still have two other hypotheses. Their data should support the acceptance of only one of them. We have experienced this situation and students often think they have done the experiment improperly when in fact they have done it correctly. Worse yet, when students write only one hypothesis, they often bias their data to support their hypothesis. Unfortunately, we have even seen students change their data to allow them to accept their single hypothesis. So having students consider all possible outcomes when developing hypotheses is a useful strategy that allows them to accept one hypothesis when the testing is completed. After examining the hypotheses below, write three hypotheses for the question, "Do pill bugs display a preference for damp and dry conditions?"

Examples: Hypotheses

H_1: If skin cancer is associated with ultraviolet light, then people with more exposure to ultraviolet light will have a higher frequency of skin cancer.

H_2: If skin cancer is associated with ultraviolet light, then people with less exposure to ultraviolet light will have a higher frequency of skin cancer.

H_0: If skin cancer is not associated with ultraviolet light, then there will be no change in the frequency of skin cancer in people with different levels of exposure to ultraviolet light.

H_1: If fermentation of yeast is affected by temperature, then increasing temperature increases carbon dioxide production.

H_2: If fermentation of yeast is affected by temperature, then decreasing temperature increases carbon dioxide production.

H_0: If fermentation of yeast is not affected by temperature, then there will be no change in amount of carbon dioxide production with changes in temperature.

Variables

It is not always easy to identify the variables of an experiment, but as students move through elementary school their ability to identify variables of scientific testing is critical to their ability to carry out full inquiry and design fair tests. We find it useful to begin by having students practice identifying the independent variable in experiment descriptions. The independent variable (manipulated) is the variable that can be attributed to the change in the test results if a change occurs. The independent variable is what you are testing and is "associated" with the outcome. Think about the pill bug tests. What is the independent variable? What was being tested? First, we tested whether the covered or uncovered halves of the dishes made a difference in the distribution of the pill bugs in the container. The amount of light as demonstrated by the covered or uncovered sides of the dish represents the independent variable. That was the variable we wanted to know about and we tested it. So what was the dependent variable? The dependent variable points to what is being measured or observed. We measured or counted the numbers of pill bugs found on the covered and uncovered sides of the dish after ten minutes. The number of the pill bugs on the covered or uncovered sides of the dish was the dependent variable. So, in summary, the experiment allows us to attribute pill bug behavior (preference) to the amount of light, using the number of pill bugs (dependent variable) located in the covered or uncovered sides (independent variable) of the dish. Of course, we can only make this attribution if all other variables remain the same (constants). Constants are variables that stay the same so the testing is fair and the results can be attributed to the independent variable. What types of constants (sometimes called controls) should remain the same with the pill bug experiment? With the pill bug experiment you would use the same type of pill bug for each trial, the same number of pill bugs for each trial, the same timeframe for testing, you would place the dish in the same area, and you would use the same dish for repeated trials. Now think back to the second pill bug experiment using damp and dry environments. What was the independent variable? What was the dependent variable? What were the constants? When teaching students to conduct experiments, remember that only one variable (independent) can be changed at a time. By keeping all the other variables the same, we can attribute the results of the experiment to the only independent variable that is changed.

Example: Identifying variables

Do pink hydrangea flowers change color in a 3% alkaline water solution?

Eight hours of light, same type of soil, and one cup of solution per day were administered to 2 sets of twelve pink flowering hydrangea plants that were observed for flower color changes over six weeks. One group of plants was given 100 milliliters of 3% alkaline water solution, and a second group was given 100 milliliters of a neutral solution.

Constants: amount of light, soil type, amount of solution, number of plants per group, timeframe

Independent variable: 3% alkaline solution

Dependent variable: Flower color change observed

Operational Definitions

Operationally defining terms and processes in an experiment is critical so that other individuals may repeat your experiment in the same manner you conducted it. Operational definitions clarify exactly how the variables in the experiment are to be observed and measured, and how the procedures are to be conducted. This brings to mind a story of five-year-old Eddie who was starting kindergarten. His father, a career Marine, told Eddie that since he was starting school, he would pay him a quarter every day he made his bed. So, on the first day of school Edward excitedly came bounding down the stairs and said, "Daddy, come look at my bed. I earned a quarter." His dad climbed the stairs, and when he reached the bed, he took out a quarter. He flipped the quarter high into the air above the bed and it fell with a plop, sinking into the covers. He said, "Son, you can't have a quarter today. Your bed isn't considered made until a quarter bounces off of it. So, let me show you how to make a bed so the quarter bounces." Clearly, the definition of a "made bed" was different for father and son. An operational definition was required and communicated so that they both understood the meaning of "making a bed" so it could be repeated. Operationally defining bed making was made observable by bouncing a quarter off the surface. Defining terms and processes operationally through observations or measurements in an experiment is critical for repeated testing. Other operational definitions can be viewed in the examples.

Example: Defining operationally

(a) The speed of absorption is operationally defined by timing (measured in seconds) how long it takes colored water to move from point A to B on a paper towel.

(b) Fingernail growth is operationally defined as measuring in milliliters the distance from a mark made on the nail base at the start of the test to the cuticle at one-week intervals for four weeks.

Collecting, Recording, and Interpreting Data

Determining what data to collect and organizing it with the use of drawings, tables, charts, graphs, and photographs are process skills that cross other disciplines and are used frequently in daily life. In scientific research, collecting and organizing data allows scientists to quickly search for anomalies and trends, and to draw conclusions from their data (evidence). Examining data for patterns and trends that explain the results is a lot easier if data are collected and organized in systematic ways. Though students generally have good intuitions about fair testing, it is not always easy for them to decide what data to collect or how to organize it. Teaching students what to collect and how to organize their data is a skill that takes frequent discussion and practice. For younger students, teachers often give students tables and charts first to introduce these skills and direct the data collection. However, as they continue to conduct inquiry activities, students should learn to make data tables or graphs. This requires you to explicitly teach them how to develop charts and graphs as tools of inquiry. We recommend discussing and having students develop charts, tables, and graphs several times a year. The following examples require students to develop charts and interpret data as part of conducting experiments.

Example: Collecting and recording data

(a) Make a table for weekly recordings of the number of *Planaria* that regenerated in water containing caffeine in contrast to the number of *Planaria* regenerated in water without caffeine. Data will be collected for a period of five weeks.

(b) Record weather data by drawing a sun or clouds and rain symbols for a month on a provided chart.

(c) Make a graph showing the amount of mass (g) needed to separate two magnets with one, two, three, and four spacers between them.

Example: Interpreting data

(a) Calculate the average number of regenerated *Planaria* in the water with vitamin B and in the water without vitamin B. Interpret the results and draw a conclusion accepting only one hypothesis.

(b) Examine the graph plotting the temperature of the yeast solution and the production of carbon dioxide. What trends in the data do you observe? What conclusion can you draw from the data? Which hypothesis is accepted?

Recording observations about natural phenomena is a common method of individual and team data collection.

Creating Models

Models can be mental or physical. Scientists may create models for conceptual representations of phenomena, objects, concepts, or processes. They may also develop models to explain a set of observations, inferences, ideas, objects, or events. Do you recall making a model of what you thought the creature looked liked from the reconstruction of the images of fossil bones in Chapter 1? In your science courses, we suspect you have been exposed to many scientific models, including models of an atom, the solar system, the human body, flower parts, and many others. As a teacher you may have students create models to better understand abstract concepts and processes that are difficult to see or experience. Furthermore, model making can be used to uncover prior knowledge that students have about science concepts. In fact, if you think about it, much of science is taught using models and analogies.

Scientifically speaking, models are often used by scientists for rigorous testing against the data to see if they hold up. For instance, the structure of the DNA double helix was first a mental construction created inductively by scientists Francis Crick, James Watson, and Maurice Wilkins from data, observations, and inferences from work of other scientists, in particular Rosalind Franklin. The mental model was then translated into a physical model which is accepted today. Watson, Crick and Wilkins received the Nobel Prize for their work. Franklin's work was critical to Watson and Crick conceptualizing the DNA double helix though she did not receive a Nobel Prize. (For more about the discovery of the DNA double helix, see http://nobelprize.org/educational/medicine/dna_double_helix/readmore.html). Below are a couple of examples of models students can create to better under the phenomena.

Example: Creating models

(a) Ms. Skelton was preparing to teach a lesson on atomic structure. She gave her sixth-grade students different colors of clay and asked them to create a model of what they think an atom looks like. She wanted to use their models to help her understand their prior ideas of atoms. After instruction she had the students reconstruct their models to represent what they had learned about atoms.

(b) Mr. Winston asked his students to examine cells under a microscope. The fifth-grade class talked about the size of the cells and how scale models are used for a variety of purposes. They discussed scale models as either larger or smaller copies of actual objects created in the same proportions. Mr. Winston had students create a cell model in a zip-lock bag and discuss how it was different from the scale models they made of the planets. Information on the cell model activity can be found at http://library.thinkquest.org/19037/making_a_cell.html or http://www.enchantedlearning.com/subjects/animals/cell/jello/.

In summary, remember that in selecting science content, you need to be alert to ways that you can teach the process skills while teaching content. The two go hand in hand. We cannot expect students to learn these skills if they do not experience or practice the skills often. Teaching science using inquiry approaches and having students learn science process skills are fundamental to students becoming scientifically literate. You may be surprised, however, to learn that inquiry-based science has been found to improve skills in reading as well (Bredderman, 1982; Morgan, Rachelson, & Lloyd, 1977; Wellman, 1978). Table 6.4 shows the process skills in science aligned to reading skills also taught in elementary classrooms. Therefore, by working with the process skills in science you reinforce skills in reading, a high priority in classrooms today.

Table 6.4 Comparisons of Reading Skills and Science Process Skills

Reading Skills	Science Process Skills	Reading	Science (investigation/text)
Note the details	**Observe, measure**	Noting details in story scenes or the behaviors of characters	Observing and measuring changes in chemical reactions, motion of objects
Compare/ Contrast	**(Classify)**	Listening to opposing arguments of characters or scenes in a story	Classifying based upon similarities/difference: predators and prey or magnetic/nonmagnetic materials
Predict	**Predict**	Predicting plots in a novel	Predicting outcomes based on data
Sequence events	**Design test procedures**	Compiling clues to solve a mystery or posed problem	Developing steps in experiments
Link cause and effect	**(Identify variables)**	Recalling why an event or person acted in a certain way	Developing hypotheses: if/then statements for experiments
Distinguishing fact from opinion	**(Analyze data)**	Discussing the use of evidence in a reading or newspaper article	Discussing the use of evidence in a science text, article or experiment
Link words with precise meanings	**(Operational definitions)**	Learning words through experience-definition/context	Developing operational definitions. Defining the "period of a pendulum" as the time it takes a pendulum to swing from Point A to Point B to Point A again.
Make inferences	**Make inferences**	Using observation and evidence	Based on observation and evidence
Draw conclusion	**Draw conclusions**	Using data for purposes of explanation	Using data for purposes of explanation

Note: Modified from Their, M. (2002), *The New Science Literacy: Using Language Skills to Help Students Learn Science.* Portsmouth, NH: Heineman

Is It an Experiment or an Investigative Activity?

Thus far, Chapter 6 has focused on teaching strategies for inquiry and has described process skills students need for conducting a variety of science inquiry activities and experiments. Before going further, we would like for you to consider inquiry once again in terms of investigative activities and experiments. We often hear teachers say to students, "Let's experiment," when they really mean, "Let's do an investigative activity." This may seem like a small detail but it is important you understand the difference. So how is an **experiment** and an **investigative activity** different? An investigative activity always starts with a question, followed by a set of procedures, and an outcome known to the teacher. For example an investigative activity may begin with, "How can we find our pulse rate?" Next students are given step-by-step procedures on how to find their pulse, record their findings, and calculate pulse rates. The teaching objective is that the students learn how to take a pulse rate and understand that an individual's pulse is caused by the heart pushing blood through the arteries. Thus, an investigative activity began with a question, followed a set of procedures, and led students to learn about concepts related to human pulse rates and the processes for taking pulse rates (a known outcome). Does this sound like an experiment in the true sense of the word? As you may have guessed, it is not. It is an example of directed inquiry and doesn't involve the integrated process skills such as hypothesizing, operationally defining, identifying variables, and other integrated process skills associated with an experiment. Let's go a step further: now suppose that the students have learned how to take someone's pulse rate, but a new question arises. Suppose a student asks, "What happens to the pulse rate of an individual lying down compared to standing?" To answer the student's question, the teacher may decide to have the class conduct an experiment to answer the question. The teacher has students assist in the designing the experiment (development of hypotheses, procedures, variable identifications, operational definitions, data collection, data interpretation, and conclusions). The beauty of investigative activities is that they can lead to experiments that students may pursue. Unlike investigative activities, the outcome of the experiment may not be known to the teacher. Thus, inquiry moves from investigative activities to experiments shifting from teacher centered to student centered activities based upon the skills of the students. Teaching science as inquiry fosters student inquiries that come in many variations with different intents. The next time you pick up a science textbook, look at the activities and ask yourself, Are the activities structured (directed), guided, or full inquiries? Are they investigative activities or experiments?

Elaborate

Analyzing Science Textbooks for Inquiry Activities and Science Process Skills

Let's take inquiry and process skills into an authentic context. Because of your knowledge of inquiry approaches and process skills, you've been asked by the principal to serve on the school district's K–8 science textbook selection committee. The textbook selection process is an intensive and time-consuming process, so subcommittees have been established. You have chosen to serve on the subcommittee responsible for reviewing potential science textbooks for their coverage of inquiry approaches and student activities. Take what you have learned in this chapter about inquiry and conduct an analysis of the text you have agreed to review.

Before you begin your review, consider the key elements you believe demonstrate a strong presence of inquiry approaches and process skills in a science textbook. For this task the subcommittee has decided to address the following: (a) identify the types of inquiry approaches (direct, guided, full), (b) identify the activities as investigative activities or experiments, (c) include the frequency of inquiry activities found in each of the three randomly selected sample chapters, (d) identify the process skills required for students to complete the activities, and (e) describe the overall range of process skills used in the activity as either basic or integrated. Before you begin collecting data, create a table or spreadsheet for recording your data and include the name, publisher, grade level, and publication date for each of the texts you review. You may have access to science textbooks in your science methods course; if not, see the "Selecting Your Science Textbook for Analysis" for other options. In order for you to compare more than one science textbook, we recommend that you partner with a classmate and exchange textbooks. Each of you can independently evaluate the same chapters, then you can compare your findings and determine which of the science textbooks is better in terms of inquiry and process skills.

Evaluate

5E

Can You Change a Directed Inquiry Activity Into a Guided or Full Inquiry?

> ### SELECTING YOUR SCIENCE TEXTBOOK FOR ANALYSIS
>
> For this activity, you will need to obtain a contemporary (2005 or later) science textbook for any K–8 grade level. There are several options for obtaining the text.
>
> 1. Borrow a science textbook from a local school where you had a practicum experience. Your instructor may also have science textbooks.
>
> 2. Many college or universities libraries and public libraries have a collection of science textbooks; check to see if they are available in your school library.
>
> 3. Some education programs have a curriculum library; check with your education department to see if any science texts are available.
>
> 4. Go to www.pearsonschool.com then click "Register" and fill out the short online form. Once you have registered, use your password which will allow you access online samples. Select a science textbook to view on line.

Refer back to the pill bug lesson in this chapter. As discussed in the explain section, the pill bug lesson was predominately a directed inquiry. Your task is to modify the pill bug activity into either a predominantly guided or a full inquiry. To assist you in this task, use the essential features of inquiry (Table 6.2), which include (a) engages in questions, (b) designs procedures, (c) gives priority to evidence, (d) formulates explanations from evidence, (e) connects explanation to scientific knowledge, and (f) communicates explanations.

Rewrite the activities of the pill bug experiment to make the teaching approach a guided inquiry or an **open (or full) inquiry**. Make a list of the changes and describe how the changes you made make the lesson more guided or open.

Summary

Over the past couple of decades, research has supported teaching science using an inquiry-based curriculum. The groundwork has been laid for inquiry approaches that encourage students to become active investigators.

BULLETIN BOARD

Research-Based Benefits of an Inquiry-Based Science Curriculum

1. Increases science achievement

2. Improves attitudes toward science

3. Enhances creativity in problem solving

4. Improves visual perceptions

5. Enhances reading readiness skills

6. Enhances language development

7. Improves process skill development

8. Improves mathematics achievement

9. Improves logical thinking

10. Improves laboratory skills

Haury, D., & Rillero, P. (1994). *Perspectives of Hands-On Science Teaching*. North Central Regional Laboratories. Columbus, OH: ERIC Clearinghouse for Science, Mathematics, and Environmental Education.

For students to become active inquirers in your science classroom, your role is to provide experiences and content that allows students to build new knowledge and skills for conducting inquiry. This does not mean that students should be left to their own means to discover everything themselves. Instruction using many variations of inquiry also helps students to focus on the science process skills; in doing so they recognize that the science knowledge emerging from their inquiries is valid and powerful. Inquiry-based approaches carried out effectively assist students in learning important concepts, processes, and ways of thinking in science. Consequently, when students participate in inquiry, they experience science as a human enterprise that is ongoing and complex, and as something they can do. Students acquire this understanding on their own, by doing what scientists do—using their intellect and creativity in processes that both generate knowledge and test knowledge about the world around them.

Annotated Resources

Seeing, wondering, theorizing, learning: Inquiry-based instruction with Kishia Moore by Dan Lewandowski

http://www.learnnc.org/lp/pages/6429.

This website provides an article of first-grade teacher Kishia Moore's inquiry-based classroom. Ms. Moore shares candidly the ups and downs of teaching by means of inquiry approaches with first graders related to the properties of rocks involving hands-on activities, notebook observations by means of drawings, graphic organizers, and KWL charts.

FOSSweb, Foss website

http://www.fossweb.com/

This website offers a series of interactive demonstration clips on a variety of topics from weather to magnets. The clips are arranged by grade levels and give a glimpse of what their interactive website offers in conjunction with the science kits it produces.

Online School Yard and Classroom Investigations (Google Science Experiment Page)

Search browser for "Online Schoolyard and Classroom Investigation" also found at www.ux1.eiu.edu/~cfkp2/CoilsHome.htm entitled the "Science Experiment Page."

This website includes a large variety of lesson ideas. The lessons are teacher tested with experiments for K–8 students. This site provides outdoor activities for those looking for environmental activities.

Ostlund, K., & Mercier, S. (1999). *Rising to the challenge of the National Science Education Standards: The processes of science inquiry (primary grades).* **Fresno, CA: S & K Associates.**

This is an excellent book that embeds process skills with content using inquiry approaches. The book includes process skills that can be used as posters, assessments, and inquiry activities with embedded process skills on seeds, matter, and dinosaurs.

Ostlund, K., & Mercier, S. (1996). *Rising to the challenge of the National Science Education Standards: The processes of science inquiry (grades 4–8).* **Fresno, CA: S & K Associates.**

This is a favorite inquiry resource. It includes inquiry activities with embedded process skills on shells, rocks, and sound. The authors also include handy cooperative learning role cards and assessment formats.

Yockey, J. A. (2001). A key to science learning. *Science & Children, 38*(7), 36–41.

This article focuses on the elementary school level, and describes a simple writing technique to help students communicate the important science concepts they have learned.

Goldston, J. M., Marlette, S., & Pennington, A. (2001). Centimeters, millimeters, & monsters. *Science & Children, 39*(2), 42–47.

This engaging article targets K–6 learners while using a creative and integrated approach for teaching students on how to measure using metric units. Using a storyline setting, students become tailors and take measurements to design clothing for some interesting creatures.

Stein, M., McNair, S., & Butcher, J. (2001). Drawing on student understanding. *Science & Children, 38*(4), 18–22.

This article describes how elementary school children can use drawings to communicate their understanding of animals. The strategy enhances student learning: They are encouraged to think deeply about what they know and have observed.

References

Bredderman, T. (1982). What research says: Activity science: The evidence shows it matters. *Science and Children, 20*(1), 39–41.

Colburn, A. (2008). An inquiry primer. In E. Brunsell (Ed.), *Readings in science methods K–8* (pp. 33–36). Arlington, VA: NSTA Press.

Hodson, D. (1988). Toward a philosophically more valid science curriculum. *Science Education, 72,* 19–40.

Misiti, Frank (2001, February). Standardizing the language of inquiry. *Science and Children, 38*(5), 38–40.

Morgan, A., Rachelson, S., & Lloyd, B. (1977). Sciencing activities as contributors to the development of reading skills in first grade students. *Science Education, 61*(2), 135–144.

National Research Council (NRC). (1996). *National science education standards.* Washington, DC: National Academies Press.

National Research Council (NRC). (2000). *Inquiry in the National Science Education Standards: A guide for teaching and learning.* Washington, DC: National Academies Press.

Ostlund, K. L., & Mercier, S. (1996). *Rising to the challenge of the National Science Education Standards: The processes of science inquiry.* Fresno, CA: S & K Associates.

Ostlund, K. L., & Mercier, S. (1999). *Rising to the challenge of the National Science Education Standards: The processes of science inquiry (primary grades).* Austin, TX: S & K Associates. Available at www.nsta.org.

Padilla, M. (1990). The science process skills. *NARST: Research matters . . . to the science teachers.* #9004. Available at http://www.narst.org/publications/research/skill.cfm.

Pomeroy, D. (1993). Implications of teachers' beliefs about the nature of science: Comparisons of scientists, secondary science teachers, and elementary teachers. *Science Education, 77,* 261–278.

Slotta, J. (2004). The Web-Based Inquiry Science Environment (WISE): Scaffolding knowledge integration in the science classroom. In M. Linn, E. Davis, & P. Bell (Eds.), *Internet environments for science education* (pp. 203–232). Hillsdale, NJ: Lawrence Erlbaum.

Their, M. (2002). *The new science literacy: Using language skills to help students learn science.* Portsmouth, NH: Heinemann.

Weiss, I. (2006). A framework for investigating the influence of the national science standards. In D. Sunal & E. Wright (Eds.), *The impact of state and national standards on K–12 science teaching* (pp. 51–79). Greenwich, CT: Information Age Publishing.

Welch, W., Klopfer, L., Aikenhead, G., & Robinson, J. (1981). The role of inquiry in science education: Analysis and recommendations. *Science Education, 65,* 33–50.

Wellman, R. T. (1978). Science: A basic for language and reading development. In M. B. Rowe (Ed.), *What research says to the science teacher,* Vol. 1 (pp. 1–13). Washington, DC: National Association of Teachers. ERIC Document Reproduction Service No. ED 148 628.

Wells, G. (1995). Dialogic inquiry in education: Building on the legacy of Vygotsky. In C. D. Lee & P. Smagorinsky (Eds.), *Vygotskian perspectives on literacy research* (pp. 51–85). New York: Cambridge University Press.

Wittrock, C., & Barrows, L. (2008). Blow by blow inquiry. In E. Brunsell (Ed.), *Readings in science methods K–8* (pp. 43–50). Arlington, VA: NSTA Press.

Wolff, M., & Roychoudhury, A. (1993). The development of science process skills in authentic contexts. *Journal of Research in Science Teaching, 30*(2), 127–152.

Inquiry Lesson Planning

5E Inquiry Instructional Model

Learning Objectives

After reading Chapter 7, students will be able to

- describe key elements of each phase of the 5E inquiry approach,
- compare and contrast the learning cycle to the 5E inquiry approach, and
- evaluate a science lesson using characteristics of the 5E phases (rubric) of an inquiry lesson.

NSES TEACHING STANDARDS ADDRESSED IN CHAPTER 7

Standard B: Teachers of science guide and facilitate learning. In doing this, teachers

- focus and support inquiries while interacting with students;
- challenge students to accept and share responsibility for their own learning; and
- recognize and respond to student diversity and encourage all students to participate fully in science learning.

Standard D: Teachers of science guide and facilitate learning. In doing this, teachers

- structure time available so students are able to engage in extended investigations; and
- ensure a safe working environment.

Source: Reprinted with permission from the National Science Education Standards, copyright 1996, by the National Academy of Sciences, Courtesy of National Academies Press, Washington, DC.

Introduction

Have you considered how many lessons you have been taught during your K–12 school experiences? If you estimate an average of six lessons per day with an average of 180 school days per year, by the time you graduate from high school you have experienced approximately 12,960 lessons. If you average one science lesson a day (a high estimate for elementary grades) you have experienced around 2,160 lessons. Having experienced many science lessons, can you tell the difference between an effective science lesson and one that is not quite so effective? What factors contribute to an effective science lesson? No matter what factors are identified, if a lesson is poorly planned, the chances of it being successful are low. As a teacher you will design many lessons on a daily basis, so thoughtful planning is important if the lessons are to promote learning science.

Because inquiry is central to the science standards, it is essential that you become very familiar with lesson planning designed for inquiry. Because inquiry lesson planning is a bit different from what you may have learned in other classes, we think it is important to tell you that as you become more experienced in using an inquiry approach for teaching science, the process of planning gets easier. You may also wonder when you'll have time to write all the detailed lesson plans that you are required to develop in your teacher preparation. Just remember, this is a process designed to get you to think through and articulate the key components of effective inquiry science lessons. The detailed lesson plans of your teacher preparation and first years of teaching will eventually be transformed into notes on your planner. When this occurs, these notes serve only as reminders because you have already internalized inquiry teaching into your actual practice. Effective science teachers make teaching science look easy because they have carefully planned and internalized the essential parts of the lesson so the focus in the classroom is on student learning.

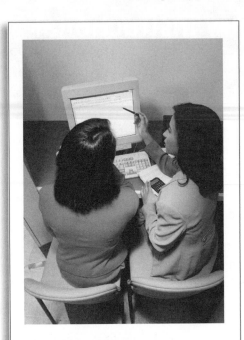

Planning with colleagues often generates new and exciting ways to present and teach science.

At this point you recognize the 5E approach because each chapter in this book is organized using it. The phases are Engage, Explore, Explain, Elaborate, and Evaluate. It's impossible to fully model each of these elements within a chapter without the opportunity to engage in discussion with you personally, but if you have paid attention to the structure of the phases in each chapter, you may have already begun to internalize some of the elements of the 5E inquiry approach. Now it's time to examine 5E inquiry lessons in more detail.

Experience is a hard teacher because she gives the test first, the lesson afterwards.

Vernon Sanders Law

Do you think experience is the best teacher? Do you think an individual can become an effective science teacher without experience? Explain your reasoning. How might the quote from athlete, Vernon Law, lead to the importance of teachers reflecting on their science teaching?

Engage

What Makes an Effective 5E Inquiry Lesson Plan?

Imagine this: You've successfully completed your teaching degree and have a job teaching a rambunctious but always curious group of sixth graders. You've decided that you're going to focus on experiments, with special attention on controlled and manipulated variables because your students struggle with identifying variables. You found a great lesson plan from a colleague's book using paper helicopters to explore variables in experiments. You copied it and left it sitting on your desk. You liked the lesson plan so much that you've invited your principal to observe you teach it. You prepare carefully, gather all the materials, and are ready to go. Unfortunately, the following week when it's nearly time for the lesson, you can't find the lesson plan anywhere. You search through the papers on your desk, but find no trace of it. Then you vaguely recall one of your students asked for some scrap paper earlier in the day to cut into strips for science vocabulary flash cards. You go to the recycle bin, find the flash cards and sure enough, when you turn over the strips, there's your lesson plan in pieces. Your task is to reconstruct the sequence of the inquiry lesson from the following six sections found in the recycle bin (see Figure 7.1 on pages 152–155).

The helicopter lesson uses a 5E inquiry approach to explore variables influencing the motion of a paper helicopter. At this point, it doesn't matter if you get all the parts in the proper sequence. What is important is that you examine the elements of what is found within each section or phase. We will return to the engage phase and the arrangement of the lesson phases later in the chapter, but in the meantime consider this question: "What does a teacher need to know about each of the phases in planning a 5E inquiry science lesson?"

Explore

A Closer Look at the Phases of the 5E Inquiry Instructional Model

At the very least, most of us think of a lesson plan as having a beginning, middle, and end. The order of the sections in the lesson plan you just organized is important if you are to orchestrate an inquiry lesson.

However, planning and teaching an inquiry lesson is more than using a simple sequence of the inquiry stages: It is also critical to understand the specific characteristics of each stage. With the helicopter lesson plan, you probably began with standards and objectives. It is a logical place to begin, given that instructional objectives serve as the guide for the expected learning outcomes (see Appendix A). Next you may have looked at how to organize the sections for the lesson to flow in a logical sequence, again an effective strategy.

> **TECH CONNECT: Tools for 5E Lesson Planning**
>
> Exploring the Internet for templates that you can modify to meet your needs can be a useful resource. For example, general templates for creating a 5E lesson plan may be found at http://www.emints.org/tools/constructivistlessonplanform.doc or at "Assignment: Lesson Planning (5E Model)" located at coe.csusb.edu/Jesunathadas/lesson_plan_format.doc or "Teachers' Network Elementary Science: The Five E's: A Lesson Plan Model" located at http://teachersnetwork.org/NTNY/nychelp/science/five_e.htm.
>
> These templates may be useful once you become familiar with and use the 5E model. When designing forms, activity sheets, and other teaching materials, consider the Internet to find useful templates for your science classroom that need only minor modifications. Always take the time to analyze web-based materials and templates to ensure they are accurate and meet your needs.

Figure 7.1   Paper Helicopters: A Lesson Plan

SECTION 1

Follow these steps:

Helicopter model templates

(a) Cut out the five paper helicopters on the solid lines. Cut on the solid lines in each paper helicopter.

(b) Fold the flaps back along the dotted lines of each paper helicopter.

(c) Fold the blade on the right side toward you on the dotted line. Fold the blade on the left side away from you on the dotted line.

(d) Attach a paper clip at the bottom of each paper helicopter.

(e) Complete the **Helicopter Comparisons** Table (answers in italics).

Helicopter Comparison			
Paper helicopter	Width of each blade	Length of each blade	Area of each blade
A	*2 units*	*6 units*	*2 × 6 = 12 units²*
B	*2 units*	*8 units*	*2 × 8 = 16 units²*
C	*2 units*	*4 units*	*2 × 4 = 8 units²*
D	*3 units*	*4 units*	*3 × 4 = 12 units²*
E	*3 units*	*8 units*	*3 × 8 = 24 units²*

(f)   For each pair of models listed in **Helicopter Investigations**, identify the controlled variable—how the two helicopters are the same (width or length of the blades); and the manipulated variable: how the two helicopter are different (width or length of blades). Then drop the models listed under the Investigation column from as high a position as possible. When comparing the two models, drop them at exactly the same time and from exactly the same height. Observe and compare the rate of spin and drop for the two models (responding variables). Give each cooperative group member a turn to drop the models while the other group members observe.

Helicopter Investigations			
Investigation drop models	Controlled variables (same)	Manipulated variable (different)	Observations (responding variables)
A and B			
A and C			
B and C			
C and D			
D and E			
Drop model A with blades folded first in one direction and then in the reverse direction			

(g)   Design two graphs to show your observations. The manipulated variable (what was different in the helicopter designs—width or length of blades) will be on the horizontal axis and one of the responding variables (spin rate or drop rate) will be on the vertical axis.

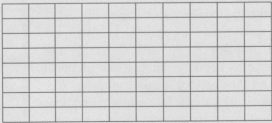

(h) Observations of the paper helicopter investigations demonstrate cause-and-effect relationships between the manipulated (cause) and responding (effect) variables. For each change in the design of the helicopter, give the effect (answers in italics).

Cause	Effect
A has shorter blades than B	*A spins more than B*
C has shorter blades than A	*C spins more than A*
C has shorter blades than B	*C spins more than B*
C has narrower blades than D	*C spins more than D*
D has shorter blades than E	*D spins more than E*
B has longer blades than A	*A reaches the ground before B*
A has longer blades than C	*C reaches the ground before A*
B has longer blades than C	*C reaches the ground before B*
D has wider blades than C	*C reaches the ground before D*
E has longer blades than D	*D reaches the ground before E*
Right blade folded forward & left folded backward	*A spins counterclockwise*
Right blade folded backward & left folded forward	*A spins clockwise*

SECTION 2:

Given a set of materials, each student will complete and answer the following:

1. What do you think will happen if you add extra clips to the models?
   The helicopters will drop faster.

2. Make a paper helicopter that will drop slowly.
   The model has long, wide blades.

3. Make a paper helicopter that will drop fast.
   The model has short, narrow blades.

4. What do you think will happen to a model with very long, wide blades?
   The model would float like a parachute. If the blades were wide enough, the spin would decrease to nearly zero.

5. What do you think will happen to a model with very short, narrow blades?
   The model would drop in less time and spin more.

6. What do you think will happen if both blades were folded in the same direction?
   The model would not spin.

7. What do you think will happen if two paper helicopters have blades with the same area but different lengths and widths?
   The model with the shortest blades will drop first.

8. What other changes might affect the drop and spin of a paper helicopter? Make two models to test your predictions.
   (Change shape of blade, change materials, etc.)

9. Identify the independent variable, dependent variable, and constants in your models for No. 8.

(Continued)

Figure 7.1 (Continued)

SECTION 3

Paper Helicopters

Modified activity originally developed by Karen Ostlund, Department of Biology, Southwest Texas State University, San Marcos, TX; Reprinted from CESI Science, Summer 1996.

Content Standards:

K-4 Physical science - Position and Motion of Objects
5-8 Physical science - Motion and Force

Objectives:

- Students will be able to identify manipulated (independent) variables, responding (dependent) variables, and constants.
- Given various scenarios, students will be able to extrapolate from data findings to make accurate predictions and apply the knowledge to make paper helicopters perform in certain ways.
- Students will be able to explain the reason behind (a) clockwise and counterclockwise spin and (b) the relationship between surface area of wing to drop rate and spin rate.

Process Skills

Observing, comparing, making models, investigating (identifying and controlling variables), predicting.

Materials

- patterns for paper helicopters
- scissor
- paper clips

SECTION 4:

Show students the two-winged maple seeds. Pass some around. Ask them what they have observed with the winged maple seeds. Have them use what they have learned through their experimentation to redesign one winged seed to make it (a) spin faster and one winged seed to make it (b) drop faster using paper models of the wings. They will draw their redesigns and write about their rationale in their science notebooks.

SECTION 5:

Fold a piece of construction paper in half. Fold it in half again. Fold it once more. Then take another piece of unfolded construction paper of the same size. Hold the folded construction paper in one hand and the full sheet of construction paper in the other keeping them at the same height. Ask each student in class to vote on which paper will hit the floor first if released at the same time at the same height. Students will make a choice by putting a slip of paper in the jar representing what they think will happen. Jar A: the flat paper hits the floor first, Jar B: the folded paper hits the floor first, or Jar C: both hit at the same time. Then have students discuss the reasons associated with their choices for each potential outcome.

SECTION 6:

Have students discuss their findings using the following Helicopter Investigation Table and subsequent questions:

Helicopter Investigation Table			
Investigation drop models	Controlled variables (same)	Manipulated variable (different)	Observations (responding variables)
A and B	*width of blade*	*length of blade*	*A spins more than B* *A reaches the ground before B*
A and C	*width of blade*	*length of blade*	*C spins more than A* *C reaches the ground before A*
B and C	*width of blade*	*length of blade*	*C spins more than B* *C reaches the ground before B*

C and D	length of blade	width of blade	C spins more than D C reaches the ground before D
D and E	width of blade	length of blade	D spins more than E D reaches the ground before E
Drop model A with blades folded first in one direction and then in reverse direction	width and length of blade	direction blades are folded	Right blade folded forward & left folded backward—counterclockwise spin; right blade folded backward & left folded forward—clockwise spin

- What variables appear to affect the rate at which the helicopter drops? *The width and length of blades.*
- Explain how these variables affect the rate at which the helicopter drops. *The wider and longer the blade, the slower the drop rate.*
- Why do you think these variables affect the way the helicopter drops? *There is more air resistance on wider and longer blades, therefore more buoyant force. The terminal velocity is lower with the drop.*
- What variables seem to affect the rate at which the blades spin? *The width and length of blades.*
- Explain how these variables affect the rate at which the blades spin. *The narrower and shorter the blade, the more times the helicopter spins.*
- Why do you think these variables affect the rate at which the blades spin? *The wider and longer the blade, the more **Bernoulli's principle** is a factor. As the velocity of the particles of air around the blades increases, the pressure of the air particles on the blades decreases.*
- What variable appears to affect the direction the helicopter spins? *The direction that the blades are folded.*
- Explain how this variable affects the direction of spin. *If the right blade is folded forward and the left blade is folded backward, the helicopter spins counterclockwise. If the blades are folded in the opposite directions, the helicopter spins clockwise.*

Explanation of the wing-folding variable on the direction of spin.

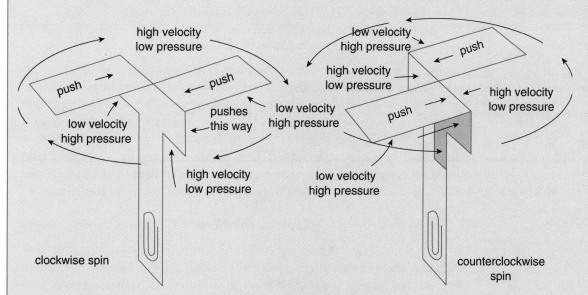

Source: Helicopter Lesson originally developed by Karen Ostlund, Department of Biology, Southwest Texas State University, San Marcos, TX. Reprinted with permission from the Council of Elementary Science International. Copyright 1996.

The helicopter lesson is a 5E inquiry lesson, which means it follows an Engage, Explore, Explain, Elaborate, and Evaluate phase sequence (Trowbridge & Bybee, 1996). It's now time for you to examine firsthand the characteristics of the 5E phases. In the following examples, select from each pair of phases the better representative of each one. As you do so, consider what makes one example better than the other.

Examine the arranged pairs of 5E phases and determine which of each pair you think is the better example. If needed you can refer to the descriptions of the 5E phases described in the rubric (see Table 7.4 on page 171).

Engage: First Grade

Ask students where they think a seed comes from. Tell students they will be dissecting a seed to see its parts. Tell students they will be comparing the findings to the drawings that they completed in an earlier activity.

Engage: Fifth Grade

Give students world maps and ask them to place sticky dots on the areas they think most volcanoes can be found. Also, ask students to use a sticky star on the places in the United States where they think there are volcanic eruptions. The teacher will collect the maps and ask students to share some of their ideas about areas of high volcanic activity. The teacher and students will return to the ideas after class activities.

Explore: Fifth Grade

Arrange students into six groups of four and give each group information about twelve different volcanoes located on the Circum-Pacific Belt, known as the Ring of Fire. The groups will read the information together. Each group will be given two mystery volcanoes to identify. Give each group clues about their particular volcanoes. The groups must use their clues and a map to determine which volcanoes they have. Once they have figured out which volcanoes they have been given, they must locate the volcanoes on the map and mark them with map flag pins. Groups defend their volcano identification and location by providing evidence to support their decisions.

Explore: Third Grade

Discuss how color and hardness are used to identify minerals. Next, talk about how hardness is often a better physical property test than color for identifying minerals. Demonstrate a mineral streak using graphite on an unglazed porcelain plate, then give students a sheet with questions. Using the textbook, students will answer questions about the physical properties of various minerals.

Explain: Third Grade

After students collect samples of their own fingerprints and those of their classmates, ask them to look at their classmates' fingerprints and group them based on similarities and differences. (They should have three groups: arches, whorls, and loops.) Then ask, "Using our class data, what are some patterns we see in our data?" (Rank the types based on the numbers of each type in the class.) Ask if any of the fingerprints look exactly alike. They will have similarities but no two fingerprints are alike. Even identical twins that look exactly alike from head to toe have different fingerprints. Ask the students to describe the similarities they notice in the fingerprints. Using their ideas, clarify the basic pattern of fingerprints. Arch patterns have lines that start at one side of the print and then rise toward the center of the print and leave on the other side of the print. Whorl patterns have a lot of circles that do not leave either side of the print. Loop patterns have lines that start on one side of the print and then rise toward the center of the print and leave on the same side of the print they start on. Now label the class chart with these terms and have the students identify their fingerprint type. Ask students to write down their fingerprint type and find two classmates who have the same type. In their science notebook, students sketch each category of fingerprints. Ask, "Okay, so who would like to summarize some of the ideas we have discussed?" (What was the most common print found in class? What was the least common print? How are fingerprints useful in solving crimes?)

Explain: First Grade

When students have completed their activity sheet on magnets, discuss as a class what they did and what they learned. Ask students what they learned about magnetic and nonmagnetic materials, how magnets move things, and how magnets interact.

Elaborate: Fourth Grade

Say, "Now that you can describe and identify each type of simple machine, I am going to assign you another task. Within this classroom there are examples of four simple machines. Team 1: Find an example of a wedge. Team 2: Find an example of a lever. Team 3: Find an example of a wheel and axle. Team 4: Find an example of a pulley." The items are visible, so have the students walk quietly around the room as a team until they locate their assigned machine. When they find it, they should make sure all team members agree before submitting the name of the object. Students will be expected to explain their selection.

Elaborate: Second Grade

Remind students of how animals and humans use plants. Have students write or draw pictures that show or describe how we use plants and why they are important not only to animals, but also to humans.

Evaluate: First Grade

Evaluate students based on how well they completed their partner activity sheet. Also, evaluate them on their participation.

Evaluate: Third Grade

Pass out diagram of a seed. Have students label each part of the seed (seed coat, root, cotyledon, and embryo) and explain the function of each part. The following rubric is used to evaluate student work (see Table 7.1).

Student name _____

Table 7.1 Scoring Rubric

Category: Seed Parts	Superior	Satisfactory	Needs Work
Seed coat Root Cotyledon Embryo	Students label four of four seed parts correctly.	Students label three of four seed parts.	Students label two or fewer seed parts.
Seed coat Root Cotyledon Embryo	Students describe four of four seed parts correctly.	Students describe three of four seed parts.	Students describe two or fewer seed parts.

Which examples were easier to identify as the better one of the pair? Did using the 5E rubric (see Table 7.4) assist in clarifying the differences between the examples to identify the better one? Were the characteristics of the phases clear? These samples were from actual lesson plans from individuals like you who were just beginning to write 5E lessons. Even without access to the entire lesson plan for each of the phases, we are confident that you could select the better example from each pair. In the next section, you will examine the characteristics of each 5E phase in detail. You will then have the opportunity to reexamine and check your original selections.

> *To accomplish great things, we must not only act, but also dream; not only plan, but also believe.*
>
> Anatole France

What do you believe about teaching science as inquiry? What great things do you aspire to accomplish in teaching science? How important are your beliefs in accomplishing your aspirations?

Explain

Focus Questions

1. What makes an effective 5E inquiry science lesson?

2. What are the characteristics of the phases of a 5E inquiry approach to teaching?

3. What is a teacher's role during the phases of 5E inquiry instruction?

4. What is the student's role during inquiry?

Inquiry as a Way of Teaching Science: 5E Inquiry Instructional Model

There are probably as many lesson plan formats as there are disciplines, but the one you have seen throughout this book is a modification of the learning cycle. The **learning cycle** instructional model has been viewed as an effective instructional model for science teaching by means of inquiry since the 1970s (Atkin & Karplus, 1962; Karplus, 1979; Karplus & Thier, 1967; Lawson, 1995; Settlage, 2000). The learning cycle phases were originally described as "exploration, invention, and discovery" (Karplus & Thier). Because of confusion over the meaning of the original terms, they were renamed. Today, the terms "exploration, concept introduction, and concept application" are most frequently used (Karplus et al., 1977).

No matter which label is used, the three phases are grounded in Piagetian theory and are linked to one another specifically for experiencing science as inquiry (Marek, Maier, & McCann, 2008; Maier & Marek, 2006). During the exploration phase of the learning cycle, students are involved in activities that provide knowledge for constructing the concepts or skills. During the exploration phase, interactive discussion that draws on the students' experiences with the activities links it to the introduction of concepts phase for concept development. The last phase, application of concepts, links to the previous stage by giving students opportunities to apply the newly developed ideas in a different context. Within the design of each phase, the learning cycle can incorporate a variety of tools and methods of teaching (Marek, Laubach, & Pederson, 2003).

A popular modified version of the inquiry learning cycle is known as the 5E model (Trowbridge & Bybee, 1996). The 5E model comprises the three phases of the learning cycle plus two additional phases, engage and evaluation.

If you teach science using the 5E model, you will find it very different from many traditional approaches you may have experienced. For instance,

BULLETIN BOARD

Comparing the Learning Cycle to the 5E Inquiry Instructional Model

Learning Cycle	5E Inquiry Instructional Model
Exploration	Engage and Explore
Concept introduction (Invention)	Explain
Concept application (Expansion)	Elaborate and Evaluate

with traditional instruction science concepts, vocabulary, and processes are usually introduced to students first, followed by an activity or discussion that reinforces the concepts already discussed. Inquiry approaches such as the 5E model and the learning cycle do the opposite. These allow students to experience science concepts and processes first. Following the student exploration activities, students are introduced more fully to the concepts, vocabulary, and processes through a variety of approaches during the explain phase. These approaches may include the use of technology, questions, demonstrations, models, charts, graphs, think-pair-share strategies, and whole class discussions that draw on the information students gathered as a result of their activities during the explore phase.

Phases of the 5E Inquiry Instructional Model

Engage

The 5E inquiry approach begins with the engage phase, during which the teacher creates student curiosity and interest, elicits students' questions, and ascertains students' prior knowledge with respect to the concept(s) to be taught. In planning this stage, it is critical to ascertain what students already know about the topic (prior knowledge) and simultaneously create curiosity or motivate students to want to know more about their ideas and those to be explored. A variety of tools can be used in the engage phase such as reading a book passage, creating story lines, posing problem-based scenarios, conducting demonstrations, giving preassessment prompts or quizzes, and using quick writes, graphic organizers, brainstorming, discrepant events, and KWL charts, to name a few. Let's examine each of the phases for a couple of lesson plans to discern the phase's key characteristics. The 5E phases for the volcano lesson plan is for fifth grade while 5E phases for the mineral lesson plan is for fourth grade. Now, begin by examining the engage phase of the lessons.

Engage 1: The teacher shows pictures of volcanic mountains (land and sea) and different types of volcanic eruptions. (Pass around pictures and use them at a science center later.) Prepare a KWL chart in advance for class viewing and have students make one of their own. Then ask students, "What do you know about volcanoes?" Students write down on their chart what they know about volcanoes (prompts: Where are volcanoes found? What do they look like? What do you know about eruption materials?). Students will share their ideas and they will be recorded for class viewing under the "K" of the chart. Then say, "Next we will discuss what we want to know about volcanoes including any questions students have about volcanoes. This will be recorded in the charts under the 'W' of the class chart." After filling out the class chart, tell the students that you will return to the chart after the activities so the class can record what students have learned and compare it to early ideas about volcanoes.

Engage 2: The class will be shown samples of quartz, mica, calcite, talc, galena, sulfur, scoria, granite, sandstone, and schist. Samples will be set up in a science center. Give each student ten small sticky notes. On a prepared graph listing each mineral sample, make a class bar graph by asking the students to place a sticky note by each item they think is a mineral (have them put their name on the sticky notes). They do not have to use all the sticky notes. The sticky notes will make a bar graph showing students' ideas of which samples are minerals. Then ask students to answer the question, "How do we know when something is a mineral?" in their science notebook. Scan notebooks for students' ideas. Before discussion, remind students that all ideas are acceptable at this point and that we will be doing investigations to help answer these questions. Now ask students about the trends seen in the class bar graph and about their definitions of "a mineral." Ask, "Did you label all the samples minerals?" "Which ones did most of you think were not minerals?" List them on poster paper. Ask, "What are your ideas about the items that are not minerals?" Conclude by making a list of any questions the students have about minerals. Move to the explore phase by saying, "We are going to explore some properties of minerals and will come back to our ideas and chart after we finish our activities."

If you carefully examine the engage phase from the examples provided you will find that in each case the teacher provides an activity that uncovers the students' prior knowledge of the science concepts to be explore. Furthermore, the engage phase examples involve the students in making tangible their ideas and sets the stage to motivate them to participate in what's to come. In the engage phase, the teacher should be a keen listener to student ideas to find out what they know of the concepts and also what they do not know. During the engage phase all ideas are accepted and the teacher needs to create an environment for this to occur. This is important so that students feel free to share their ideas. After all, the main focus of the engage phase is to find out what students "think" about the topic to help you address misconceptions and gaps in their knowledge later as part of the instruction. Encouraging students' questions is appropriate in all phases; the engage phase is not the time to tell the students the answers to their questions or to correct their ideas. The bulk of their questions should be addressed later, during the explain phase.

Explore

The engage phase connects to and paves the way for the next phase, the explore phase. During the explore phase teachers encourage students to actively participate in learning tasks independently, and, more often than not, cooperatively with other students. During the explore phase the teacher provides directions and responds to students' questions regarding aspects of their investigative activities or experiments. Teachers are facilitators during the explore phase assisting students in seeking their own answers through the lesson's activities. During the explore phase, teachers are facilitators who observe and interact with students, asking questions and redirecting the students' learning or activities as appropriate. Remember, during this phase you should avoid giving answers or explaining concepts; instead, encourage and provide guidance for students to investigate on their own and seek solutions to the questions either collaboratively or on their own. Provided next are two examples of the explore phase.

Explore 1: Four students form a team. Give each team information about twelve different volcanoes located on the Ring of Fire. Give each team information clues on four volcanoes, but not the names (each student is responsible for taking the lead on one of the assigned volcanoes). Each member of the team must then verify that they agree with the lead investigator on the final identification of the volcano. Students will be given characteristics and important facts about these particular volcanoes. The students must use the information given to them and a map to determine which volcanoes they have. Give students resource sheets (volcano information, maps, a clues list and a list of computer websites). Once students have figured out which volcanoes they have been given, they must locate the volcano on the map and mark it with a stick pin. Safety: Students can pick up stick pins only after the teacher has verified their volcano location. No playing with pins. They are sharp!

Explore 2: Teacher will partner students and pass out the activity sheet for the students to complete for each mineral. Inform students they will be given six labeled mineral samples: calcite, talc, quartz, mica, sulfur, and galena. They are to become mineralogists and explore the properties of these six known minerals. Their work as mineralogists is to conduct tests to determine the hardness of their minerals using a penny, a nail, a fingernail, a microscope slide, an unglazed streak plate, and a steel file. Using Moh's Scale of Hardness and a mineral guide handout, teams will test and record their results in a table. Students will also determine and record other physical properties (crystal shape, streak, color, smell, and double refraction) of the minerals using their mineral guide handout. Safety: Wear safety goggles. Use the tools only as instructed. Handle materials carefully. Nails and files are pointed and slides can break. No eating or tasting in science labs. Report any accidents immediately.

The centerpiece of the explore phase is a student-centered activity that can take on a variety of forms and use a variety of equipment. During the students' activities, your role is to facilitate the activity by observing, listening, and questioning to assist students in developing and clarifying their understanding of the concepts or processes. Sometimes you may need to redirect or stop students and ask them questions as a check on their idea development and progress, but this is still not quite the time to fully explain the concepts. A favorite response to student questions during this phase is, "Great question. What do you think? How do you think we could find out?" You want to continue to encourage the students to seek answers on their own even though you may find them a bit resistant to do so. From our experience, we find this to be the case. Children very early on view the teacher as having all the answers and they quickly become programmed to having teachers "tell them the answer." Rarely are students given opportunities to carry out activities where they are expected to seek answers on their own. So if it feels like a new way of teaching for you, it is also a new way of learning for the students. Again, your questioning during the activity is critical in guiding students toward acceptable understandings of the science being explored.

An inquiry center allows students to explore an unseen world through a microscope.

The lesson examples demonstrate that the explore phase is about students learning in active ways. Also recognize that if you were a substitute teacher in either class, you would have a good idea of what the students are going to do by reading the explore phase of each lesson. Why? Because there are sufficient details included to make the explore phase clear. So when writing your lessons, remember to include enough details. It is useful to include student activity sheets and relevant handouts as well as safety notes because these items provide additional insights about the activities in the lesson (see Appendix B). Last, but not least, what you cannot see because it occurs in the classroom is that during this phase the teacher is actively listening, observing, and questioning students as they carry out the activity.

Explain

The third phase is known as the explain phase, but be warned—it does not mean that you, the teacher, do all the explaining. In fact, within the explain phase the teacher encourages students to explain concepts through a thoughtful line of questioning. The questions developed and asked by the teacher prompt students to respond using data they collected during the activities. Furthermore, the teacher encourages the students to give evidence to support their ideas. It is during the explain phase that teachers introduce formal definitions and explanations of concepts, drawing on students' experiences during the explore activities. Examine the following.

Explain 1:

1. Use a class map to show the teams' work on finding the names and location of their volcanoes. Using the finished map ask, "What patterns do you see?" Wait for student responses. (Students should say that they notice that the location of the volcanoes form a ring or curve, or are found along plate boundaries.) Ask other questions depending on where the students have placed their stick pins to indicate volcanoes.

2. Now let's look at a different map (crustal plate map with all U.S. volcanoes listed).

   Ask, "What do you notice about the location of U.S. volcanoes? Where is the highest concentration of volcanoes in the United States?" Wait for student responses. (Answer: Volcanic activity occurs on coastal areas or borders of crustal plates.) "We refer to this area as the Ring of Fire." (Show the area.) "How are U.S. volcanoes located with respect to the Ring of Fire?"

3. "What is your best thinking about what causes more volcanoes to be located along the crustal plates?" Wait for student responses. (Answer: Unstable land or crustal plate borders shift.) "What mainland U.S. volcano located on the Circum-Pacific Belt/Ring of Fire erupted in 1980?" (Answer: Mount St. Helens.) Use a Mount St. Helens video clip. "What type of explosion occurred at Mount St. Helens? What other types of materials can spew from volcanoes?" (Answer: volcanic bombs, ash, lava, foam in addition to lava, etc.)

4. "Let's recall what we learned earlier about the crustal plates and volcanoes. Does anyone remember what the top layer of the Earth is called?" (Answer: the crust.) "The crust of our planet is made up of sheets or slabs called plates. If we look at the map, what do you notice about how they fit together?" (Answer: jigsaw puzzle.)

5. "What is the layer underneath the crust called?" (Answer: mantle, athenosphere.) Using large rectangle clear glass baking dish, put cardboard pieces (crust) on a mixture of cornstarch and water (mantle), and demonstrate the meeting of crustal plates floating on the mantle. These plates sometimes move because the mantle has the property of plasticity. It can flow. To demonstrate, push down on one crustal plate edge and push the two plates together to show the plate changes (the cornstarch will push up between the plates). "Between the Earth's crust and the mantle is a substance called magma made of melted rock and gases. When two plates collide, one slides on top of the other; the one underneath is pushed down and magma may be squeezed up between two plates (with lava at the surface)." Discuss and demonstrate the plasticity of the cornstarch mixture and the subsequent movements. "Now, the Ring of Fire is where the North American and Pacific plates meet and it is an important area where shifts occur and magma can be pushed up. How else might the plates move?" (Answer: shift side by side or apart.)

6. "What other kind of Earth activity do you think might occur along the Ring of Fire (Answer: earthquakes, tsunami.) "Why do you think this is the case?" Discuss that there are often faults (large breaks in rock layers that can extend deep into the Earth) associated with volcanoes, especially along the Ring of Fire. Earthquakes may occur in an area before, during, and after a volcanic eruption, but they are the result of the forces connected with the eruption, and not the cause of volcanic activity. On the other hand, there is some evidence that earthquakes can trigger volcanic explosions.

"Let's return to our KWL chart and see how our new ideas now compare to our earlier ideas."

Explain 2: When students have completed testing the hardness of calcite, talc, quartz, mica, sulfur, and galena, and conducting other physical property tests, discuss their findings using a class chart for observing student team findings.
Questions to ask:
"What was the hardness of sulfur? How do you know this? What was the hardness of quartz? What is your evidence? What is the hardness of galena? What is the hardness of calcite? What is the hardness of talc? What is the hardness of mica? What is the hardest mineral we have? What is the hardest mineral on Moh's scale? How does Moh's scale of hardness help us identify minerals?" Ask these questions and then explain how Moh's scale works.

"Now let's focus on the findings you made using streak plates, color, smell, and crystal shape properties. What physical properties are found for sulfur? What did the streak test show for sulfur? What do you notice about the odor of sulfur? Did any of the other minerals you tested have an odor? What does streak tell about the mineral? What did you notice when you put the clear calcite on a piece of newspaper? Does calcite have a metallic or a nonmetallic property? What did you notice about the way mica breaks? Which minerals have obvious crystal shapes? What did you notice about talc?

"What we have examined in the activity is known as the physical properties of minerals. How would you define a physical property? Why do you think we need to use more than one property to identify a mineral? Which of the tests are most useful? Why?" Bring out other quartz samples of different colors. Show them to the students and ask if they see a problem with using only color to identify minerals. "Do you have any questions about any of the tests or physical properties of minerals? Okay, so look at the class bar graph we made at the start of the lesson and compare it to what we have learned about minerals. What have we learned to help us distinguish between the items we thought were minerals and those we thought were not? Now, look at the samples that are not minerals. What are these samples if they aren't minerals?" (Answer: rocks.) Highlight the difference between minerals and rocks. Concept: Physical properties of minerals are used by mineralogists to help determine the identity of a specimen. Some of the tests or observations can be conducted easily (such as streak, color, luster), and others require laboratory equipment. In general, a single property is not enough to identify the mineral because many minerals share the same physical properties. Examination of several of a mineral's physical properties often results in a unique set of physical properties that can be used to identify the mineral. Common physical property tests include hardness, color, luster (indicates how much the surface of a mineral reflects light and whether it is metallic or nonmetallic, greasy, silky, etc.), odor, streak (refers to mineral in powder form, which is the true color), crystal shape, and cleavage (refers to how minerals break—e.g., along the flat planes or angles).

You have undoubtedly noticed that the explain phase is dominated by the use of questions associated with the explore phase activity and with the concepts to be taught. The questions should evoke students' ideas and explanations of the activities as well as provide explanations for new concepts or processes. By careful selection of questions, a teacher can encourage students to use their evidence (from the activity or other resources) to justify what they know and have found. The questions in the volcano example were developed around the information sheets on volcanoes, maps the students worked on, and information from a website students explored. In the mineral example, the questions focus on data from testing mineral characteristics and other resources to draw out their ideas of physical properties tests for identifying minerals. Neither sample of the explain phase includes all questions asked during the actual lessons, but each sample uses questions that draw out students' explanations, leading to concept development, which is central to this phase.

Besides questioning, the teacher's role during the explain phase is to provide students with complete explanations, definitions, and vocabulary associated with the concepts explored by the students. You may have noticed that the volcano example used a demonstration to enhance student understanding of the process of plate movement associated with volcanic activity. Furthermore, with the volcano and mineral explain phases students return to the engage activity to reflect on their earlier ideas, which may include misconceptions or gaps in understanding. This strategy gives students the opportunity to rethink their prior ideas. For teachers, this strategy is an opportunity to challenge students' earlier ideas based on new information. Finally, you may have noticed a brief concept description with the mineral example that could also be used by the teacher to bring the explain phase to a close with a summary of the key ideas. The volcano example embeds the concepts within the question-and-answer sequence. Both ways are useful and serve to focus and guide the teacher in developing the concepts with the students. So, remember during the explain phase to carefully craft questions. Well-crafted questions assist students in constructing science concepts using their experiences, data, and evidences, while also providing appropriate vocabulary and explanations needed for students to develop the key ideas.

Elaborate

The fourth phase is the elaborate phase. In this phase of the lesson, students use knowledge of the concepts, vocabulary, and processes learned during earlier phases of the lesson. With that in mind, the purpose of the elaborate phase is to have students apply or extend their newly constructed knowledge in a different context. Consider the following:

Elaborate 1: Students will work with their teams using the Smithsonian–United States Geological Survey website, which updates international volcanic activity weekly. Students will create an international newscast updating the audience (class) on current volcanic activity in their assigned region. Students will use maps to present volcanoes found in their assigned region, give a brief overview of each volcano's past and current activity (including earthquakes), as well as its location relative to crustal plate borders. Resources: The Global Volcanism Program at http://www.volcano.si.edu/ and the Smithsonian/USGS Weekly Volvanic Activity Report at http://www.volcano.si.edu/reports/usgs/.

Elaborate 2: Student teams of three will be given an activity sheet that lists the minerals corundum, beryl, and quartz. They will use what they have learned about minerals to research and identify what gemstones come from each of the minerals. (Answers: rubies and sapphires are extracted from corundum, emeralds are from beryl, and amethyst is a form of quartz.) Each student will take the lead on researching library resources and websites for one of the minerals, and must teach the team members about the mineral (its streak, hardness, luster, etc.) and describe the gemstone associated with it.

During the elaborate phase, the science teacher asks questions and monitors students' use of the concepts, ideas, and processes during the student activity. In each of the elaborate examples, students use previous terms and concepts, as well as previous data and skills in a new context. At its best, the elaborate phase allows students to apply the ideas and processes in an authentic or everyday context. For instance, the elaborate phase of the volcano lesson asks students to use an active website, the Global Volcanism Program, to explore current volcanic activity. The elaborate phase in the mineral lesson creates a problem for the student mineralogists to solve.

Evaluate

The last phase of the 5E model is the evaluation phase. Before going further, we need to point out that to be able to write an effective evaluation, a lesson must have instructional objectives. Objectives are the road maps for a lesson plan and serve to keep you focused on the learning outcomes. For examples of effective instructional objectives and the essential characteristics of objectives see Appendix A. So how do we know if the students have learned what we wanted to teach as stated in the instructional objectives? If you are thinking it is time to assess or evaluate students, then you are correct. Formative assessment, as a practice, should be ongoing throughout the lesson. Effective science teachers formatively observe and assess students' learning throughout inquiry lessons. In the evaluation phase, the focus is on finding out whether and how well the students have achieved the instructional objectives. The evaluation phase must align with the objectives to demonstrate the degree to which students' have achieved the objectives of the lesson. You simply cannot create an effective evaluation or a lesson without knowing the objectives and designing activities around them. Therefore, we have included the objectives and the evaluations for the lessons in the following examples.

Go to the SAGE Study Site at **www .sagepub.com/ goldston** to access the 5E Lesson Plan that accompanies this lesson.

Volcano lesson objectives

1. Students will be able to explain the Ring of Fire as an area of frequent volcanic activity associated with movement of plates at the crustal boundaries.

2. Using a map, students will be able to locate the Ring of Fire.

3. Students will be able to apply the terms "magma," "lava," "crustal plates," "mantle," "crust," and "plasticity" while describing volcanic activity.

4. Students will be able to give a rationale for earthquake activity along crustal boundaries.

Evaluation 1

Students will complete the following written evaluation:

1. Mark two areas of volcanic and earthquake activity on the map given to you. Write your reasons for selecting the areas and give a rationale for the earthquake and volcanic activity in the areas you marked.

2. What is the Ring of Fire? Using your map locate the Ring of Fire. (Have students circle A, B, C, or D marked on the map.)

3. Using the terms "magma," "lava," "crustal plates," "mantle," "crust," and "plasticity" explain the processes that contribute to increased volcanic activity along the Ring of Fire. The following rubric is used for scoring the evaluation exercise (see Table 7.2).

Table 7.2 Volcano Lesson Rubric

	5 Points	3 Points	1 Point	0 Point
Question 1	Identifies two areas correctly	Identifies one area correctly		Does not identify any areas correctly
Question 1	Explains causes for volcanic/earthquake activity	Partially explains (few errors) causes for volcanic or earthquake activity	Partially explains (major errors) causes for volcanic or earthquake activity	Gives inaccurate causes for volcanic /earthquake activity or makes no attempt
Question 2	Gives complete description of the Ring of Fire	Partial description of the Ring of Fire (few errors)	Partially describes the Ring of Fire (major errors)	Gives inaccurate description of the Ring of Fire or makes no attempt
Question 3	Uses all five to six terms correctly in explanation of volcanic activity along Ring of Fire	Uses at least three to four terms correctly in the explanation of volcanic activity along the Ring of Fire	Uses at least one to two terms correctly in the explanation of volcanic activity along the Ring of Fire	Lacks correct use of terms in the explanation of volcanic activity along the Ring of Fire

Mineral Lesson objectives

1. Students will be able to explain how each physical property (hardness [Moh's scale of hardness], streak, crystal shape, and luster) is used to identify minerals.

2. Students will be able to state the benefits of using more than one physical property when identifying a mineral.

3. Given necessary guides for physical properties of minerals, students will be able to apply the appropriate tests to identify unknown minerals and explain how they are determined.

Go to the SAGE Study Site at **www .sagepub.com/ goldston** to access the 5E Lesson Plan that accompanies this lesson.

Evaluation 2

Students will complete the following written evaluation:

1. Describe the following:

   Moh's scale of hardness
   Streak
   Crystal shape
   Luster

2. Why do mineralogists examine several physical properties to identify minerals?

3. You will be given four numbered unknown minerals. (They are feldspar #1, gypsum #2, graphite #3, salt #4.) Your job is to determine the physical property requested for each mineral below and describe how you determined the identity of your mineral. You have information sheets on Moh's scale of hardness and materials for testing hardness, streak, crystal types, cleavage, and luster. Record your answers in Table 7.3.

Table 7.3 Mineral Identification Response Sheet

Physical property	Answer	Name the mineral	Describe what you did to determine each physical property
What is the hardness of mineral 1?			
What is the streak of mineral 2?			
What is the luster of mineral 3?			
What is crystal shape of mineral 4?			

In the volcano and mineral evaluation examples, you find that each evaluation item corresponds to each of the objectives. This is imperative, because this allows you to determine if each of the objectives is met. Furthermore, because the items of the volcano evaluation are student-generated responses there is a need for a **rubric** with criteria to determine the level of the student's proficiency. With student-generated responses there may be partially correct responses that warrant criteria to assess them. Because of the potential variations in student answers, a rubric is useful to provide the learner with feedback. The mineral evaluation answers are either correct or incorrect for two categories so there is no need for criteria. However, look at the last category in the table. Would a rubric with criteria be useful for determining a student's level of proficiency in describing the physical properties? Possibly, but the teacher is looking at which tests the students conducted to ascertain the mineral identification. Thus, the rubric is not critical because the responses are limited.

Now, return to the paired examples of the 5E phases earlier in the chapter. If you chose Engage fifth grade, Explore fifth grade, Explain third grade, Elaborate fourth grade, and Evaluate third grade as the better examples of the phases, you are on target. If you look at the correct choices and identify the characteristics of each phase it will be clear what makes it the better choice. Finally, were you wondering if you put the helicopter lesson back into the proper sequence for inquiry? If you chose Segments 3 (Introduction), 5 (Engage), 1 (Explore), 6 (Explain), 4 (Elaborate), and 2 (Evaluate) in that order, you have the proper sequence for inquiry. Congratulations! You're on your way to creating effective science inquiry lesson! The completed lessons plans on mineral and volcanoes can be found at the end of the chapter. Now it is time to see if you can apply what you have learned about the 5E inquiry lesson.

Elaborate

A Lesson Redesign: 5E Inquiry

As teachers, we do not always write lessons from scratch. In fact we often modify activities or other lessons from textbooks, trade books, and other resources. This authentic assignment is one you will probably do many times throughout your teaching career.

For this task you are challenged to take a lesson plan or an activity and turn it into your own 5E inquiry lesson. Go to Science NetLinks at www.sciencenetlinks.com and locate the lessons tab. There you will find a large variety of science lessons for Grades K–2, 3–5, and 6–8.

Your assignment is to select a lesson and modify it to fit the 5E inquiry model. As you modify the activities, consider whether you are making the lesson a directed, guided, or full inquiry lesson. Include the appropriate National Science Education Standards (NSES) (National Research Council [NRC], 1996) or state standards (most states display their standards on the state department of education websites; a few states may not have state standards so you may have to refer to local standards). Because you are modifying a lesson created by someone else, don't forget to cite the source. In your lesson include the grade level, instructional objectives, and the 5E stages of the inquiry model. Also make sure to modify the evaluation phase to match your objective(s); if you use the evaluation phase presented, make sure the objectives are written to match. You may do this by using **backward planning**. This means to simply start with writing or revising the objectives and then go directly to developing the evaluation phase (and a rubric if needed) to match the objectives. Last, complete the rest of the lesson. After you complete your modified lesson, take a moment to reflect on the original plan. What stages of the 5E were easy to identify in the original lesson? What stages were missing in the original lesson? What other elements of an effective science lesson may be missing in the original lesson? What is the advantage of using a 5E model over the way the lesson what originally presented. What phase modifications were easy to make? Why do you think this is so? What phase modifications were more difficult? Why do you think this is so?

Evaluate

Evaluating a 5E Inquiry Lesson Plan

Part1: To evaluate your knowledge and skill in using a 5E inquiry model for lesson planning, your instructor may give you a lesson plan to evaluate using the 5E inquiry lesson plan rubric. If not, take the lesson you just modified and switch with a partner to become a critical reviewer. To evaluate the lesson plan use the 5E inquiry lesson plan rubric (Goldston, Day, Sundberg, & Dantzler, 2010), which contains the characteristics of the 5E inquiry phases as well as other elements normally found in written lesson plans, see Table 7.4. Examine the 5E inquiry lesson plan rubric. How does it compare to the learning cycle? What are the key characteristics of the phases? After evaluating the lesson answer the following: "Did using the rubric help in conceptualizing the aspects of each stage of the inquiry model? What feedback would you suggest for the lesson? What score did you give the lesson plan? What are the strong points of the lesson? What are some benefits for using rubrics?"

Managing Science Inquiry Activities

As you may have guessed, managing inquiry lessons involves more than what is seen during the actual teaching process. Inquiry-oriented science teachers know that most of the preparation for inquiry lessons is done in advance of teaching. In general, when preparing to conduct any inquiry activity it is useful to ask yourself, "How can the classroom space be made suitable for the activities? Does the activity or laboratory space need to be different from a discussion area? What do I need to consider if students are rotating through inquiry stations? How may I use science centers? How should the materials be arranged for accessibility? What safety issues should be addressed?" A primary means of anticipating how to design effective inquiry lessons is to make sure that you try out any activities you use with students before doing them with students. Your familiarity with the activities will help you to anticipate many of the management or safety issues related to the lesson (see Appendix B). The following additional tips are not intended to be comprehensive, but will address some of the common issues associated with managing science inquiry activities.

When you use hands-on activity stations with teams of students rotating through them in a given timeframe, it is important to set them up in different areas around the room with space provided for teams to work. In addition, take care to set up the activities in each station to take about the same amount of time to complete. Just consider for a second what would happen if a team of students finishes their station and has to wait ten minutes to proceed. It doesn't take much of an imagination to foresee problems that can occur. So, design stations in such a way that the teams finish in about the same time; you might also design a couple of "Wait Stations" with additional activities for teams to do if they finish before the allotted time.

From an instructional standpoint, before you begin any hands-on inquiry activity, give directions to students before handing out materials to avoid unnecessary distractions. Given the choice of exploring the materials or listening to you, the materials will always win. In addition, set expectations for behavior before starting the activities and remind students to return materials to their original condition when done. When giving directions for rotational activities, explain the rotational sequence and model how students

Table 7.4					5E Inquiry Lesson Plan Rubric (ILP)
0	1	2	3	4	Concepts and/or skills selected for the lesson align with National Science Education Standards and relevant state/local standards.
0	1	2	3	4	The lesson plan contains objectives that are clear, appropriate, measurable, and align with the assessment/evaluation.
0	1	2	3	4	Materials list is present and complete.
					Exploration—Phase 1
					(Engage and Explore)
					Engage item 1
0	1	2	3	4	The **engage** of the exploration phase: Raises student interest/motivation to learn. Raises questions from children. Elicits students' prior knowledge. Leads into the exploration.
					Explore item 1
0	1	2	3	4	During the **explore** phase, students are actively working on the learning task. When appropriate, teacher questions evoke the learners' ideas and/or generate new questions from students. Student inquiry may involve student questioning, manipulating objects, developing inquiry skills (as appropriate) and developing abstract ideas.*See list of typical inquiry skills.
					Explore item 2
0	1	2	3	4	Learning activities in the **exploration** phase are student centered and involve hands-on/minds-on activities.*** See NOTES for examples of activities.
					Explore item 3
0	1	2	3	4	The inquiry activities show evidence of student learning for formative/authentic assessment.** See NOTES for a list of formative assessment methods.
					Invention—Phase 2
					(Explain)
					Explain item 1
0	1	2	3	4	There is a logical transition from the exploration phase 1. There are questions (mixed divergent and convergent) for interactive discussion led by teacher or students. Questions (regarding the activity/or data collected) lead to the development of concepts and skills. Includes a complete explanation of the concept (s), terms, and/or skill(s) taught.
					Explain item 2
0	1	2	3	4	The explain phase provides a variety of approaches to explain and illustrate the concept or skill. For example approaches might include but are not limited to the use of technology, virtual field trips, demonstrations, cooperative group discussions, panel discussions, interview of guest speaker, video/print/audio/computer program materials, teacher explanations.
					Explain item 3
0	1	2	3	4	The discussions or activities allow the teacher to assess students' present understanding of the concept or skill through appropriate formative/authentic assessment.

(Continued)

Table 7.4	(Continued)				
					Expansion–Phase 3
					(Elaborate and Evaluate)
					Elaborate item 1
0	1	2	3	4	There is a logical transition from the explain phase.
					The elaborate learning activities provide students with the opportunity to apply and extend the newly acquired concepts and skills into new areas.
					Elaborate item 2
0	1	2	3	4	The elaborate learning activities encourage students to find real-life (everyday) connections with the new concepts or skills.
					Evaluation item 1
0	1	2	3	4	The lesson includes summative **evaluation**, which can include a variety of forms/approaches.
					Evaluation item 2
0	1	2	3	4	The **evaluation** matches the objectives. **See NOTES for list of some methods of evaluation.
					Evaluation item 3
0	1	2	3	4	The **evaluation** criteria are clear, appropriate, and measurable (i.e., rubrics).

_____ Points

Scoring Criteria

4	Excellent	All elements are present, complete, appropriate, and accurate, with rich details. Another teacher can use the plan as written.
3	Good	Most of the elements are present, complete, appropriate, and accurate, with rich details. Another teacher could use the plan with a few modifications.
2	Average	Approximately half of the elements are present, complete, appropriate, and accurate, with some details. Another teacher could use the plan with modifications.
1	Poor	Few of the elements are present, complete, appropriate, and accurate, with few details. Another teacher would have to rewrite the lesson in order to implement the lesson.
0	Unacceptable	Key elements are not present. Descriptions are inappropriate. Plan lacks coherence and is unusable as written.

Notes:

*Typical inquiry (process) skills include predicting, hypothesizing, observing, measuring, testing, recording, graphing, creating tables, and drawing conclusions.

**Typical formative assessment methods: activity or data sheets, science journals, concept maps, writing assignments, art work, drawings/charts, graph, quiz, test, PowerPoint presentation, I-movie, movie, cartoons, KWL charts (three column chart with headings: a) What I know about X; b) What I want to know about X; and c) What I learned about X). Recall that evaluation comes from the culmination of the formative assessments used during the lesson.

***Examples of appropriate experiences are the use of technology, Internet field trips, field trips, hands-on/minds-on learning activities, cooperative group discussions, panel discussions, interview of guest speaker, video/print/audio/computer program materials, teacher explanations, Webquest, TrackStar, I-movie, and PowerPoint.

Source: With kind permission from Springer Science+Business Media: *International Journal of Science and Mathematics Education, 8*(4), 2010, Goldston, M. J., Day, J., Sundberg, C., Dantzler, J., Psychometric analysis of a 5E learning cycle lesson plan assessment instrument.

change stations. Assigning the stations a number assists students in staying in the proper sequence. Timing is critical when setting up inquiry activities or stations, so use a timer or assign students as time keepers to signal when it is time for teams to clean up and change stations. One last point: Provide enough time for the teams to complete the activities or stations. If it takes you fifteen minutes to complete the center, it usually takes students longer to complete it. In addition to stations, you may wish to set up science inquiry learning centers where students can work on a variety of content and science process skills individually or in teams. They can be set up in a variety of ways to enhance student learning (see Appendix C).

Inquiry activities in K–8 classrooms are most frequently carried out by grouping student's desks in clusters of two to four students each. You may already have observed such desk arrangements in classrooms. As with the inquiry stations, managing the activities means you need to determine the individuals in each team. Using cooperative strategies and assigning each student a role in the team is important to ensure all students are actively engaged in their learning. Another decision you must make is to determine whether students pick up materials in a central location or have sets of materials for each team. Finally, from experience, we recommend that you always build in extra time when doing inquiry activities. They take longer to complete than traditional approaches.

Sometimes you will find students' desks arranged in rows; while not as easy, hands-on activities can still occur. However, seeing desks arranged in rows typically implies a teacher-centered, whole-class instructional approach. For instance, the teacher may need to present a demonstration, lead a discussion, give out instructions, or simply gain students' attention. While you can easily engage in a whole-group discussion with student desks clustered in groups, it is much more difficult to conduct inquiry activities with students sitting in rows and facing the teacher. The point here is that room arrangement can help or hinder learning tasks, so consider the physical arrangement of the room as you plan your lessons.

You may find that doing inquiry activities with students presents some challenges with classroom management. Noise, movement, and activity are to be expected. However, it is nothing that cannot be addressed with some advanced planning. Suppose second-grade students have finished making and identifying fingerprints types to solve a crime. You are ready for them to discuss their findings, but as is often the case with inquiry activities, the students are really "into the activity" and not ready to stop. You ask for their attention; unfortunately it is noisy and they continue without hearing you. There are many approaches you could use to get their attention, so be clever and make it fun. You could do the clap-pat-finger, snap, ring a bell, whisper, or turn the light off and on a couple of times. These approaches will gain students' attention faster than raising your voice. If you start off the year teaching an attention getting strategy, students quickly learn it so when you clap-pat-finger snap it means, "Please stop and look at the teacher." With the finger snap, students will even join in to help get everyone's attention. Okay, now that you have the second graders' attention, you probably won't keep it long. Why is that? Remember, they still have all those "cool" materials in front of them. To prevent students from continuing to play with materials, you can ask that they put the materials back in the tub or container, put the items in the center of the table, or you can simply collect the materials. If your classroom has a laboratory or activity area separated from the discussion area, then all that is needed is to move students to the discussion area, which signals a different kind of activity. There are many aspects to managing inquiry instruction, but if you plan in advance for the inquiry activities, arrange the room for interactive discussions of ideas, and support students' independence with hands-on tasks, then your classroom can become an exciting, positive community for learning science.

Summary

In this chapter, we have taken the journey into planning 5E inquiry lessons with a detailed focus on each of the five phases, guided by the lesson's objectives for learning. Each phase has its own characteristics; when sequenced appropriately, it leads to an active inquiry approach. The 5E inquiry approach gives students the chance to experience science processes and concepts firsthand. In doing so, students construct their own ideas based on the activities and their findings. Their ideas are then heard, challenged, clarified, and the concepts further developed during an interactive, teacher–student discussion as part of the 5E lesson approach. As a teacher, shifting your thinking away from didactic approaches where you explain the concepts first followed by activities to one where students explore first with the teacher assisting them in constructing science concepts is nothing short of conceptual change in your view of science teaching. Have patience: With time and practice you will find using inquiry a motivating and effective approach for teaching science.

By now you know that inquiry instruction in science takes much more than constructing a lesson plan. In fact, it means carefully thinking about the ways you will manage students, materials, and the physical arrangement of classroom. Furthermore, you need to make sure you have a safe learning environment that promotes effective science learning for all students. Safety considerations about the physical arrangement of the room and how students work with materials and science equipment, as well as planning accommodations for learners with special needs, are all important for science inquiry instruction. In closing, as you begin effective planning for science inquiry activities, remember to extend your planning to include the physical and social aspects of the environment, thus ensuring that all students will have access to a supportive and productive learning climate.

Annotated Resources

ScienceNetLinks (American Association for the Advancement of Science)

http://www.sciencenetlinks.com/matrix.php

Science Link: Lesson Index is a website that includes a large number of lesson plans. Many lessons are inquiry based, but there are also lessons that are not inquiry based. In addition to science resources, standards, and benchmarks, this site offers a large variety of science lessons cross-indexed by grade level, topic, or title. The ScienceNetLinks website also has a variety of other teacher resources, tools, and benchmarks.

The Educator's Reference Desk

http://www.eduref.org/cgi-bin/lessons.cgi/Science

This website provides many science lessons across the K–12 grade spectrum. Many of the lessons are inquiry based but are written in a variety of formats. In general, all of the lessons include a brief overview and have generally well-written objectives, activities, lists of materials, and resources. In some cases, assessment tools are also available.

Konicek-Moran, R. (2009). *More everyday science mysteries: Stories for inquiry-based science teaching.* **Arlington, VA: NSTA Press.**

This resource book is the second volume by the author. It includes fifteen stories to springboard teachers and their students into science inquiries as they make sense of the science that may explain the mysteries posed in the text.

Konicek-Moran, R. (2008). *Everyday science mysteries: Stories for inquiry-based science teaching.* **Arlington, VA: NSTA Press**

This resource book is a wonderful way to incorporate challenge and problem solving into science inquiry. There are fifteen stories in the text that span Earth, life, and physical science concepts. The author suggests using open-ended science stories to invite students and teachers into a journey of investigating, discussing, and writing about the concepts of science that help explain the mysteries. This is excellent for making literacy connections while staying focused on science.

Montana State University & the Council for Environmental Education (1995). *Project WET.* **Bozeman, MT: The Watercourse and the Council for Environmental Education.**

Project WET is an excellent resource for student activities, many of which can be conducted outdoors. The resource is for teachers and is designed to infuse innovative water-related activities into the classroom curriculum. The text has seven units or themes that include numerous creative, exciting activities for K–12 students. The hands-on activities incorporate different formats (whole- and small-group exercises, laboratory activities, and even service learning projects), all of which have been tested and used by teachers. This activity guide is available for low-cost or free workshops only. To find a workshop in your area, go to www.projectwet.org.

American Forest Foundation (2010). *Project Learning Tree.* **Washington, DC: American Forest Foundation.**

Project Learning Tree is a favorite resource for us! It includes ninety-six PreK–8 activities divided into five major themes: (1) diversity, (2) interrelationships (3) systems, (4) structure and scale, and (5) patterns of change. Each theme provides several activities for inquiry that are organized with background content, objectives, and interdisciplinary connections, to name a few. Activities use a variety of teaching formats to address environmental literacy and values of stewardship. This activity guide is available for low-cost or free workshops only. To find a workshop in your area, go to www.plt.org.

Bosak, S. (2010). *Science is. A source book of fascinating facts, projects and activities.* **Markham, ON, Canada: The Communication Project.**

Science Is. is a large collection of hands-on investigations, experiments, and projects that can readily be used in any K–8 science classroom. This resource book is a must for your classroom. The activities range from very short, quick activities that introduce basic concepts, and other activities that require more planning and more time. The book is divided into ten areas with forty topics filled with numerous fun-filled inquiries for you and your students to explore.

Kessler, J. (1997). *The best of wonderScience: Elementary science activities,* **vols. 1 & 2. New York: Delmar Publishing.**

The Best of WonderScience is a well-organized, two-volume resource for science teachers at the third- to eighth-grade levels. It is a must-have item for your classroom. Both volumes include activities covering ninety-seven different topics. All activities have been examined for safety and use inexpensive easy-to-find materials. The colorful illustrations of kids doing the activities and step-by-step directions make the activities easy and fun to do.

References

Atkin, J., & Karplus, R. (1962). Discovery or invention? *Science Teacher, 29*, 45–51.

Goldston, M. J., Day, J., Sundberg, C., & Dantzler, J. (2010). Psychometric analysis of a 5E learning cycle lesson plan assessment instrument. *International Journal of Science and Mathematics Education, 8*(4), 633–648.

Karplus, R. (1979). Teaching for the development of reasoning. In A. Lawson (Ed.), *1980 AETS yearbook: The psychology of teaching for thinking and creativity* (pp. 149–172). Columbus, OH: ERIC/SMEAC.

Karplus, R., Lawson, A., Wollman, W., Appel, M., Bernoff, R., Howe, A., et al. (1977). *Science teaching and the development of reasoning: A workshop.* Berkeley: Regents of the University of California.

Karplus, R., & Thier, H. (1967). *A new look at elementary school science: New trends in curriculum and instruction series.* Chicago: Rand McNally.

Lawson, A. E. (1995). *Science teaching and the development of thinking.* Belmont, CA: Wadsworth.

Maier, S. J., & Marek, E. A. (2006). The learning cycle: A re-introduction. *The Physics Teacher, 44*(2), 109–113.

Marek, E., Laubach, T. A., & Pederson, J. (2003). Preservice elementary school teachers' understandings of theory-based science education. *Journal of Science Teacher Education, 3*(14), 147–159.

Marek, E., Maier, S., & McCann, F. (2008). Assessing understanding of the learning cycle: The ULC. *Journal of Science Teacher Education, 19*(4), 375–389.

Settlage, J. J. (2000). Understanding the learning cycle: Influences on abilities to embrace the approach by preservice elementary school teachers. *Science Education, 84*, 43–50.

Trowbridge, L., & Bybee, R. (1996). *Teaching secondary school science: Strategies for developing scientific literacy* (6th ed.). Englewood Cliffs, NJ: Merrill.

Chapter 8

Assessment and Evaluation

A Guide for Science Instruction

Learning Objectives

After reading Chapter 8, students will be able to

- describe and distinguish between forms of assessment (alternative, authentic, performance, traditional),
- distinguish between assessment and evaluation, including the roles each holds in teaching and learning,
- demonstrate the alignment of instructional objectives with assessment,
- describe the purposes and uses of analytic and holistic rubrics, and
- apply the use of a rubric with assessment.

NSES TEACHING STANDARDS ADDRESSED IN CHAPTER 8

Standard C: Teachers of science engage in ongoing assessment of their teaching and of student learning. In doing this, teachers

- use multiple methods and systematically gather data about student understanding and ability;
- analyze assessment data to guide teaching;
- guide students in self-assessment;
- use student data, observations of teaching, and interactions with colleagues to reflect on and improve teaching practice; and
- use student data, observations of teaching, and interactions with colleagues to report student achievement and opportunities to learn to students, teachers, parents, policy makers, and the general public.

Source: Reprinted with permission from the National Science Education Standards, copyright 1996, by the National Academy of Sciences, Courtesy of National Academies Press, Washington, DC.

Consider students' reactions when you return their scored work or a test. There may be a range of reactions but most assessments are connected to a student's emotions.

Introduction

Take a moment to think back on your school experiences. Recall your thoughts and emotions when a teacher returned your graded work. Were you excited, unconcerned, or fearful of the results? Whatever the outcome of your assignment, good or bad, it is probable that you saw the grade as a personal and emotional reflection on you. Assessment, evaluations, and grades are connected to the affective domain. This connection often triggers feelings related to self-esteem and the way one views the discipline being graded. In fact, children may form a disposition toward science simply because of the grades they make in the discipline.

Remember, assessments and evaluations are more than red pens, happy faces, gold stars, and grades. So it is important for teachers to consider carefully why, how, when, and what we assess or evaluate because at some point, very early in formal schooling, the impact of assessment and evaluation affects the learner. The following quote by Albert Einstein is one that challenges teachers to really consider "what" we assess or evaluate.

> *"Not everything that counts can be counted and not everything that can be counted counts!"*
>
> —Albert Einstein

How might this relate to your experiences with assessment or evaluation? What examples can you describe to illustrate the quote?

Einstein's quote may well have captured the essence of how important it is for teachers to make clear to students why and how a task for assessment or evaluation "counts." While Einstein's quote reflects "what" counts, Ms. Wilson's narrative in Your Science Classroom: Team Meeting and Planning, portrays a different stance on "how" assessment for learning counts.

YOUR SCIENCE CLASSROOM:
Team Meeting and Planning

Ms. Wilson wanted all her students to meet her learning outcome. She announced to her fourth-grade students that if their reports on the electricity (circuits) investigation was accepted, they would receive an A, and if it was not accepted they would receive it back for revisions. After revisions, if it was accepted then they would also

Teaching Standard B: 1 & B: 2

How does this scenario reflect these standards?

receive an A. Now, as you might expect, some children asked what would happen if they still needed further revisions. Ms. Wilson replied that they could redo it until it was accepted. At that time they would receive an "A," because they had met the standards. She said, "Because I wasn't lowering the score for each retry, I worried there would be complaints that I wasn't being fair, but I had none."

Another concern for Ms. Wilson was time. She knew it would take more time to assess multiple submissions but decided to do it anyway. She created the rubric and went over it with the students. The rubric focused on students' demonstrating their knowledge of electrical flow in series and parallel circuits by means of drawing and writing. She waited for the completed projects and found that eleven of the eighteen children achieved the standards. Not great, but at least there were only seven to reassess. When the students' work was returned she said, "I was delighted to see children working and talking with others about ways to make it correct. Mind you, they were not copying— they were talking about what was weak or incorrect and discussing how it should be!" Only two children made revisions a third time. Though it did take more time, there were fewer reviews because only the parts that needed improvement were examined. All students succeeded and were actively focused on learning. At her team meeting she shared what she had done and asked, "Give me some feedback—what do all of you think about using this strategy?"

What are the trade-offs of assessing in this manner for students? What are the trade-offs for teachers? Would you like to be a learner in Ms. Wilson's classroom? Explain.

This short narrative shared by a practicing teacher profiles a teacher who is interested in all children learning science content and achieving success while developing positive dispositions toward science. Her emphasis, like that advocated in the National Science Education Standards (National Research Council [NRC], 1996), has shifted from assessment *of* learning, which creates an image of learning as defined by a grade, to assessment *for* learning, which creates an vision of learning with ongoing assessment used to modify teaching strategies that provide optimal learning opportunities for student success.

Consider your own experiences: Were your assignments focused on assessment *of* learning or assessment *for* learning? We hope the assignments were more in line with assessment *for* learning. In either case, assessment has already played a large role in your school experiences. It will play an even larger role in your career as a teacher. Assessment and evaluation are deeply embedded within the fabric of the educational system and throughout society. After all, don't we all assess ourselves and others from time to time? Of course we do, but in science education, assessment and evaluation are defined more specifically, as you will find in this chapter. At this point, however, it is important to recall that no matter how one assesses, our purpose is to find out what students know and what we can do to continually enhance their opportunities to learn science. In your journey to become an elementary or middle school teacher of science, we encourage you to reflect on issues of assessment by pondering the following: Can any assessment ever completely reflect another person's knowledge or skills? How does a score reflect a learner's knowledge? How many times have you looked at your own scored work and realized that you knew more than the task demonstrated? How do you decide how much is learned? What does an "A" or "B" student look like? Can you tell the difference? Yes, we ask many questions because assessment in any form is an extremely important aspect of teachers' work and a skill you must continually develop and refine. As you read this chapter and carry out the activities in the 5E model, the question remains: "How do we find out what students know and can do in science to continually enhance their opportunities to learn?" Once we have addressed this question, the next step is recognizing that assessment and instruction are unsurprisingly connected within the instructional setting.

Engage

What Is Assessment? What Is Evaluation?

Quick write: Take a minute and write down your description or definition of assessment. After you complete your ideas on assessment, write down your description or definition of evaluation. Diagrams or drawings will work as well. Keep your descriptions for comparison later as you complete the chapter. The next step is to explore assessment in a classroom activity.

Explore

Assessing Student Work

Your fourth-grade cooperating teacher has asked you to assess Laura Kate's work using the rubric she designed for the activity.

The activity: The letter-writing assessment is embedded within a two- to three-day classroom module during which students explore the circulatory system and health. The assessment is designed to challenge students to write and draw their understanding of the processes and science content knowledge learned during the activities within the structure of writing a letter.

Directions Given to the Students

You will write a letter to someone who is important to you (parents, grandparents, friend, teacher, or someone else you select). The letter should tell about the science you have been studying and what you have learned or found out. You may include drawings, calculations, diagrams, or tables. You may also include questions you have about the science content or processes you have been learning.

Students were given the rubric. The instructor discussed the rubric and the assessment with the children. The criteria in the rubric included the following (see Table 8.1):

(1) Explain the heart rate or pulse activity.

(2) Use the appropriate vocabulary.

(3) Incorporate three elements of letter writing (see below).

Letter-writing elements include (a) using correct standard English, (b) using correct letter form, (c) expressing opinions, (d) supporting arguments, (e) suggesting alternative procedures or

> **Teacher's Desk Tip: Addressing Diversity in Your Classroom**
>
> In this assessment example, be aware that it's important to be inclusive and sensitive to students from nontraditional families.

Table 8.1 Letter Writing Assessment Rubric for Heart Rate

Rubric	Quality			
Criteria	4	3	2	1
Understands and explains how to take a heart rate or pulse rate	Clear description of taking pulse rate; no errors in reporting; details and connections made to other learning	Some evidence of taking a pulse rate; some errors in reporting, and some connections to other learning	Description of pulse rate not fully explained, many errors in reporting, few to no connections to other learning	Description of pulse rate unclear, many errors, few details and few to no connections to other learning
Uses appropriate vocabulary	Use of scientific terms (four or more); no errors in term usage	Use of scientific terms (at least three); minor errors in term usage	Use of scientific terms (at least two); major errors in term usage	Use of at least one scientific term; errors in usage

solutions, (f) making writing consistent with the relationship between the writer and the addressee, and (g) expressing feelings about the meaningfulness of the activity. Now examine the letter by Laura Kate (see Table 8.2).

Laura Kate's Work Sample

On the back of her work, Laura Kate draws a picture of how a person takes a pulse rate (see Figure 8.1).

Now that you have analyzed the work given to you by your cooperating teacher, consider the following questions: What challenges or problems did you have in completing the rubric? What would you do to improve the task or rubric? What did learn about what Laura Kate can do or has learned from the task? Would you consider this an assessment or an evaluation? Explain.

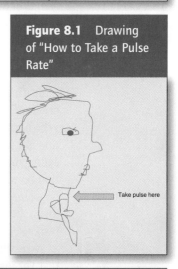

Figure 8.1 Drawing of "How to Take a Pulse Rate"

Take pulse here

Table 8.2 Laura Kate's Work Sample

Dear Mom,

For homework I have to take your pulse. we learned how to take your Pulse in school. All you have to do is take your two fingers your point & middle fingers and put them below the side of your face (ether side).Then leave them there for a minite and count. The more food that you eat that put's fat on your body is the more the arteries are going to glog up. your arteries are the blood veins and when you put your fingers on your pulse you fill them going in and out. They are pumping blood. When you are finish with doing your pulse three thimes you have to average them. When you average you add all the numbers up. Then the you divide the answer and the numbers that you added you count them up. Well here is an example

$$23$$
$$24$$
$$\underline{26}$$
$$3/113$$

That is how you average. Now here is example of how you do your pulse. on back drawing

Love,

Laura Kate

Explain

Focus Questions

1. What is assessment? What is evaluation?
2. Why is assessment important?
3. What role does assessment play within the classroom, school, and community?
4. What forms can assessment and evaluation take?
5. What types of assessment strategies are appropriate in an inquiry-based classroom?
6. What are the advantages and limitations of various assessments?

Assessment or Evaluation: What's the Difference?

In general, **assessment** is viewed as the act of collecting and interpreting information about students, whereas **evaluation** is passing a judgment (Northwest Regional Educational Laboratories, 1994, 1998). Consider for a moment that a student receives an 81% on a task; that score represents a measure of the student's knowledge for that given task. However, when evaluating the student's work a teacher asks, "Is this good enough to meet the designated criteria?" Decisions about the quality of students' assessments are considered evaluations. Whether the assessment represents a happy face, numerical score, or a letter grade, evaluation is a judgment on the quality of the learning. Assessment and evaluation are often used synonymously and indeed the difference between them is subtle. If you don't make a distinction between the two terms, and many people do not, keep in mind that assessment is an ongoing, systematic process. Both assessment and evaluation should include a variety of forms, both traditional (e.g., multiple-choice tests) and alternative (e.g., student-generated responses).

Assessing and measuring knowledge in any form is never complete nor is it totally objective. For instance, if you create a multiple choice test or develop criteria for a student project, the test items you select or the questions you pose for the project are based on the subjectivity of what you find important for the students to know. So, in this sense objectivity is a myth. However, that doesn't mean that assessments cannot be effective. Effective assessments of learning can be accomplished by collecting assessment data from many sources. Multiple assessments give teachers a more comprehensive understanding of what students know and can do. Finally, effective assessments require that the assessment administered to students align with the learning objectives and instructional approach while recognizing and valuing the different learning styles of the students.

Assessment and Its Role in Supporting Education

Assessment is a predominant feature of education in the United States. It is a mechanism for meeting standards and objectives, and measuring student learning. It takes on a variety of forms, both alternative and traditional, and in some cases the assessment becomes evaluation as seen in state-mandated, standardized testing. Good or bad, make no mistake, test score results affect individuals, programs, schools, and the community. With the reauthorization of the Elementary and Secondary Education Act of 1965, known today as No Child Left

Behind (2002), traditional standardized testing results are paramount to a student's success and are the measures that determine successful schools and the teachers therein. Clearly, it is essential that assessment, whether traditional or alternative, mirror the curriculum and comprehensively measure students' knowledge and skill. Within an inquiry science classroom where children are actively and creatively engaged in problem solving and critical thinking, you will find that alternative and traditional assessments provide useful data on student learning, albeit with different purposes. In preparing students for science in the twenty-first century, we must recognize that mandated testing is primarily based on lower levels of cognition. As the educator Kingman Brewster stated, "To many students of proven intellectual capacity, the prospect of 20 years of competition for nothing worthier than test scores dampens all inspiration." (*New York Times*, January 2, 1991). We must strive to assist students in acquiring the necessary skills of critical thinking for problem solving and use assessments appropriate to accomplish this goal and ignite intellectual inspiration.

Given the impact of legislation through No Child Left Behind (2002), and the accountability issues associated with national standards-based initiatives, it is important to understand the impact of assessment and ultimately evaluation from the perspectives of the various stakeholders (students, teachers, community members, administrators, and departments of education, to name a few). Therefore, we begin with the rationales driving assessment at the local school level that include the following:

- To make sure teachers have met the local or state standards, or both
- To make sure students meet local or state curricular objectives, or both
- To determine whether students have the skills and knowledge needed to proceed
- To make curricular decisions at the school-wide level
- To determine the quality of teaching and schools

External assessment at the state or national level communicates to students, teachers, parents, and the public what the state or nation considers important to teach and learn in school (Bond & Cohen, 1991). This broad public communication does the following:

- Validates what disciplines are important by assessing those disciplines as a part of the school function
- Influences policy to monitor the outcomes of instruction
- Shapes curriculum in both positive and negative ways

With the implementation of No Child Left Behind in 2002, these communications have been clearly demonstrated by the singular emphasis in our schools on reading and mathematics, both of which are highly monitored and tested throughout the year. Science and other disciplines have been marginalized in the elementary curriculum, and in some cases are rarely taught in the K–6 grade levels. In some states science testing in the elementary grades was not part of the No Child Left Behind mandate

BULLETIN BOARD

Assessment and Research

- Effective assessment is at the heart of successful decision making (Anderson, 2003).

- Assessment is derived from the Latin *assidere*, "to sit with" meaning to sit with the student. "It is something we do *with* and *for* a student, not something we do *to* them" (Wiggins [1992], cited in Green [1998]).

- "Teachers make somewhere between 800 and 1,500 decisions every day" (Kauchak & Eggen, 2005, p. 55).

- "Most teachers do not see assessment as part of decision making or something that makes them better teachers, but something they have to do to grade students and please parents or administrators" (Arends, 2003).

BULLETIN BOARD

Assessment and Communicating With Parents

The lists of words and phrases below are a sample from Shafer's (1997) publication *Writing Effective Report Card Comments* (pp. 42–45). She suggests the avoidance of some terms and the careful use of others when assessing children or communicating with parents can create a more supportive and a less stressful encounter.

Terms to Avoid	Positive Terms	Needs Improvement Terms
unable	thorough	could profit by
can't	caring	has trouble with
won't	excels at	benefits from
always	shows commitment	needs reinforcement in
never	has a good grasp of	shows a need for

between 2002 and 2007. During that time, the message to teachers was that their teaching priority was reading and mathematics. Now with renewed state testing of science in the fifth grade, science is again considered a valued part of the elementary curriculum. Students' science scores on standardized tests clearly influence local school systems' policies; decisions regarding instruction, professional development, and school improvement are made based on the analysis of student data as schools strive to meet annual yearly progress.

National and statewide assessments have become an important process within education. Ultimately for teachers, however, assessment is important in communicating to children and parents ways in which learning can be supported and enhanced for student success in the classroom. Therefore it is important for teachers to ask the question, "How is assessment used to improved instruction?" There are numerous responses to this question but the following are ones that we find teachers cite as the most important. Teachers state that assessment (a) serves to find out students' prior knowledge, (b) clarifies students' conceptual understanding, (c) shapes instructional decisions, (d) assists in placing students in productive learning groups, (e) communicates to students the teacher's expectations, (f) documents student learning, and (g) provides feedback to students and their parents.

In this section we have discussed the differences between assessment and evaluation, uses of assessment at the national and statewide levels, and uses of assessment by teachers to improve instruction. The next section addresses the important connection between classroom assessment and instruction.

Connecting Assessment and Instruction

As you have probably experienced as students yourselves, assessments can range from traditional multiple choice tests to alternative assessments. No matter what form assessment takes, the key to effective assessment is to align the assessment to the teaching objectives and the instructional approach used. In the following narrative, Ms. Lyle, a first-year teacher, shared her experience with assessment when using an inquiry science activity with her fifth-grade students.

Learning objectives can and should be assessed in a variety of ways. When choosing an assessment consider the balance between selecting an assessment that measures what is being taught and what can be learned about the students' knowledge against the time constraints associated with using the assessment. In other words, if you're going to use student interviews, which are time-consuming to develop and conduct, then use them to assess long-term gains of

YOUR SCIENCE CLASSROOM:
Matching Instruction to Assessment

Ms. Lyle was a first-year fifth-grade teacher and a science enthusiast. The next topic in her curriculum was on characteristics of invertebrates. Rather than teach directly from the text, she decided to explore invertebrates in the children's neighborhood, and she was very excited to begin. She planned various activities with insects, arachnids, and worms, activities that included collecting and examining samples of grasshoppers, beetles, spiders, praying mantises, bees, hummingbird moths, cabbage butterflies, and sulphur butterflies. She discussed safety, including handling animals with care and washing hands well after handling them. The children also created a worm habitat while observing and reporting on the behaviors of worms and changes they saw in the compost habitat. The children keep journals with drawings, generated questions (How does a worm poop? How do you know which end is which? What are the rings? How do grasshoppers lay eggs? What do the eggs look like? Who is Polyphemus? How are cocoons and chrysalises different?), participated in grand discussions, read the textbook, and conducted research to learn about the various invertebrates they collected. After two weeks, Ms. Lyle gave the children a multiple-choice test taken from their fifth-grade textbook. Throughout the explorations, Ms. Lyle was excited about all that she observed taking place with her students. They were engaged and learning! She just knew her students would do well on the test. After she scored the tests, she was heartsick. About two thirds of the class made very low scores on the test, and the highest scores were no more than average. She wondered where she'd gone wrong and couldn't understand the discrepancy of what she'd seen them do in the classroom with what they did on the test. So at the next team planning meeting, Ms. Lyle shared her story with her mentor who listened and then asked her what she thought went awry.

> **Teaching Standard C: 4 & C: 5**
>
> How does this scenario reflect these standards?

What do you think might account for Ms Lyle's students' poor test scores? As a member of Ms. Lyle's team, what feedback and suggestions would you offer Ms. Lyle to alleviate or prevent this problem from happening again?

---

key concepts or skills. For instance, it is more practical to use interviews as an assessment for students' mastery of key concepts at the end of a unit rather than to use them to assess a few science concepts taught within a lesson. In broad terms, effective assessment strategies do not just happen by luck. Effective assessment involves aligning the instructional approach and the objectives to the task or test to ascertain a comprehensive understanding of what students know balanced against the time it takes to develop, administer, and score it.

Assessments for Inquiry

Recall Ms. Lyle's story. On the one hand, she implemented student-centered inquiry strategies; on the other hand, though, when it came time to assess, she used a traditional multiple-choice assessment that was not tailored to her inquiry strategies and possibly not aligned to her learning objectives, which are not identified in the narrative. Teaching science as inquiry, by its nature, prompts the teacher to explore alternative ways to find out what students have learned and can do. This often requires assessments that go beyond those traditionally used. What other methods, besides traditional (multiple choice, True/False) assessments may be useful for science inquiry approaches in the classroom? During inquiry lessons students frequently learn through active, hands-on, minds-on activities and traditional tests often do not adequately assess these types of learning activities. For example, when we teach an inquiry-based sound lesson to second graders, we address the National Science Education Standard, "Properties of Objects and Materials," for K–4 grade levels (NRC, 1996, p.106). One learning objective is that students describe how sound is created by vibrations of various materials. A second learning objective is that children build a sound instrument (given a variety of items) and apply their knowledge of sound to change the pitch and volume of their instrument. Traditional tests are valuable for measuring factual knowledge, but here is a case where there is little match between a traditional assessment and the learning objectives. Consider for a moment how a classroom of students studying sound might appear. Imagine the students exploring sound activities in centers located around the room. In the centers, students use straws, balloons, string, cups, tuning forks, combs, and cans to identify characteristics of pitch and volume. Can you envision an assessment for this kind of instruction? Did you consider a task where student match pitch to its definition, or did you consider something else? The instructional objectives and pedagogical approach described in the sound activity are perhaps better suited to an alternative assessment such as the performance-based assessment described below.

Second-Grade Performance Assessment on Sound

Objective 1

Children will be able to demonstrate orally and in a written report that they understand sound is created by vibrations of materials using a self-made sound machine.

Objective 2

Given a variety of items, children will be able to (1) build a sound machine and (2) demonstrate orally and in a written report how to change the pitch and volume using a self-made sound machine.

National Science Education Standards: K–4 Properties of Objects and Materials. Sound is produced by vibrating objects. The pitch of sound can be varied by changing the rate of vibration.

Teacher Preparation

Children will explore sound activities in science centers, hold lively discussion regarding their explorations, and conduct additional activities to answer their questions.

After all the activities are completed, the teacher will ask the children to design and make a sound machine that has variable pitch and volume. A table will be set up with materials for the children to use. Other items for making a sound machine requested by students will be provided if available. They will be given sufficient time to create their machines and write their reports.

Go over the sound rubric to be used on the task with the students (see Table 8.3).

Directions to Students: You will make a sound machine from the available materials on the table. Your machines cannot be identical to any of the sound examples used in your previous activities. Your machine should be original in some manner. Your machine must do the following:

1. Produce sound

2. Demonstrate a change in volume

3. Demonstrate a change in pitch

When you complete your machine, be ready to present and explain how it works to the class.

1. Describe how your machine makes sound.

2. Demonstrate how your machine changes pitch and volume.

3. Complete the report (see below).

Table 8.3 Second-Grade Sound Analytic Rubric

Criteria	2	1	0	Comments
Did I tell how the sound machine works to make sound?	Clearly states how the sound is produced by a vibration of your machine	Not sure, not clear	Didn't state it	
Did I tell what pitch is?	Demonstrates a complete description of pitch (refers to the high/low sounds)	Vague description of pitch	Missed it or forgot it	
Did I show how to change pitch with my machine?	Demonstrates two or more pitch changes with the machine	Discussed some but slipped up on some of it	Missed it or left it out	
Did I tell what volume is?	Demonstrates a complete description of volume (refers to loudness)	Slid over volume	Didn't tell about it	
Did I show how to change volume with my machine?	Discussed and made two or more volume changes with the machine	Discussed in part but was not clear	Skipped it or missed it	

Alternative Forms of Assessment

In the example of inquiry presented, the alternative assessment and rubric are designed to assess students on the instructional objectives in a way that is similar to the way in which they were taught. It doesn't mean that a matching test would not work, but it does mean changing the objectives. The objectives as stated make it clear that the purpose of the activity is to ascertain the learners' knowledge of sound and their ability to apply that knowledge. This assessment makes transparent what they know and what they can do. We refer to assessments seen in the example as an alternative assessment.

MY SOUND MACHINE

Student name: _____

My sound machine is named _____

Draw a picture of your sound machine.

What do you need to do so that your machine will make sound?

How do you change the pitch?

How do you change the volume?

In general, **alternative assessment** is an umbrella term that defines those forms of assessment whereby students generate a response instead of selecting an answer (i.e., multiple choice, true/false, matching). Alternative assessments include any student-generated response seen in essays, short answers, oral presentations, demonstrations, photogalleries, and portfolios. In essence, alternative assessment is a broad term that encompasses both performance and authentic assessment, which are not mutually exclusive.

Performance assessment refers to direct, systematic observations of actual student performances and to the rating of those performances according to preestablished criteria. Some would argue that all assessments are performance assessments. However, we argue that not all alternative assessments are performance assessments. For instance, an essay is an alternative assessment but it is not a direct and systematic observance of a performance. When a performance assessment activity is embedded within a science unit it does not necessarily appear to be an assessment, we refer to this type of assessment as an **embedded assessment**. It may actually appear to be just another inquiry activity that students complete without teacher assistance. Could the sound machine assessment discussed earlier be an embedded performance assessment? Yes, it could, and it looks just like one more activity that is usually given during the middle or at the end of the unit.

Another form of alternative assessment is authentic assessment. **Authentic assessment** focuses on the learner's demonstration of content knowledge and skill in ways that resemble real life as closely as possible. Products of authentic assessment include oral tasks, written tasks, performances, or interviews, to name a few. The following illustrates an authentic assessment used with fifth-grade students.

Fifth-Grade Authentic Performance Assessment

Properties and Changes in Matter

Objective 1: Given a variety of materials, students will identify color change in their scientific report as evidence of chemical change.

Objective 2: Given a variety of materials, students will design a test, conduct the test, and explain in a scientific report which of the antacids tested is best in lowering the pH of stomach acid.

National Science Education Standards 5–8 grade levels

Physical Science

- Properties and changes in matter

  Substances react chemically in characteristic ways

  Scientific inquiry

  Abilities necessary to do scientific inquiry

  Design and conduct a scientific inquiry

  Develop descriptions, explanations, predictions, and models using evidence

  Communicate scientific procedures and explanations

Teacher Preparation

After a series of activities exploring acid–base interactions, pH, and neutralization reactions, students are directed to complete the following task. Provide materials and set up the equipment in an area that is accessible to all students. Go over the directions and safety procedures with the students and discuss using small amounts of substances in the tests. Prior to students beginning the activity go over the rubric with them so they understand how they are being assessed (see Table 8.4).

Safety

Wear safety glasses.

No eating or tasting in science labs.

Report any spills to the teacher immediately.

Table 8.4 Fifth-Grade Properties and Changes in Matter Analytic Rubric

Criteria	3	2	1	Comments
Did I describe what I observed when the chemicals reacted?	Observations were drawn or written with complete details	Observations were drawn or written with moderate details	Observations were drawn or written with few to no details	
Did I explain what happens when an antacid (base) is added to an acid?	Explained in detail the changes that occur (amounts added, color changes)	Explained most of the changes that occur (amounts, color changes)	Explained few of the changes that occur (amounts, color changes)	
Did I describe the test design completely?	Included all of the details in the report	Included most of the details in the report	Included only a few details in the report	

Directions to students

Your dad has been complaining about indigestion and takes an antacid. From the various materials available, your task is to design a test to demonstrate which antacid is best and explain how the antacid works.

Students are given an indicator (radish or red cabbage juice) and pH strips. They also receive a sample of vinegar or lemon juice. Students select two different antacids (crushed to powder) to use in their tests. Other necessary equipment (balances, filter paper, testing trays, tweezers, etc.) will be available for them to use. Students are encouraged to use only very small amounts of materials in their tests. Students write a report using the experiment guidelines that include the necessary components needed to conduct the tests to determine which antacid is best for their dad to use and describe how they know a chemical change occurred.

Students are assessed using a rubric that reflects the learning objectives of the task. As with the second-grade sound example earlier in this chapter, the rubric and report form were discussed in advance with the students. In this example, as you probably recognized, the students were applying their acquired knowledge of chemistry and scientific inquiry in an authentic, real-life application.

Alternative assessments, whether authentic, performance, or both, require products or processes that are often more open-ended than traditional assessment. Therefore, alternative assessments are viewed by some as more subjective than traditional forms because the task can be completed successfully in more than one way. Alternative assessments generally require rubrics that can take considerable time to create and often require several revisions. However, alternative assessments with sophisticated tasks can be useful in examining higher-order thinking and levels of learning that traditional tests cannot examine. In addition, well-developed alternative assessments generally provide opportunities for more authentic, interdisciplinary applications of science concepts than traditional assessments. However, the scoring of alternative assessments, without a doubt, takes much more time and often involves

FIFTH-GRADE SCIENCE EXPERIMENT: CHEMICAL CHANGE

Name:_____

1. What is the question you are trying to answer?

2. Remember to state how we operationally define "best."

3. Did I write my hypotheses?

4. Did I describe the variables?

   Independent

   Dependent

   Constants

5. Did I write the steps used in the experiment?

6. Did I write how I recorded data and observations?

7. Did I write a conclusion and state which hypothesis is accepted?

developing a scoring rubric in advance of the task assignment.

No matter what form of assessment is used, the following guidelines are suggested for creating effective assessment in your classroom (Wiggins, 1992).

- Provide opportunity for the learners to exhibit worthwhile knowledge and skills
- Foster the development of the learners' strengths
- Involve collaborative peer–peer and teacher–student interactions
- Strive for inviting, real-world application contexts
- Aim for "big ideas" or concepts in science
- Include challenges that integrate knowledge across disciplines
- Target the development of a quality product, not a single answer

As a novice, strive to use one or two or these guidelines when developing your assessments. It is difficult for even an experienced teacher to incorporate all of the guidelines into every assessment used. In either case, using the guidelines as a referent can assist teachers in creating effective assessments when selecting, designing and incorporating tasks for their science classroom. Bulletin Board: Alternative Assessment Products offers many examples that are appropriate for use in K–8 science classrooms.

Learning requires communicating with yourself, your peers, and informed others. It requires effort and a meaningful assessment of the effort. In the following sections on portfolios, self-assessment, and science journals, we examine alternative assessments that provide a venue for communicating one's learning.

BULLETIN BOARD

Alternative Assessment Products

A letter	Oral presentation
Advertisement	Pamphlet
Animated movie	Survey
Photonarratives	Play
Gallery (art, photographs, etc.)	Skit
Block picture story	Poetry
Chart or concept map	Press conference
Model	Prototype
Collage	Riddle
Comic strip	Science story
Demonstration	News story
Web quest	Slide show
Storyboard	Song
Puzzle	Television program
Journal	Video clip
Diary	Time line
Diorama	Brochures
Editorial essay	Create a rule
Experiment	Science tale
Family tree	Flip book
Game	Graph
Labeled diagram	Interview
Map with legend	Maze
Mobile	Instrument (sound)

Portfolio: Assessment Using Collections of Student Work

The key to assessing student's learning and the success of a science curriculum lies in the methods that assist a teacher and student in measuring progress toward instructional

TECH CONNECT: Online Student Portfolios

Portfolios can be powerful assessment tools and an exciting way for teachers, students, and parents to see the work and progress of the student. To find out more and view examples of portfolios, see Portfolios for Students and Teachers (K–12): TeacherVision.com located at http://www.teachervision.fen.com/assessment/teaching-methods/20153.html.

Read about how to create and use eportfolios for K–8 grade levels at Education-World.com located at http://www.educationworld.com/a_tech/tech/tech111.shtml. In addition here are a few sites with tools for creating electronic student portfolios:

Mahara Open Source eportfolios located at www.mahara.org

http://eportfolio.org/

http://docs.moodle.org/20/en/E-portfolio

goals. A large amount of a teacher's time is related to assessing student learning. To make science learning meaningful, it is important to frequently collect both formative and summative data about what children can do. Recall that **formative assessment** occurs during learning process, is often ongoing, and used to guide instruction. In short, formative assessment is assessment *for* learning. **Summative assessment** is assessment to determine whether the instructional objectives have been met. It is assessment *of* learning. Given the current testing climate, it is common in classrooms to see worksheets and tests composed of multiple choice, true/false, or matching items—all of which emphasize low levels of cognitive engagement, whether summative or formative in nature. This approach is entrenched in a history of educational evaluation that views these items as objective, equitable, and easy to score. Despite continued historical trends and the emphasis on standardized testing, talented teachers manage to provide students with a variety of assessment opportunities. In fact, after years of talking and working with creative teachers, we have found that many believe effective assessment should challenge students intellectually, engage them in the task, bring forth what they know and can do, measure student growth over time, and provide learners with authentic, real-world contexts. A portfolio is an effective assessment based on the teachers' criteria. Portfolios are challenging assessment tools that give students the opportunity to showcase their best efforts in a collection of their work.

The use of portfolios to assess students' performance received considerable attention in the mid 1990s along with the science reform initiative, Project 2061 (American Association for the Advancement of Science; AAAS, 1991). Since that time, portfolios permutated into many forms and there is no single design. They do not all look alike, nor should they. There is no formula for designing portfolios. The purpose and design can be determined by the teacher, student, or both. The versatility of the portfolio is considered one of its strengths. In general, portfolios are collections of students' work that are gathered over time to portray the learners' knowledge and skills. A portfolio is a representation of a learner's growth and provides rich opportunities for students to reflect on their own learning.

Just as a scientist decides what evidence is necessary to support a hypothesis, students also can decide what evidences of work represents their knowledge and skills. When they do so, a portfolio becomes a reflective, metagcognitive tool providing them with intellectual independence and autonomy regarding their own learning.

Because portfolios represent a range of work collected over time, both teacher and student gain insights into the individual's learning patterns and those experiences that influence the learning, not to mention the power they hold in demonstrating the learner's progress to parents. Despite the variations found in portfolios that are usually negotiated between the student and teacher, there are some common elements. For instance, portfolios have a purpose (content or skills specific), are dynamic (flexible), are student centered, and are a tool for reflecting on learning. In addition, a portfolio's adaptability is based on the criteria selected for its construction. In other words, its uniqueness is determined by its purpose, its use, its appearance, and its intended audience. The adaptability of portfolios makes them effective assessment tools that are used to help students assess their own progress; assist teachers in making instructional decisions; communicate student growth to parents, teachers, and administrators; and help educators assess their program and curriculum goals.

Journals or Science Notebooks

Journals, also known as science notebooks, are practical, versatile tools for the science classroom. Entries can be structured by having students write a response to a specific question or content topic. They also can be unstructured with reflective writing of personal choice. In either case, science provides exciting content for connecting to language arts through expository writing in journal entries. In addition, the writing process provides a means for communication between the teacher and student or, if journal buddies are used, student to student. Many educators find that journal writing strengthens children's cognition by fostering the organization of language. Writing can prompt links to new information while helping students construct meaning of the classroom experiences and the natural world. Students build concepts by collecting information and applying their new ideas in this case through writing. Journal entries provide teachers with a practical tool for viewing students' thinking, dispositions, and skills. Writing about science content or processes can evoke metacognitive thinking in students, a form of internal dialogue that can develop deeper understanding. Journals or science notebooks enable students to describe their own ways of seeing and thinking about the science concepts constructed through their individual or shared experiences. In addition, teachers can use journals or science notebooks as an assessment tool for inquiry by having students include investigation notes like observations, drawings, charts, graphs, diagrams, and calculations (Klenchy, 2008; Shepardson & Britsch, 2001).

The following is an example of a journal entry written by a first grader. Ashia's class was exploring the question of which type of ball (ping-pong ball and golf ball) has the better bounce. The students were given two different kinds of balls to create a fair test to determine which ball bounces higher. They conducted four trials, spotting the height each time the ball bounced. They spotted how high the ball bounced by making a mark on a piece of chart paper taped to the wall. After the testing, Ashia wrote in her journal,

BULLETIN BOARD

Science Portfolio Ideas

Introduction

Table of contents

Lab reports (experiments or investigations)

Unit or chapter tests

Project examples of best work (self or teacher selected)

Photonarratives

Photographs of performance assessments

Written report

Book reports (on scientists, science concepts)

Samples of science journal entries or reflections

Drawings, diagrams, or models

Interactive historical vignette scripts

Options for selection:

(1) teacher-selected works to show snapshots of student work,

(2) teacher-determined assignments placed in the portfolio (i.e., All end-of-unit projects are placed in portfolio), or

(3) student-selected work demonstrating best efforts

TECH CONNECT:
Elements of Science
Notebooks

What might your K–8 students' science notebooks look like? Teachers from all over the country have uploaded examples of science notebook entries scanned from original student work. You can explore entries by topic and grade and find useful resources like assessment tools for science notebooks and lesson plans at http://www.sciencenotebooks.org/.

A relly good bouncer goes the highest. The pingpong was good bouncer. I think it bounce to the highest line. I think it bounced high because It is made of hard plastc because plastc can bounce good. The pingpong bal bounces better it bounced to the high line 4 times.

Ashia's entry describes the test her team conducted. Through this structured entry, asking the student's to use their data to determine which ball is the better bouncer, a teacher can gain important information on a student's knowledge of experimentation. Analyzing Ashia's entry, we find that she gives an operational definition of a "good bouncer." Can you find her definition? Yes, a good bouncer reaches the highest line. Furthermore, she shows the use of data (bounces to the highest line four times) to support the conclusion that a ping-pong ball is a good bouncer. Entries such as this one enable students to demonstrate their ideas about science content in a form that they can examine and even reconsider.

Journals or science notebooks can also be a source for questions that can inform subsequent teaching opportunities while capitalizing on the child's interests. The following questions were taken from student journal entries:

I learned that we can see layers of rock along side the roads, but why are some of the layers wavy? (Includes a drawing of a folded rock layers)
    Shauntae, sixth grade

Why does the moon follow us in the car?
    Tricia, second grade

How do cranes work? They can lift cars in the junk yard.
    Cesar, fifth grade

What do baby spiders look like?
    Brandon, Kindergarten

How do antibiotics work on germs?
    Kenny, seventh grade

In some science classes, a teacher begins class by writing a question on the board. Students are given time to respond to the prompt at the beginning of the class. The journal prompt question can be designed to ascertain what students recall from an earlier lesson. They can also provide the teacher with important assessment into what the students already know about a topic that the teacher is preparing to teach.

Here are a few examples of science question prompts we have seen teachers use effectively in classrooms.

Yesterday we investigated changes in states of matter. What was the most difficult idea to understand?

If you had to describe a chemical change to your younger brothers or sisters, what would you tell them?

You have two metals. One is a magnet and one is magnetic material. Can you describe how you could tell which one is the magnet?

Describe places around your home and neighborhood that show weathering.

As you consider these prompts, look at each one and ask yourself what assessment data the teacher is trying to ascertain. Is there a question that seems to focus on improving instruction? Is there a problem-solving question? Is there a question assessing students' ability to apply knowledge? At other times, you may not want to focus on a specific content question; in that case, you might prefer to use general journal prompts such as the following:

What were the main points of the activity?

What did you enjoy most about the activity?

How might you use what you learned in the activity?

Did this activity make you think of any questions you would like to study?

Whether you choose to call these tools journals or science notebooks, they can make assessing science content an experience that is natural and personal. As you may have already figured out, however, it is impractical to assess all of the students' entries on a regular basis. A solution is to assess random entry selections, which, depending on the teacher's purpose, can serve as a formative assessment for guiding and improving instruction or as a summative assessment used at the end of a unit.

Alternative assessments, such as journaling about science, can be valuables tools for finding out what students know and are thinking.

Self-Assessment

Self-assessment refers to students judging the quality of their own work, based on evidence and explicit criteria, for the purpose of doing better work in the future. When we teach students how to assess their own growth, with known criteria, there is much to gain. Self-assessment influences learners' performance by improving self-confidence and motivation. Self-assessment is a critical skill for developing independent, lifelong learners. Unfortunately, it is often a neglected form of assessment. Through self-assessment, students may become aware of how their thinking can be applied in future work. Self-assessment can range from simple to complex, but effective self-assessment involves discussing with students how to use or apply the criteria. Using examples helps students to understand what the criteria mean. With older students, the criteria can be negotiated, which fosters satisfaction and ownership. Finally, giving students' feedback on their self-assessments is an important step that assists them in setting improvement goals and plans to accomplish the goals. A general example of self-assessment is seen in the following:

SELF-ASSESSMENT

Date: _____ Topic: _____

Name: _____

Check one that best describes you:

____ Hey! I really was not very interested in the task (I did not want to do it).

____ My interest was "so so," or somewhat neutral (I could take it or leave it).

____ I was pumped! I couldn't wait to get started! (I was ready to do it).

What would you do to make it more interesting to you?

Check one of the following categories to describe yourself on the activity:

____ I did not do the work because_____

____ I only spent a little time thinking about the task because_____

____ I did it, but I had problems with _____

____ I did it and I think I understood it.

____ I completed it.

____ I completed the assignment and did more than was required.

How can I improve my work? My goals for improvement:

1.

2.

3.

What's a Rubric?

While discussing alternative assessments, we have used the term "rubric" many times. At this point, you might be wondering just what a rubric is or how one might use it. A rubric is an assessment tool created to analyze students' work.

A rubric is a guide for both teachers and students. It is shared before the task is assigned and the criteria are discussed so that the students are well versed on what is expected with the task. A rubric and its criteria are designed to provide students with specific feedback information regarding their strengths and weaknesses. It also provides the teacher with a clearer analysis of where instruction has been successful and where there may be weaknesses or gaps. Keeping in mind that rubrics provide students' feedback here are two general types of scoring rubrics: holistic and analytic.

Holistic scoring rubrics provide a single measure of mastery related to the quality of the students' work or performance as a whole. **Analytic scoring rubrics** provide separate measures based on criteria for several important dimensions of performance. So, how do I know when to use each one? There is no set rule: It depends on your instructional objective and your purpose. In general, holistic rubrics are used more often with younger students, in part because they contain less detail and are easier for young students to comprehend. The analytic rubric includes more criteria and detail, which makes it useful for assessing knowledge or skills that are more complex. Suppose students have been asked to design an experiment, similar to the test design in the fifth-grade exploration of changes in matter seen earlier in the chapter. The following are examples of holistic and analytical rubrics that could be used to assess students' skills in designing experiments (see Table 8.5).

Meaningful learning involves the use of a variety of assessments, both traditional and alternative. We believe that variety in assessment approaches is important in science classrooms. Though not addressed here, traditional testing is important, given the prevalence of statewide testing. Students must be taught to take traditional tests: To do less is to do them a disservice. So use both alternative and traditional assessments and evaluations, but remember no matter which type you use it should align to learning objectives and the instructional approach.

BULLETIN BOARD

Common Elements of Rubrics

- Rubrics measure stated learning or instructional objective(s).

- Rubrics display a range of levels of performance.

- Rubrics identify specific criteria or characteristics that determine the level at which the objective has been ascertained.

TECH CONNECT:
Web-Based Rubric Generators

A variety of web-based tools exist for developing your own rubrics for your science classroom. The following sites are useful resources for creating rubrics; many include examples of rubrics that you can modify to meet your needs:

Rubistar (http://rubistar.4teachers.org/)

TeAchnology (www.teach-nology.com)

Tech4Learning (www.tech4learning.com)

Advantages of Using Rubrics

Developing a rubric is not easy, and takes preparation time in advance of the task. Furthermore, it often undergoes repeated revisions (a work always in progress) with

Table 8.5 Examples of Holistic and Analytic Rubric

Example of Holistic Rubric Experimental Design		Example of Analytic Rubric Experimental Design				
CRITERIA	**Scale**	**CRITERIA** **4-Excellent; 3-Superior;** **2-Average; 1-Needs work**	**4**	**3**	**2**	**1**
Hypothesizes, explains procedures, observes results, records results accurately, analyzes results, and draws conclusions accurately.	5	**Problem or Questions**: Clearly stated, complete, appropriate				
Missing one of the above criteria	4	**Hypotheses**: Provides testable, clear, multiple hypotheses				
Missing two to three of the above criteria	3	**Variables**: Identifies independent and dependent variable				
Missing four of the above criteria	2	Identifies control variables				
Missing more than four of the above criteria.	1	**Operation Definitions:** All pertinent operational definitions are identified, appropriate for the design, and observable or measurable				
		Procedures: Procedures are clearly stated. found in the appropriate sequence, can be repeated, and are appropriate for the question				
		Results and Conclusions: Records data, makes charts, and draws appropriate conclusions correctly				

continued usage. However, despite the preparation time and continued refinements, there are several advantages to using rubrics.

- Rubrics can help learners judge how well they have done.
- Rubrics make clear what is expected through specified criteria for both students and parents.
- Rubrics provide more learner feedback (both strengths and areas for improvement).
- Rubrics emphasize clear, specific criteria. The more details, the better.

Creating a rubric with effective criteria requires the use of clear, specific language. Using fuzzy terms in developing the criteria such as "a student writes an innovative question" causes confusion. The term "innovative" is difficult to define. Instead, use the term "testable question," which is clear and less subjective. Also, defining levels of quality in a rubric is often difficult, so spend time in advance thinking about how to describe the levels for clear understanding.

As you can see, there are many dimensions and elements to consider when choosing and designing assessments. From our own teaching experiences and conversations with teachers, we have compiled practical tips and important ideas about assessments for you (see Bulletin Board: Dee and Laura's Top Ten Assessment Tips).

As we move from the discussion of assessment in the explain stage, the next step in examining assessment is to have you take what you have learned and use it.

Elaborate

Course Evaluation Instrument: Is It Good Enough?

As students, you are all familiar with the course or instructor evaluations given at the end of your course. Your instructor should be able to supply a copy of the evaluation instrument to you. Examine the course or instructor evaluation form. Develop a holistic or analytic rubric for assessing the quality of a course evaluation instrument. Justify your selection of rubric, discussing its purpose and use. You might begin by examining the evaluation instrument in terms of the information it provides to the instructor for improving their course, or you might consider the instrument from the students' standpoint: Does the instrument provide opportunities or items that students think would be useful to the instructor? These are just a couple of questions to get you started, so do not be limited by them.

Evaluate

YouTube Media: Make an Assessment Video

This is a team project and it will involve self-assessment and group assessment. You and your team will create a short YouTube.com video or a PowerPoint slideshow (your choice) that addresses three of the chapters' objectives.

BULLETIN BOARD

Dee and Laura's Top Ten Assessment Tips

10. KISS (Keep It Simple Silly) Keep the assessment short; remember, you have to provide feedback or score it, or both.

9. Use a variety of assessments, keeping in mind the diversity in your classroom.

8. Let the students know when and what you are assessing; rubrics demand that you do this.

7. Give positive feedback as well as feedback on areas for improvement.

6. Give frequent and timely feedback.

5. Use bright standout colors other than red for grading (red can signal negativity).

4. Use positive terms when conveying progress to the child and parents (see Bulletin Board: Assessment and Communicating With Parents).

3. Provide opportunities for self-assessment; cooperative teams need group and self-assessment.

2. Always balance the time for assessment preparation against what you can learn from the assessment.

1. Don't fall into the trap of grading all the students' work. Be selective and tell them when the assignment is important. With homework, randomly select work to grade.

1. Distinguish between assessment and evaluation and the roles they hold in teaching and learning.
2. Describe and distinguish between forms of assessment (alternative, authentic, performance, traditional).
3. Demonstrate the alignment of instructional objectives with assessment.

You and your team members will need to discuss the objectives and the elements you wish to highlight in the project. You will need to assign roles and tasks to each member and set a timeline for completion. After the completion of the project, you will assess your own understandings and contributions to the group. You will also assess your team members. The final product will be uploaded on YouTube.com for class members to view.

Summary

In summary, assessment as discussed in the explain phase of this chapter places a demand on teachers to develop assessment literacy themselves. According to Rolheiser and Ross (2003), assessment literacy has been defined as (1) the capacity to collect and analyze students' data, (2) the ability to interpret the data, (3) the ability to make changes to improve teaching derived from those data, and (4) an openness to engage in external assessment discussions that have an impact on classrooms and schools. Developing assessment literacy facilitates teacher confidence about the defensibility of their evaluation practices and reduces feelings of vulnerability. It means that teachers are able to provide parents, students, and administrators with clear and detailed assessments, and are able to provide a rationale for the assessment choices they make in their classrooms. Educators who can clearly and respectfully discuss assessment issues with noneducators and educators are better able to link student learning and instructional approaches for the purpose of continuous improvement.

Annotated Resources

Miami Museum of Science

http://www.miamisci.org/ph/lpexamine1.html

This is an exciting web resource for alternative assessments for K–8 students. The site includes performance, authentic, portfolio, and journal assessment ideas and activities. The pH factor theme activities on acids and bases are engaging and appropriate for classroom use. Remember safety rules. The activities include web searches. A teacher's guide is available, but you will need to create your own rubrics.

Kathy Schrock's Guide for Educators: Assessment and Rubric Information

http://school.discoveryeducation.com/schrockguide/assess.html

This site has a tremendous amount of information on assessments and rubrics. You will find an assortment of alternative assessments for Sink and Float and Mystery Powder activities, as well as rubrics for oral presentations, self-assessments, and team assessments. A wide range of materials ready for use or easily adapted for the classroom is suggested.

Rubrican.com

http://www.rubrican.com

This site is designed for educators as a guide to creating project evaluations. It features rubrics for a range of subjects, including science. Click on the menu tab and you will find thirty or more rubrics associated with science experimentation or science content.

Edutopia (The George Lucas Educational Foundation)

http://www.edutopia.org/assessment

This is an exciting website with videos using top researchers on a variety of educational issues. You will hear and read about assessment from inside the classroom as well as from a leader in the assessment and evaluation field, Grant Wiggins. Check out Wiggins' presentation, "The idea of authentic assessment." This is an excellent website for preservice and inservice teachers.

Internet4Classrooms (Helping you use the Internet effectively)

http://www.internet4classrooms.com/

This site is useful for teachers and parents. The table of contents is divided by grade levels, with standardized testing examples for students. The site is intended to reinforce students' skills and content knowledge based on Tennessee standards. Don't let that deter you, if you are not in Tennessee: this is a very good site for students to practice traditional testing with good science examples. Simply cross-check the state standard and grade level you are interested in working with to those on the site.

National Science Education Standards, National Academies Press

http://books.nap.edu/openbook.php?record_id=4962&page=104

This site offers a free download of the *National Science Education Standard* text. Chapter 5, Assessment in Science, "provides criteria to judge progress toward scientific literacy. The assessment standards describe the quality of assessment practices by teachers and agencies to measure student achievement and opportunity provided students to learn science" (NRC, 1996, p. 75).

Assessing science learning: Perspectives from research and practice (2008) Edited by J. Coffey, R. Douglas, and C. Stearns

http://www.nsta.org

This book resource available at the Science Store at www.nsta.org is appropriate for preservice and inservice teacher. It runs the gamut of issues surrounding assessment and evaluation with authentic examples and applications for the classroom. The book is divided into four areas of focus: (1) formative assessment in the service of learning and teaching, (2) classroom-based strategies for assessing students' science understanding, (3) high-stakes tests, and (4) assessment-focused professional development.

References

American Association for the Advancement of Science (AAAS). (1991). *Benchmarks for science literacy: Project 2061.* New York: Oxford University Press.

Anderson, L. W. (2003). *Classroom enhancement: Enhancing the quality of teacher decision making.* Hillsdale, NJ: Lawrence Erlbaum.

Arends, R. (2003). Jacket quote in *Classroom enhancement: Enhancing the quality of teacher decision making.* Hillsdale, NJ: Lawrence Erlbaum.

Bond, L. A., & Cohen, D. (1991). The early impact of Indiana statewide testing for educational progress on local education agencies: Administrators' perceptions. In Robert Stake (Ed.), *Advances in program evaluation: Effects of changes in assessment policy* (pp. 75–100). Boston: JAI Press.

Elementary and Secondary Education Act of 1965. (1965). Available at http://www.k12.wa.us/esea/.

Green, J. (1998, February). *Constructing the way forward.* Keynote address: "Innovations for effective schools." Office of Economic and Co-operation and Development (OECD) Conference, Christchurch, New Zealand.

Kauchak, D., & Eggen, P. (2005). *Introduction to teaching: Becoming a professional.* Upper Saddle River, NJ: Prentice-Hall/Merrill Publishing.

Klenchy, M. (2008). Using science notebooks in elementary classrooms. Arlington, VA: NSTA Press.

National Research Council (NRC). (1996). *National Science Education Standards.* Washington, DC: National Academies Press.

No Child Left Behind Act of 2001. (2002). Pub. L. No. 107-110, 115 Stat 1425 (2002).

Northwest Regional Educational Laboratory Program on Science and Mathematics Alternative Assessment. (1994). *Improving science and mathematics education: A toolkit for professional developers: Alternative assessment.* Portland, OR: Northwest Regional Educational Laboratory. Available at http://www.eric.ed.gov/PDFS/ED381360.pdf.

Northwest Regional Educational Laboratories. (1998). *Improving classroom assessment: A toolkit for professional developers.* Portland, OR: Author.

Rolheiser, C., & Ross, J. (2003). *Student self-evaluation: What research says and what practice shows.* Center for Development and Teaching. Available at http://www.cdl.org/resource-library/articles/self_eval.php?type=author&id=28.

Shafer, S. (1997). *Writing effective report card comments.* New York: Scholastic.

Shepardson, D., & Britsch, S. (2001). The role of children's journals in elementary school science activities. *Journal of Research in Science Teaching, 38*(1), 43–69.

Wiggins, G. (1992). Creating tests worth taking. *Educational Leadership, 49*(8), 26–33.

PART IV

The Nature of Diversity in Science Teaching and Learning

Chapter 9

Learning Styles and Diverse Learners

Learning Objectives

After reading Chapter 9, students will be able to

- discuss key learning modalities,
- compare and contrast learning style models currently used today, and
- synthesize findings on learning styles and argue for and against the use of learning styles when teaching science.

NSES TEACHING STANDARDS ADDRESSED IN CHAPTER 9

Standard A: Teachers of science plan an inquiry-based science program for their students. In doing this, teachers

- select science content and adapt and design curricula to meet the interests, knowledge, understanding, abilities, and experiences of students.

Standard B: Teachers of science guide and facilitate learning. In doing this, teachers

- recognize and respond to student diversity and encourage all students to participate fully in science.

Standard D: Teachers of science design and manage learning environments that provide students with the time, space, and resources needed for learning science. In doing this, teachers

- create a setting for student work that is flexible and supportive of science inquiry.

Source: Reprinted with permission from the National Science Education Standards, copyright 1996, by the National Academy of Sciences, Courtesy of National Academies Press, Washington, DC.

Introduction

Second-grader Brandon is wiggling in his seat as Ms. Hocutt starts to talk to the class about the rocks they are preparing to study. He cannot wait to get his hands on the rocks she passes out. In fact, he is so excited to explore the rocks he hears very little she is saying. Jane, listening intently, answers a question the teacher asked about how to use the magnifying glasses. On the other side of the room, Timmy blurts out a response without waiting for the teacher to call on him. The names may be different, but we suspect you've seen Brandon, Jane, and Timmy before. Maybe you recognize yourself or a student you have worked with in one of these students. Clearly, individuals respond to learning opportunities and teaching approaches in their own ways. Some students thrive on lecture, some are thoughtful listeners, some prefer working collaboratively with others, and still others desire hands-on or kinesthetic approaches. These behaviors represent only a few of the ways that individuals prefer to engage in the learning process. These preferred approaches to learning are often referred to as **learning styles**. We make a distinction here between learning styles and learning theories. Though some may consider learning styles to be learning theories, most educators consider learning as the process that draws together cognitive, emotional, and environmental variables and experiences for acquiring, enhancing, or changing one's knowledge, skills, values, and views of the world (Illeris, 2000; Ormorod, 1995). As such **learning theories** are explanations of what occurs or what happens when learning takes place. In this chapter, we examine learning styles that center on "how students prefer to learn," as opposed to learning theories that attempt to explain "how learning actually occurs."

A Brief History of Learning Styles

The idea that individuals have preferred learning styles and are more comfortable learning in some ways and not others has a long history. This chapter gives a brief overview of the history of how personality types, first described by the early Greeks, gave rise to present-day examples of learning styles, multiple intelligences, and brain-based research findings that are important to science teaching today.

In both education and psychology, views on learning styles have roots deep in the past. Today concepts of learning styles can be traced back to personality types described by the Greek physician, Hippocrates (460 BC–377 BC). He described personalities as melancholy (somber), sanguine (cheerful), choleric (enthusiastic), and phlegmatic (calm). Since the time of Hippocrates, many individuals have explored personality types; these explorations paved the way for Carl Jung's work in the 1920s. Jung's work began with connecting personality types to the ways in which people behave. Later, building on Jung's work, Isabel Briggs Myers and Katherine Briggs shifted the focus of their research from personality types to thinking or cognitive styles. A result of their work is an instrument you may have heard about still in use today. The instrument, called the Myers-Briggs Cognitive Inventory, was developed in 1943, but continues to be popular and is still in use more than sixty years later. During the 1970s, further examination of personality types and cognitive styles were often linked with school environments and student learning resulting in several related terms. One such term, **learning modality**, is associated with perceptual sensory paths (auditory, tactile, kinesthetic, and visual) whereby students input or output information. Learning modalities are channels whereby individuals give, receive, and store information. In general, the learning modalities of students in K–12 classrooms are generally found to be about 30% visual, 25% auditory, 15% kinesthetic, and 30% mixed modalities (Barbe & Milone, 1980). **Cognitive style** refers to the way a person processes, uses, and thinks about information. Today, learning modalities associated with sensory pathways and cognitive styles that refer to how an individual processes information, have been subsumed under the much broader term of "learning style." This broader term, learning style, in general represents consistent ways in which an individual operates within a learning space. This involves a variety of aspects that are perhaps best viewed by science teachers through asking questions such as, "Is the learner one who learns in a random manner or a step wise linear fashion? Is the individual more convergent or divergent in their thinking? Is the learner more logical or more guided by emotions when taking on a challenging task? Does the learner prefer guidance or prefer to work it out alone? Would the learner prefer working in the morning or in the afternoon?" All these questions suggest that learning styles draw on cognitive, affective, and physiological dimensions of the individual that provide a relatively consistent indicator of how he or she perceives, interacts with, and responds in the context of learning (Keefe, 1979).

Engage

What's Your Most Memorable Learning Experience?

Frequently in this book, you are asked to reflect on your own learning. Please do so again. Think for a moment about a learning experience that stands out for you. Recall a memorable time when you were learning something, either inside or outside of school. Maybe it was creating a science project in school, or maybe it was when you learned to ride a bike, or the time you had to memorize your role for a school play. Whatever memorable experience you choose, represent it in light of the way you perceived and responded to it at the time of the experience. Your representation can take on any form you choose (i.e., cartoons, drawings, writing, diagrams, etc.). After you represent your experience, record your answers to the following questions in parts one, two and three below:

Part 1: Consider the cognitive dimension of your memorable learning experience. What aspects made it easy or difficult to learn? What does the experience reveal about how you learn? Describe how you think you learn best. When learning new materials, do you need concrete examples, lectures, or other experiences? If you said other experiences, what are they? How do you think you process new information? Do you process the information in a linear fashion one step at a time, or do you approach the learning randomly? Explain.

Part 2: Now think about the **affective** dimension of your learning experience, which includes motivation, values, emotions, and judgment.

What aspects of the memorable learning experience motivated you the most? What kinds of learning experiences motivate you the least? What learning experiences make you uncomfortable or nervous? What motivates or emotionally hooks you into tackling a task? How do you tackle learning difficult material? Do you approach it logically or from an emotional stance? Explain.

Part 3: Finally, think about the physiological dimension of your learning experience.

What physical aspects of your memorable learning experience felt comfortable? Where were you during the experience? Was it a familiar location or a new place? Was it quiet? Was it noisy? Were you indoors or outdoors? Do you prefer learning when there is music or other sounds in the background or when it is quiet? Explain. What is your ideal environment for learning (lighting, eating, seating, location, temperature)? What time or times of day do you do your best work?

Explore

What's Your Learning Style Preference?

Your reflections and responses in the engage phase were intended to make you aware of some of the factors that influence learning. As you work with your students, one of your tasks as a teacher is to help them to reflect on how they learn science. So, let's explore dimensions that affect learning science in terms of individual learning styles. Over the years, many researchers have developed several learning style instruments to explore the way individuals learn. Many of the instruments have common elements that address the perceptual and the cognitive dimensions that also contain unique elements. Before you begin, remember that all learning style preferences are created equal and none is considered better than others. Furthermore, note that neither the learning style inventory nor its results should label a learner or the learner's learning style(s). That is not the intent of such inventories, nor should it be. However, the inventory results can provide insights about how individuals may prefer to learn and that can be very beneficial for you as a science teacher. What better way to explore learning styles than to examine your own? What are your preferred learning styles? Do you know? Go to the following websites and take the three learning style inventories. After you take the inventories, identify your dominant learning style(s). In addition, read about all the preferred styles of learning associated with each inventory.

Howard Gardner's Multiple Intelligences
Located at http://www.lth3.k12.il.us/rhampton/mi/MI.html

Personality Pathways (Myers-Briggs Test)
Located at http://www.personalitypathways.com/type_inventory.html

Modified Gregorc Learning Style
Located at "Check Your Personal Thinking Style: The Learning Web" at http://www.thelearningweb.net/personalthink.html

After completing the inventories, what stands out about learning styles in general? What did you find out about your learning style(s)? Were you surprised by the outcome or were you aware of the conditions needed to optimize your learning experience? How do your reflections on how you learn (from the engage phase) compare to the results of your inventory? How might knowing more about your learning style and other learning styles influence the way you teach science to students?

Explain

Focus Questions

1. What is intelligence?

2. How is knowledge of learning styles important for effective K–8 science teaching?

3. How can a science teacher incorporate knowledge of learning styles in the science classroom?

4. What controversy surrounds learning styles and brain-based education research?

Snow's Law of Conservation of Instructional Effectiveness: "No matter how you try to make instruction better for someone, you will make it worse for someone else."

Richard Snow, Educational Psychologist (1989)

Recognizing that students in your classroom will have their own individual ways of learning science, where do you stand with respect to the quote? Take a stance and explain your position.

Styles of Learning

If you were wondering why you were asked to examine your own learning styles, it is because it has often been stated that teachers tend to teach the way in which they themselves prefer to learn. What follows is that teachers may find it difficult to reach students who learn in ways different from their own. When pedagogical approaches do not match the way a student learns best, the student may fall short of the learning objectives. Specifically, when teaching science to students, we should support their learning style strengths as well as the learning preferences in which they are not as strong. To do this, it is important that teachers use a variety of strategies that address the different learning styles represented in their classroom. Making ourselves aware of various learning styles is one way to effectively address the needs of all science learners.

Before we begin delving into learning styles, here are a few caveats for you as a K–8 science teacher. As mentioned earlier, learning styles are ways individuals consistently respond and use stimuli in a learning context. In other words, learning styles represent the educational conditions, whereby students are most

Providing diverse approaches for the same task allows students to engage in learning experiences in different ways.

likely to learn. When dealing with learning styles, be cognizant that they are not representative of who or what students are or are not. It is important not to label individuals as certain kinds of learners, such as a visual or kinesthetic learner. Instead, science teachers should recognize that within positive learning environments students are all able to learn, no matter what their learning styles. It is also important to recognize that while students might have a preferred ways of learning, they also need to be comfortable using a variety of learning styles. As discussed, learning styles have been around a long time with a substantial literature base that supports them. However, there is ongoing disagreement on how learning styles are measured in the research literature (Coffield, Moseley, Hall, & Ecclestone, 2004; Pashler, McDaniel, Rohrer, & Bjork, 2009). For instance, Coffield and colleagues examined learning style research findings and found that there was not enough evidence to support the connection between matching teaching and learning styles as an effective way to improve student learning. Despite the controversy, it is important for K–8 science teachers to understand learning styles for a couple of reasons. First, most individuals would agree that students approach learning differently and having knowledge of these differences helps teachers to be more effective. Second, most learners are not aware of their learning styles. Having such personal knowledge has the potential of making students more proactive in learning. Assisting students to become aware of their learning styles or learning preferences can also foster metacognition about their strengths and weaknesses as learners (Merrill, 2000). For science teachers, the key point is to use a wide variety of approaches when teaching science. Using an array of learning approaches gives students opportunities to learn in their own preferred ways at different times.

Over the past three decades several inventories for determining learning styles have emerged. Some learning style inventories are appropriate for students in Grades 3–12; though not a common practice, some schools have used learning style inventories to assess each student's learning style strengths and weaknesses. Teachers armed with this information are better able to provide versatility in teaching that addresses student diversity. An example is seen in Teacher's Desk Tip: Addressing Diversity in Learning Styles in Your Classroom, with Mr. Kim's assessment strategy that provides students' multiple options for completing the task.

By providing students with choices as seen in the Teacher's Desk Tip: Addressing Diversity in Learning Syles in Your Science Classroom, students can demonstrate what they have learned in ways that may draw on their preferred learning styles. So, how do

---

Teacher's Desk Tip: Addressing Diversity in Learning Styles in Your Classroom

Mr. Kim's fifth-grade class has been studying sound, vibration, pitch, frequency, and volume, and waves and their characteristics. To address various learning preferences, his students work with partners and select a final activity from the following:

- Make a sound machine using a minimum of four properties of sound that we have studied in class. Each student must demonstrate and discuss one of the sound machine's properties.
- Write a poem using four of six terms associated with sound. Illustrate the properties of the terms used in the poem.
- Create a video or digital photostory that represents the development of a musical instrument highlighting four to six properties of sound.
- Create a diagram for building a futuristic musical instrument that operates by shaking, stroking, and blowing. The labeled diagram must describe how and what is needed for the instrument to produce sound in the three ways given.
- Develop a song that explains four of six properties of sound.

you become more informed about the variety of learners found in your classroom? In the next section you will examine popular learning style inventories, the key modalities on which each learning style is based, and the application of these learning styles to science teaching.

Learning Style Inventory Approaches

Dunn and Dunn Learning Style Model

A contemporary model used today for assessing learning styles was developed by Dunn and Dunn (1993a, 1993b). With regard to learning styles, Dunn and colleagues point out that it is important to recognize that individual behaviors are only part of the story; it is important to explore and examine the whole of each child's dispositions toward learning (Dunn, Thies, & Honigsfeld, 2001). Based on this premise, the Dunn and Dunn learning style model is sophisticated, using five categories and twenty-one elements that influence each individual's learning. The five categories include emotional, environmental, sociological, physiological, and psychological.

A. Emotional

This category encompasses an individual's motivation, responsibility, structure, and persistence for learning. For example, in the area of structure, you may find some learners prefer to finish one project before continuing to the next, whereas other students prefer to work on multiple projects at the same time.

B. Environmental

Environmental elements are rarely addressed in public schools. Environmental elements are associated with sound, light, temperature, and physical room design. For instance, does a student prefer bright or soft light, warmer or cooler temperatures, silence or background noise to study or work?

C. Sociological

Sociological elements are those that refer to how one learns relative to others. With this element, one might ask if the student learns better with (a) peers, (b) alone, (c) adults who structure the learning, or (d) adults who provide student choices in learning.

D. Physiological

Elements of **physiology** refer to a student's perceptions (visual, tactile, auditory), energy levels associated with time of day, food consumption while studying, and whether the student prefers to move around or remain sedentary while learning.

E. Psychological

These elements correspond to how students process and internalize information. They include impulsive–reflective, global–analytical, and right–left brain processing. With impulsive–reflective elements, one might ask whether the student takes a long time before making a move or decision quickly. The global–analytical elements compare groups of elements associated with the other four categories and are discussed next, Right–left brain processing is discussed in the Gregorc Style Delinator below.

Based on the Dunn and Dunn learning style model, when learners are presented with stimulating, thought-provoking material, individuals fall into two styles of processing: global or analytical. Global learners prefer comfortable, informal, and softly lit environments. Analytic learners operate best in formal, brightly lit, quiet environments with few interruptions or snacking. In general, children tend to be more global in processing information. Gender differences in boys and girls typically find that males prefer freedom to move and that they learn well in informal environments. Females prefer auditory, quiet formal environments (Dunn & Griggs, 1998). Considering the differences in boys' and girls' learning preferences, ask yourself who is most likely to do well in schools.

According to Dunn and Griggs (1998), gender, age, academic achievement, and global or analytical processing are different among individuals and groups. They point out that learning styles change with age and elementary children more often than not show a preference for working with peers and authoritative adults, however, their preferences may certainly change as they mature. Given these findings, understanding the various ways in which students learn is invaluable for you as a K–8 science teacher. Before you look at the next inventory, ask yourself, What are some of the classroom applications of Dunn and Dunn's model?

> **TECH CONNECT:**
> **Webquests**
>
> Webquests are inquiry-based explorations where students can search out and discover various answers on the Internet. With some creativity, a webquest can be constructed that allows for many of the preferred learning styles to be addressed. There are many webquests already created or you can create your own. More information can be found at http://webquest .org.

Gregorc Style Delineator

Anthony Gregorc's (1984) learning style model is based on hemispheric brain research. Hemispheric brain research refers to the right- or left-brain dominance, which is a way of looking at learning styles. Neurobiological research findings show that the left hemisphere is associated with language and logic, whereas the right hemisphere is associated with nonverbal, intuitive, holistic thinking. Though both hemispheres work together in all that humans do, it is generally thought that most people have a dominant side. In other words, when learning new or difficult tasks individuals prefer to learn in certain ways that are linked to the brain's dominant side. With Gregorc's Style Delineator, learning preferences fall into two categories: perceptual quality and ordering ability. Both perceptual quality and ordering ability is present in each individual but some may emerge as more dominant than others. Gregorc suggests that an individual's perceptions fall along two continua. One continuum spans concrete to abstract thinking, and the other continuum deals with how individual's order information (sequential to random). The two continua intersect to generate four learning styles (Gregorc, 1984): concrete sequential, concrete random, abstract sequential, and abstract random.

A. Concrete sequential

Concrete sequential learners are students who prefer to learn from authentic experiences, real objects, and hands-on activities, and when information is fashioned in a logical order.

B. Concrete random

Concrete random students prefer stimuli-rich environments. Real events and objects are preferable while they tackle the information in a haphazard, trial-and-error approach (randomly).

C. Abstract sequential

Abstract sequential learners prefer traditional pedagogical approaches (lecture, readings, outlines) that are ordered in a logical, systematic manner.

D. Abstract random

Learning is best for abstract random learners when information is delivered by means of abstract presentations (video clips, guest speakers, group discussions) with the learners chunking and ordering the information in their own way (randomly). To view the graphically displayed results from a Gregorc Style Delineator see Table 9.1.

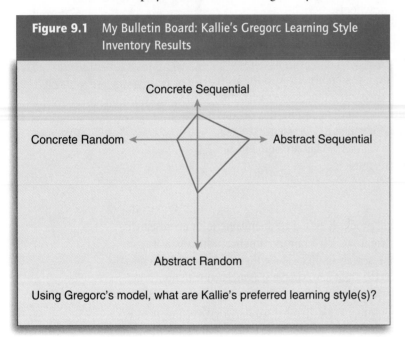

Figure 9.1 My Bulletin Board: Kallie's Gregorc Learning Style Inventory Results

Concrete Sequential

Concrete Random ←→ Abstract Sequential

Abstract Random

Using Gregorc's model, what are Kallie's preferred learning style(s)?

Think back to the explore activity and your results on the modified Gregorc's Style Delineator. Consider your results and the categories discussed in the chapter: It should be obvious that, like other learning style inventories, the Gregorc inventory is intended to show stronger and weaker preferences related to learning. Do you recall your dominant learning style preferences using the modified Gregorc Style Delineator instrument? How do Kallie's results compare to your dominant learning style (see Figure 9.1)? Contemplate the learning preferences that are represented in Kallie's inventory. How might you support her learning science in your classroom?

Hanson, Silver, and Strong Learning Preference Inventory

Hanson, Silver, and Strong's (1991) Learning Preference Inventory is similar to the other inventories presented in this chapter proposing four learning style dimensions. The dimensions in the instrument refer to two ways of perceiving (sensing and feeling) and two ways of judging data (thinking and intuitive). Based on Carl Jung's theory (1971), the Learning Preference Inventory examines four learning styles that include (a) sensing–thinking, described as realistic, practical, and results-oriented; (b) intuitive–thinking which is a tendency to be theoretical, logical, and knowledge-oriented; (c) intuitive–feeling, a self-expressive style characterized as imaginative, insightful, and future-oriented; and (d) sensing–feeling, an interpersonal style that seeks learning that is personal, experiential, and socially oriented (Silver & Hanson, 1998). In addition to Hanson and colleagues' inventory, David Kolb's Experiential Learning Theory instrument is also a popular learning style used among educators.

Kolb Experiential Learning Styles

This contemporary learning style model is based on *Experiential Learning Theory* by David Kolb (1984). Kolb views the human mind as having perceiving and processing abilities, much as Jung (1971) viewed the mind. The perceptual dimension like the Gregorc learning style, involves a continuum from concrete (feeling) to abstract (thinking). The processing dimension ranges from active (doing) to reflective (watching) and is unique to the model. The two dimensions combine to represent the following four types of learning preferences.

A. Converging Learning Style (Abstract Conceptualization vs. Active Experimenter)

Students with this learning preference are drawn to practical applications of ideas and technical tasks with a single correct answer. They use reasoning skills in problem solving and are comfortable with new ideas and applications.

B. Diverging Learning Style (Concrete Experience vs. Reflective Observation)

Students with a preferred diverging learning style are sensitive and often view events concretely using multiple viewpoints. They are data gatherers and use imagination to solve problems. You may recognize them as students who like to brainstorm, generate ideas, work in groups, and listen with an open mind.

C. Accommodating Learning Style (Concrete Experience vs. Active Experimenter)

Students with this learning style prefer direct experiences, hands-on activities, and teamwork. They tend to act on their intuition instead of logic, and are drawn to new challenges involving action and initiative.

D. Assimilating Learning Style (Abstract Conceptual/Reflective Observation)

Learners of this preferred learning style focus more on ideas and abstract concepts than on people. They prefer concise, clear logical pathways. Students with this learning style prefer lectures, examining models, reading, and time to think.

Hansen, Silver, and Strong's and Kolb's learning style inventories draw heavily on Carl Jung's work and address different ways of exploring preferred learning styles within the context of the three primary modalities—auditory, tactile, and visual. These inventories and the others discussed are just a sample of many learning style inventories that have been applied across the educational field. Given the preponderance of learning style inventories, it is unsurprising that some researchers posit that when science teachers use a style that matches the student's preferred learning style the student generally finds greater satisfaction and has a more positive attitude toward the experience. However, there is considerable debate about the degree to which teaching and learning style matching affects a student's achievement (Coffield et al., 2004). Findings are mixed and inconclusive. For now, it is more important to first consider the instructional strategies that are most appropriate to the content and then consider learning styles as ways to refine and select instructional strategies (Merrill, 2000). Again, what this means for you as a science teacher applying knowledge of the learning styles to your classroom is to provide a variety of approaches in your science classroom so students experience all types of learning styles. More recently, learning styles and the ideas behind them have been expanded on with the Theory of Multiple Intelligences (Gardner, 1983).

Figure 9.2   Teacher Timeout—Coffee Cup Humor

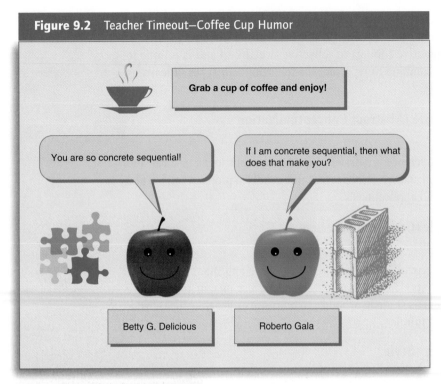

TECH CONNECT:
Technology Tools
for Multiple Intelligences

How might you use technology tools to maximize students' learning style strengths and build areas that are weaker? This website takes each of Gardner's intelligences and provides examples of technology tools for each:

http://eduscapes.com/tap/topic68.htm

Gardner's Theory of Multiple Intelligences

Howard Gardner's multiple intelligences theory was described in his book, *Frames of Mind* (1983), and from that time it has become a popular model for understanding learning styles, personalities and behavior. Gardner describes intelligence as "the capacity to solve a problem or to fashion products that are valued in one or more cultural setting" (Gardner & Hatch, 1989, p. 5). Gardner's work with multiple intelligences emerged out of psychology, but he also drew on biological and cultural research. If someone asked you to define intelligence, what would you say? In general, if you consider all the tests given to determine the intelligence of a student, you will find that intelligence is defined by an individual's verbal and mathematical ability. Gardner's (1983) stance embraces a different view that all individuals have multiple intelligences. He proposes that individuals have stronger and weaker intelligences, and moves beyond a limiting definition of intelligence to frame eight areas of intelligences: (1) verbal–linguistic, (2) logical–mathematical, (3) visual–spatial, (4) bodily–kinesthetic, (5) musical–rhythmic (6) intrapersonal, (7) interpersonal, (8) naturalist; a ninth is sometimes included: (9) existentialist intelligence.

A. Verbal–Linguistic Intelligence

Linguistic intelligence refers to the use of language. Students who demonstrate this intelligence show strength with written and spoken forms of communication as well as the interpretation, retention, and explanations of information or concepts.

B. Logical–Mathematical Intelligence

Students with the ability to detect patterns, reason, and think logically represent logical–mathematical intelligence. This intelligence is often associated with scientific and mathematical thinking.

C. Visual–Spatial Intelligence

Visual–spatial intelligence in students is linked with their ability to manipulate and internally create images necessary for solving problems. It involves imagination and pictorial expression portraying understanding between images to meanings.

D. Bodily–Kinesthetic Intelligence

Bodily–kinesthetic intelligence is a student's mental ability to coordinate bodily movements. It involves physical agility and balance as well as hand, eye, and body coordination.

E. Musical–Rhythmic

Musical–rhythmic intelligence centers on a student's appreciation and skill in producing music. A student with this intelligence exhibits thinking in terms of sounds, auditory patterns and rhythms.

F. Intrapersonal Intelligence

Intrapersonal intelligence refers to a student's awareness of his or hers inner state of being. Students displaying this intelligence have the ability to self-reflect and recognize their own inner feelings, relationships with family and other individuals, and their strengths and weaknesses.

G. Interpersonal Intelligence

Interpersonal intelligence encompasses a student's perceptions of other people's feelings and the student's ability to relate to others. Interpersonal intelligence also consists of the ability to understand relationships between individuals and the behaviors of those individuals.

Outdoor explorations provide unique opportunities for students to engage in multiple ways of learning.

H. Naturalist Intelligence

Naturalist intelligence relates to a student's skill in discerning among living organisms with sensitivity to objects of the natural world.

I. Existentialist Intelligence

Existentialist intelligence refers to a student's ability or inclination to seek connections by wondering about human existence within a grand scheme through inquiries of a philosophical nature.

Many teachers normally work with and are comfortable with one or two of the intelligences and even on occasion may try three intelligences with activities. It requires flexibility and the willingness to take a bit of risk to try to integrate skills of other intelligences into science classroom activities. Though it is not always necessary to integrate all the

BULLETIN BOARD

Gardner's Multiple Intelligence Strategies for the Science Classroomn

Verbal–Linguistic: Conduct interviews about frogs, create a quote about earthquakes, write a story problem on metamorphosis, write the script and present a weather forecast, lead a discussion group on the rock cycle

Logical–Mathematical: Collect and analyze data on motion, calculate formulae for density, use deductive reasoning to solve a crime scene, solve nonroutine problems, design and conduct experiments on shadows

Visual–Spatial: Plan and create a storyboard for describing cellular respiration, make a mobile to illustrate levels of cellular organization, create a digital photonarrative of local pollution, create charts, graphs, and maps

Bodily–Kinesthetic: Act out a story of water movement in a plant, create a simulation for photosynthesis, make a model of internal leaf structure, make model cell parts for a game

Musical–Rhythmic: Create a jingle for planetary traits, rewrite the words of a song for predator–prey relationships, generate rhythms for the producers, consumers, and decomposers of a food chain.

Intrapersonal: Critique your own work, determine how you feel about science, identify what you are capable of contributing to a team task, journal your thoughts regarding cloning

Interpersonal: Teach a partner how use a balance, provide constructive feedback on a project, ponder multiple views on deciding if foam is a solid, liquid, or gas, work collaboratively with a team in building a machine using three different simple machines

Naturalist: Collect natural objects (insects, rocks, leaves), photograph spider webs, care for classroom organisms, classifying leaves, study ponds for pH levels, study birds

Existentialist: Create flyers as well as research and report on local environmental issues, campaign school administration for healthy foods and exercise programs, actively participate in service learning projects for recycling and clean up of polluted areas in the community

intelligences, it is recommended that teachers include at least four intelligences when designing and assessing activities. When you integrate four intelligences into the experiences, students have four chances to learn and present their knowledge of content. Of course, this kind of integration also challenges teachers to teach in new ways, which may create a bit of anxiety. However, if a teacher consistently incorporates several intelligences into lessons and assessments it will eventually become part of his or her teaching repertoire. Now go back and read the Teacher's Desk Tip featuring Mr. Kim. Identify the multiple intelligences Mr. Kim uses in his assessments. What are some other assessment options that would emphasize other intelligences? So far we've taken a look at some of the more popular learning style approaches. In the next section, we will discuss brain-based research, an emerging field that bridges research in the biological sciences with education and learning.

Brain-Based Research and Education

For many years scientists studying the brain (neuroscientists) have been exploring how the brain operates. Over the past twenty years, neuroscientific findings have piqued the interest of cognitive scientists, psychologists, and educational researchers who are striving to find ways to apply what we know about how the brain works to teaching and learning. Since the brain is always involved in what students are engaged in, to ignore such findings would be ridiculous. In 2008, Eric Jensen made the case that merging the findings of **neuroscience**, cognitive science, and educational research can support education. He stated that brain-based education has accumulated enough empirical and experimental evidence that a new model for education should be considered. In this model, Jensen proposes that we consider aligning what we have learned about how the brain works with teaching—in this case teaching science. In order to do this, Caine and Caine (1994) developed some core principles regarding neurological functions that may be applied to the educational setting. Here are a few of the brain-based principles that are relevant to teachers and the field of education:

- The brain is designed to search for meaning; it is innate.
- The brain can do many things all at once; it is a highly developed, adaptive system.
- The brain engages the body and vice versa; there is a reciprocal communication between the two, which affects learning.
- Emotions are central to our patterning and they power attention, meaning, and memory.
- The brain perceives wholes and parts.
- Information is stored in multiple areas of the brain and can be retrieved through multiple neurological pathways.
- The brain works best when there is social interaction, one might say, "Two brains are better than one."

BULLETIN BOARD

Brain Trivia

1. The brain weighs about three pounds.
2. The brain is the fattiest organ in the body.
3. There are no pain receptors in the brain.
4. The brain is 75% water.
5. The brain continues to grow until the individual reaches about age eighteen.

As professionals, it is important to stay abreast of research findings that come from other disciplines and reflect on how these findings can improve science teaching in K–8 classrooms. Drawing on neuroscientific findings, Caine and Caine (1991, 1994) identified three principles of curriculum, instruction, and assessment that influence learning related to K–8 science teaching: orchestrated immersion, relaxed alertness, and active processing.

1. Orchestrated immersion occurs when science teachers create environments that immerse students in their learning. For example, Ms. Young's first-grade classroom is learning about tadpoles. As a student in her class, you would find an aquarium with tadpoles and you would be encouraged to draw pictures in a journal about the changes you observe in your science notebook (Klenchy, 2008). You would visit a pond and take photos of the habitat where tadpoles develop. Within the classroom, you would find a variety of age-appropriate books that explore the life cycles of amphibians. You and other students would listen to a tape of sounds from a wetland and try to identify the organisms making the sounds. In a culminating activity, you would work in a group to create a puppet show that demonstrates the life cycle of a frog, using colorful backdrops and other props.

2. Relaxed alertness requires the science learning environment to support a sense of calm confidence where students are challenged and supported in learning. This is demonstrated in Mr. Jimenez's sixth-grade class, where students have been studying cell structure and function. Over the week, their activities have included creating edible cell models in baggies with a legend to represent the cell organelles, examining various types of cells under microscopes, researching cell organelles on computer simulations, and team presentations of findings with options to present the material in creative ways such as collages, poems, posters, models, skits, and demonstrations. With Mr. Jimenez facilitating, students created graphic organizers that represented various plant and animal cells and their functions. In preparation for the final task, Mr. Jimenez designed a classroom environment that set a calm ambiance with soft music playing in the background. The shades are partially drawn and the room is warm, neat and orderly. Mr. Jimenez speaks with a

Teacher's Desk Tip: Addressing Diversity in Your Classroom

Read this chapter's elaborate task: What if the task could only be completed as a poem? How comfortable would you be with accomplishing the task? How confident would you be? How would writing the poem relate to your preferred learning styles? What happens when teachers use only one or two approaches in their classrooms? Should one always work in a preferred learning style?

calm voice and hands out the test saying, "Over the past week, you've shown me already how well you know the material. I am confident you will all be successful with this task."

3. Active processing refers to attaching new information to prior knowledge when setting the stage for science learning. In Ms. Jones' third-grade classroom, students are studying a unit on rocks. Ms. Jones begins by showing students a pebble, a boulder, a piece of concrete block with embedded pebbles, and the dust created when she rubs two rocks together. She asks them to describe what a rock is and what makes it up. She records students' responses on chart paper to revisit after they have finished their unit. From their responses, she recognizes that the students do not differentiate between naturally formed and human-made rocks. Students don't mention the term "minerals," either. Now that she knows some of what students understand about rocks, she can use that information to develop lessons that connect new information she wants to teach with what they already know. She also uses tools like concept maps and word webs to help students make visual connections among the ideas.

As seen here, each of the principles has direct application for science teaching and yet brain-based research, like learning styles, also evokes controversy among educators. There are many people that believe neuro-science research and education are not easily linked. Although Jensen (2008), Caine and Caine (1994), and others have proposed ways of apply-ing brain-based research to education, some have criticized the linkages as doing nothing more than supporting educational practices that have been used by effective teachers for decades. The point is that past practices used by teachers were, for lack of a better term, intuitive, and were not supported with the empirical findings—findings that neurosciences today support. If one keeps an open mind, it is easy to see that brain-based research findings have the potential to improve science education practices as they seek to bridge what we know about the brain and how it functions with direct applications for learning in the sci-ence classroom. In Bulletin Board: Brain-Based Findings you can read more about what is new with brain-based research. What applications do you think the research findings might have for you in your future science classroom?

Elaborate

Compare and Contrast Your Learning Style to Science Instructional Approaches

Think about a science class (not a methods class) you took in either high school or col-lege. Think about the ways in which the materials were presented (books, lecture, labs, discussions, group work, individual work, etc.). What tasks were you given (reading assignments, writing assignments, labs, group projects, individual projects, tests, etc.)?

Write down all the various instructional strategies that were used to teach the topics and how you felt as a learner in that class. Now think about the learning style inventories you took. You should have identified your preferred learning styles using the modified Gregorc, Myers-Briggs, and Gardner's Multiple Intelligences instruments. Focusing on the descriptions of the science class you recall, compare and contrast that class to your inventory results. Consider the following: What was the predominant instructional strategy of the science course? Did it match your preferred learning style(s)? If so, which one(s) did it match? Explain. If it did not match your preferred learning style(s) what learning style(s) does the science class seem best suited for? How do you know? How successful do you feel you were in learning the material within the science class? Describe changes you would make to address a broader diversity of learners.

Evaluate

Lesson Critique: Learning Modalities and Learning Styles

Now that you've spent some time thinking about your own learning style preferences and your experiences as a student, take a look at the following modified lesson plan from Project Learning Tree, a nationally available environmental education curriculum. If you want to know more about Project Learning Tree visit their website located at www.plt.org.

BULLETIN BOARD

Brain-Based Findings

- The human brain grows new neurons. We find that new neurons are highly correlated with memory, mood, and learning.

- The growth of neurons can be regulated by daily activities (exercise, low stress, good nutrition). Kempermann, Wiskott, & Gage (2004)

- Social contexts influence the brain. The discovery of "mirror neurons" suggests imitative reciprocity in our brain. Social structure in schools can influence a sense of acceptance, sadness, joy, connectedness, and stress so social grouping of students should be reflective and planned. These are inactive in autistic individuals. Iacoboni and colleagues (2005)

- Neuroplasticity is the ability of the brain to reroute connections. Verified studies show that appropriate skills development, art, music, and technical preparation in schools can make changes in the brain. Kilgard & Merzenich (1998); Temple et al. (2003); Mahncke et al. (2006)

- Long-term stress influences the brain in terms of "memory, attendance, social skills, and cognition." Allostasis is an adjusted new baseline for stress found in brains of individuals with stress and anxiety problems. McEwen & Wingfield (2003, p. 411)

- What we eat influences our brains. Evidences show the effects of nutrition on memory, attention, and stress.

Source: Findings cited within Jensen, E. (2008). A fresh look at brain-based education. *Phi Delta Kappan, 89*(6), 411–412.

After reading the lesson, Birds and Worms, your task is to complete the following three evaluation tasks:

Task 1: Analyze the lesson to identify the learning modalities (kinesthetic or tactile, auditory, and visual) emphasized in the lesson.

BIRDS AND WORMS LESSON

Grade 4
NSES: K–4 Characteristics of organisms, and organisms and environments
Objective: Students will describe camouflage as a characteristic of animals for protection (shape, color, and size) and survival.

Engage: Provide students with pictures of various animals such as a fox, coyote, snake, deer, frog, or a rabbit. Then provide students with several pictures of various habitats including a pond or wetland area, a forested area, a grassy area, a rocky area, and so on. Have students work in small groups to try to pick out the best habitat for each animal, making sure that students recall that habitats provide food, water, shelter, and space. Engage students in a discussion of why they chose the habitats that they did for their animal and what the habitat provides the animal. Ask the students if the coloration of the animals influence the habitat they chose. If so, how?
    Materials: Pictures for engage; sixty beans of each type; string to mark off area

Explore: Divide the students into two to four groups with the same number of students in each group and take students to a marked grassy area (3m x 3m) outside where four different colors of dried beans (red, white, black, and split peas) have been randomly scattered. Show a sample of each bean to the students and tell them that the beans represent worms and that they, as birds, are going to be hunting for food (beans which represent worms) within the designated area. Teams must line up; when the signal is given, the student in the front of each line will "fly" over the area and hunt for a "worm" (bean). When she or he finds one, the student returns to the line, taps the next person in line, and move to the end of the line. Each student will fly over to hunt three times. When each bird on the team has three worms, the team should sit down to signal they are done.

Explain: Have students bring their worms and place them on a large piece of chart paper to create a bar graph, counting the final totals for each "worm" type. Explore the following questions with the students: What were your observations about the birds as they hunted? What trends in the data do you see? Which colors of worms were found most often by the birds? Which color were found least often? What are possible reasons for the trends you see? If you were a worm, which color would you want to be? Why? Introduce the word "camouflage" (color, shape, size) to students if they do not introduce the word themselves Can you think of an example of camouflage that happens in nature?. Discuss how they would define camouflage. Ask students if they have any questions about camouflage. Ask if they can think of real examples of animal camouflage in nature. Create a class list of their examples of camouflage.

Elaborate: Now that students have defined camouflage, give them white beans to represent an organism like a worm. Have the students identify a new habitat on the school grounds that would provide a suitable habitat for the white beans (worms) to be camouflaged from the birds, Repeat the activity and have students examine whether their selection was beneficial in camouflaging the white beans and what evidence they have to support their ideas.

Evaluate: Using various art supplies, have the students create their own birds and describe a habitat that would provide camouflage from predators for their created birds. Remind students that a habitat, such as a forest, might provide the best camouflage near the ground or within the branches of trees, so they should be specific and include a description of how the habitat they chose helps to camouflage their created birds. They should also describe how the habitat would provide food and water for their bird.

Permission to adapt the Birds and Worms Activity (© 2011, American Forest Foundation) from Project Learning Tree's PreK–8 Environmental Education Activity Guide has been granted by the American Forest Foundation to Sage Publications, Inc. Educators can receive the complete guide by attending a Project Learning Tree workshop. Contact the PLT National Office at 202-463-2475 or information@plt.org. For more information about Project Learning Tree, visit www.plt.org.

Task 2: Analyze the lesson using Howard Gardner's Theory of Multiple Intelligences. Which of the intelligences does the Birds and Worm lesson address? Describe how intelligences are addressed within the lesson. Which intelligences are not represented and how could the lesson be modified to include some of them?

Part 3: Look at the Gregorc's abstract random learning style preferences and analyze the lesson based on the descriptions. What aspects of the abstract random learning style preference are represented in the lesson? Which are not? How does this lesson compare to the concrete sequential learning style? How can your knowledge of learning styles, multiple intelligences, and brain-based research help you address learner diversity in your classroom practices?

Summary

Think back to the introduction. Do you remember Brandon, Jane, and Timmy? What can you infer about their preferred learning styles? You may never conduct learning style inventories with students, but you should be aware of the full range of learning style preferences you will find in your science classroom. Therefore, a strategy to keep in mind when teaching science is to select and use a wide variety of different kinds of activities in your classroom. This affords opportunities for your students to strengthen their preferred learning styles while experiencing other learning styles during the year.

Staying informed of current trends in educational research is a part of your ongoing professional development and growth as a teacher. This chapter began with the origins of personality inventories that metamorphosed into learning styles. By exploring some of the more prominent learning style inventories, you delved deeper into and reflected on your own learning style preferences. The chapter concluded with a brief discussion of the principles of brain-based education research, an emerging field with great potential to have an impact on science teaching and learning. Though controversial, having knowledge of learning styles, multiple intelligences, and brain-based findings can give you a breadth of understanding into how different learners approach learning. As a result, you become a more informed, savvy teacher. Taking away the key elements of this chapter, you should be reminded to use a variety of teaching strategies that address a range of intelligences and learning styles. Work at not relying solely on those learning style preferences you hold and always remember to teach the whole child, which includes addressing the physical, emotional, and cognitive dimensions as part of their science experiences.

Annotated Resources

Brain rules: 12 principles for surviving and thriving at work, home, and school, by John Medina. Seattle, WA: Pear Press (2008).

http://www.brainrules.net/

This website by Dr. John Medina includes important neuroscience findings that apply to professionals and schools. This is an interesting and very informative site about the applications of brain-based finding using power points, video clips, and readings.

Edutopia.org (The George Lucas Educational Foundation)

http://www.edutopia.org/search/node/multiple%20intelligences

This website is committed to publishing stories of innovations in schools. It contains video clips, blogs, and articles that provide cutting-edge or creative approaches in education.

Elementary School Kids Show Their Multiple Intelligences

http://www.edutopia.org/multiple-intelligences-immersion-enota

This narrative account is about Enota Multiple Intelligence Academy in Georgia. As noted by the school name, it uses Howard Gardner's Theory of Multiple Intelligences. The article addresses how teachers at Enota encourage their students to use a variety of multiple intelligences to succeed in their classes.

Brain-Based Research Prompts Innovative Teaching Techniques in the Classroom

http://www.edutopia.org/brain-based-research-powerful-learning

Building a Better School With Brain-Based Technology

http://www.edutopia.org/brain-based-learning-key-largo-school-video

This short article and video focus on new strategies used by teachers in Key Largo, FL. Teachers work to integrate technology where principles of brain-based research are being implemented. These nontraditional approaches use the principles of how the brain learns and of multiple intelligences with positive results. This site includes a video clip of how the Key Largo schoolteachers carry out their innovative strategies.

How people learn: Brain, mind, experience and school **(2000) by the Committee on Developments in the Science of Learning John D. Bransford, Ann L. Brown, and Rodney R. Cocking. Washington, DC: National Academies Press, http://www.nap.edu/catalog .php?record_id=9853.**

You can locate the text by going to National Academy Press Library at www.NAP.edu/ and search the book title. The book is a free download. The text discusses current research on how the brain functions and applications to teaching and learning. The book spans aspects of learning with broad implications for the classroom including memory and the structure of knowledge, analysis of problem solving and reasoning, early foundations, metacognitive processes, and self-regulatory capabilities and cultural experience and community participation. In conjunction with the book is an audio Podcast regarding how people learn at http://www.nap.edu/catalog.php?record_ id=9853#podcast.

YouTube Video: Introduction to 4MAT by Bernice McCarthy

http://www.youtube.com/watch?v=cpqQ5wUXph4 and alternative

McCarthy uses four learning styles in a program that crosses the curriculum with many strategies that are teacher and learner friendly. This video describes the learning styles as four quadrants of a circle that supports the ideas that teachers should use activities that enhance students' learning styles while also having students experience other styles.

References

Barbe, W. B., & Milone, M. N. (1980). Modality. *Instructor, 39*(6), 45–47.

Caine, G., & Caine, R. (1991, Winter). The use of brain research as a basis for evaluating integrative approaches to education. *Journal of the Society of Accelerated Learning and Teaching, 16*(4), 365–382.

Caine, R., & Caine, G. (1994). *Making connections: Teaching and the human brain.* New York: Addison-Wesley.

Coffield, F., Moseley, D., Hall, E., & Ecclestone, K. (2004). *Learning styles and pedagogy in post-16 learning: A systematic and critical review.* Learning and Skills Research Centre. Available at http://www.lsda.org.uk/files/PDF/1543.pdf.

Dunn, R., & Dunn, K. (1993a). *Teaching elementary students through their individuals styles: Practical approaches grades 3–6.* Boston: Allyn & Bacon.

Dunn, R., & Dunn, K. (1993b). *Teaching secondary students through their individuals styles: Practical approaches grades 7–12.* Boston: Allyn & Bacon.

Dunn, R., & Griggs, S. (1998). Learning styles: Link between teaching and learning. In R. Dunn & S. Griggs (Eds.), *Learning styles and the nursing profession* (pp. 11–23). New York: NLN Press.

Dunn, R., Thies, A. P., & Honigsfeld, A. (2001). *Synthesis of the Dunn and Dunn learning-style model research: Analysis from a neuropsychological perspective.* Jamaica, NY: Center for the Study of Learning and Teaching Style, St. John's University.

Gardner, H. (1983). *Frames of mind: The theory of multiple intelligences.* New York: Basic Books.

Gardner, H., & Hatch, T. (1989). Multiple intelligences go to school: Educational implications of the theory of multiple intelligences. *Educational Researcher, 18*(8), 4–9.

Gregorc, A. (1984). *Gregorc style delineator: Development, technical, and administration manual.* Columbia, CT: Gregorc Associates.

Hanson, R., Silver, H., & Strong, R. (1991). *The learning style preference: User's manual.* Trenton, NJ: Silver Strong & Associates.

Illeris, K. (2000, November). *Trends and perspectives on learning, knowledge and skills development.* Presentation at the Opening Conference of Learning Lab, Denmark, Copenhagen.

Iacoboni, M., Molnar-Szakacs, I., Gallese, V., Buccino, G., Mazziotta, J. C., & Rizzolatti, G.

(2005, February 22). Grasping the intentions of others with one's own mirror neuron system. *PLoS Biology*. Available at http://biology.plosjournals.org/perlserv/?request=get-document&doi=10.1371/journal.pbio.0030079.

Jensen, E. (2008). A fresh look at brain education. *Phi Delta Kappan*, *89*(6), 409–417.

Jung, C. (1971). Psychological types. In *Collected works of C. G. Jung*, Vol. 6. Princeton, NJ: Princeton University Press.

Keefe, J. W. (1979) Learning styles: An overview. In NASSP's *Student learning styles: Diagnosing and proscribing programs* (pp. 1–17). Reston, VA: National Association of Secondary School Principals.

Kempermann, G., Wiskott, L., & Gage, F. (2004). Functional significance of adult neurogenesis. *Current Opinion in Neurobiology*, *14*(2) 186–191.

Kilgard, M., & Merzenich, M. (1998). Cortical map reorganization enabled by nucleus basalis activity. *Science*, *279*, 1714–1718.

Klenchy, M. (2008). *Using science notebooks in the elementary classroom*. Arlington, VA: NSTA Press.

Kolb, D. (1984). *Experiential learning: Experience as the source of learning and development*. Upper Saddle River, NJ: Prentice Hall.

Mahncke, H., Connor, B. B., Appelman, J., Ahsanuddin, O. N., Hardy, J. L., Wood, R. A., et al. (2006). Memory enhancement in healthy older adults using a brain plasticity-based training program: A randomized, controlled study. *Proceedings of the National Academy of Sciences* (August), 12523–12528.

McEwen, B., & Wingfield, J. (2003). The concept of allostasis in biology and biomedicine. *Hormone Behavior* (January), 2–15.

Merrill, D. (2000). Instructional strategies and learning styles: Which takes precedence? In R. Reiser & J. Dempsey (Eds.), *Trends and issues in instructional technology* (pp. 96–106). New York: Prentice Hall.

Ormorod, R.J. (1995). Putting soft or methods to work: Information systems strategy development at Saninsbury's. *Journal of the Operational Research Society*, *45*, 277–293.

Pashler, H., McDaniel, M., Rohrer, D., & Bjork, R. (2009). Learning styles: Concepts and evidence. *Psychological Science in the Public Interest*, *9*(3), 105–119.

Silver, H., & Hanson, R. (1998). *Learning styles and strategies* (3rd ed.). Woodbridge, NJ: Thoughtful Education Press.

Snow, R. E. (1989). Cognitive-conative aptitude interactions in learning. In R. Kanfer, P. L. Ackerman, & S. Cudeck (Eds.), *Abilities, motivation, and methodology: The Minnesota symposium on learning and individual differences* (pp. 435–474). Hillsdale, NJ: Lawrence Erlbaum.

Temple, E., Deutsch, G. K., Poldrack, R. A., Miller, S. L., Tallal, P., Merzenich, M. M., et al. (2003). Neural deficits in children with dyslexia ameliorated by behavioral remediation: Evidence from functional MRI. *Proceedings of the National Academy of Sciences*, *4*(March), 2860–2865.

Chapter 10

Addressing Student Diversity

Science for All

Learning Objectives

After reading Chapter 10, students will be able to

- synthesize key issues related to learning science for students with disabilities, female students, diverse students, and English language learners (ELLs),
- create a toolkit describing successful strategies that address students with disabilities, female students, minority students, and ELLs in the science classroom, and
- modify K–8 science lessons to ensure that instruction supports the learning of all students in a diverse science classroom.

NSES TEACHING STANDARDS ADDRESSED IN CHAPTER 10

Standard A: Teachers of science plan an inquiry-based science program for their students. In doing this, teachers

- select science content and adapt and design curricula to meet the interests, knowledge, understanding, abilities, and experiences of students.

Standard B: Teachers of science guide and facilitate learning. In doing this, teachers

- recognize and respond to student diversity and encourage all students to participate fully in science learning.

Standard D: Teachers of science design and manage learning environments that provide students with time, space, and resources needed for learning science. In doing this, teachers

- make the available science tools, materials, media, and technological resources accessible to students.

Source: Reprinted with permission from the National Science Education Standards, copyright 1996, by the National Academy of Sciences, Courtesy of National Academies Press, Washington, DC.

Introduction

Each of your science classrooms is unique, because each of your students is unique. Factors such as the geographical location of your classroom, the social and cultural populations of the school community in which you work, and the individual students who make up your class will all affect your science classroom. As a K–8 teacher, it's your responsibility to teach science to every one of your students. This is underscored in the National Science Education Standards (National Research Council [NRC], 1996), that state, "The intent of the *Standards* can be expressed in a single phrase: Science standards for all students. The phrase embodies both excellence and equity. The *Standards* apply to all students, regardless of age, gender, cultural or ethnic background, disabilities, aspirations, or interest and motivation in science" (p. 2). The importance of "science for all" also draws attention to the projected increased need in the United States for a science, mathematics, engineering, and technologically skilled workforce to keep the United States globally competitive. This societal need makes clear the importance that science education experiences prepare *all* of our students. This is summed up in a 2000 report issued by the Congressional Commission on the Advancement of Women and Minorities in Science, Engineering and Technology (SET) Development (2000), which states, "Obviously, the current and projected need for more SET workers, coupled with the fact that women, underrepresented minorities, and persons with disabilities comprise an increasing proportion of the labor pool, argue for policies that support greater participation by these underrepresented groups in SET education and careers" (p. 11).

There is no easy way of addressing the learning needs of all the diverse students you will have in your classroom. There are, however, strategies that can assist you in facilitating students' learning of science in a classroom rich in diversity. Becoming aware of your own experiences and views of science, understanding the needs of diverse learners, removing barriers for learners, and developing a repertoire of strategies that foster success can make science for all an achievable goal. In this chapter, we will explore the background of the **Individuals with Disabilities Education Improvement Act** (IDEIA; 2004), as well as gender, cultural, and linguistic diversity coupled with teaching strategies for promoting success with diverse learners in your K–8 science classroom.

> *We need to give each other the space to grow, to be ourselves, to exercise our diversity. We need to give each other space so that we may both give and receive such beautiful things as ideas, openness, dignity, joy, healing, and inclusion.*
>
> Max de Pree
>
> Consider this quote in light of diversity in your classroom. What ideas do you draw from these words that may be useful to you as a K–8 science teacher?

Engage

My Science, My World

For this engage phase, you will be doing something a bit different. You will create a digital story of "My Science, My World." According to the Center for Digital Storytelling, a digital story is a short, first-person image-based narrative created by combining recorded voice, still and moving images, and music or other sounds. The Center for Digital Storytelling can be located at http://www.storycenter.org where you can view examples. Another resource you can examine and use is a free downloadable program, Photo Story 3, located at www.micro soft.com (or search for "photostory").

Your digital story should present your experiences, views, attitudes, and beliefs about science and some representation of how your culture, ethnicity, race, gender or abilities have influenced the ways in which you view science in your world. Your digital story should be short (two to four minutes long) and should tell your story of science with pictures, words, narration, and music. Your instructor may provide a space on a classroom webpage or Wikispace for you to post and share your stories, or you may be asked to share them in your class. To get you started on your digital story "My Science, My World," consider the following questions: What does science mean to you? What images portray science as you see it? Is it a positive image, a neutral image, or a negative image? What images come to mind that represent how you interact with science in your world? What images have shaped and influenced the way you view science? What images, words, or music portrays how your gender, race, ethnicity, social class, abilities, culture, family, or community mirror your experiences and views of science? As a teaching strategy, how do you think digital stories could benefit diverse learners?

When you have completed your digital photostory, reflect on the following questions: How do the images you incorporated represent science and you? In other words, answer this question by considering your gender, your racial and ethnic background, your socioeconomic status, the geographic location of your upbringing, and so forth. How does your digital story reflect your community, culture, schooling, and experiences growing up? How are they influenced by your access to and participation in science? How might your past experiences and views of science influence who you are as a K–8 science teacher?

One strategy to become a teacher who effectively addresses diversity in the classroom is reflective thinking (Gay, 2002; Villegas & Lucas, 2002). If we simply represent—or *re*-present—science only as we know it, we run the risk of marginalizing all those students in our classrooms whose cultures and experiences are rich, yet different from our own. By becoming conscious of how culture and experience shape the ways we personally view science, we become more purposeful in recognizing the cultures, experiences, and abilities of our students to maximize their opportunities to access and learn science in our classrooms and beyond.

> **TECH CONNECT: Digital Storytelling**
>
> What stories could your K–8 students tell using digital stories in your science classroom? How could your students use photos to convey science ideas and concepts in new and unique ways? Maybe your students could find examples of potential and kinetic energy in their world, or perhaps they could create a photo story that documents the changes in a tree they've adopted through the seasons.

Explore

Each Student Is Unique

Now that you've have reflected on the ways you have experienced science and how those experiences may have shaped your views of science, consider the question, "How do my views influence the way I teach science and students learn science?" Let's begin to think about these questions in the context of diversity with Ms. Peters. Ms. Sylvia Peters, an experienced teacher who has taught in an urban setting for many years, will tell you that she has seen a lot of changes in her school during her career. The single biggest change that has personally influenced her view on teaching and learning is the increased diversity and unique needs of students in her classroom. She is also a part of a team working on various state standards and curriculum units for sixth-grade science. Out of interest in presenting the contributions of diverse cultures in science, Ms. Peters and her colleagues developed a teaching unit called "The Chemistry of Adornment." The unit explores the physical and chemical processes involved in creating and using dyes to color yarns and cloth that were an integral part of the ancient cultures of Peru, West Africa, India, and the Navajo. Ms. Peter's current sixth graders represent a wide range of learners. She shares the following about some of the diverse students that make up her classroom:

(a) Jesus Morales is an ELL who has recently arrived in her class. He was born in Juarez, Mexico. He predominantly speaks Spanish but knows a few English words.

(b) Chin Li and Maria Chan are from Taiwan. Both were born in the United States and are first-generation U.S. citizens. Both girls speak English and are highly motivated to do well in school.

(c) Jacob Castillo is a wonderful child with enough energy for the entire class. He has a quick wit, is very articulate, loves science, but is highly distracted and is always on the move. Keeping him focused on a task to completion without him rushing through the work is a challenge. He has been diagnosed with attention deficit hyperactivity disorder (ADHD). His mother is not eager to put him on medications and is currently trying to work with you to find strategies for Jacob to be successful in school without medication.

(d) CJ Monahan is an intelligent gifted child who is dyslexic. He struggles with written language. He has learned to read aloud but struggles to comprehend what he reads. He can comprehend if you read aloud to him, but he can't read text himself and comprehend at the same time. Kinesthetic activities need to be modeled for him from his position. In other words, when you're showing him how to hold science equipment, for instance, he has difficulty if you stand in a mirrored position. In addition, he views himself as "dumb" and often gets frustrated with learning tasks and is prone to giving up quickly, thinking himself not capable.

(e) Tenisha Owens is a bright student who excels in reading and writing, but who struggles with math and science. The mere thought of a science test makes her anxious and upset. Although she's quick to respond in Ms. Peter's language arts lessons, when it comes to science time, Tenisha is quiet and does not often participate in class.

Ms. Peters knows that the unit is a good start, but that there are improvements that can be made to the lessons within the unit to create opportunities for all her students to be successful in her class. She starts with the following lesson:

Peru

Background: The Incas have a long and rich history in the use of dyes for textiles. The textiles have been remarkably preserved due to two important factors: (1) clothing was very important to the culture of the Incas and people of importance were buried wrapped in several layers of clothing and adorned cloth, and (2) the dry and sandy conditions of the burial sites have kept the garments in relatively good condition. The oldest evidence of the use of dyes in the area is documented at 2500 BC, with dyes used extensively around 1000 BC. The dyes from the area were remarkably varied, with one historian documenting the use of 190 different hues. This variety was not produced by different dyes, but rather from three main dye colors that were top-dyed (layered colors, one over the other to produce a new hue). The three primary dye colors were red, yellow, and blue. The blues came from an indigo plant native to the area and the reds from the cochineal insect or Nopal cacti from the region; the exact source of the yellow is not known. It is believed that the yellows were produced from any of a variety of leaves or barks from the area. However, the most commonly used dye was from local walnut trees. The walnut husk was used to produce a brown dye. The appearance of decoration with dye emerged around 1000 BC. Textiles have been recovered that depict stylized feline gods, birds, and snakes that were painted on cloth, as well as on pottery and stone using the same dyes.

Objectives

1. Working cooperatively, students will research and present a physical representation (poster, diorama, etc.) of Incan life, including three important details about the daily life of the Incas and a statement of the role of adornment in Incan life.

2. Students will be able to describe the preparation and application of a dye created from walnuts to create a depiction of a symbol important to Incan culture on cloth.

3. Students will be able to design an experiment to show that the walnut dye produces a chemical change.

Activities

Engage: Ask students to select an image they think best represent themselves. Allow students to share their responses and rationales for their choices. Ask students to think about their state and what images come to mind when they think of their state. These might be buildings or landmarks, flags, state symbols, plants or animals found within the state, famous people who were born in the state, and so on. Relate to students that these images are symbols. Ask them to make a list of everyday symbols and put these on the board. Have students write down their ideas of what these symbols are and what they are used for ? (A symbol represents something more than just an image.) State that in this activity you'll be exploring the symbols of an ancient people, their culture, and the science involved in creating their symbols.

Explore

Group Presentations: To give students a better picture of the Incan culture, divide students into cooperative learning groups of four and assign roles. Provide students with the challenge of researching Incan culture and constructing a physical

Quilt created from student dye samples of Incan symbols.

representation of their research findings, making certain to include at least three important details about the Incas in their representations. Important details might include the sources of food for the Incas, living structures, governance, community roles, important symbols, and religion.

Physical representations may be either two or three dimensional, such as a model of an Incan village or a poster that represents the elements of daily life for an Incan. Each student must have a part in the presentation. Provide groups with a rubric that will be used to assess the assignment. During discussions, make certain that students are aware of the historical timeframe they are exploring to present a history of the creation and use of dyes in the region (see background above).

Walnut Dyeing and Top Dyeing

Safety

Wear rubber gloves, goggles, and protective smocks.

No eating or tasting in science labs.

The students will prepare a substantive dye, or one that does not require a process known as mordanting. This process is the application of a fixative to the dye bath, typically a metal salt, in order for the dye to be permanent. The Incas used walnuts as the source of the brown dyes they created. Although the exact species of walnut that was used by the Incas may not be available, any walnut will work. However, you must use either the leaves or the green husks on the walnuts to create the dye. Black walnuts are especially easy to use and the husks will produce a much richer dye than the leaves. If possible, distribute plastic gloves and have students help to collect about three-fourths of a peck of green hulls and place them in a pot. Instruct students to barely cover the hulls with water and allow them to soak for thirty minutes, then to bring the water to a boil for fifteen minutes. After the water cools, tell students to remove the hulls and add enough water to create four and a half gallons of the dye bath. While students are waiting for the dye to be prepared, have them create stencils of an animal that was important to the Incan culture. Stencils may be created out of file folders or plastic used for stenciling, which you can find in hardware or craft stores. There are several good examples of actual animal symbols that were used in Incan fabrics found in reference books. When the dye is ready, have students paint using their stencils on dry cloth (cotton works well). If time allows, provide students with additional dyes (purchased) to explore top-dyeing methods described in background above.

Note that other natural materials would have been used by the Incas to produce these colors. Ask students to think about what natural materials might produce some of the colors they are using. Allow the cloth to dry overnight.

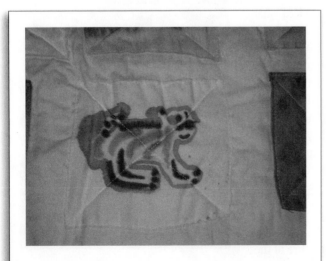

A student's walnut-dyed animal print.

Explain

Chemical or Physical Change? After students have made and applied walnut and top-dyeing methods used by the Incas, lead them in discussion using the following questions: "What is a physical change? What is a chemical change? Knowing what you know about physical and chemical changes, do you think that the dyeing techniques we used involved a physical change, a chemical change, or both?"

In cooperative groups, your team will create tests to determine whether the change was physical or chemical. Note: Students will probably want to rinse or wash the dyed fabrics and may be reluctant to do so with their own creations, so you may want to have additional samples they can test available. The groups should come up with an experimental design that includes multiple hypotheses, procedures with operational definitions, data, data analyses, and summaries of findings. Provide groups with team roles and the assessment rubric that will be used to evaluate their experimental designs.

Elaborate

Exploring Other Dyeing Techniques: In the same cooperative learning groups, have students explore other assigned dyeing techniques, and ask them to determine whether the dyeing process is a physical or a chemical change. If time permits, allow students to investigate with actual dyeing techniques.

Evaluate

Using a rubric, evaluate group presentation and experimental design.

Thinking about this lesson and Ms. Peters' sixth-grade students (CJ, Jesus, Jacob, Tenisha, Maria, and Chin) what lesson modifications would you recommend to Ms. Peters? What strategies do you think might help each of these students be more successful? Write a brief lesson modification for each of the students and include a discussion of the following:

1. What components of the original lesson do you think would be of benefit to CJ, Jesus, Jacob, Tenisha, Maria, and Chin? Why?

2. What modifications, changes, or adaptations do you think could be made to help each of these students have a successful science experience with this lesson? What is your rationale for these changes?

Explain

Focus Questions

1. How does culture affect learning in the science classroom?
2. How do factors such as gender, race, ethnicity, and language affect learners in the science classroom?
3. What might limit students with disabilities in the science classroom and how do I make accommodations to reduce barriers to learning?
4. How do I adapt my science teaching to meet the needs of all my students?

Teaching All Students Science

Before we delve into important background information and discussion of teaching strategies that can help you to be successful in achieving the goal of "Science for All," we begin with words of caution. You may have heard teaching referred to as both an art and a science. And indeed, we'd agree that it is. Teaching is a science—each day you are experimenting with combinations of research-based strategies applied to the unique students in your classroom. You outline procedures, collect data, and analyze results. However, the variables are constantly changing when dealing with human beings, each with unique backgrounds, experiences, and abilities as well as ever-changing conditions and environments for learning. As teachers, we understand that even research-supported strategies will not be effective with every single child and we may have to try several different strategies to be effective in facilitating the learning of all our students. As a professional, you will use your expertise, experience, and creativity to find those combinations that work—and that's where the art of teaching comes in. It requires *knowing* your students and *responding* to their needs as learners. The ways in which we weave these strategies together creates a unique and constantly changing tapestry for our science classrooms. We teach human beings. While it is useful to categorize students to better understand some of their needs and strategies that can help to facilitate learning, there is no one "typical" student with learning disabilities, or one "typical" student who is an ELL, nor is there one strategy that works for these students. It's important that we keep in mind they are individuals first, and are not the labels assigned them. We present the information in this section as a guide to build your awareness and skill with learners that have traditionally lagged behind their peers in the science classroom, however, it is in no way comprehensive. It will be up to you to seek resources and understand the unique needs of the students in your science classrooms to achieve the goal of science for all.

Individuals With Disabilities Education Improvement Act (IDEIA)

One of the first pieces of legislation in the United States that directly addresses the needs of diverse student was the Education for All Handicapped Children Act (EAHCA), signed into law in 1975. Prior to that time, only one in five students with disabilities was educated in public schools. Some states even had laws that prohibited children with certain disabilities from attending public schools, including those students who were blind, deaf, "emotionally disturbed," or "mentally retarded" (U.S. Department of Education, n.d.). EAHCA mandated that all schools accepting public funds provide equal access to education for children with physical and mental disabilities. This act has been revised over time, with the most recent substantive revision in 2004, at which time the act was renamed the Individuals with Disabilities Education Improvement Act or IDEIA. This legislation is often referred to by its original name, the Individuals with Disabilities Education Act (IDEA).

Individuals with Disabilities Education Improvement Act
http://idea.ed.gov/explore/home

Read more about IDEIA including who is covered under the act, as well as webcasts, training, and models of forms used with students with disabilities.

IDEIA requires that special education services meet the unique needs of disabled students from preschool through age twenty-one, and that students with disabilities receive services in public schools that prepare them for further education, employment, and independent living. More specifically, IDEIA requires that an **individualized education plan** (IEP) be developed for each student that qualifies for special education services under federal or state guidelines. The IEP includes assessments of the student's current level of performance and provides a description of how the student's disability(ies) affects academic performance. The IEP also identifies type and frequency of services provided to the student with specific accommodations and modifications. The IEP must be developed by a team of school personnel including the student's regular and special education educators, a school psychologist, and the child's parents. The team must provide educational services in the least restrictive environment, ideally in a regular classroom, when appropriate.

YOUR SCIENCE CLASSROOM:
IEP Team Meeting: Modification vs. Accommodation

In his first year of teaching fifth grade, Mr. Salas encountered his first Individualized Education Plan (IEP) for a student in his classroom who had been diagnosed with attention deficit hyperactivity disorder (ADHD). The IEP required annual revisions; the school special education coordinator called together a team planning meeting to revisit and revise the student's IEP. The team included Mr. Salas, the student's classroom teacher; Ms. Grover, the school special education coordinator; Ms. Taylor, the special education teacher who was to work directly with Mr. Salas and this student to provide services; and Mr. Hinton, the school psychologist. The school-based team was meeting to draft initial updates and revisions to the student's IEP prior to meeting with the student's parents to gain input and finalize this year's IEP. Mr. Salas carefully read through the existing IEP prior to the meeting, but had many questions. As the meeting began, the team spent time reviewing the previous year's IEP and assessment data. Though he was feeling a bit embarrassed that he didn't know, Mr. Salas believed that in order to provide the best possible education this year for this student he needed some clarification regarding the language found in the IEP. Specifically, he wasn't certain what the difference was between an accommodation and a modification, so he asked the team to help him understand by explaining the difference.

Ms. Grover smiled and reassured Mr. Salas, saying, "I know all of this can be a bit overwhelming and we want you to ask as many questions as you have! This is a team effort and so we're all here to help each other. Let me try to explain the difference and the rest of you feel free to jump in." In this student's case, most of the strategies in his IEP are accommodations. Accommodations are changes in the *ways* the learning is facilitated with the student, not in the content he is expected to know; it amounts to doing "whatever it takes" to facilitate the student's learning. So, in this IEP, you can see that one of the accommodations is preferential seating, which means that when we're directing instruction, we keep this student in closer physical proximity to the teacher; also, when the student is completing learning tasks, we do our best to provide a learning environment that

(Continued)

(Continued)

minimizes distractions. So for instance, we face him away from the windows or hallways where he can be distracted by students walking by when he's completing assignments is an accommodation. He also has the choice of picking his quiet area for work or going to the resource room to complete the assignment. Another accommodation is that this student is given additional time to complete assignments. He is still expected, however, to learn the same material. We make accommodations in how we teach and the materials we use to teach such as assignments and assessments, the learning environment, time demands, scheduling, and special communication tools (e.g., charts, diagrams, trackers, and so on). You might notice that these are things we adjust for all students at different times, depending on their learning needs. Modifications are changes to *what* we expect a student to learn. So for instance, with a student that has a more severe learning disability, we might make a modification to the science content within the classroom. It is a little more challenging to give an example of a modification. Ms. Taylor jumped in: "Remember last week when you were having the students create an experimental design to test the strength of the bridges they'd constructed? You had them create their designs from scratch. A modification for a student with a more severe learning disability would be to provide the student with the experimental design you created and guide them through conducting the experiment rather than expecting them to create the design." "Exactly," said Mr. Farnsworth. He went on to say, "It is important to try accommodations before modifications. We're striving to make sure that all our students are achieving at the highest level possible."

> **Teaching Standard
> B: 1 & D: 1**
>
> How does this scenario reflect the standards?

Adapting Science for Special Needs Learners

Teaching science has an advantage over other subject areas because it naturally lends itself to strategies that work well with students with different abilities. For instance, because of its hands-on nature, science requires less reading and offers opportunities for those students with challenges in reading to excel in learning. Also, as we noted in Chapter 1, science is a human endeavor, and the use of cooperative learning groups in the science classroom is a common practice. The use of cooperative learning allows the teacher to construct groups that match students with differing strengths so that everyone contributes and succeeds. Also, cooperative learning is a strategy that lends itself to peer mentoring, giving students more learning opportunities with their peers.

BULLETIN BOARD

Cooperative Learning: Strategies for Diverse Learners

Cooperative learning is an instructional strategy involving grouping students in small groups (usually three to five) working interdependently to accomplish a learning task. It is more than simply putting students into groups and allowing them to talk to each other. Johnson and Johnson (1994) identify five key elements for effective cooperative learning:

1. **Positive interdependence**. In short, this term means students need each other to achieve their goal. Strategies for promoting positive interdependence include

   (a) creating a common goal;

   (b) giving group grades and rewards for individual achievement of goals (e.g., if all group members score at least 90% on the individual assessment, the group receives bonus points);

   (c) creating resource interdependence so that groups have to rely on the materials of each team member to achieve a goal (sometimes called a jigsaw or assembly line method); and

   (d) assigning roles for each group member (e.g., investigation director, data recorder, lab materials manager, lab reporter, etc.) that require working together to achieve goals.

2. **Face-to-face interaction**. Working cooperatively in groups creates opportunities for students to support each other's learning through activities such as explaining how to solve problems, teaching skills or content to each other, checking for understanding, and discussing concepts or results while connecting new learning to past learning.

3. **Individual accountability**. Students also need a clearly perceived personal accountability to the group in cooperative learning tasks. Encouraging individual accountability may occur by giving individual assessments, randomly calling on one group member to discuss the group's results of a learning task, or having students teach what they learned to team members.

4. **Interpersonal and small-group skills**. Effective cooperative learning requires interpersonal and small-group skills that need to be taught and supported. An important part of cooperative learning is teaching and nurturing social skills, leadership, decision making, trust building, communication skills, and conflict resolution with students.

5. **Group processing**. To maximize the benefits of cooperative learning, it is important to include opportunities for groups to debrief learning activities, discuss what worked well and what didn't, and brainstorm ways to improve the group for future learning activities.

Finally, you will recall in Chapter 7 that teaching science using inquiry methods can be open ended. By fostering open-ended inquiry you can challenge students to create and explore their own questions, tapping into individuals' interests and providing multiple means for learning science content. For example, suppose you are teaching about circuits in a science unit on electricity. You may have students manipulate wires, a battery, and a light bulb to create a completed circuit, make diagrams of circuits, run computer-based demonstrations on circuits, read about circuits in science trade books, write about the construction of circuit boards, use circuits to create a game, and so on. Providing choices creates multiple pathways for learning science content and opportunities for accommodations that help to ensure that all students may have success in learning science.

TECH CONNECT:
Computer-Based Demonstrations

Check out an example of a computer-based demonstration on circuits: http://www.brainpop.com/science/energy/electriccircuits/. How could you use computer-based demonstrations in your science classroom?

Using multiple pathways for learning is often referred to as **differentiated instruction**. Differentiated instruction is not a single strategy; rather, it is an approach to teaching that combines a variety of strategies to meet individual student needs. Using a differentiated instructional approach works well for all students, but is especially appropriate for differently abled students. It allows all students to access the same science content and learning by providing different points of entry, associated learning tasks, and specific outcomes that are tailored to students' needs (Hall, Strangman, & Meyer, 2003). As K–8 science teachers, we should be differentiating instruction for all students, but it is helpful to explore in more detail some general strategies for differentiated instruction in the science classroom as it relates to students with different learning needs.

BULLETIN BOARD

Accommodations for Students With Disabilities in Your Science Classroom

Reading Accommodations for Science Texts, Trade Books or Other Written Materials

- Highlight important science textbook and handout passages. Remind students to focus on the highlighted material first.
- Provide students with a study guide with key words missing to complete as they read.
- Provide students with partners who read the material out loud.
- For students with sight impairments, provide text in Braille or provide a magnifier.

Accommodations for Directed Instruction, Lectures, or Discussions

- Use visuals (e.g., charts, diagrams, data tables, pictures, webs) to accompany instruction or discussion and to reinforce key ideas.
- Tap into prior knowledge to connect with new ideas.
- Provide students with an overview before beginning the lesson (also called an advanced organizer).
- Allow students to audio or video record instruction or discussion.
- Write key phrases on the board to emphasize their importance; use a color to highlight key terms.
- Summarize all important points and rephrase key ideas.
- Provide students with note outlines with key words or ideas missing to use during instruction, or provide the student with a notetaker or a copy of notes.
- Use a sign language interpreter for students with hearing disabilities.
- Use cooperative learning to create opportunities for active participation in the experiment as opposed to roles that require extensive reading or writing.

Accommodations for Writing

- Allow students to use a word processor to complete lab sheets, science journals, and other key written assignments in class.
- Use a partner to write down student responses.
- Use adaptive devices such as special writing instruments, papers with raised or colored lines, and so on.
- Use adaptive technologies such as a voice recognition system that allows students to verbally respond and see their words recorded as text on a computer.

- Grade content and mechanics separately on written assignments.
- Provide alternative assessments for assignments that include opportunities for students to represent their ideas in ways other than writing.
- Use cooperative learning groups in science labs that allow students who struggle with writing.

Accommodations for Labs, Investigations, or Assignments

- Have students repeat directions in their own words and demonstrate to you what they're being asked to do.
- Model what you are asking students to do.
- Model metacogntive processes, and "think out loud" for students.
- Provide directions in alternative forms such as pictures or, when given orally initially, in written step-by-step instructions.
- Have students work with learning partners or in cooperative learning groups.
- Break investigations, data collection, and other learning tasks into smaller chunks to help maintain focus.

General Accommodations for Organization

- Use color-coding systems to help students organize different types of information (e.g., green = vocabulary, red = key ideas, blue = important names or dates).
- Make sure the written materials you provide students are uncluttered, have a clear starting point, and follow a logical order.
- Provide students with organizational tools such as lab notebooks where they can organize their materials and color code their notes.
- Allow students extra time to complete learning tasks, assignments, and tests when appropriate.
- Use assistive technologies when appropriate.
- Break down larger tasks or assignments into smaller tasks and give students a timeline and checkpoints.

Adapted from *Accommodations and Modifications: What Parents Need to Know* (Florida Department of Education, 2003).

You may recognize many of the strategies discussed in this chapter as those mentioned in previous chapters, including the use of varied and diverse learning activities in the classroom to tap into preferred learning styles, alternative assessments, and cooperative learning techniques. So, think back on the students in Ms. Peter's class. Do you have any new ways to adapt the lesson plan to meet the needs of some of her students? We have only touched on a few effective strategies for differentiating instruction for differently abled students. It is important for you to recognize that there are a variety of resources available to you within your schools. Seeking out the expertise of your fellow classroom teachers, special education instructors, and specialists, as well as making use of resource materials in your school and district, will assist you in achieving the goal of science for all in your classroom.

Gender and Minorities in Science

Have you ever wondered about diversity within the fields of science? If so, you probably know that women and minorities are underrepresented in science, technology, engineering, and mathematics (STEM) career fields. An analysis of 2006 data found 18.9 million jobs in the United States in the fields of science and engineering; women

If this picture were in a science textbook, what message might it give to girls about doing science? What other message might it send to diverse students?

held only 8.2 million (43%) of those jobs, yet make up about 50% of the population. A larger gap exists in the number of minorities working in science- and engineering-related fields, with minorities holding only about 4.5 million of the 18.9 million jobs (National Science Foundation [NSF], 2009). Minorities currently represent just over one third of the U.S. population, but hold fewer than 25% of the science and engineering jobs. Although strides have been made in closing these gaps, it is clear that there is still much work to do be done. Paying special attention to how we facilitate learning opportunities in our K–8 science classrooms can have a powerful impact on the involvement of women and minorities in the future. First, let's take a look at gender in the science classroom.

Gender Equity in the Science Classroom

Gender stereotypes for females and males in schools can limit educational opportunities for our students. In science we've become primarily concerned with how gender bias affects females. Both overtly and inadvertently, girls have been sent the message that STEM subjects are for boys, not girls. That message has appeared in numerous forms. For instance, it has been seen in the ways males and females are portrayed in science textbooks, how parents and teachers encourage students, the interactions between teachers and students in science classrooms, and the differing experiences or opportunities for boys and girls in science both in and out of the school setting (Bailey, 1992; Zittleman & Sadker, 2010). As teachers, becoming aware of our often unintended and subtle messages is a critical component to promoting effective learning and engagement of both boys and girls in your science classroom.

Strategies for Teaching Science to Female Students

Science teachers unintentionally reinforce the stereotype that science is for males by calling on boys more than girls during science discussions, paying more attention to boys, providing more encouragement for boys in the science classroom, and not monitoring the roles that boys and girls perform in science inquiry activities (Bailey, 1992; McCormick, 1995). Incorporating strategies in your science classroom such as using wait time (discussed in Chapter 6), being purposeful about calling on different students, and using classroom materials such as textbooks, trade books, and bulletin boards that reflect diversity and include images of women doing science will help to reduce gender bias. In addition, make sure that you're providing equal assistance and support for both boys and girls as they

BULLETIN BOARD

Research on Gender in STEM Fields

- Teachers tend to pay more attention to boys than girls, calling on boys more frequently, interacting with boys more than with girls, and giving boys more encouragement than girls (Einarsson & Granström, 2002; Lockheed & Harris, 1984; Massey & Christensen, 1990; Rodriguez, 2002; Sadker, Sadker, & Bauchner, 1984).

- Books perpetuate stereotypical images of gender, or underrepresent females both in text and images (Zittleman & Sadker, 2002–2003).

- Fifty-one percent of boys, compared to 37% of girls, have used a microscope by the end of the third grade (Jones & Gerig, 1994).

engage in hands-on science experiences. The use of these strategies can go a long way in helping girls develop positive attitudes about science and experience more success in your science classroom. Furthermore, these steps help to debunk the stereotype that science is for males. More specifically, "Encouraging Girls in Math and Science," a U.S. Department of Education publication produced by the Institute of Education Sciences of the National Center for Education Research (Halpern, Aronson, Reimer, Simpkins, Star, & Wentzel, 2007), makes five research-supported recommendations for promoting gender equity in science and math (Table 10.1).

Again, we remind you that these are just some of the recommendations to foster success for girls in your science classroom.

Recall your digital photostory (this chapter). Were there images selected that reflect gender bias in science? If so, did you recognize it? You must be cognizant of such biases to create a positive learning environment free of gender bias. Incorporating the strategies and recommendations mentioned in this section can foster equity for males and females and ultimately encourage more students (especially women) to pursue science-related careers. Numerous reports indicate that in order to meet the STEM workforce needs of the twenty-first century, it is critical that we increase the involvement of women (American Association of University Women [AAUW], 2010). We have made strides in leveling the academic achievement of females in the science classroom. Today there are only small differences between girls' and boys' science and mathematics scores, according to the National Assessment of Educational Progress (NAEP) (Grigg, Lauko, & Brockway, 2006). However, according to a 2010 report issued by the AAUW, "Despite the tremendous gains that girls and women have made in education and the workforce during the past 50 years, progress has been uneven, and certain scientific and engineering disciplines remain overwhelmingly male" (2010). By working to keep your science classroom free of gender bias and creating a learning environment that fosters a variety of interests, participation and equity for all students in your classroom, you can play an important role in the continued progress and advancement of women in science. Revisit your initial modifications of Ms. Peter's lesson plan. In light of the information presented, what additional ideas do you have to modify the lesson for the girls in her classroom?

Students Who Are Culturally and Linguistically Diverse

Unfortunately, students with disabilities and girls aren't the only audience we need to pay special attention to in the science classroom. Similar challenges in science education exist among minority cultures, especially Black students and Hispanic students. That is not to say that Black and Hispanic students constitute the range of cultural diversity that you may find in your classroom. It is important to recognize that cultural diversity refers to culture in its broadest sense. Culture includes beliefs, values, traditions, religion, social expectations, and shared behaviors or practices of a group, so it encompasses not only race and ethnicity, but also local and regional cultures. However, in the United States, Black and Hispanic students represent the largest groups of minority students in public schools.

To understand the issue better, it is useful to once again look at the Nation's Report Card, also known as the National Assessment of Academic Progress (NAEP) (Grigg et al., 2006). The most recent (2006) NAEP results indicate there has been some improvement in fourth- and eighth-grade science scores for minority students. However, an analysis of science scores from 1996, 2000, and 2005 indicates there was no significant change or improvement for Black students or Hispanic students at twelfth grade between 1996 and 2005 (Grigg et al.). This means we've done little over the past decade to narrow the gap between White students

Table 10.1 Promoting Gender Equity in Science

Recommendation 1: Teach students that academic abilities are expandable and improvable.

- Teach students that working hard to learn new knowledge leads to improved performance.
- Remind students that the mind grows stronger with use and with continued effort understanding the material will get easier.

Recommendation 2: Provide prescriptive, informational feedback.

- Provide students with feedback that focuses on strategies used during learning, as opposed to simply telling them whether they got an answer correct. This strategy encourages students to correct misunderstandings and learn from their mistakes.
- Provide students with positive feedback about the effort they expended on solving a difficult problem or completing other work related to their performance.
- Avoid using general praise, such as "good job," when providing feedback to individual students or an entire class.
- Make sure that there are multiple opportunities for students to receive feedback on their performance.

Recommendation 3: Expose girls and young women to female role models who have succeeded in math and science.

- Invite older girls and women who have succeeded in math- or science-related courses and professions to be guest speakers or tutors in your class.
- Assign biographical readings about women scientists, mathematicians, and engineers, as part of students' assignments.
- Call attention to current events highlighting the achievements of women in math or science. When talking about potential careers, make students aware of the numbers of women who receive advanced degrees in math- and science-related disciplines.
- Provide girls and young women with information about mentoring programs designed to support students who are interested in mathematics and science.
- Encourage parents to take an active role in providing opportunities for girls to be exposed to women working in the fields of math and science.

Recommendation 4: Create a classroom environment that sparks initial curiosity and fosters long-term interest in math and science.

- Embed mathematics word problems and science activities in contexts that are interesting to both boys and girls.
- Provide students with access to rich, engaging relevant informational and narrative texts as they participate in classroom science investigations.
- Capitalize on novelty to spark initial interest. That is, use project-based learning, group work, innovative tasks, and technology to stir interest in a topic.
- Encourage middle and high school students to examine their beliefs about which careers are typically female-oriented and which are typically male-oriented. Encourage these students to learn more about careers that are interesting to them but that they believe employ more members of the opposite gender.
- Connect mathematics and science activities to careers in ways that do not reinforce existing gender stereotypes of these careers.

Recommendation 5: Provide spatial skills training.

- Recognize that children may not automatically recognize when spatial strategies can be used to solve problems and that girls are less likely to use spatial strategies than boys. Teach students to mentally image and draw spatial displays in response to mathematics and science problems.
- Require students to answer mathematics and science problems using both verbal responses and spatial displays.
- Provide opportunities for specific training in spatial skills such as mental rotation of images, spatial perspective, and embedded figures.

Note: From Halpern, D., Aronson, J., Reimer, N., Simpkins, S., Star, J., & Wentzel, K. (2007). *Encouraging girls in math and science* (NCER 2007-2003). Washington, DC: National Center for Education Research, Institute of Education Sciences, U.S. Department of Education. Retrieved from http://ncer.ed.gov.

and minority students, especially Black students and Hispanic students. In fact, some suggest that there hasn't been any significant progress in closing the achievement gap for Black students for more than twenty years (Barton & Coley, 2010). The gap in science achievement translates into underrepresentation of minority populations in science-related fields (NSF, 2009). This trend is summed up in the following: "Achievement and participation data tell us that it scarcely matters whether underrepresented students of color have an interest in SET [science, engineering, technology] careers. Because of the inadequate education received, low achievement levels often preclude their successfully attempting a SET career" (Congressional Commission on the Advancement of Women and Minorities in Science, Engineering and Technology Development, 2000, p. 18).

So why do some minority students lag behind in science achievement? That's a complex problem with no clear answers. Factors such as higher levels of poverty among minority students, attitudes and beliefs of teachers and school administrations, lack of resources in schools that serve minority populations, family structures, lack of high-quality teachers, and cultural factors that discourage students from engaging in learning all contribute to the challenge. What is perhaps a more important question to you as a K–8 science teacher is, How can we work to decrease this gap in science achievement among our culturally diverse students? One response is, we can implement a **culturally responsive pedagogy** (Villegas, 1991). Culturally responsive pedagogy "recognizes and utilizes the students' culture and language in instruction, and ultimately respects the students' personal and community identities" (Richards, Brown, & Forde, 2006, p. 7).

Before engaging in culturally responsive teaching, you should start by examining your own attitudes and beliefs about different cultures, especially as they relate to science. Consider the following: "Because teachers' values impact relationships with students and their families, teachers must reconcile negative feelings towards any cultural, language, or ethnic group. Often teachers are resistant to the notion that their values might reflect prejudices or even racism towards certain groups. When teachers are able to rid themselves of such biases, they help to create an atmosphere of trust and acceptance for students and their families, resulting in greater opportunity for student success" (Richards et al., 2006, p. 5).

Understanding our own values and counteracting any stereotypes or negative feelings we might hold about cultural, language, or ethnic groups can help to pave the way toward creating positive relationships between you and all your students. Research suggests that as much as our negative stereotypes can disenfranchise students and limit learning and participation in science, meaningful student–teacher relationships can have a positive impact, helping culturally diverse students to be successful (Brand, Glasson, & Green, 2006). Often neglected, but important to culturally responsive teaching, is learning about the culture of the students through their family and community. Strategies such as making home visits and visits to community organizations or other local gathering spaces can help you to gain critical insight into what may influence students' attitudes and behaviors. Furthermore, such culturally responsive activity opens the door to involve families and community members as resources in your science classroom (Richards et al., 2006).

In addition to developing an awareness of culture (both your own and that of your students), there are additional strategies that can promote success for diverse learners in your science classroom. You will notice that many of the strategies overlap with those stated previously for students with different abilities and girls. Effective science teaching incorporates many of the

YOUR SCIENCE CLASSROOM:
Grades 3–5 Science Team Meeting:
Culture and Communication

Teaching Standard B: 1

How does this scenario reflect this standards?

As the third- to fifth-grade science team met for its weekly planning session, Ms. Able, a first-year teacher, began discussion about a frustration she was experiencing with some of her students. She related to her team members that during her science lab last week on simple machines, it was clear that one of her students, Jaime, was struggling with the concepts. Ms. Able described how as she began to draw some diagrams and use them to explain the concept of a fulcrum, Jaime was looking down and wasn't paying attention to a word she was saying. "How am I supposed to get through to him?" she asked of the team. Ms. Gomez responded, "Jaime was in my class last year and one thing that might be helpful for you to know is that Jaime comes from a fairly traditional Mexican family. In that culture, it's disrespectful to make eye contact with someone who is viewed as an authority figure such as a parent or teacher. By not looking at you when you speak, he's showing respect. But he is listening. If you're checking for understanding, try checking in with Jaime verbally and asking him to explain it back to you in his own words." "Um, I never thought of it that way—that's an important thing to know! Thank you for explaining this to me without making me feel stupid. I really appreciate that."

elements that have been found to promote success in science for diverse students. These strategies include (a) constructivist approaches to teaching, especially tapping into prior knowledge and experiences, (b) teaching for conceptual change (see Chapter 4), (c) using cooperative learning groups, (d) using a variety of learning styles with hands-on science activities and experiments, especially those that tap into cultures, (e) using alternative assessments, and (f) ensuring that texts, books, pictures, bulletin boards, and any other visual information reflects diverse participation in science. In addition to these general strategies, the Bulletin Board: Checklist for Culturally Responsive Science Classrooms reveals ways for creating a science classroom that is culturally responsive to diverse learners.

BULLETIN BOARD

Checklist for Culturally Responsive Science Classrooms

1. Does the culture of my classroom reflect the language and culture of the community?

2. Do my science instructional materials
   - present diverse images and content that celebrate the rich history and contributions of diverse cultures to the field of science?
   - portray diverse people actively engaging in science in an authentic way?
   - present positive images of diverse people?
   - undergo evaluation for stereotyping, bias, racism, underrepresentation, and other inaccuracies?

3. Do I use a variety of science teaching methods to accommodate the diverse learning styles of my students? Do I use hands-on learning opportunities whenever possible?

4. Do I encourage students to take pride in their culture and provide opportunities for inclusion of students' culture in learning tasks?

5. In my school and classroom, are community celebrations and important cultural events observed?

6. Do I use community as a classroom resource (places, people, materials) when appropriate and possible?

7. Am I careful to avoid cultural bias in my evaluations and assessments? Do I make use of a range of learning styles and alternative assessments that allow diverse students to represent their learning in different ways?

8. Do I take time to learn more about community culture by visiting with students, parents, families, and community members?

9. Do the parents of my students feel welcome in my classroom? Do I send written or electronic communications to parents in their native language whenever possible?

10. Do I make a point to regularly contact all my students' parents with positive messages about their children?

11. Am I aware of the way cultures represented in my classroom affect communications and interactions?

12. Is my classroom a place where equity and mutual respect are practiced?

13. Are students encouraged to lead discussion in my science classroom?

14. Am I aware of and do I interact with students in ways that respect preferences for speaking that may be different from my own, such as wait time, eye contact, turn-taking, or spotlighting?

15. Do I encourage my students to use science content vocabulary to express their understanding of ideas?

16. Do I promote written and oral language development using strategies such as modeling, eliciting, probing, restating, clarifying, questioning, praising, and so on, in purposeful discussion and writing?

17. Do I use communication styles appropriate for students' cultural preferences, such as co-narration, call-and-response, and choral, among others?

18. Do I set high expectations, use praise, and encourage all of my students?

Modified from Assessment Checklist, Indian and Metis Staff Development Program, Saskatchewan Education, 1995, p. 243.

The strategies presented for diverse learners help to achieve the dual mission of boosting achievement and stimulating interest in science for all students. This is not, however, a comprehensive list of strategies and your continued exploration of culturally responsive pedagogies will be critical as classrooms become increasingly diverse. In using culturally responsive approaches to teaching, your goal is to create a science learning environment that capitalizes on the diversity of students' interests and experiences, promotes beliefs in students that science is for everyone, and provides multiple and diverse opportunities for students to learn. Remember that a powerful teaching tool you have for ensuring student success in science is tapping into your students' culture and community. How well did you do in modifying Ms. Peter's lesson plan to be culturally responsive? Are there any changes you'd make now?

Science and English Language Learners

Classrooms in the United States are becoming more diverse not only in terms of culture, but also in terms of language. Increasingly, our science classrooms have students whose first language is not English. Recent census data show that over the past twenty-five years the number of ELLs from ages five to seventeen grew from 3.8 million to 9.9, million or approximately 10% of the entire U.S. school population (Grigg et al., 2006). As a K–8 science teacher, you will need to develop skills and strategies that meet the needs of the ELL student. At the risk of sounding like a broken record, much of what we have already discussed as important strategies for learning science, such as tapping into students' prior knowledge, using varied teaching approaches, particularly those that rely on visual or kinesthetic learning, using guided inquiry, scaffolding instruction, and using alternative assessments, are all strategies that support ELL students' learning in the science classroom. It is, however, also important that you address the language needs of ELL students, and science offers unique opportunities to do so. The active science classroom is rich with learning that engages students in small-group discussions, whole-group discussions, demonstrations, explaining, inferring, hypothesizing, describing, elaborating, and synthesizing. The language of science is both a challenge and an opportunity. The language opportunities embedded within hands-on explorations, demonstrations, and experiments in the science classroom provide relevant and real-life opportunities to not only learn the content of science, but also to acquire a greater facility with languages (Buxton, 1998; Laplante, 1997; Wellington & Osborne, 2001).

Science vocabulary presents challenges for many students but it can be even more challenging to ELL students. Many words such as "energy" or "family" are technical or specialized terms in science, but have different meanings in conversational English. In the process of language acquisition, it is important to remember that it takes ELLs about one to two years to acquire conversational language, but up to five to seven years to acquire academic language (Cummins, 1984). The ability to effectively communicate with fellow students in the lunchroom doesn't mean ELL students are proficient in classroom communications. Corder (2008) advocates specific strategies for the integration of language acquisition in the science classroom that include (a) setting language objectives in addition to science content and process objectives, (b) supplying background information (e.g., modeling steps for complex tasks, thinking out loud, word walls and using visuals with new vocabulary), and (c) modifying written materials (e.g., highlighting key words, writing notes in the margin, including illustrations with directions, or rewriting text in different words without "dumbing it down"). The use of graphic organizers (e.g., webs, concept maps, T-charts, feedback diagrams), in particular, can be an important tool for ELL students. Graphic organizers serve three functions for ELL students. They generate understanding as students fill in organizers, help to scaffold learning, and serve as an assessment of student understanding (Díaz-Rico, 2008; Verplaetse & Migliacci, 2008).

Additional strategies for ELL students include (a) introducing vocabulary during or after hands-on experiences that help to illustrate the words or contextualize the language, and (b) using charts and graphs to illustrate ideas and encourage students to use vocabulary in different contexts as well as during investigations and experiments in the science classroom (Jarrett, 1999). The key is embedding the language within a context, rather than focusing on vocabulary development in isolation. If you think about your own experiences, you may recognize times when you've encountered unfamiliar vocabulary that you were able to figure out because of the context. If you continue to encounter and use that new vocabulary, it is much more likely that you will retain its meaning. Also, by presenting material (both oral and written) in language that matches the ELL student's level of competence, including sentence length, complexity, and levels of abstraction while gradually altering language to be just a level above the student's language abilities, the science classroom can become an effective place for language acquisition (Lee & Avalos, 2003).

Again, you may recognize that there are several strategies for diverse learners that also facilitate learning for ELLs. It makes sense that many of the strategies presented for diverse learners are applicable for ELLs. In particular, connecting with the family can be especially important. Parents of ELL students can provide you with invaluable information about their child's learning styles, interests, and previous experiences, as well as their hopes and goals for their child (Jarrett, 1999). Additionally, the use of study guides that prompt students to fill in missing words, as mentioned earlier for students with disabilities, can also be a useful strategy for ELL students. "Of particular use to ELL students are partial 'sentence chunks' that scaffold the types of sentences students should use to communicate their scientific knowledge. Sentence chunks allow students to express their scientific learning without being hindered by a lack of language skills—they also model the types of scientific language students can use in the future. As students become more proficient less scaffolding is required" (Ballantyne, Sanderman, & Levy, 2008, p. 49). The use of cooperative learning or paired learning opportunities can be especially important for ELL students because they create opportunities for small-group contextualized discussion, which can be a more comfortable environment than whole-class discussion for ELL students to practice their language acquisition (Gersten, Baker, Shanahan, Linan-Thompson, Collins, & Scarcella, 2007).

It is important to note that silence is a strategy that ELL students often use in the classroom. ELL students may focus on comprehending language prior to speaking or writing. It takes time for them to compose their thoughts prior to speaking, or they just take time out from the focus required to learn in another language. Furthermore, it is important with ELL students that both you and your students focus on *what* fellow classmates are saying, not on *how* they say it. There is some evidence to suggest that constant corrections to ELL students discourage dialogue. Creating an environment where ELL students are encouraged to practice with language skills without fear of correction or embarrassment supports stronger language acquisition (Crawford & Krashen, 2007; Díaz-Rico, 2008).

At this point, it may seem the challenge of meeting all students' needs is overwhelming, but remember that many of the strategies for both effective science teaching and diverse learners overlap. Teaching for conceptual change, and using constructivist-based approaches, cooperative learning strategies, and inquiry approaches are all effective strategies for students with special needs as well. Perhaps the most valuable lesson for a teacher in addressing the needs of all your students is to use a variety of approaches that facilitate differentiated instruction. The background information and strategies presented here for students with unique learning needs in your science classroom are intended to raise your awareness and provide you with some initial tools for your teaching toolbox, but they are in no way exhaustive. Utilizing additional school and community resources, such as special education or ELL teachers, and engaging in professional development to develop your skills will help you to achieve the goal of "science for all" in your K–8 science classroom.

Elaborate

Science in a Foreign Language

Now it's time to take some of what you've learned about meeting the needs of diverse learners and apply it to a new setting. While many of you may already fall into the category of one of the diverse learners discussed in this chapter, in this elaborate phase you're going to experience what it's like to be an ELL student. Go to www.youtube.com and search for "Step T for ELLs: Teaching Science to Diverse Students." As you watch this video, consider the following questions:

- What are you feeling as you try to understand the concepts being taught?
- What do you think is the concept being taught in this lesson?
- What strategies are used by the teacher in this video to assist you as a learner?
- What strategies in the video make learning more difficult?
- What additional strategies could the teacher use to further facilitate learning? In answering this question, consider strategies for the wide range of diverse learners.
- What additional "best practices" in science teaching could be applied to make learning more meaningful for all students?

While viewing this video, you may have a better understanding of some of the experiences of ELL students in a science classroom. It is, however, important to remember that you only experienced nine minutes, whereas the ELL student's experience it throughout the school day. You also have a very different cultural background that influences your science understandings, so recognize that this task is not intended to be comparable to the experiences of an ELL student.

Evaluate

Creating a "Science for All" Toolkit

For the evaluate phase, you're going to create a "Science for All Toolkit." In the spirit of alternative assessments, you may choose to create your toolkit in a way that you feel best represents your learning. You might, for instance, choose to create your toolkit as a concept map, a toolkit notebook, a file box with note cards, a poster, a PowerPoint presentation, or a video. Your Science for All toolkit should contain the following:

1. Information on at least six science classroom strategies for each of the following diverse learner audiences: students with disabilities, female students, students from diverse cultural backgrounds, and ELLs. At least one of the strategies for each group needs to come from your own research and not have been previously identified in this chapter. A useful place to start your search is with the annotated bibliography located at the end of the chapter.

2. A list of at least three famous or real-world scientists from each of the following categories: scientists with disabilities (learning or physical), female scientists, and scientists from diverse cultures (aim for diversity here). Include a brief biography for each scientist you select that includes a description of the work each scientist does and a picture, if available, and discuss how you might integrate the inclusion of these scientists in your science classroom.

Summary

Real education should consist of drawing the goodness and the best out of our own students. What better books can there be than the book of humanity?

César Chávez

It might seem to you that this chapter presents some tremendous challenges for you as a K–8 science teacher in addressing the needs of diverse learners, yet there are also tremendous opportunities that diversity brings to your science classroom. Consider for a moment the field of ecology. Ecology is the study of organisms and their environment. Community ecology focuses on the study of species that function together as a unit; this interdependency forms a community. A benchmark in the ecology of a strong community ecosystem is biodiversity. Biodiversity is often a measure of the health of an ecosystem. For example, when biologists study stream ecosystems, one indicator of a healthy stream is evidence of macroinvertebrates diversity. A similar principle applies to K–8 science teaching and learning. Your science classroom is a richer community when there is evidence of diversity—diversity in your students, diversity in your students' interests, diversity in the learning strategies that you use to teach science, and diversity in the ways you assess science learning. If you work with, rather than against, the diversity in your classroom, you open up opportunities for actively engaging students in their own learning. By drawing on the rich diverse backgrounds of your students, you can create enthusiasm and excitement for learning science in a climate fostering success for all your students.

Success in your science classroom for all students is especially important in light of concerns about America's ability to remain competitive in the global economy, which are directly connected to the increasing need for a STEM-related workforce. If we, as a country, are to remain competitive in the global economy, it is imperative that all students are achieving at high levels in science and math and that we encourage our students to pursue STEM-related careers. It is only through this diverse representation in STEM-related careers that we will continue to be a vibrant and strong country.

Annotated Resources

Center for Research on Education, Diversity, and Excellence (CREDE)

http://gse.berkeley.edu/research/crede/standards.html

This website contains standards that represent a research consensus designed to create the ideal conditions for instruction of all cultural, racial, and linguistic groups in the United States, all age levels, and all subject matters.

National Clearinghouse for English Language Acquisition

http://www.ncela.gwu.edu/

This website offers a rich resource library for teaching ELLs, as well as a state information system that provides you with state-based resources, contacts, and standards. Some of the resources are specific to science.

SciTrain

http://www.catea.gatech.edu/scitrain/

This website contains modules for learning more about meeting the needs of students with disabilities. Included is a section that lists specific accommodations for students with special needs in the science classroom.

Teaching Diverse Learners

http://www.lab.brown.edu/tdl/

The Teaching Diverse Learners website offers background information and strategies for addressing the needs of diverse learners, including a section devoted to culturally responsive pedagogy and creating strong relationships with families and communities.

SciGirls

http://www.pbs.org/teachers/scigirls/

This website is part of the SciGirls project of the Public Broadcasting System (PBS). The teacher site includes resources for engaging girls in science. A companion site for kids, found at www.pbskids.org/scigirls/, has videos of girls doing science, science activities, and a social networking opportunity where girls create a profile and become a part of an online community, all designed to promote girls' interest and involvement in science.

References

American Association of University Women (AAUW). (2010). *Why so few? Women in science, mathematics, engineering and technology.* Washington, DC: Author.

Assessment Checklist, Indian and Metis Staff Development Program. Saskatchewan Education, 1995. Available at http://www.newteachersnwt.ca/culture_based_education2.html.

Bailey, S. (1992). *How schools shortchange girls: The AAUW report.* New York: Marlowe & Company.

Ballantyne, K. G., Sanderman, A. R., & Levy, J. (2008). *Educating English language learners: Building teacher capacity.* Washington, DC: National Clearinghouse for English Language Acquisition. Available at http://www.ncela.gwu.edu/practice/mainstream_teachers.htm.

Barton, P., & Coley, R. (2010). *The black white achievement gap: When progress stopped.* Princeton, NJ: Educational Testing Service. Available at http://www.ets.org/Media/Research/pdf/PICBWGAP.pdf

Brand, B. R., Glasson, G. E., & Green, A. M. (2006). Sociocultural factors influencing students' learning in science and mathematics: An analysis of the perspectives of African American students. *School Science and Mathematics, 106*(5), 228–236.

Buxton, C. A. (1998). Improving the science education of English language learners: Capitalizing on educational reform. *Journal of Women and Minorities in Science and Engineering, 4*(4), 341–369.

Congressional Commission on the Advancement of Women and Minorities in Science, Engineering and Technology Development. (2000). *Land of plenty: Diversity as America's competitive edge in science, engineering and technology.* Washington, DC: Author.

Corder, G. (2008). Supporting English language learners' reading in the science classroom. In J. Brunsell (Ed.), *Readings in science methods* K–8. Arlington, VA: NSTA Press. Originally published in *Science Scope,* May 2007.

Crawford, J., & Krashen, S. (2007). *English learners in American classrooms: 101 questions, 101 answers.* New York: Scholastic.

Cummins, J. (1984). *Bilingualism and special education: Issues in assessment and pedagogy.* Clevedon, UK: Multilingual Matters.

Díaz-Rico, L. T. (2008). *Strategies for teaching English language learners* (2nd ed.). New York: Pearson.

Einarsson, C., & Granström, K. (2002). Gender-biased interaction in the classroom: The influence of gender and age in the relationship between teacher and pupil. *Scandinavian Journal of Educational Research, 46,* 117–127.

Florida Department of Education. (2003). Bureau of Instructional Support and Community Services & Florida Developmental Disabilities Council, Inc. *Accommodations and modifications: What parents need to know.* Available at http://www.fldoe.org/ese/pdf/ac-mod-parents.pdf

Gay, G. (2002). Preparing for culturally responsive teaching. *Journal of Teacher Education, 53*(2), 106–116.

Gersten, R., Baker, S. K., Shanahan, T., Linan-Thompson, S., Collins, P., & Scarcella, R. (2007). *Effective literacy and English language instruction for English learners in the elementary grades: A practice guide* (NCEE 2007-4011). Washington, DC: National Center for Education Evaluation and Regional Assistance, Institute of Education Sciences, U.S. Department of Education. Available at http://ies.ed.gov/ncee.

Grigg, W., Lauko, M., & Brockway, D. (2006). *The nation's report card: Science 2005* (NCES 2006-466). U.S. Department of Education, National Center for Education Statistics. Washington, DC: U.S. Government Printing Office.

Hall, T., Strangman, N., & Meyer, A. (2003). *Differentiated instruction and implications for UDL implementation.* National Center on Accessing the General Curriculum. Available at http://www.k8accesscenter.org/training_resources/udl/diffinstruction.asp.

Halpern, D., Aronson, J., Reimer, N., Simpkins, S., Star, J., & Wentzel, K. (2007). Encouraging girls in math and science (NCER 2007-2003). Washington, DC: National Center for Education Research, Institute of Education Sciences, U.S. Department of Education, Washington, DC. Available at http://ncer.ed.gov.

Individuals with Disabilities Education Improvement Act (IDEIA). (2004). Pub. L. No. 108-446, 118 Stat. 2647. Available at http://frwebgate.access .gpo.gov/cgi-bin/getdoc.cgi?dbname=108_cong_public_laws&docid=f:publ446.108.

Jarrett, D. (1999). *The inclusive classroom: Teaching mathematics and science to English-language learners.* Portland, OR: Northwest Regional Education Laboratory.

Johnson, R., & Johnson, D. (1994). An overview of cooperative learning. In J. Thousand, A. Villa, & A. Nevin (Eds.), *Creativity and collaborative learning* (pp. 30–32). Baltimore: Brookes Press.

Jones, G., & Gerig, T. (1994). Silent sixth-grade students: Characteristics, achievement, and teacher expectations. *The Elementary School Journal, 95,* 169–182.

Laplante, B. (1997). Teaching science to language minority students in elementary classrooms. *New York State Association for Bilingual Education Journal, 12,* 62–83.

Lee, O., & Avalos, M. (2003). Integrating science with English language development. *SEDL (Southwest Educational Development Laboratory) Letter 15*(1, December). Improving Achievement in Mathematics and Science. http://www.sedl.org/pubs/sedl-letter/v15n01/6.html.

Lockheed, M., & Harris, A. (1984). A study of sex equity in classroom interaction. Final Reports #1 and #2. Princeton, NJ: Educational Testing Service.

Massey, D., & Christensen, C. (1990). Student teacher attitudes to sex role stereotyping: Some Australian data. *Educational Studies, 16,* 95–107.

McCormick, P. (1995) Are girls taught to fail? *U.S. Catholic, 60*(2), 38–42.

National Science Foundation (NSF). (2009, January). *Women, minorities, and persons with disabilities in science and engineering: 2009.* NSF 09-305. Arlington, VA: Division of Science Resources Statistics. Available from http://www.nsf.gov/statistics/wmpd/.

National Research Council (NRC). 1996. *National Science Education Standards.* Washington, DC: National Academies Press.

Richards, H., Brown, A., & Forde, T. (2006). *Addressing diversity in schools: Culturally responsive pedagogy.* Tempe, AZ: National Center for Culturally Responsive Educational Systems.

Rodriguez, N. (2002). Gender differences in disciplinary approaches. ERIC Document SP041019.

Sadker, M., Sadker, D., & Bauchner, J. (1984). Teacher reactions to classroom responses of male and female students. Washington, DC, National Institute of Education, ERIC Document ED245839.

U.S. Department of Education. (n.d.). Office of Special Education and Rehabilitative Services. History: Twenty-five years of progress in educating children with disabilities through IDEA. Available from http://www.ed.gov/policy/speced/leg/idea/history.pdf.

Verplaetse, L. S., & Migliacci, N. (2008). Making mainstream content comprehensible through sheltered instruction. In L. S. Verplaetse & N. Migliacci (Eds.), *Inclusive pedagogy for English language learners* (pp. 33–53). New York: Lawrence Erlbaum.

Villegas, A. M. (1991). *Culturally responsive pedagogy for the 1990s and beyond.* (Trends and Issues Paper No. 6). Washington, DC: ERIC Clearinghouse on Teacher Education.

Villegas, A. M., & Lucas, T. (2002). Preparing culturally responsive teachers: Rethinking the curriculum. *Journal of Teacher Education, 53*(13).

Wellington, J., & Osborne, J. (2001). *Language and literacy in science education.* Philadelphia: Open University Press.

Zittleman, K. & Sadker, D. (2002, December/2003, January). Teacher education textbooks: The unfinished gender revolution. *Educational Leadership, 60*(4), 59–63.

Zittlemen, K., & Sadker, D. (2010, December/January). *Gender bias is alive and well affecting our children.* Online PTA: Every child, One voice. Available at http://www.pta.org/3734 .htm.

Chapter 11

Interdisciplinary Connections

Science Across the Curriculum

Learning Objectives

After reading Chapter 1, students will be able to

- describe integration and each of the broad categories that encompass most types of integration approaches,
- apply the processes of integration to create a lesson as part of an integrated unit, and
- take a position on integrating curriculum and defend it by analyzing arguments for and against integration.

NSES TEACHING STANDARDS ADDRESSED IN CHAPTER 11

Standard A: Teachers of science plan an inquiry-based science program for their students. In doing this, teachers

- select science content and adapt design curricula to meet the interests, knowledge, understanding, abilities, and experiences of students; and
- work together as colleagues within and across disciplines and grade levels.

Standard F: Teachers of science actively participate in the ongoing planning and development of the school science program. In doing this, teachers

- plan and develop the school science program;
- participate in decisions concerning the allocation of time and other resources to the science program; and
- participate fully in planning and implementing professional growth and development strategies for themselves and their colleagues.

Source: Reprinted with permission from the National Science Education Standards, copyright 1996, by the National Academy of Sciences, Courtesy of National Academies Press, Washington, DC.

Introduction

According to the National Science Education Standards (NSES; National Research Council [NRC], 1996), planning and working with colleagues is a "vehicle for professional support and growth" (p. 32). More specifically, collective and individual reflective planning is essential for continued growth in teaching science. With this in mind, we are reminded of the value of **professional learning communities** (PLCs). PLCs created in schools are usually teams of teachers and administrators formed for any number of different purposes—all of which ultimately focus on student learning (Dufour, Eaker, & DuFour, 2005). PLCs may use book studies, lesson studies, or even developing and testing a particular strategy for improving student achievement. For example, at some time in your career you may find yourself part of a PLC comprised of an administrator and teachers of science, mathematics, and technology. Together, members of the team learn more about each discipline and jointly design a coherent unit of inquiry that assists students in constructing knowledge with connections across the disciplines. After all, isn't this how most of us go about addressing issues and problems in our lives? Most of us use diverse forms of knowledge without separating them when addressing daily issues. Working professionally with other teachers to develop units that cross content areas is often referred to as multidisciplinary, interdisciplinary, or parallel design (Jackson & Davis, 2000). Though these terms represent subtle differences, they frequently are used interchangeably.

When planning curricular units with other teachers or planning science lessons on your own that make connections with other content areas, you are using an **integrated approach** to teaching. According to the NSES, creating curriculum that is integrated opens up learning so students view the "big picture of scientific ideas" (NRC, 1996, p. 104). Today with No Child Left Behind legislation emphasizing reading and mathematics, keeping the big picture of scientific ideas in the curriculum is a challenge. In many elementary classrooms, science only exists as a vestigial organ in the elementary curriculum body (Goldston, 2005). As such, this chapter presents an overview of some of the most frequently observed approaches that teachers use to integrate science and other content into the curriculum. One common method of implementing a multidisciplinary approach is known as a thematic unit, in which a theme is studied in more than one content area (Barton & Smith, 2000). In this chapter, we take you through the process of creating a thematic unit inspired by children's literature. Finally, a discussion of different types of integrated approaches as well as the pros and cons associated with integration are presented. To begin, consider the challenge of teaching inquiry science that Ms. Young is facing in the following narrative of Your Science Classroom: Finding Curriculum Connections.

YOUR SCIENCE CLASSROOM:
Finding Curriculum Connections

Jill Young was in her second year of teaching first graders at Red Rock Elementary School. It was the end of the day, and she was sitting at her desk surrounded by books and stacks of papers that needed to be assessed. She wasn't, however, contemplating grading papers. She could smell springtime in the air and was thinking how quickly the year would be coming to a close. She anxiously looked over her curriculum guide again and panicked at the number of science concepts

(Continued)

(Continued)

she still needed to teach. She wondered where time had gone and why she hadn't taught more science. Since the implementation of federal legislation No Child Left Behind (2002), teachers in her school spend two to two and half hours daily teaching reading and another hour or more teaching mathematics to meet the annual yearly progress goals. This left little time to teach science. She

> **Teaching Standard A: 1 & A: 2**
>
> How does this scenario reflect these standards?

didn't want to admit it, but when she did teach science it was mostly through reading trade books. She was really struggling with what to do.

As Ms. Young sat contemplating, Ms. McCord, Mr. McCullough, and Ms. Robards walked down the hall and stopped by to say hello. Ms. McCord said, "Hi, Ms. Young, how are things going?" Jill said, "Not, so good. I need some guidance." Ms. McCord replied, "Well, let's have it, what's on your mind?" Jill paused and said, "I need to teach more science and want to do inquiry activities, but I can't ever seem to find enough time. Do you have any ideas?" Ms. Robards in a quiet, confident manner asks, "What are the concepts you want to focus on?" Jill stated, "I want to focus on the standards that address the characteristics of organisms and their habitats, but I have to find time for reading and mathematics, too. How do you do it?" Ms. McCord chimed in, "Why don't you consider integrating the three content areas? There are some trade-offs, but it can be time efficient if you do it carefully. There really is no single approach to integration—it can occur in several ways. You could design it to be multidisciplinary by drawing on concepts of each discipline like thematic units. Or you could also make it project based. Or you could identify a skill that crosses all the content areas. Not to mention that you could set up stations with any of the approaches as well as conduct the activities with the whole class or in teams. How you decide to approach it is your call. You already know what big ideas you want to teach. From there you can either identify the specific concepts in each content area you wish to address or you can generate activities for the content areas. It doesn't matter which you do first because you will eventually do both at some point." Ms. Robards, who has a passion for literacy quietly offers, "Yes, you could have students read several books related to organisms and their characteristics and still get your reading time into the unit. I even have some first-grade trade books on that topic you are welcome to borrow." Mr. McCullough, also nods in agreement. "I sometimes use items in trade books to help my students learn how to collect data. If you are exploring organisms, for starters you might have students group the different kinds of organisms in the books. For instance, have the students count the number of different organisms for each group in the book and then have them snap colored cubes together to represent the number of organisms in each group. Then they can use them to color in the number for each group in bar graphs for comparisons. Of course you can decide what hands-on science activities you want them to do, but some of these ideas may work for you. Hey, I remember when I first started integrating some of my lessons. I suspect you have as many questions as I had back then. Maybe we can help you out with this. Let's get the team together."

> If you were in Ms. Young's situation, what might you do to try to incorporate more science inquiry into the school day? Wh\at questions should Ms. Young ask her colleagues about integration? What do you think may be some of the trade-offs when integrating curriculum instead of teaching content areas separately?

It was an initiation into the love of learning, of learning how to learn . . .
as a matter of interdisciplinary cognition—that is, learning to know
something by its relation to something else.

Leonard Bernstein

What would Bernstein say about how schools are structured to teach science and other content areas as distinct disciplines? How might he suggest that schools be reformed so that they inspire a love of learning and learning to learn?

Engage

What Do You Think About Integrating Curriculum?

We would all probably agree that learning makes more sense and new knowledge is often retained longer if it is learned within a context that connects to other knowledge. If this is the case, you may wonder why we don't see more integrated curriculum in science classrooms. To begin to examine this question and others related to the use of integration, consider the following statements and decide whether you agree or disagree with each one. Be prepared to explain your choices.

Integrating Curriculum: A Survey

Given the following statements on integrated curriculum, decide if you agree or disagree (A-agree, D-disagree) and explain your choices.

Integration of curriculum

_____ 1. fosters sustained enthusiasm in students, parents, and staff.

_____ 2. increases students' school attendance.

_____ 3. shortchanges some disciplines.

_____ 4. may not prepare students for high-stakes testing, affecting teacher accountability.

_____ 5. creates a positive work environment for schools that use teacher teams.

_____ 6. falls short of teaching in-depth content.

_____ 7. allows teachers to look more deeply into multiple content areas.

_____ 8. often attempts to relate unrelated subjects with little attention to students' prior knowledge and interests.

_____ 9. allows students to work with multiple information sources.

_____10. allows students to engage in studies that aligns with their interests, skills, and experience.

_____ 11. improves standardized test scores, especially with students who traditionally do poorly on standardized tests.

_____12. may originate from students.

As you consider your position on each of these statements, ask yourself if integrating science with other content areas is an efficient and effective way to teach K–8 science. Furthermore, keep these statements in the back of your mind as you read more about the various approaches and issues surrounding the practice of curriculum integration.

Explore

Children's Literature: A Springboard for Integration

In this explore, you take on the persona of a fourth-grade teacher who is preparing to address two science standards that are part of the science curriculum. These standards are "objects in the sky and changes in earth and sky" (NRC, 1996, p. 107). In addressing these standards you want your students to focus on the moon, its properties, and its motions relative to the Earth and sun. As part of the unit, an objective is to have students acquire knowledge about the moon and the moon's phases. As an elementary science teacher with a busy schedule of activities, you have to make time for inquiry science during the school day.

As seen with Jill Young in the narrative, you are considering integrating across some of your disciplines to make time for science.

You, like your colleagues, find with the emphasis on reading that children's literature might provide a way to integrate other disciplines with science. In this explore, go to www.child renslibrary.org and find "First Time Visitors" and click "Read Books." Then search for the book *Cry-Baby Moon* (Mataira & Kemp, 1992) and read the book online. As you read this book, you'll notice that the story is built around the phases of the moon and other natural phenomena like rain, clouds, thunderstorms, and rainbows.

Any or all of the natural phenomena found in the book could become a central theme for an integrated unit. However, for this activity the focus is on the moon, the central character in the story. Because the moon is the focus, the theme selected is "Moon Changes." First, brainstorm possible activities from across the various fourth-grade disciplines that you think connect to the theme.

Book cover for *Cry-Baby Moon*.

To get started we have begun the brainstorming process describing a few activities in science and one for language arts. For instance, in science, students will keep a moon journal for a month, make drawings of their observations, and note changes over time. In another science activity, students compare their observational data to a calendar that tracks the moon phases. The third activity invites students to investigate the phases of the moon using a light source (sun) and spherical models of the Earth and moon. In language arts, students read other 'origin tales' about the moon from different cultures and explore the role of origin tales as a central focus in children's literature. Many teachers use webs or other graphic organizers to visually lay out their ideas and activities for integration.

You will find a graphic organizer started for you below. Your task is to add other activities that connect to the moon theme. We recommend that you use textbooks, the Internet, and other resources to find a variety of

TECH CONNECT:
Electronic Books

Many local libraries are now offering books in digital formats. Take a moment to explore your local library's offerings. Are there digital books you might use in an integrated unit available through your local library?

Author's Note:

www.childrenslibrary.org

content area activities that make connections to the theme. This is a brainstorming process, so think broadly and include all possible activities, even though you may not include all of them in the completed unit. Using the Curriculum Connections Planning Wheel (Jacobs, 1989; Maute, 1992) as a graphic organizer—generate and write down possible activities in each subject area that will allow you to teach content area concepts and also make connections to the theme (see Figure 11.1). If you think of activities that connect the theme to disciplines other than those listed on the graphic organizer, then add them.

Now, look at your curriculum wheel. Your next step is to take some time to describe the activities you have listed in more detail. Once you have done that, examine each activity carefully and identify the concepts or skills to be taught in each subject area. As you identify the concepts, always consider whether the concepts or skills support the theme. Finally, reflect on whether the activities build content knowledge in each discipline and contribute to the theme.

> **TECH CONNECT:**
> **Graphic Organizer Technology Tools**
>
> There are numerous software and online tools that can be used to create graphic organizers with your students. Check out http://www.diagram.ly/ as one example. What are the benefits of using technology to create a graphic organizer with K–8 students?

Figure 11.1 Thematic Integration: Developing Activities for "Moon Changes"

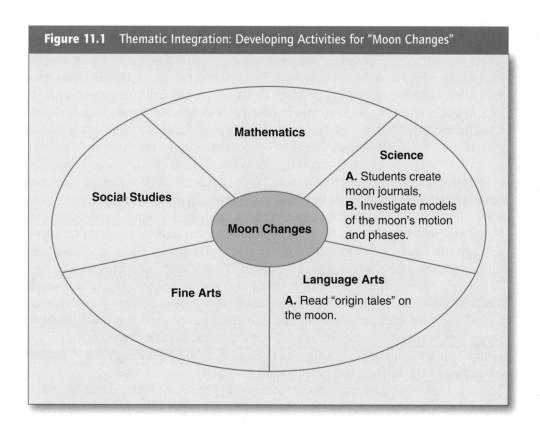

How well do you think your activities connect to the theme? In which subject area(s) did you find the most connections? What gaps do you feel you might have in your brainstormed ideas? Is there another way that you might begin the process of creating a thematic unit?

Explain

Focus Questions

1. What is a main focus of integration?

2. What are some common types of integration?

3. What is meant by multidisciplinary, interdisciplinary, and transdisciplinary integration?

4. How might you begin integrating two separate disciplines?

5. What are the arguments for integration? What are the arguments against integration?

Thematic Integration: A Common Approach

Integration means different things to different people: Just ask several teachers what integration means and you will quickly find that they don't agree on its description. This is probably due to the fact that there are so many types of integration. Despite that, most teachers will gladly share and describe the integrated units they use with their students. Many of them are thematic in nature. If you ask teachers about how they created the integrated unit, again you will get many different approaches. The point is that no matter how the process of integration unfolds, what educators do agree on is that any effective integrated unit must have clearly identified concepts, connect to the standards, and contain well-thought-out activities if it is to make explicit connections between concepts or skills across the disciplines.

Many times a thematic unit arises from and is most powerful when it centers on questions from students. Savvy teachers, whether alone or in teams, often use their students' questions as a springboard for developing integrated units. When reading *Cry-Baby Moon* to students, we find students often ask questions such as, "What causes the moon to change? Why does the moon disappear?" or "Why can we see the moon in the daytime?" to name a few. As noted earlier, the Moon Changes unit was motivated by children's literature, however, we find changing the topic or theme into an open-ended question that addresses students' questions is an authentic way to guide a thematic unit's inquiries and activities. For instance, using the students' questions above we can change the theme, "Moon Changes" into a question such as, "How does the moon change?" or "What are moon changes?" either of which is broad enough to address the motions of the moon and its actual surface features. "How does the moon change," a guiding question, is open-ended, succinct, and unbiased. It provides multiple entry points to engage students and gives a purpose to the inquiries. In the following, we modify the moon theme into a guiding question and share some of the activities to demonstrate how an integrated unit may develop (see Figure 11.2).

As noted earlier, there are many other ways to start and create an integrated unit. Some K–8 teachers begin the integration process with a broad topic such as sound, natural disasters, or problem solving, while others begin with a particular standard such as "organisms and their environments" or the "transfer of energy." From a broad topic, standard, or theme question teachers may decide on possible activities to use or they may move directly to identifying specific concepts from the disciplines linked to the theme (Jacobs, 1989). In our example, the process began with a theme that evolved into a guiding question followed by brainstorming and selecting activities for the unit. Our next step is to identify the concepts and skills associated with the activities that we want students to learn and develop (see Figure 11.3 on page 258).

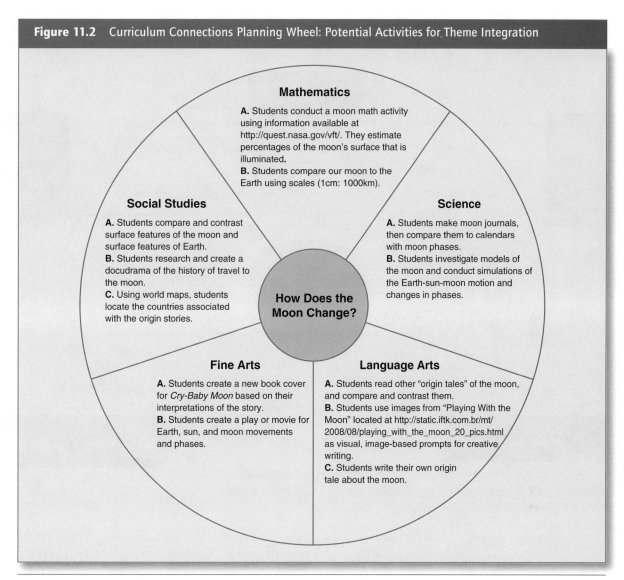

Figure 11.2   Curriculum Connections Planning Wheel: Potential Activities for Theme Integration

Note: This figure is a modification of a Curricular Connections Planning Wheel, Maute, J. (1992), Cross-Curricular Connections. In J. H. Lounsbury (Ed.), *Connecting the curriculum through interdisciplinary instruction* (pp. 73–77). Columbus, OH: National Middle School Association.

From the activities generated for the moon unit, we identified the concepts and skills that students are expected to know or do. For instance, in science the concepts and skills associated with the moon journals include being able to make accurate observations of lunar changes over time and to identify patterns in the observations to conceptualize the process of cycles related to the moon and the Earth. Other science concepts associated with the activities in the unit include examining the positions and motions of the Earth, sun, and moon, as well as describing the phases of the moon. In mathematics, the concepts of ratios and proportions focus on students calculating changes in an individual's weight relative to his or her mass on the moon and the Earth. In another mathematics activity, students estimate the percentage of the moon in shadow prior to observing the moon each day using a percentage wheel. Social studies concepts focus on changes in the geographic features of the Earth through erosion and weathering contrasted to the moon's surface

Figure 11.3 Curriculum Connections Planning Wheel: Thematic Activities, Concepts, and Skills

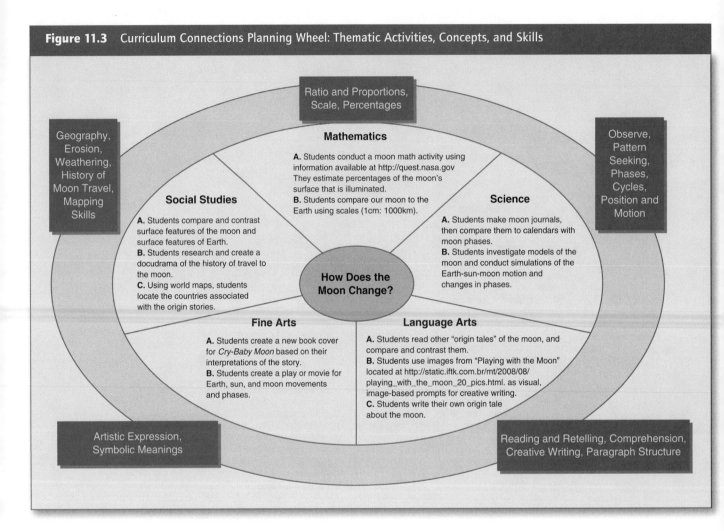

features. In addition, the history of technology and societal influences leading to moon travel in the United States will be part of the unit. Language arts concepts include retelling origin stories, comparing, contrasting, comprehending, and developing writing skills with a creative writing assignment using photographs from "Playing With the Moon" located at http://static.iftk.com.br/mt/2008/08/playing_with_the_moon_20_pics.html. In the final language arts activity, students write and illustrate their own origin tale. Art concepts will evoke students' artistic impressions and prompt exploration of symbolic meanings through the book's visual images. Students will redesign the cover of the book to reflect how they interpret the story's thesis. Finally, we use a moon ball game as a physical education activity for students with emphasis on team building, but it is perhaps the least connected to the theme. In the moon ball activity, students compete in teams to see how long the moon ball can be kept in the air without touching the floor. There are several variations of the activity that can be found online. If the activity cannot be conducted in physical education classes, keep in mind that it can be an exciting recess activity or can be used at the end of the unit as a celebration activity.

Author's Note:

For moon ball activities, search "moon ball." This activity is a document file at sitemaker.umich.edu/adventuretherapy/files/moon_ball.throwables.doc.

Thus far, we have discussed the activities for the "How Does the Moon Change?" unit and identified the concepts that will be taught in each discipline while supporting the thematic question. According to Jacobs (1989) the next step is to create a concept map to visualize how the different subject areas merge to address the unit's theme. A concept map helps in determining if the concepts, activities, and processes connect across the disciplines in effective, relevant ways to support the thematic question. Figure 11.4 represents a partial concept web for the unit "How Does the Moon Change?"

Now that the concepts and skills associated with the activities on a concept web have been identified, the following sections describe the activities and concepts of the disciplines in the developing unit.

Science

The moon's orbit around the Earth illuminates portions of the moon due to the positions of the Earth, sun, and moon. As the moon reflects light from the sun, the percentage of

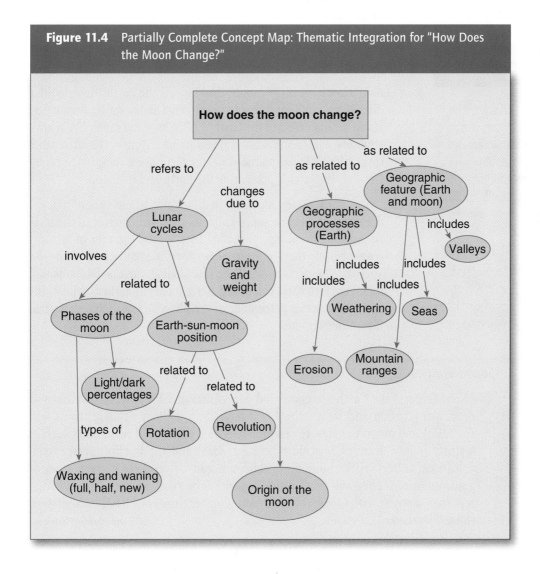

Figure 11.4   Partially Complete Concept Map: Thematic Integration for "How Does the Moon Change?"

illumination changes as viewed from the Earth during the moon's orbit around the Earth, which results in the phases that appear in its monthly cycle.

(1) Students will use models and light sources to explore, explain, and draw the positions of the Earth, sun, and moon representing full, new, and half moons. They will also explore the processes of the moon waxing and waning as they work through conceptualizing the "moon's cycle."

(2) Students will make a moon journal from sheets of the premade circles that students shade daily to reflect the lit surface, write in the date, time, and an estimated percentage of illumination. To promote home and school connections, a letter will be sent home to encourage parents and guardians to be part of the activity. Students will compare their journal drawings to lunar phases at http://stardate.org/nightsky/moon (word search: lunar star chart) that gives monthly lunar cycles, or to NASA Moon Phases: Calendar at http://www.calculatorcat.com/moon_phases/moon_phases.phtml. After students have completed all the activities, teams will be given the challenge of creating a skit to demonstrate their knowledge of the lunar cycle and its phases based on the positions of the Earth, sun, and moon.

TECH CONNECT: Virtual Tools for Faraway Places

Seeing pictures of stars, the moon, planets, or even places on the Earth that would not normally be accessible are possible through the Internet. For instance, students could take a virtual field trip to Glacier National Park or see invasive species in the Everglades National Park. What other ways might you use virtual field trips in your K–8 science classroom?

Mathematics

(1) Ask, "How large is the moon? How large is the Earth? How do their diameters compare to each other? What is meant by diameter?" Using the diameters of the Earth (12,756 km) and moon (3476 km), students will create scale models using a 1cm = 1000km scale ratio. After calculating the scale, they will use a compass to create circular diagrams representing the Earth and its moon.

(2) Using grid paper students will overlay their moon journal drawings and count approximate nonshaded squares to the total squares. By dividing nonshaded by the total number of squares coverage of their moon drawings, students will find the approximate percentage of the illuminated surface. Students will then compare their calculated percentages to earlier estimations and to the actual percentage of the phase's illuminated surface at the online website.

Social Studies

(1) The moon and the Earth are compared and contrasted for surface features and processes (erosion and weathering) that have shaped them. Student teams will use NASA and moon websites to research specified features of the moon's surface features (e.g., volcanoes, lava flows, craters, seas) and the Earth's surface (e.g., volcanoes, craters, rifts, mountains, valleys, oceans, rivers, etc.), given a set of guide questions. They will present findings either by creating a brochure, written report, or a poster with Glogster (http://edu.glogster.com/) or PREZI presentation (http://prezi.com/).

(2) Using classroom resources, library materials, and the NASA website entitled StarChild: Space Travel located at (http://starchild.gsfc.nasa.gov/docs/StarChild/space_level2/ travel.html) teams of students will summarize the history of space travel, noting the successes and tragedies associated with travel to the moon by creating a time line. The time lines will be compared across teams and a class time line will be created for display in the classroom.

Language Arts

(1) Students will read silently with their partners various short books or stories that are origin tales of the moon. Examples might include selections from Caduto and Bruchac's *Native American Stories* (1991), Belting's *Moon Was Tired of Walking on Air* (1992), or McCaughrean's story "The Raven and the Moon" (1996).

Students and their partners will read the selected stories and the teacher will conduct choral readings of passages from them. After reading the stories, partner teams will be assigned two stories and will make a list of how the two moon origin stories are alike and how they are different. These lists will be displayed on butcher-block paper and will be shared with the class. Students will write their own origin story with illustrations if they so choose. Origin stories selected from different parts of the world will be linked back to geography, and students can locate and put sticky flags on the map where the specific folktale originated.

This activity is one that helps students to connect the term "origin" to its meaning in the phrase "origin tales." The activity also will include discussion of the origin of the moon viewed from the scientific explanation. Finally, students will select one photograph from the website "Playing With the Moon" where they will find interesting and unique photographs of the moon. Students will use the photograph they select as a creative writing prompt telling the story of the picture.

Fine Arts

Students will examine the illustrations in *Cry-Baby Moon*, specifically examining how the artist created movement in the illustrations and how they evoke the connectedness between the Earth, sea, and space. Discussion will focus on how the text and the colorful illustrations portray symbolically the phases of the moon. Students will design and color a new illustrated cover, based on class discussions and their interpretations of the story and its illustrations.

BULLETIN BOARD

Origin Tales for the Moon

Adler, N. (1996). The rabbit in the moon. In *The dial book of animal tales from around the world*. London, UK: Penguin, Grades 4–6.

Belting, N. (1992). Moon was tired of walking on air, The traveling sky baskets, Why sun has a headdress and moon has none. In *Moon was tired of walking on air: Origin myths of South American Indians*. Willmington, MA: Houghton Mifflin, Grades 3–6.

Caduto, M. J., & Bruchac, J. (1991). *Native American stories (myths and legends)*. Golden, CO: Fulcrum Publishing.

McCaughrean, G. (1996). The raven and the moon. In *The silver treasure: myths and legends of the world*. New York: Simon & Schuster, Grades 4–6.

Zwerger, L. (1989). Aesop. The moon and her mother. In *Aesop's fables*. Saxonville, MA: Picture Book Studio, Grades 3–5.

At this point, it is important to note that the example of integration described in this chapter does not present a completed thematic unit. As you may have noticed, the unit still requires other activities and fully developed lesson plans for each of the activities. The intent and purpose of this chapter was to introduce you to strategies used for integrating curricula. Developing effective integrated units is no small task, so start small by integrating concepts or skills across a couple of disciplines. Creating a full unit may not be practical until you have a few years of teaching experience. Teaching experience gives you familiarity with the concepts and skills associated with all disciplines in your grade level. This knowledge is essential in building connections necessary for effective integration.

In summary, the "How Does the Moon Change?" unit was designed centered on the properties of the moon and its phases. We chose a thematic question that was open-ended enough to include features of the Earth, its moon, and their motions. Furthermore, the connections across the content disciplines were considered in thoughtful and logical ways without being forced. As a result, student's knowledge of science becomes linked with the contexts of language, art, social studies, and mathematics in a variety of ways. Student learning can occur in greater depth when students view the big ideas or a theme from many entry points of engagement across several disciplines. According to Beane (1997), a leader in the area of interdisciplinary studies, having multiple points for student engagement is one of the important reasons for using integrated approaches. With this in mind, we now examine three types of integration.

A visually impaired student is locating a story's origin using a relief globe inscripted with Braille labels.

Other Ways of Looking at Curriculum Integration

No matter how you begin an integrated unit, the objective is to make connections among a wide variety of concepts or skills to build students' understanding. Therefore, an integrated science unit should never simply be a collection of lesson plans—it should be a thoughtful, dynamic, coherent series of inquiries for students. In fact, many integrated units resemble "works in progress" because they are always open to new activities that foster even greater depth of understanding through new connections.

Because integrated curriculum can be developed in a number of ways, you will find several descriptions, types, and levels of integration discussed in the literature. For instance, Jacobs (1989) identified six levels of integration ranging from no cross-curricular connections to fully integrated curriculum that originates from students and their daily experiences. Fogarty and Stoehr (2008) present ten views or levels of curriculum integration, starting with nonintegrated to immersed and networked curriculum. More recently, other researchers have presented views of integration that are described and represented along a continuum.

Despite the numerous types of integration, in Drake and Burns' (2004), *Meeting the Standards Through Integrated Curriculum*, the authors state that nearly all types of integration can be explained by three views of integration: (1) multidisciplinary, (2) interdisciplinary, and (3) transdisciplinary, as seen in the following.

Multidisciplinary: Focus on the Disciplines

With **multidisciplinary approaches** like "How Does the Moon Change?," two or more content areas are taught using a shared theme, topic, or guiding question (Travers, 1998). The purpose is to make overt connections across the disciplines. In the upper grades or elementary schools where subject areas are departmentalized, you may find that teachers within a given grade level collaborate to teach the same theme within each of their content areas. Another popular **thematic approach** seen in elementary schools is the use of learning centers. With multidisciplinary integration, a teacher may select a topic (e.g., "interdependency" or "problem solving") or question and set up different learning centers for each discipline over a period of several weeks. Students explore the topic, theme or question from the perspective of each discipline. According to Drake and Burns (2004), other examples of multidisciplinary approaches are referred to as **intradisciplinary approaches,** which link subdisciplines within a discipline (e.g., chemistry and biology in the study of cellular function); **fusion,** which refers to the blending of content knowledge, skills, and other dispositions into the school-wide curriculum (e.g., character-building programs such as Project Wisdom); and **service learning**, which is associated with community-based projects that provide assistance and service as part of the learning process. In each case, the multidisciplinary focus on integration is on developing relationships and associations across two or more disciplines.

Interdisciplinary: Focus on Common Skills and Concepts Within the Disciplines

Interdisciplinary approaches are associated with capitalizing on skills and knowledge common to each. Maintaining the integrity of the disciplines is less important than teaching of common skills or concepts found within them. For example, suppose an elementary teacher has students reading a story to note details and make inferences as a way of focusing on these two reading skills. She has students look for the details and draw inferences from the story text. She makes a two-column chart listing students' details and inferences on a large poster paper

Teacher teams often plan and work together to help each other use interdisciplinary strategies effectively.

displayed on the wall. Later the same day, while teaching science, she uses the poster to point out that in reading, "noting details" and "making inferences" are the same skills used in science. She explains that "noting details" means making "observations" and the inferences mean the same in both areas. Students make an observation chart for a science activity that involves placing raisins in water and in a clear carbonated beverage. Using their recorded observations of the activity, the teacher asks the students to make inferences about what they think may cause the raisins to bounce in the carbonated beverage and not in water. Thus, interdisciplinary approaches like this means teachers, either individually or collaboratively, sequence and arrange their classroom activities around concepts or skills that are common across two or more disciplines.

Transdisciplinary: Focus on Students' Interests and Concerns

A **transdisciplinary approach** centers on students' ideas, questions, and interests, as well as real-life issues (Beane, 1995; Vars & Beane, 2000). Transdisciplinary approaches by their nature move beyond individual disciplines and embrace learning holistically— similar to how we learn and experience daily life. Most of you either have experienced or at least heard of projects where students become highly involved in a social issue or local problem. For instance, students may become intrigued with solving an issue such as an overgrowth of algae in a local lake or saving the Konza Prairie and its native grasses. With project-based integrations, students are encouraged to think critically about contemporary problems. Students apply their knowledge and what they are learning to reach a solution or attain the goals of the project. In culminating activities for a transdisciplinary unit, students often synthesize their work with a variety of products and displays that present their results and findings. Teachers using project-based integration must be willing to learn alongside their students. They listen to their students and plan activities, arrange opportunities for the students to work within the context of the issue, set up field activities, and guide students toward appropriate resources and experts as necessary. Frankly, teachers take on a role that moves them beyond just being a classroom facilitator. Transdisciplinary approaches are very inviting because they draw on the philosophy that all learning is connected and interdependent. Furthermore, it is grounded in the interests and concerns of students. However, due to No Child Left Behind with high-stakes testing and accountability, and the need for K–8 teachers to meet local curriculum objectives as well as state and national standards, carrying out transdisciplinary approaches can be problematic for teachers. Thus, transdisciplinary approaches are not used frequently. The type of integrations more commonly seen in K–8 science classrooms is usually multidisciplinary or interdisciplinary in nature. Given the three views of integration presented here, read the narrative below and determine which view of integration it represents.

In any discussion of curriculum integration, we would be remiss if we did not point out that developing effective integrated units takes time. In fact, given our experiences with integration, we highly recommend that you begin small when developing integrated units. You may find that it is easier to begin by only integrating two areas as seen in the narrative. You may find science and mathematics a good place to start. Science and mathematics have natural commonalities through process skills that make logical connections across the two disciplines (Goldston, 2004). For example, the websites Great Expectations in Mathematics

YOUR SCIENCE CLASSROOM:
Integrating Science and Mathematics

During his lunch break, Mr. Wilke, a mathematics teacher, and Ms. Delorenta, a science teacher, were discussing how their eighth-grade students often struggle with measuring, measurement units, and calculations using them. Mr. Wilkes said, "I have an idea! Why don't we organize our teaching so we align our teaching of measurement skills to give our students support in both classes and help them see that science and mathematics often go hand in hand?"

> **Teaching Standard**
> **A: 1 & A: 2**
>
> How does this scenario reflect these standards?

Ms. Delorenta said, "You know, not only is that a good idea, but I think I know where it fits into my curriculum. A couple of my units would work well with your content, I think. I use measurement in my matter unit, especially with density, which is not an easy concept for students to understand, unless they have a handle on ratios and proportions. So, what do you think? Do you think you could work with density, mass, and volume in mathematics as you teach your content on ratios and proportions?"

Mr. Wilke's smiled and said, "You bet I can. Those are excellent examples for students to use. I will need to borrow some of your materials, like balances. Is that okay?" Ms. Delorenta replied, "Absolutely, you may use them anytime. So let's discuss the content each of us will teach in conjunction with measurement skills so we can help students see the connection between our two disciplines." They agree to design activities for each of their classes to reinforce measurement skills associated with volume and mass.

Mr. Wilkes said, "I will have students measure items for volume and mass and then make calculations using the formula for density as part of my unit on ratios and proportions." He jots down some of the other activities he has in mind.

Ms. Delorenta excitedly exclaimed, "That would be great! In my class, it will help students calculate the density of various items and help them to understand density as it relates to sinking and floating. I also plan to have them explore the density of liquids, build density columns, and conduct activities that teach them about the density of water and buoyancy." She then said, "Do you think we could do this again when I teach the forces and motion unit? Students need lots of practice with measurement. This time we could focus on velocity and speed. I will be glad to share my materials."

Mr. Wilkes nodded and said, "It is certainly possible. I would be very interested in working with time, speed, acceleration, and velocity during my written problem-solving unit." With Ms. Delorenta sharing her materials (cars, ramps, stopwatches), Mr. Wilkes considered having his students collect their own data and do their own calculations using those concepts. Mr. Wilkes said, "Let's get our calendars and see when we can meet to work out our activities and time lines."

> What type of integration approach do Mr. Wilkes and Ms. Delorenta use for integrating eighth-grade science and mathematics? What is their primary focus? Explain your selection.

and Science (GEMS; www.lhsgems.org) and Activities Integrating Mathematics and Science (AIMS; www.aimsedu.org) (please see Annotated Resources) take advantage of these natural connections. Both AIMS and GEMS are highly motivating supplementary classroom materials that integrate activities that draw connections between both science and mathematics.

We have presented a brief overview of curriculum integration, but the ideas associated with integration have been around a long time. This prompts a question: Given the positive results associated with integration suggested by many, why isn't integration seen more often in K–8 science classrooms? Frankly, like many approaches today, there are arguments for and against using an integrated curriculum. As a K–8 teacher, it is important for you to be aware of both sides of the integration issue in order to make your own professional decisions about whether or not to integrate.

To Integrate or Not to Integrate? That Is the Question

Many educators claim that integration can bring relevant, real-life connections into a classroom and connect learning in science to other content areas. Other educators find themselves drawn to the use of integration for a variety of reasons. One reason is that there is a growing body of research that suggests when individuals are learning they organize and order ideas or problems as logical wholes, not pieces in isolation (Bransford, Brown, & Cocking, 2002). These scholars advocate using integration as a vigorous way to learn. Another rationale used by self-contained classroom teachers is that with the pressure of high-stakes testing in all content areas integration provides a way to actually teach all the disciplines. Many teachers find that integration may be a useful way to ensure the study of all disciplines into a busy, overloaded school day.

You may be thinking that integration is an approach you should consider when you have your own classroom. But before you do, look more closely at the integration issue. In the *Logic of Interdisciplinary Studies* (Mathison & Freeman, 1998), the authors extensively examined issues surrounding integration. Their examination of several published articles on the integration of curriculum revealed that integration supports students' learning by promoting the following:

- A greater understanding, retention, and application of general concepts
- A better overall comprehension of global interdependencies, along with the development of multiple perspectives, points of view, and values
- An increase in the ability to make decisions, think critically and creatively, and synthesize knowledge beyond the disciplines
- The increased ability to identify, assess and transfer significant information needed for solving novel problems
- Cooperative learning, promotes a better attitude towards self as a learner and as a meaningful member of a community
- increased motivation

(Mathison & Freeman, 1998, p. 19)

In addition, brain-based researchers find that integration, such as thematic approaches, support brain research, wherein individuals seek patterns and connections among ideas (Cohen, 1995; Schuster & Jovic, 2007). Still others suggest integration provides relevancy for learning as students experience real issues or current problems unlike traditional approaches to teaching (Czerniak, Weber, Sandmann, & Ahern, 1999).

It would seem that, given these outcomes, most teachers would incorporate more integration in their classrooms. The problem is that despite the positive claims, there exists limited empirical research to support the idea that integration is better than traditional approaches (Czerniak et al., 1999; Mathison & Freeman, 1998). In addition to a lack of empirical data, educators also voice other concerns about integration. In a review of literature focused on science and mathematics integration, Czerniak and colleagues pointed out that many science educators are concerned about a loss of rigor and a lack of in-depth content knowledge when science is integrated with other content areas. Simply put, they worry that science concepts will be addressed in a superficial manner. Associated with these concerns is a national push to encourage and prepare more individuals for careers within the fields of science, technology, engineering, and mathematics (STEM). Thus, there is an apprehension that if science is integrated with other disciplines in superficial ways, students may not be prepared to enter and be successful in the fields of engineering, medicine, or scientific research. Though many K–8 educators see testing and accountability as a reason for integration, others find that science integration may not prepare the students for the standardized testing that is today's accountability measure of success.

As we close this section, we return to the engage phase of the chapter and the statements posed to you about integration. Go back and review your answers. Would you change any of your initial choices after reading about integration? If you agreed with all the statements, then you have a realistic perspective of the issues surrounding integration and how the process of integration occurs. All of the statements have been noted in publication findings (Barton & Smith, 2000; Bolak, Bialach, & Duhnphy 2005; Brophy & Alleman, 1991; Czneriak et al., 1999; Flowers, Mertens, & Mulhall, 1998; Gatewood, 1998; Pumerantz & Galano, 1972; Stevenson, 1998; Wood, 1997), but whether integration fosters student learning more effectively than teaching the individual disciplines has yet to be determined.

Elaborate

It's a Teacher's Life

For the elaborate phase, your first task is to locate in a university library the following article: French (Goldston), M. J., & Skochdopole, L. (1998). It's a salmon's life. *Science and Children, 35*(4), 35. This article discusses activities that are part of an integrated unit (see references for full citation). After reading the article, answer the questions: "What type of classroom instructional approach was used for students to experience the activities? What are the integrated activities organized around? What type of integration does it represent (multidisciplinary, interdisciplinary, or transdisciplinary)?"

Teachers borrow, modify, and reconstruct lessons from other sources more frequently than you might imagine. For this task you have decided to conduct the salmon activities with your students. You just need one more lesson. You note that the article provides a few extension ideas. So you have decided to select one of the extension ideas and write a 5E lesson for use in the unit. (If you have an idea that is not listed in the article, but think your idea will connect to the unit, then develop your lesson around it.) If not, craft your lesson on one of the following activities from the article:

- A writing activity with students drawing on their experiences as a salmon in the activity as presented in the article (i.e., haiku, creative, narrative, etc.).

- An activity that compares and contrasts one or more different life cycles. The life cycle may center on a different type of fish (perch, trout, catfish, or other local fish) or another organism.
- An activity that examines fish anatomy and adaptations to their habitats.
- An activity that explores the role of salmon in the lives of Native Americans of the Pacific Northwest.

Evaluate

Where Do You Stand on Curriculum Integration?

The evaluation phase is in two parts. Part 1: Imagine that you have been working as a teacher at Bradenton K–8 Science and Mathematics Magnet School for a couple of years. Your principal has asked you and the rest of the second-grade professional learning community to do some research on the issues surrounding integration that is being considered as part of a school-wide project. As part of the principal's request, your task includes (a) defining integration, discussing examples of several types of integration, and describing the broad categories under which most integration falls. Part 2: The last part of the principal's request is that you synthesize the findings on the pros and cons associated with integrating curriculum.

Your final task is to prepare a presentation for the rest of the faculty that highlights the questions in part 1 and your team's findings on the pros and cons of integrating curriculum as well as your team's recommendation regarding integrating curriculum in the second grade as part of the school-wide project.

Summary

In light of No Child Left Behind legislation, K–8 science has generally taken a back seat to reading and mathematics. Furthermore, teachers frequently tell us that it is impossible to find enough time to teach all that is currently required. As such, many elementary and middle school teachers find themselves scrambling to find ways to help them teach what is required to meet their annual yearly progress benchmarks. Though integration of curriculum takes some time to develop, it also provides teachers a way to bring all the disciplines into the curriculum to help with the time demands. For instance, grade-level teams of teachers can work together to rearrange grade-level subject area content objectives so they are more readily integrated across the various disciplines. The possibilities for integration are only limited by the creativity of the teacher or teachers.

Though the term "integration" has many definitions, its essence is grounded in drawing out the relationships between ideas and skills while making connections within and across disciplines. Rather than a single approach to integration, there are many approaches that fall into three broad categories—multidisciplinary, interdisciplinary, and transdisciplinary. This chapter presented some strategies for integrating curricula that can support students learning of science by making connections in more than one subject area. Finally, the chapter highlights the pros and cons of integration of curriculum. Any discussion on integrating curriculum reveals that many educators favor integrating different disciplines, however, they voice caution that connections between subject areas should not to be forced. Instead, the connections should be carefully designed and thoughtfully selected, and whenever possible should be created around students' questions, concerns, or interests. On the other side of the issue, some educators find that integration can water down content knowledge of a discipline or poorly prepare students for high-stakes testing. Clearly, there is still more to learn about the impact of integration and a need for more research to assist educators in determining how useful integration of curriculum is in improving students' achievement.

Annotated Resources

GEMS: Great Expectations in Mathematics and Science

http://www.lhsgems.org/

This website is based at University of California Lawrence Hall of Science, Berkeley. GEMS produces a variety of science and mathematics materials with units that integrate the two disciplines. The GEMS program provides professional development on GEMS units. The site has networking links and also provides instructor videos to support teachers use of their units and activities.

AIMS: Activities Integrating Mathematics and Science

http://www.aimsedu.org/

This is the home page for a nonprofit organization that offers a variety of books full of activities that integrate science and mathematics based on brain-based research. The organization's mission is to assist students in developing strong conceptual understandings of both science and mathematics. They offer workshops, materials, e-activities, and activities specific to state standards, to name a few. Each month, a new activity is showcased and can be downloaded for free at the website. The activities are highly engaging supplements to any science or mathematics curriculum.

Math and science across cultures: Activities and investigations from the exploratorium. **Bazin, M., & Tamez, M. (1992). New York: The New Press.**

From NSTA Press, this book includes a series of activities that explore the science of sound from the culture of a Brazilian *carnavál* of musical instruments. Other activities include the investigation of the principles of flight using Native American arrows. Example activities such as these draw your students into science and math while connecting to other cultures.

Science & stories: Integrating science and literature: Grades K–3 **Teacher resource. Staton, H., & McCarthy, H. (1994). Parsippany, NJ: Good Year Books (Imprint of Pearson Publishing).**

This K–3 resource uses children's literature to teach oral language skills, writing, and science concepts with cooperative learning strategies and authentic assessments. The resource describes science and literacy connections associated with classic stories such as *The Legend of Blue Bonnet, Owl Moon,* and The *Very Hungry Caterpillar,* along with twenty other stories.

Science & stories: Integrating science and literature: **Grades 4–6. Staton, H., & McCarthy, H. (1994). Parsippany, NJ: Good Year Books (Imprint of Pearson Publishing).**

This teacher resource will ignite your students' interests in science and literature using activities associated with twenty-four children's books that include *Julie of the Wolves, Galileo,* and many others. Stories, activities, and skills are designed around space, ecosystems, technology, and patterns of change.

Music Through the Curriculum, by Phil Tulga

You may also Google Music through the Curriculum or to

http://www.philtulga.com

This interesting interactive website has a variety of K–8 activities that connect music with science and mathematics concepts related to sound. Students will enjoy the technology used to teach them about many cross-curricular concepts. Some of the activities include Pattern Block Rock, Science of Sound Activities, Hearing Subtraction, and many others.

Dear Mr. DeRosa **(2009, November 29). Integrating Literacy Across Your Curriculum. Go to YouTube.com and search Dear Mr. DeRosa or curriculum integrations, or to**

http://www.youtube.com/watch?v=alpd-Jrb1l4.

The short video profiles a teacher sharing how he integrates and makes connections across different disciplines in his class. He begins by identifying some examples of "common learnings" that include graphs, charts, data tables, as well as current media as an easy way to start the integration process. This is a brief video and Mr. DeRosa only shares ideas without discussion of their full development. Some of the ideas presented are interesting.

References

Adler, N. (1996). The rabbit in the moon. In *The dial book of animal tales from around the world* (pp. 14–21). New York: Penguin.

Barton, K., & Smith, L. (2000). Themes or motifs? Aiming for coherence through interdisciplinary outlines. *The Reading Teacher, 54*(1), 54–63.

Beane, J. (1995). Curriculum integration and the disciplines of knowledge. *Phi Delta Kappan, 76,* 616–622.

Beane, J. (1997). *Curriculum integration.* New York: Teachers College Press.

Belting, N. (1992). *Moon was tired of walking on air: Origin myths of South American Indians.* Boston: Houghton Mifflin.

Bolak, K., Bialach, D., & Duhnphy, M. (2005). Standards-based, thematic units integrate the arts and energize students and teachers. *Middle School Journal, 31*(2), 57–60.

Bransford, J., Brown, A., & Cocking, R. (2002). *Brain, mind, experience, and school.* Washington, DC. National Academies Press:

Brophy, J., & Alleman, J. (1991). A caveat: Curriculum integration isn't always a good idea. *Educational Leadership, 49*(2), 66.

Caduto, M. J., & Bruchac, J. (1991). *Native American stories (myths and legends).* Golden, CO: Fulcrum Publishing.

Cohen, P. (1995). Understanding the brain: Educators seek to apply brain research. *ASCD Education Update, 37*(7), 1, 4–5.

Czerniak, C., Weber, W., Sandmann, A., & Ahern, J. (1999). A literature review of science and mathematics integration. *School Science and Mathematics, 99*(8), 421–430.

Drake, S., & Burns, R. (2004). *Meeting the standards integrated curriculum.* Alexandria, VA:

Association for Supervision and Curriculum Development.

DuFour, R., Eaker, R., & DuFour, R. (2005). *On common ground: The power of professional learning communities.* Bloomington, IN: Solution Tree.

Flowers, N., Mertens, S., & Mulhall, P. (1998). The impact of teaming: Five research-based outcomes. *Middle School Journal, 36*(5), 9–19.

Fogarty, R., & Stoehr, K. (2008). *Integrating curricula with multiple intelligences: Teams, themes, and thread.* Thousand Oaks, CA: Corwin.

French (Goldston), M. J., & Downey-Skochdopole, L. (1998). It's a salmon's life. *Science and Children, 35*(4), 35.

Gatewood, T. (1998). How valid is integrated curriculum in today's middle school? *Middle School Journal, 29*(4), 38–41.

Goldston, M. J. (2004). *Exploring the natural connections: Stepping up to science and math.* Arlington, VA: NSTA Press.

Goldston, M. J. (2005). Elementary science: Left behind. *Journal of Science Teacher Education. 16*(3), 185–187.

Jackson, A. W., & Davis, G. A. (2000). *Turning points 2000: Education adolescents in the 21st century.* New York: Teachers College Press.

Jacobs, H. H. (1989). *Interdisciplinary curriculum: design and implementation.* Alexandria, VA: Association for Supervision and Curriculum Development.

Mataira, K., & Kemp, T. (1992). *Cry-baby moon.* Wellington, New Zealand: Ahuru Enterprise.

Mathison, S., & Freeman, M. (1998). The logic of interdisciplinary studies. Report Series 2.33 ERIC Education Resources Information Center #ED418434.

Maute, J. (1992). Cross-curricular connections. In J. H. Lounsbury (Ed.), *Connecting the curriculum through interdisciplinary instruction* (pp. 73–77). Columbus, OH: National Middle School Association.

McCaughrean, G. (1996). The raven and the moon. In *The silver treasure: Myths and legends of the world.* New York: Simon & Schuster.

National Research Council (NRC). (1996). *National Science Education Standards.* Washington, DC: National Academies Press.

Pumerantz, P., & Galano, R. (1972). *Establishing interdisciplinary programs in the middle school.* West Nyack, NY: Parker Publishing.

Schuster, D., & Jovic, K. (2007). Resourceful science integration. *Science and Children, 44* (6), 33–35.

Stevenson, C. (1998). Finding our priorities for middle level curriculum. *Middle School Journal, 29*(4), 55–57.

Travers, R. (1998, March). What is a good guiding question? *Educational Leadership, 55*(6), 70–73.

Vars, G., & Beane, J. (2000, June). Integrative curriculum in a standards-based world. *ERIC Digest #* EDO-OS-00-6.

Wood, K. (1997). *Interdisciplinary instruction: A practical guide for elementary and middle school teachers.* Upper Saddle River, NJ: Merrill.

Zwerger, L. (1989). The moon and her mother. In *Aesop's fables.* Saxonville, MA: Picture Book Studio.

APPENDIX A: HOW DO I WRITE AN INSTRUCTIONAL OBJECTIVE?

As a part of your teaching preparation and your work in K–8 science classrooms, you might have been asked to write lesson plans. How did you begin? A good place to start, though you can start in a number of ways, is to describe what students will be able to do or exhibit as result of the lesson or unit of study. Such statements are the focus of the instructional objectives for the lesson. According to Mager (1997, p. 4), instructional objectives are statements that include

(a) specific learning outcomes (performance),

(b) circumstances under which the learning occurs (condition), and

(c) an element that specifies a level of proficiency (criterion).

Perhaps the best way to tease out the components of effective instructional objectives is to look at them through examples. Let's start with an objective about the concept of energy.

Objective 1a: The students will understand the key types of energy transfer.

Does this objective tell you what students need to know or do? Not easy to answer, is it? Here is a suggestion. After writing an instructional objective, ask yourself if the objective provides enough information to assess it. Examine objective 1a: Is it clear enough for you to determine if your students achieved what it intends? What would your assessment look like for this objective? Would you require students to write down the ways energy is transferred? Would students describe energy transfer or would they label types of energy transfers? Do you see the problem? As written, the term "understand" lacks clarity and doesn't specify how students will show you what they know. Just try writing an assessment for the objective. It is near impossible because we don't have a clear idea of what student should know as a result of the lesson. Objective 1a does not clearly state an "action" or use an "action" verb that signifies what the students will do or know. Bloom's Taxonomy of educational objectives provides many action verbs that span Bloom's levels of cognition and that are useful in developing the performance element of an instructional objective. Take care, though: Some action verbs are far better than others (e.g., identify, analyze, examine). Avoid the terms "understand, know, appreciate, comprehend, learn, recognize," and any others that lack an action. Without an action verb, the objective does not make clear what knowledge students will have or what they should be able do at the completion of the lesson or unit. This crucial element, the essence of an instructional objective, is called a **performance element**. The performance element should be a carefully thought-out learning outcome that can be assessed. Now let's modify and improve Objective 1a to include a clearer performance element. Consider the following revision with a performance element.

Objective 1b: The students will be able to label the key types of energy transfer.

Objective 1b gives detail to the expected student performance. Students will be labeling energy types, but is the objective as clear as it can be? Could a substitute teacher look at it and know exactly what the students should know or do at the end of the lesson? At this point, a question you should ask is whether the objective gives some direction for the activities and orchestration of the lesson. Does it give specific conditions under which the students will perform a skill or demonstrate their knowledge? For instance, are the students labeling a diagram, a set of pictures, or are they labeling the ways energy is transferred with actual examples set up in the classroom? We cannot be sure from the objective as written. What's missing is another element of an instructional objective, referred to as a condition element. This element deals with what students use to carry out the task, what materials they will have available, or where the task occurs. The condition element clarifies conditions so all students know what is expected. Look at the condition element added to the Objective 1c below. Is it clearer? Now could you develop an assessment to match the objective?

CONDITION ELEMENTS OF EFFECTIVE INSTRUCTIONAL OBJECTIVES

Examples:

Given a bag of magnetic and nonmagnetic items, students will . . .

Using a graphic organizer, students will . . .

Using batteries, bulbs, and wires, students will . . .

Using a microscope, students will . . .

Using actual thermometers, students will . . .

Objective 1c: Given a set of pictures depicting types of energy transfer, the students will be able to label key types of energy transfer.

By now you probably think that this is a pretty good objective and it is, but there is more to consider. Take a minute to consider the types of energy transfer. What key types of energy transfer are intended in the objective? How would you revise the objective to clarify the key types of energy transfer? Without specifying the different types of energy transfer in the objective, how can one assess or evaluate students' knowledge? So remember to specify exactly what the key types are for your lesson. So let's revise the objective once again.

Objective 1d: Given a set of pictures depicting types of energy transfer, the students will be able to label them as convection, conduction, or radiation.

This last revision describes the "key types" of energy transfers students should know as a result of the lesson. At this point, we have an effective objective. One last element of importance to discuss is known as the **criterion element**. It refers to an observable or measurable performance level expected of the students. In our example, it is assumed that convection, conduction, and radiation will be labeled correctly by all of students, so it is not stated. In fact, if a criterion element is not stated it is assumed that students will achieve at 100%. Whether instructional objectives have conditional or criterion elements, all objectives must have a clear performance element stating specifically what students must know or what they should be able to do. Examine the following objectives for the objective elements. Notice that many are still effective objectives even with some elements absent.

1. Students will be able to explain that mass is a measure of the amount of matter in an object. (The context and criterion elements are assumed and the students will correctly write or orally explain the description of mass).

2. Using a diagram, students will be able to label cinder cone, shield, and composite volcanoes and state a characteristic for each. (The criterion element is assumed: All students should label and state a characteristic of all three volcanoes correctly).

3. Using a specified distance scale and sentence strip, students will be able to measure and place each planet's name at the appropriate distance it is located from the sun. (The criterion element is assumed that all planets are measured and placed correctly).

4. Given ten items (variety of magnet and nonmagnetic), students will be able to sort the items into two categories with 80% accuracy. (All three elements are present).

5. Using everyday items provided, students will be able to identify each item as a lever, incline, wedge, pulley, or wheel and axle. (The criterion element is assumed at complete accuracy).

Practice your skill in identifying effective objectives for each of the pair written below.

Objectives

(1a) Either in the form of drawings or digital photographs, students will identify four out of five everyday examples of simple machines: lever, incline, wedge, pulley, and wheel and axle.

(1b) Students will be able to present what they have learned to the class in order for the class to learn about their simple machines.

(2a) Students will be able to recognize objects that are and are not attracted by magnets.

(2b) Given a list of materials (paper, iron nail, rock, magnetite, plastic, wood, aluminum foil, penny, nickel, etc.), students will identify each material as magnetic or nonmagnetic.

(3a) Students will be able to state where a seed comes from.

(3b) Given a diagram of a bean seed, students will label the cotyledon, seed coat, and embryo.

(4a) Using a map, students will be able to locate areas of high volcanic activity (i.e., plate boundaries and the Ring of Fire).

(4b) Students will know how volcanoes and earthquakes are related.

We imagine you're curious to know how well you did, so here are the most effective objectives from the paired examples: 1a (contains condition and performance elements), 2b (contains condition and performance elements), 3b (contains condition and performance elements), 4a (contains condition and performance element). You will notice that many of the weaker objectives in the pairs lack specificity or the performance element is missing or unclear. Remember, objectives do not have to have all three elements but they must have a performance element; in addition, they need to be detailed enough to ascertain whether students achieve the objective through assessment.

Resources

Mager, R. (1997). *Preparing instructional objectives: A critical tool in effective instruction.* Atlanta, GA: CEP Press.

Bloom's Taxonomy of Educational Objectives

The following two webfiles contain useful action verbs for writing objectives:

http://www.llcc.edu/LinkClick.aspx?fileticket=%2F0BA4qlDaAE%3D&tabid=3938

http://www.wcu.edu/WebFiles/WordDocs/wcucfc_bloomsverbsmatrix_082409.doc

APPENDIX B: SAFETY IN YOUR SCIENCE CLASSROOM

Anytime you teach students, safety is paramount. It is especially important when teaching student-centered activities that promote student independence and that require students to manipulate equipment and materials. These materials may include live animals, plants, equipment, and chemicals. It is your responsibility to be knowledgeable about the safety guidelines for using these items and many others. Providing a safe working environment for teachers and students is an important responsibility for schools and school districts. Make sure you know your school's policies on safety and accidents. In addition, the National Science Teachers Association (NSTA) website has many practical and useful resources about classroom safety. One very useful resource compiled by the Council of State Science Supervisors, *Science and Safety: It's Elementary,* is a practical reference for teachers on safety in the science classroom. Other excellent safety websites for teacher can be found at the following:

Excellent Safety Websites

1. NSTA Portal: http://www.nsta.org/portals/safety.aspx

2. Science and Safety: It's Elementary: http://www.csss-science.org/downloads/scisaf_cal.pdf

Until you know your students and gain knowledge of safety management yourself, it is best to start slowly. So, think carefully about what you bring or allow in your classroom. Before bringing animals or plants into the classroom, make sure to check state policies, as well as your school's rules regarding animals and plants. In addition, it is important to know if your students have any allergies to certain pets or plants. If students are working with chemicals, plants, or animals, provide students with appropriate protective wear (e.g., lab aprons, plastic gloves, safety goggles) and teach them that they should not touch their eyes, nose, mouth, ears, or faces after touching the organisms or chemicals. They should always wash their hands after working with chemicals or organisms.

Despite taking the appropriate safety precautions, accidents may still occur, so be sure that you read and know about any school policies regarding accidents. Every teacher should request information on the following:

(1) School and district policies and rules regarding animals and plants in the classroom

(2) Protocols and procedures associated with accidents or injuries

(3) Professional safety training

(4) First aid and CPR training

(5) Policies for purchasing, storage, and disposable of chemicals

Know the protocol to follow in case of an accident. Report all accidents; depending on school policy, you may need to fill out an accident report. If an accident occurs and you need to remain with a student, send another student to get the school nurse or the assigned emergency person. Also, don't forget to teach students who to contact if you are the one who is injured. As a science teacher, part of your job is to provide instructions for safety and provide a safe learning environment. Begin by posting rules for students: Review them often and have students practice what to do during simulated accidents. Also teach students what is acceptable and unacceptable when using laboratory equipment and materials. This section is not intended to be comprehensive, but presents common, useful rules and tips for safety in science classroom. We highly encourage you to read safety reference materials cited in the references below. In addition, the following are general practices.

Important safety practices often posted in K–8 science classrooms:

- Wash hands before and after handling lab organisms or materials.
- Keep hands away from face, eyes, nose, mouth, and ears when handling chemicals or organisms.
- Wear goggles during laboratory activities.
- Absolutely no playing around in the laboratory.
- Follow the teacher's instructions.
- Immediately report spills or injuries to the teacher.
- No open-toed shoes in laboratory.
- Tie hair back and remove any loose jewelry when conducting laboratory activities.

Safety guidelines and tips for teachers:

- Teach safety rules and conduct periodic tests on safety.
- Use safety contracts with students and parents.
- Include safety within your lesson plan.
- Do not leave students unattended.
- In case of emergency, have a plan to contact the school nurse or someone trained in first aid and CPR.
- A first aid kit should be readily available.
- Report accidents or injuries to proper authorities.

These rules and tips are intended to make you aware of your responsibility to provide a safe environment for students, not deter you from conducting inquiries with students. Remember, safety refers to everyone. At times it may seem that attention to science safety makes it more difficult to include *all* students in laboratory or inquiry activities. This is not the case, nor the intent. What it means is that teachers need to pay careful attention to learners with special needs so that they, too, are included in the experiences. Even so, some alternatives may need to be made for those who are unable to fully participate in the hands-on experiences. With creative and thoughtful planning, accommodations for special needs students can often be made. Spending time considering alternative strategies as well as using technology can often provide safe equitable opportunities for all students to be part of science inquiry.

Resources

National Science Teachers Association (NSTA). (2008). *Safety in the elementary science classroom.* Arlington, VA: NSTA Press.

Roy, K. (2007). *The NSTA Ready Reference Guide to Safer Science.* Arlington, VA: NSTA Press.

APPENDIX C: SCIENCE INQUIRY LEARNING CENTERS

Now that you are familiar with different types of science inquiry lessons ranging from teacher-directed inquiry to student-driven full inquiry, you may find that you want students to have more time for exploring the concepts. Science inquiry centers for K–8 classrooms are useful for this purpose and can promote learning in numerous ways. For instance, inquiry centers can evoke curiosity, generate questions, and provide firsthand experience with science processes and concepts for as long as you decide appropriate. Centers provide motivating moments for students because of their self-guided nature, giving students a chance to explore in ways they choose. They also help with classroom management because they provide opportunities to keep students engaged in science learning when they have finished with other classroom activities. Science centers may be used for enhancing students' process skills development, investigating novel objects or phenomena, experimenting, problem solving, recording and collecting data, and researching by means of books and or computers.

How Do I Begin a Science Inquiry Center?

One way to think about science inquiry centers is to view them as ways to complement or reinforce your science curriculum for the year. A starting point for selecting a center topic is to look at the units in your science textbooks or a grade-level curriculum guide to identify the main topics. Once you have selected the unit topics, choose the specific science content or skills to be enhanced or reinforced in a center. Centers should be interesting and draw students into the exploration phase. Start small, develop only a few centers, and design them with storage in mind. Store center materials in labeled plastic tubs or boxes for quick setup. Try to make them reusable and continue to modify them as needed to keep them current.

What Is Needed for a Science Inquiry Center?

Teaching science by inquiry will require you to obtain some basic equipment and materials. Basic equipment for a K–8 classroom includes items such as a class set of magnifying glasses, a set of thermometers, a set of tape measures or rulers, and some balances, various measuring cups, spoons, and plastic tubs. You might also consider collecting items found in nature or around the house to be used with your inquiry lessons or in centers. Commonly collected items include a variety of shells and seeds (i.e., whirlybirds, dandelions, cockleburs, corn, sunflower seeds, marigolds, lima beans, peas, etc.), a honeycomb, small ant farm, acorns, pine cones, chicken or other animal bones (bleached), play sand, and a variety of rocks, to name a few. Consider multiple uses for typical throwaway materials (e.g., empty toilet tissue or paper towel rolls for making spectroscopes or movable arms that can support a plate of cookies). Start collecting a variety of magazines, science trade books, and nonfiction resource books. Also keep a list of interactive websites for use in appropriate centers. When you have the materials collected, you can set up directed, guided, or open-ended activities using laminated cards for instructions at the center.

How Are Science Inquiry Centers Managed in the Classroom?

Consider how you might manage students at the centers set up to enhance their study of sound. One possibility is that you may designate Monday as science center day and have individuals or teams rotate to the center throughout the day. If you have two or three centers set up and labeled, you may have teams rotate through them within a given timeframe. Use a timer, bell, or timekeepers to signal teams to move to the next center. If you have teams at the centers, use small tables which are generally more conducive for teamwork activity. Another alternative is to leave centers up for student exploration for the entire unit and have a few students use the center each day until everyone has completed them. It is our experience that teachers generally leave centers up for two to four weeks. Because science centers, like science lessons, should be inquiry-based, create your centers around a key question. Why? Well, consider a center entitled "Sound" and another center entitled "Can You Change the Pitch?" Which one would you find more appealing? Besides inspiring interest, "Can You Change the Pitch?" poses a challenge and gives purpose to the activities. Finally, centers don't have to take up much space. They can set up in drawers, cabinets, and other areas in the room. Students often enjoy naming the centers such as Discovery Drawer, Curiosity Cabinet or Engineering, and Invention Table. Below are some brief descriptions of science inquiry centers.

Sound Invention Center

Can You Change the Pitch?

A. Students use center materials to demonstrate pitch by constructing a futuristic sound instrument to attract some runaway nanobots in the room. Nanobots are attracted to particular sounds. Students must create a combination of three pitches to attract the flawed nanobots so they can be caught and redesigned. Materials include straws, scissors, rulers, balloons, wide-mouth containers, assortments of rubber bands, small boxes, and a variety of other items.

Can You Hear Me Now?

B. In the old days before the telephone and long before cell phones, children built their own phones. In this center, teams construct string phones using a variety of different types of cups, cans, string, fishing line, and wire to determine which phone is best by testing specified variables.

Resources

Awesome Experiments in Light and Sound, by Michael DiSpezio. (2006). New York: Sterling Publishing.
Hands-On Science: Light and Sound, by Sarah Angliss & Maggie Hewson. (2001). New York: Kingfisher.
Secrets of Sound, by April Pulley Sayre. (2002). New York: Houghton Mifflin.
Sound Waves, by Ian F. Mahaney. (2007). New York: PowerKids Press-Rosen Publishing.

Insect Center

What Will It Look Like?

A. Students follow the life cycle of mealworms, which are the larvae of darkling beetles (other options are caterpillars/butterflies, tadpoles/frogs, or toads) by creating and sustaining its habitat. Students examine both young and adult organisms while learning the organism's characteristics and needs. Additional specimens are added to the center as appropriate and available for other arthropod investigations (i.e., pill bugs, grasshoppers, crickets, etc.).

What Conditions Are Preferred?

B. Conduct experiments with mealworms using different variables (flour or ground rice cereal; wet or dry; light or dark; etc.). Materials include boxes, petri dishes or small containers, black construction paper, paper towels, eyedroppers, flour, ground rice cereal, and small lamps. Students use digital photographs and videos to document behaviors.

Resources

Children of Summer: Henri Fabre's Insects, by Margaret J. Anderson & Marie Le Glatin Keis. (1998). New York: Dover Publishing.
Incredible Insects Q & A: Everything You Never Knew About Insects by DK Publishing. (2009). New York: DK Publishing.

Geology Discovery Drawer

What Are My Characteristics?

A. Students make observations using a variety of rocks. Using a variety of rock identification guides students will sort the rocks into igneous, metamorphic, and sedimentary.

What Are Earth Materials?

B. Students explore a variety of earth materials (clay, sand, silt, and pebbles). Center includes a set of materials for examining soil particles (sediment) using magnifying glasses and microscopes. They will make drawings in their science notebooks and will sort the types of particles by general size. Students will predict how different-sized sediment will settle in water by adding measured amounts of each into a clear plastic jar. Materials in the jar are shaken and allowed to settle. Students make observations and drawings of the jar after a period of time.

Resources

A Field Guide to Rocks and Minerals (Peterson Field Guides), by F. Pough, R. Peterson, & J. Scovil. (1998). Boston: Houghton Mifflin.
A Handful of Dirt, by R. Bial. (2000). New York: Walker & Company.
Great Science Adventure Series: Discovering Earth's Land Forms and Surface Features, by D. Zike & S. Simpson. (2003). Melrose, FL: Common Sense Press.
National Audubon Society Field Guide to North American Rocks and Minerals, by C. W. Chesterman. (1979). New York: Alfred A. Knopf Publishing.
Soil, by C. Ditchfield. (2002). New York: Children's Press.

Magnet Center

Can Magnets Attract and Repel Through Liquids?

A. Students explore with a variety of magnets to determine if they attract or repel through various liquids (honey, water, glycerin, etc.).

How Can We Find the Strongest Magnet?

B. Students design experiments to determine strengths of various magnets. Center includes a wide variety of magnets (include some strong small magnets) in shape and size, paper clips, graph paper, string, ring stands, and assorted materials.

Resources

Magnetic Magic, by P. Doherty & J. Cassidy. (1994). Palo Alto, CA: Klutz.
Mondo Magnets, by F. Jeffers. (2007). Chicago: Chicago Review Press.
Science Projects About Electricity and Magnetism, by R. Gardner. (1994). Springfield, NJ: Enslow Publishing.

Light Center Cabinet

What Happens to Light Passing Through Different Materials?

A. Using the crystals from an old chandelier or prisms and penlights students explore refraction of light. A light ray box is a wonderful tool to explore refraction.
B. Students explore light refraction through various media (water, syrup, glycerin). Materials available include penlights, black construction paper, liquid materials, pencils, and a variety of clear containers.

Resources

Experiments With Light and Mirrors, by R. Gardner. (2006). Springfield, NJ: Enslow Publishers.
Eyewitness: Light, by D. Burnie. (1999). New York: DK Publishing.
Great Science Adventures: The World of Light and Sound, by D. Zike & S. Simpson. (2002). Melrose, FL: Common Sense Press.

Measurement Center

How Much? How Tall? How Cold?

A. Students calculate various measurements using (a) thermometers (air temp/water temp with and without ice) to measure temperature, (b) balances to measure mass (wood blocks, metal blocks), (c) tape measures to measure distances (height of a chair, length of a pencil), (d) measuring cups to measure volume (sand, rocks), (e) graduated cylinders calibrated in the International System (SI) of units (metric) and the units of the American System for comparing volume in both systems. The center's materials include sand, water, ice cubes, rice, yarn, rocks, pencils, containers, tubs, and a large variety of items for measurement. Note: This center could be developed into separate centers focusing on different types of measurement.

Are Measurements Important in the Kitchen?

B. Students measure ingredients in the SI system for no-bake peanut butter cookies. Center materials include flour, oil, salt, sugar, brown sugar, and peanut butter.

Resources

How Tall, How Short, How Far Away? by D. A. Adler & N. Tobin. (2000). New York: Holiday House.
Librarian Who Measured the Earth, by K. Lasky. (1994). New York: Little, Brown & Company.
Twelve Snails to One Lizard: A Tale of Mischi, by S. Hightower & M. Novak. (1997). New York: Simon & Schuster.

Micro Center

What's Under the Microscope?

A. Students view prepared slides and make slides themselves. Center materials include a microscope or digital microscope and computer setup. Using the microscopes, students begin with looking at the letter "e" under the microscope to examine how the lens reorients the item under the lens. Student can examine, draw, and label characteristics of insects, moth and butterfly antennae, pollen, flower parts, cloth fibers, and leaf cells. In addition, students can make slides for viewing pond water, Elodea (water plant) cells, and onion cells.

Resources

Looking Through a Microscope (Rookie Read-About Science), by L. Bullock. (2004). New York: Children's Press.
World of the Microscope (Science & Experiments Series), by C. Stockley & C. Oxlade. (1989). New York: Children's Press.

GLOSSARY

5E inquiry instructional model: Inquiry lesson design based on sequential phases of Engage, Explore, Explain, Elaborate, and Evaluate.

Accommodation: The process of adaptation whereby the learner, according to Piagetian theory, changes the preexisting cognitive scheme to align with the new encounter.

Adaptation: The ability to adjust to different environments.

Affective: The term associated with emotions or emotional responses.

Alternative assessment: Forms of assessment whereby students generate a response instead of selecting an answer.

Alternative framework or misconception: Conceptual structure that is constructed by individuals to make sense of their world. In science, misconceptions are explanations that are at variance with scientific views.

Analytic scoring rubrics: Separate measures based on criteria for several important dimensions of performance.

Assessment: The act of collecting and interpreting information about students' learning.

Assimilation: According to Piagetian theory, refers to the alignment of a new experience or knowledge with the preexisting cognitive scheme.

Authentic assessment: Forms in which the learner demonstrates content knowledge and skill in ways that resemble real life as closely as possible.

Auxin: Plant hormones or enzymes that regulate growth and other processes.

Backward planning: Lesson planning that begins with selecting the objectives, followed by designing the evaluation instrument. As appropriate, the evaluation instrument may be a rubric that reflects what the students should learn. Once the evaluation activity or task is developed, the rest of the lesson is completed.

Basic science process skills: Skills that are used daily, but when used in science become skills necessary for investigations. Basic process skills include observing, inferring, classifying, measuring, estimating, predicting, and communicating.

Bernoulli's principle: States that as the speed of a moving fluid (liquid or gas) increases, the pressure within the fluid decreases.

Binary classification: The sorting of organisms based on a single trait that is present.

Classify: System of grouping items or processes based on similarities and differences with the purpose of showing relationships.

Cognition: Mental processes or thinking to develop concepts, ideas, or processes.

Cognitive disequilibrium: A mismatch between a preexisting cognitive scheme and new experiences or encounters, creating an imbalance.

Cognitive schemes: Systematic patterns of thinking or behavior that make up the person's image of reality.

Cognitive style: The way an individual processes, uses, and thinks about information.

Communication: Takes any number of forms (verbal and nonverbal) used to convey information about processes, events, or objects.

Concept: Ideas or notions derived from generalizations of facts and experiences.

Conceptual change: Process of using instructional strategies that challenge students' misconceptions while encouraging them to rethink their ideas in light of new evidences through inquiry activities that move them to acceptable understandings of the concept.

Constructivism: An epistemology (origin of knowledge) whose premise is that all individuals actively construct or build their knowledge from their experiences as a way of making sense of the social and natural world around them.

Convergent questions: Questions that are often called closed-ended and generally have one answer.

Culturally responsive pedagogy: Teaching strategies that recognize and incorporate students' culture and language into instruction, and that respect students' personal and cultural identities.

Dichotomous classification key: A key for identifying unknown organisms using pairs of statements that represent given characteristics. One statement from each pair that identifies the unknown organism's trait is selected, leading to the next pair of statements, until the statement ends with the name of the organism.

Differentiated instruction: An approach to teaching that combines a variety of strategies to meet each individual student's needs.

Directed or structured inquiry: An inquiry teaching approach that is teacher-centered with respect to all or most of the essential features of inquiry. Direct inquiry is often referred to as a cookbook activity.

Discrepant event: An activity with an unexpected outcome or is contrary to what is predicted thereby challenging the conceptual framework of the individual.

Divergent questions: Also known as open-ended questions. Those that have multiple responses or answers.

Embedded assessment: Assessment that occurs within a unit that appears to be just another activity that students complete without teacher assistance.

Epistemology: Refers to the origin of knowledge, where it comes from, and how it is created.

Equilibration: Refers to the accommodation of disequilibrium until a balance is regained.

Estimate: Refers to a basic skill of judging an approximation of a quantity given a unit of reference.

Etiolation: The result of plants growing in reduced or the absence of light characterized by an elongated stem and small sparse leaves of yellowish color.

Evaluation: Passing a judgment on information (data) collected on student achievement.

Experiment: Asking a testable question, stating hypotheses, and conducting a fair test to answer it.

Facts: Discrete information substantiated through evidences that are supported by sensory inspection.

Fair test: Refers to an experiment in which all the variables are kept the same except for the variable being tested.

Formative assessment: Gathering data on students used to adjust teaching and learning while students are involved in learning activities.

Fusion: A multidisciplinary approach that refers to developing relationships of content knowledge, skills, and other dispositions into a school-wide curriculum.

Group processing: Strategy whereby team members debrief learning activities and each other's contributions to the goals.

Guided inquiry: An inquiry teaching approach that offers students some choice with respect to essential features of inquiry.

Holistic scoring rubric: An instrument providing a single measure of mastery related to the quality of the students' work or performance as a whole.

Hypothesis: An "if-then" statement that is testable and falsifiable. As part of an experiment, hypotheses are accepted or rejected.

Individualized education plan (IEP): Includes assessments of the student's current level of performance, a description of how the student's disability(ies) affects academic performance, type and frequency of services provided to the student, with specific accommodations and modifications.

Individuals With Disabilities Education Act (IDEA): Law passed in 1975 that requires public schools to provide special education services to meet needs of disabled students from preschool through age twenty-one that prepare them for further education, employment, and independent living.

Individuals With Disabilities Education Improvement Act (IDEIA): A modification in name of IDEA made in 2004.

Inferences: Explanations, generalizations, or conclusions a person makes based on his or her observations and experiences.

Inquiry: Seeking knowledge and understanding by questioning, observations, inferring, predicting, estimating, measuring, classifying, investigating, collecting data, analyzing, and evaluating.

Integrated approach: Teaching approaches that make connections with other content areas.

Integrated process skills: Include skills used for experimentation hypothesizing, identifying variables, controlling variables, operationally defining objects or processes, designing procedures, testing, collecting data, organizing data, drawing conclusions, communicating findings (oral, graphical, pictorial), and even making models.

Intellectual independence: The ability to judge the evidences and findings of research for one's self.

Interdisciplinary approach: An approach that focuses on teaching skills and concepts that are common to two or more disciplines.

Intradisciplinary approach: An integrated approach that connects subdisciplines within a given content area.

Investigative activity: Involves a stated question, procedures, and a known outcome. Textbooks generally include many examples of investigative or directed inquiry.

Learning accommodation: Changes in the ways that learning is facilitated with the student, not in the content he or she is expected to know.

Learning cycle: Inquiry lesson design that includes the phase exploration, concept introduction, and concept application.

Learning modalities: Channels whereby individuals give, receive, and store information (visual, auditory, kinesthetic/tactile).

Learning modifications: Changes to what we expect a student to learn.

Learning styles: Refers to an individual's learning condition preferences.

Learning theory: Explanations of what occurs or what happens when learning takes place.

Measure: Refers to quantifying the dimensions of an object, event, or process, and using appropriate units.

Metacognition: Refers to thinking about thinking.

Misconceptions: Conceptual frameworks that are constructed by individuals to make sense of their world. In science, misconceptions are explanations that are at variance with scientific views.

Model: Refers to mental of physical conceptualizations of objects, ideas, or processes of phenomena.

Multidisciplinary approach: Involves two or more content areas taught using a shared theme, topic, or guiding question (Travers, 1998). The purpose is to overtly make connections across the disciplines.

Nature of science: A way of knowing, guided by commonly held principles that underpin the emergence scientific knowledge.

Neuroscience: A scientific discipline involving exploration of nervous system and the brain.

Objectivistic approaches (Objectivism): refers to an epistemology that knowledge exists outside the individual. Knowledge is separate from the knower and in teaching encourages learners to examine the natural world with an objective mind—separate from imagination, intuition, emotion, beliefs, or values.

Observation: Any information gathered through your senses or with instruments to extend the senses.

Open or full inquiry: An inquiry teaching approach that is highly student-centered with students making the decisions with respect to the essential features of inquiry. The teacher's role is to guide and facilitate students' experimentation.

Operational definition: Defines variables, processes, or object in observable or measurable ways to determine its presence or quantity.

Pedagogy: Refers to teaching strategies or approaches.

Performance assessment: Refers to direct, systematic observations of student performances and rating those performances according to preestablished criteria.

Performance element: Refers to the element of instructional objectives that states what a learner is doing that demonstrates mastery.

Physiology: Refers to the body processes or functions of an organism.

Positive interdependence: In cooperative learning, it refers to students needing each other to achieve a team goal.

Predictions: Statements of a future event based on a pattern or consistency of evidence seen in data.

Principles: Ideas that describe the often multifaceted relationships among related concepts.

Professional learning community: Teams created in a school (teachers, administrators, or relevant others) formed for any number of different purposes, all of which ultimately focus on student learning.

Qualitative: Descriptive characteristics or attributes.

Quantitative: Numerical or measurable characteristics.

Rubric: A tool that includes a set of criteria used in assessing or evaluating student work.

Scaffolding: A strategy whereby a student is supported by a teacher, strategies, or content as he or she builds knowledge of a specified goal.

Scientific laws: Statements or descriptions of the relationships among observable phenomena.

Scientific literacy: Knowledge and understanding of scientific concepts and processes required for personal decision making, participation in civic and cultural affairs, and economic productivity (National Research Council [NRC], 1996, p. 2).

Scientific theories: Explanations for observable phenomena.

Service learning: Involves community-based projects centered on providing assistance and service as part of the learning process while developing relationships and associations across two or more disciplines.

Summative assessment: Assessment to determine whether the instructional objectives have been achieved by students.

Tabula rasa: A Latin term that refers to the mind as a "blank slate," a reference that individuals are born without innate ideas.

Thematic approach: Is a multidisciplinary approach where different content area activities and associated concepts support learning in each discipline and students' understanding of the theme.

Transdisciplinary approach: Centered on students' ideas, questions, and interests, as well as real-life issues; also embraces learning holistically stepping beyond the boundaries of the disciplines.

Unifying concepts: Ideas or processes that connect scientific ideas across the disciplines.

Variables: In an experiment, variables refer to independent (manipulated) or dependent (responding) which is the variable being measured or observed. Constants or controls are variable that are kept the same.

Wait time: A questioning technique with five seconds or more of silence after a question has been asked. A second wait time should occur after a student has responded to a question.

Zone of proximal development: Refers to what a learner can produce without assistance and what the learner can produce with assistance

Resources

National Research Council (NRC). (1996). *National Science Education Standards.* Washington, DC: National Academies Press.

Travers, R. (1998, March). What is a good guiding question? *Educational Leadership, 55*(6), 70–73.

INDEX

ABOUT THE AUTHORS

M. Jenice "Dee" Goldston

Dr. Goldston, "Dee," is a past president of the Council of Elementary Science International (CESI) and a professor of science education in the Department of Curriculum and Instruction at The University of Alabama. Her passion over the last thirty years has been and still is teaching science to both K–8 students and preservice elementary and middle school teachers. She was the recipient of the Outstanding Undergraduate Educator at Kansas State University, Mortar Board's Outstanding University Educator, and the Kappa Delta Phi Outstanding Educator in the field. Most recently she received a commendation from the Alabama State Board of Education for Leadership and Service to elementary science education. Dr. Goldston has edited *Stepping Up to Math and Science: Natural Connections*, is the author of articles in *Science Education, Journal of Research in Science Teaching, Journal of Science Teacher Education, International Journal of Science and Mathematics, Science Teacher, Science and Children,* and *Physics Teacher,* and in addition is the author of several book chapters. In addition, she is an author for an elementary science textbook series, *Seeing Science: Learning in a Whole New Light.* She conducts local, state, national, and international presentations and workshops on a variety of science topics for teachers and science educators. In addition, Dr. Goldston has been project investigator and codirector for numerous state and national grants fostering professional development of K–12 teachers of science. She is currently associate editor for the *Journal of Science Teacher Education.* She has served on the advisory board of *Science and Children.* Currently she serves on the review panel for *Journal of College Science Teaching* and *Science and Children.* She has served on various committees in state and national organizations such as the National Association for Research in Science Teaching, Association for Science Teacher Education, American Educational Research Association, and National Science Teachers' Association.

Laura Downey

Laura's first love is teaching. With a bachelor's degree in elementary education (minor in math and science) from Michigan State University, a master's in educational administration and supervision from Roosevelt University in Chicago, and a PhD from Kansas State University in curriculum and instruction, Laura has taught in Spain, the Chicago Public Schools, and in Manhattan, Kansas, at the elementary, middle, and preservice levels. During the ten years that Laura taught in the elementary or middle school classroom, her experiences included teaching middle school math and science and teaching elementary school as first-grade teacher. Laura has a diverse background working in several school settings with a wide variety of populations. Laura is currently the executive director for the Kansas Association for Environmental Education (KACEE). KACEE is a statewide nonprofit organization that provides professional development and support for both formal and nonformal educators in environmental education. She has been acknowledged for her leadership in the field of environmental education with a variety of honors from the U.S. Environmental Protection Agency and the North American Association for Environmental Education. Laura is also involved in the formal science education community, as a former board member and membership chair for the Council for Elementary Science International and a frequent presenter for the National Science Teacher's Association's conference. Laura knows what teaching and learning look like from a variety of perspectives through her distinctive combination of experiences teaching science, science methods, or environmental education to both children and formal and informal educators in diverse settings.

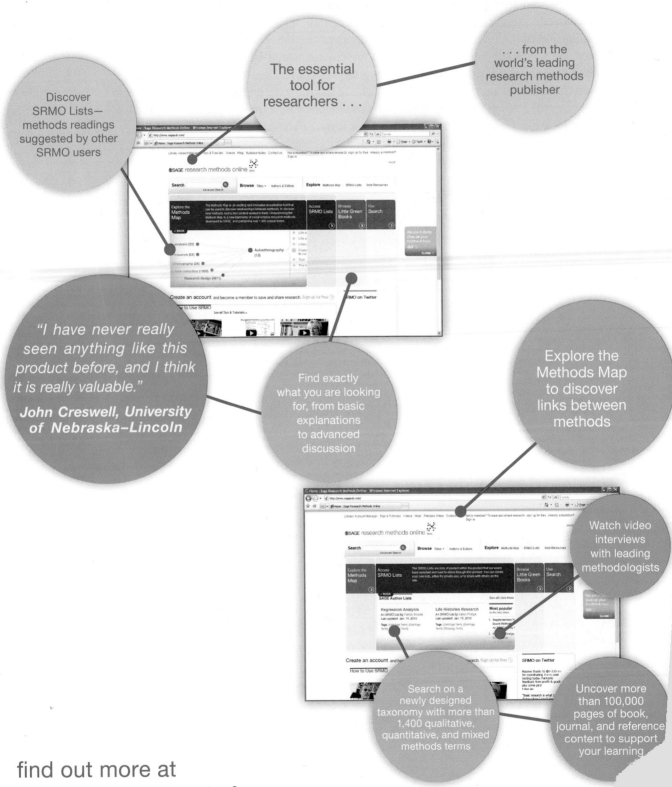